Dream Big!

Dream Big!

O's Guide to Discovering Your Best Life

Oxmoor House®

contents

here we go

HOW FANTASTIC WOULD YOUR LIFE LOOK if nothing were holding you back? That's the million-dollar question, and we're here to help you answer it with *DREAM BIG: O's Guide to Discovering Your Best Life*. With more than 75 articles drawn from the pages of *O, The Oprah Magazine*, this best-of-the-best collection of inspiration and advice gives you our recommended daily allowance of breakthroughs, insights, and laughter—and of course, for all you big dreamers, a triple dose of "wow."

In this dazzling volume, we've assembled proof that anyone can change ("I Was a 51-Year-Old Desk Muffin," page 10)...reminders that you're already far more fabulous than you think ("Great Moments in Self-Esteem," page 107)...and irrefutable evidence that it really is okay to make room in your world for the things that truly matter ("Urgent! Urgent! Or Is It?" page 64). We've examined the mysteries of money ("What's Standing Between You and—Ka-ching!—Financial Security?" page 232). We've looked deep into the minds of men ("Why Don't You Notice My Hair? & Other Frequently Asked Questions," page 169). We've figured out the absolute best way to respond when people are mean ("Crouching Tiger, Hidden Dragon Lady," page 196) and even when life is ("You Can't Possibly Let Cancer Have Its Way," page 45).

I've always believed that becoming your best self involves looking beyond yourself; so this book also includes stories—you'll want some tissues handy—about everyday heroes ("An Operation Called Hope," page 306) and the extraordinary things that ordinary women can do when they put their minds to it ("Band of Sisters," page 285). Finally, you'll get to meet some of the people who have expanded my own horizons: Eckhart Tolle, who has taught so many of us so much about freeing ourselves from unhappiness (page 133); Denzel Washington, who brings such passion to his work (page 298); and my dear friend Maria Shriver, whose life is a shining example of the importance of following your heart (page 110).

It's all right here, just waiting in this big, bright, beautiful book. Ready to dream it? Ready to live it? Watch out world, here you come.

Oprah

YOUR MIND/ YOUR BODY

diet and exercise

The moral to this tale of the tape: A bread roll can equal a belly roll.

"I Was a 51-Year-Old Desk Muffin"

After 23 years at a computer, she'd chalked up five novels, one Pulitzer, and 19 extra pounds, all wadded around her middle. Then Geraldine Brooks found a solution that's given her speed, endurance, and hips like a Spanish waiter.

Doctors warn that moving can be one of the chief causes of stress in life, right up there with changing a job or a partner. To move, you have to confront the past. You never know what you're going to find in the garage or the basement. It might be something poignant, like the favorite baby outfit, lovingly put away for the second child you never managed to have. Or something enraging, like the copy of the memo you sent to an abusive boss. When I was packing up to

move in December 2006, what I unearthed was a fitness assessment from the day I joined a gym in Cleveland in March 1984, when I was 28.

Talk about stressful. Suddenly, there it was, in black-and-white; the quantification of my physical decline over the previous 23 years. Could it possibly be true that I once weighed only 104 pounds? Leaving cardboard boxes gaping and bits of Bubble Wrap strewn across the floor, I went hunting for the bathroom scale. Part of me hoped I'd already packed it.

No such luck. I stepped on the scale and watched the needle travel in a wide arc around the dial. In the second it took to find its resting place, some very good meals flashed before my eyes. Steaming plates piled high with linguine. Crispy fried chicken and mounds of mashed potatoes. Succulent shellfish glistening with butter. The result of all this culinary indulgence glared at me in big black numerals under the shuddering needle: In 23 years, my petite, five-foot-two-inch frame had gained 19 pounds. And thanks to the careful measurements noted on my fitness evaluation, I was able to ascertain exactly where those pounds had landed. Braving withering looks from my spouse, who wondered why I wasn't getting on with the job at hand, I started rummaging around in the packing boxes until I located my tape measure.

It's not the easiest thing, taking one's own measurements, but this was hardly information I wished to share with anyone, especially a husband. I tried not to cheat by pulling too hard on the tape. Biceps, chest, thigh, and calf...so far, the news was surprisingly good. But that 19 pounds had to have gone somewhere. I slung the tape around my midriff. Ahhhhrrrgggh. Then my hips. Eeeeek.

In 1984 I'd been an hourglass. Now I was a brandy snifter.

In the hourglass days, I'd worked as a newspaper reporter, assigned to *The Wall Street Journal*'s Cleveland bureau. My boss had an aversion to seeing reporters sitting at their desks. He believed, quite rightly, that the news was happening elsewhere. So in those days I'd done quite a bit of pavement pounding. But now I'm a novelist, an occupation that is almost entirely sedentary. In the morning I walk the dogs. In the evening I weed the garden. In between I just sit, on what I now was forced to recognize had become my ample backside. You can't get a novel written without a great deal of sitting. Bum glue, as a colleague once indelicately put it, is a necessary material for the writing of any book. For almost ten years, I'd spent my days staring into space, trying to work out what my characters were going to do next. Now I had to decide what I was going to do next. Going through the rest of my life shaped like a Bosc pear was not an attractive option.

The problem I faced was twofold: I love to eat and I hate to exercise. But all was not lost. The move we were making was taking us from rural Virginia to downtown Sydney for a three-month sojourn in my sun-drenched, surf splashed hometown before we relocated

Try this diet rule: Look at the food and ask, *"Do I want that glued on my butt?"*

to our new, permanent place on Martha's Vineyard. Surely, in the sparkling days of an antipodean summer, I could exercise without effort. Regular trips to the beach, pitting myself against the strong Sydney surf, would sweep some pounds away.

Actually, what got swept away was me. After years of summering on gentle Atlantic coves, I'd lost my healthy childhood respect for the Pacific Ocean. I plunged into the invigorating brine, powering out past the breakers, out past the last line of surfers, slicing through the water like a seal. *This,* I thought, *is easy. Fun. Exhilarating.* Eventually, as my arms started to feel heavy, I turned to shore. Which suddenly seemed rather distant. Caught in a powerful current, I made no headway, no matter how hard I thrashed and kicked. Had it not been for a 12-year-old surfer who paddled out to rescue me, my pear-shaped corpse might have washed up in New Zealand. Sprawled on the hot sand, humiliated and waterlogged, gasping for enough breath to thank my pint-size savior, I realized I was going to have to try something else.

Yoga seemed a safer bet. I admired the toned, flexible bodies of friends who were devotees. After consulting a bewildering menu of choices—Bikram, vinyasa, vindaloo—I set out for a studio located superconveniently close to our Sydney home. I enjoyed the evocatively named poses: warrior, downward dog, cobra, plow. But as I lay in corpse pose at the end of each class, struggling to clear my mind and follow my breath as the instructor advised, all I could think of was looming deadlines and shopping lists. Instead of rising calm and centered to face my day, I'd bolt out of the studio, wild-eyed with guilt and anxiety over all the tasks awaiting me. An hour and a half, I realized, was an unrealistic time commitment for someone trying to be both a full-time writer and a full-time mom.

A friend, lean and fit well into her 70s, recommended Pilates: "You'll love it. It's yoga, speeded up and stripped of all the BS. And it takes only an hour."

Maybe. But what a boring hour. It was too rote, too predictable for me. I found myself sneaking glimpses at my watch: Can we really be only ten minutes into this? It feels as if I've been sucking in my belly button and neutralizing my spine for, like, ever....

Three months later, our Sydney intermezzo had come to an end and I was packing to move again. I pulled the old fitness report from the place I'd stashed it, at the rear of a file drawer, and realized I was still nowhere: still a slightly mushy, 123-pound pear with the cardiovascular capacity of an aging hippo. I needed help.

Fortunately, on Martha's Vineyard, that help was at hand. There was a bewildering array of options, from $1,000 a week detox sessions to inexpensive, pay-by-the-class aerobics. A number of my new neighbors on the Vineyard were avid tennis players. Encouraged by their enthusiasm, I signed up for a women's beginners class under an instructor whose e-mail address, LatinAce, sounded promising. LatinAce sent me out on the court with the racket I'd borrowed from my husband and started lobbing balls gently in my direction. Ten minutes later, he shook his head sadly. "Sorry, but you're not good enough for this group. The other ladies in beginners, they know how to hit the ball."

Stinging from this rejection, I began to consider drastic measures. A couple of different fitness instructors offered programs billed rather ominously as "boot camps." I had rejected these as too GI Jane for me. I asked a friend who'd tried one. She wrinkled her nose. "Very talky and huggy." That didn't sound like me. And then, one morning at 5 past 6, I awoke to the sound of raucous laughter just outside my bedroom window. Irritably, I got up to see what was going on. A large group of women, all shapes, sizes, ages, and colors, were running up and down the hill oppo-

Arrghh! What's that? A tumor? I thought the day I made reacquaintance with my long-lost biceps.

site my house. Weirdly, they seemed to be enjoying it.

A little research revealed that this was the boot camp of Nisa Counter, a 38-year-old certified fitness trainer. I called her. "Is it, you know, talky and huggy?" I inquired. "Absolutely not. That's the other boot camp. My motto is: Your body is my problem, your mind's your own."

I made an appointment to show Nisa my long-ago fitness assessment. She frowned. "This is ancient stuff. Nobody does these tests anymore. Like, 'grip strength'? What is that? 'Flexibility'— how did they measure that?" I explained that I'd had to sit on the floor with my legs extended and reach past my toes. "That's not even a safe stretch!" she exclaimed, appalled.

I told her about my extra pounds acquired since then, and how I'd located them with some precision.

"Okay, so you now know that your entire weight gain has gone to your middle. The bad news is there's no such thing as spot reducing. Seventy percent of that weight is what you put in your mouth. You'll have to work on that. I'll work on the other 30 percent." I asked her for diet advice.

"Sure. I've got a diet: Eat five almonds a day for a month and you'll get thin. No question. But no one can live like that, and it's the same with all these crazy, stupid diets. My rule is simple: Look at the food and ask yourself, *Do I want that glued on my butt? Is a minute of yum in my mouth worth a month of working it off?*"

KNEAD VIGOROUSLY:
Turning doughy muscles into toned arms.

4 Ways to Put Your Diet First

A Boston College study of dieting women found that more than half reported feeling pressure to eat in all social settings. But there was a crucial difference in the way they responded: Sixty percent of successful dieters used positive statements to shore up their resolve, while nearly two-thirds of the failed dieters reported worries about what other people were thinking (and half looked for reasons to rationalize overeating). Here, examples of the psychological traps we set for ourselves and how to respond.

YOU FEEL: Concerned that people will notice you're not eating as much.
TELL YOURSELF: *So what? I'm entitled to eat however I please.* And if someone wants to know why, you can say, "I'm trying to eat healthier," and change the subject.

YOU FEEL: Rude for turning down a second helping.
TELL YOURSELF: *Taking care of my health is more important than pleasing the host.*

YOU FEEL: That you've been good and deserve a treat.
TELL YOURSELF: *Every decision I make about food counts. I can find other ways to celebrate a special occasion.*

YOU FEEL: Everyone is staring at you, pressuring you to eat.
TELL YOURSELF: *Be strong— smart eating is more important than everyone's approval.* Follow that with a firm, "No, thanks." Repeat if necessary.

—**Suzette Glasner-Edwards**

Suddenly I found myself looking at a muffin and realizing it looked just like a curvaceous deposit of midriff fat. And that mound of orzo bore a striking resemblance to cellulite....

Armed with this new dietary perspective, I set out to let Nisa take care of the other 30 percent. Six A.M. is an hour with which, until three months ago, I was not that well acquainted. Now that hour found me up, dressed, and moving. Fast. For an hour, Monday through Friday, we'd meet up at a prearranged location to discover what Nisa had in mind for us. Spinning one day, kayaking the next, aquarobics the day after, lunging along the seawall the day after that, working out with weights, a step class, a power walk along the beach while the sky put on a dawn extravaganza. Every day was a different activity, so I didn't have a chance to get bored. I've learned that variety is key to a program I can stick with. Camaraderie helped, too. For someone who spent her working hours alone in a room, it was fun to start the day with a bunch of supportive, non-competitive women. It was amazing how fast an hour of lunges went by if, between grunts and gasps, there was a juicy morsel of local or celebrity gossip to chew over.

But after a month, I hadn't had a trumpets-blaring, Rocky-like transformation. I called Lisa Sanders, MD, a physician with a special interest in obesity and the author of *The Perfect Fit Diet*. I wanted to know what I was up against, metabolically. Is it really harder to shed midlife weight, or is that just a myth we use to excuse our failure?

"There's some metabolic reason, but it's not huge," she said. "As you age, you lose muscle mass, and muscle is a much more effective user of sugar than any other part of you. Also, as you approach menopause, some of your hormones peter out, and that can impact muscle growth." The new hormone environment in your body tends to send fat to the area around your internal organs, which helps explain why the waistline expands. And all this is happening at an age when most of us begin to exercise less, Lisa explained: "You're busier; your life gets in the way." Ideally, she says, the opposite should happen. Women preparing for the onset of menopause should exercise more and eat smaller portions. The easiest way to control weight is to avoid gaining too much in the first place. When you put on a lot of weight, you start adding new fat cells, which, once acquired, never go away. "You can empty them, but they hang around, just waiting to fill up again, and that happens a lot more quickly and easily than a cell that has to build itself from scratch."

This advice, of course, had come about a decade too late for me. I had to deal with fat cells I'd already acquired. So I signed up for another month of boot camp. And another after that. Gradually, I've discovered, I can run farther, lift more weight, do more jumping jacks. The gym equipment that used to make me think of medieval torture chambers now looks quite inviting. Recently, my jeans have acquired a pleasant latitude in the waistband, and my upper arms no longer jiggle so much. (*Arrghh! What's that? A tumor?* I thought the day I made reacquaintance with my long-lost biceps.) Inch per inch, Nisa reminds me, muscle weighs more than fat. And while I haven't dropped pounds, the really good news is the inches. I've lost nine and a half of them from a variety of places. My hips are now an inch and three-quarters narrower than they were when I was 28, and my waist has only an inch more to go. If I'm not quite back to being an hourglass, neither am I any longer a brandy snifter. More, I like to think, a champagne flute. Cheers. ◍

Avoiding the Holiday Spread

Ahhh, the good cheer, the family gatherings, the gift giving—and the extra pound or two that appears just in time for New Year's. **Suzette Glasner-Edwards's "assertive dieting"** techniques will help you survive your holiday season with no pain and, best of all, no gain.

I t's the holidays. I can always restart my regular eating habits come January." Whether my patients say it or hear it from others, that sentiment can sabotage smart eating plans. And it helps explain why this particular time of year marks the beginning of irrevocable weight gain. Research published in the *New England Journal of Medicine* suggests that while people tack on only about a pound at the holidays, they don't lose it—the gain just stays through the winter and accumulates, year after year.

To avoid that trap, you'll need to gird yourself against the temptations at parties and family dinners. That's where assertive dieting comes in: I teach my patients how to anticipate problems and effective ways to say no—and mean it. The decision to give in to or resist an impulse often comes down to a split second. Taking charge in that moment with grace is a skill that requires preparation, rehearsal, and a handful of strategies that you can use in any social situation.

Practice "No" Well-meaning friends and relatives will go to what often feels like malicious lengths to get you to overeat. Some of the pressure is understandable. After all, food has become mixed up with demonstrations of affection; think of not just holidays but

STAY CONSCIOUS: A few simple tricks can help you negotiate all that tempting food.

weddings, Bar Mitzvahs, and even wakes—they all prominently feature food. As a result, rejecting a second helping can feel as if you're rejecting a loved one. Cathleen Adams, a systems analyst in Los Angeles who has dieted on and off throughout her life, knows that feeling well. "It's very hard for me to say no to anyone. Finding ways of doing it without hurting people's feelings has been a challenge."

Jeffery Anne Bellows, a mother of three who lives in Denver, feels guilty when declining a home-cooked meal. "If someone has gone to a lot of trouble to make a special dinner, I don't want her to think I didn't like it," says Bellows. That worry has led to some regrettable diet lapses for her.

Adams uses a technique I teach: practicing assertive statements. Working on this with dieting buddies or other supportive friends is a great way to build the skill. Alternatively, you can polish your assertive style in front of the mirror. The trick is to strike the right note—regardless of how someone's offer of food may feel, their intentions are usually pure. I recommend people comment on how delicious the food looks and recognize the effort that went into preparing it: "Wow, that looks fabulous! You must have spent a lot of time making it." And yes, definitely practice until you find a way to sound natural and convincing—"I think I'll pass this time," for example.

Put Your Needs First You don't gain immunity from peer pressure when you graduate from high school. Studies have found that even adults feel the need to conform, and it's so automatic that it barely enters our conscious thought. Many of my patients report that fear of attracting attention or having to explain that they're dieting has led them to make food choices that are inconsistent with their goals.

I tell my would-be assertive dieters that weight and health goals have to take precedence over the reactions and feelings of others. When Adams senses her willpower wavering, she reminds herself about her family's history of diabetes and weight problems, both of which make her concerns about offending a friend seem insignificant. With those priorities in mind, she can trump her need to please others and politely decline.

Letting go of others' opinions has been another valuable technique for Bellows. Even though it makes her feel self-conscious, she'll typically eat only half of what she's

> If you feel as if saying no puts you in the spotlight, you're probably overestimating how much attention others are paying.

served. "I've noticed that people overserve their guests, the same way restaurants do," Bellows says. She puts the fork down and resists eating more by telling herself, *This doesn't work with my calorie count for the day; I'm just going to stop, and that's of primary importance.*

If you still feel as if saying no puts you in the spotlight, you're probably overestimating how much attention others are paying. I like to remind my patients that at social gatherings, most people—hosts included—are too busy socializing to see what other partygoers are eating. And even if someone does take notice, successful assertive dieters learn to shrug it off. Bellows's daughter, Anne, a project director in Los Angeles, maintains a "so what" attitude by reminding herself of the most important asset she brings to any social event: herself. "Coming to the party, having fun, and being me is what matters, not what I eat when I'm there."

Make a Plan Turkey and stuffing? Check. Mashed potatoes, check. Pie, check. Within reason, you know what will be on the table before you arrive for most big meals, and if you're not sure, call ahead. Then you'll be able to sit down ahead of time and plan out what—and how much—you can eat. (Be sure to save a few calories for the unexpected treat just in case someone offers your own personal kryptonite—egg nog, say, or pecan pie.) This is a great assertive dieting tactic you can employ year-round. Before dining out, Bellows sometimes looks up a restaurant menu online and decides in advance what to order. When she's at the restaurant, she requests a to-go container when the food arrives so that when she hits her portion limit she can immediately pack away the leftovers. At a large holiday gathering, the food will be sitting in front of you for a while, but with a little preparation you can make sure you don't overload your plate. If you're at a buffet, prior to serving yourself, scan the selections carefully for what you can eat to squelch impulsive food choices. And assertive dieters tell themselves that the first selections are final; no going back for seconds.

Having lost 63 pounds, Bellows now knows she can learn something new from every experience, even if she does make an error. And her experience has taught her that the most important thing is to be forgiving: "There are times when you'll succumb to the temptation and times that you won't. But beating yourself up about it will only make you eat more." ⬡

Dan Ariely, PhD,
decision scientist

Michael Gonzalez-Wallace,
personal trainer

David L. Katz, MD, *O*'s
nutrition columnist

Got 10 Minutes?

We've got a radically fun, totally painless plan to get you in shape—inside and out.

You can skip this section if you (a) are passionately devoted to exercise, (b) have laserlike discipline, and (c) can't imagine what it's like to fall compulsively in love with a certain ice cream.

Now, for every other woman who would kill to unearth the healthier her—if only she had time—we have a proposition: Just give us ten minutes and we'll get you in shape, mentally and physically. Not that we're pretending you can perfect a well-lived-in butt and testy disposition in ten minutes—you wouldn't fall for that anyway.

But here's the thing: If you can find a little window each day to do something for yourself—and who doesn't have ten minutes?—whether it's doing yoga, exercising, or fixing a nutritious lunch, you'll feel a difference that will make you want to pry another ten minutes from your schedule. And then another. You see where we're going. And for an extra boost, we've got eight of the world's top coaches and inspirational figures offering an irresistible dose of motivation. Ten minutes, we promise....The clock is ticking!

3 Upgrades for a Well-Behaved Mind

Don't put off reading this!

Since the late 1980s, Nike has been telling us, "Just Do It!" If only we simply needed a sneakered kick in the butt. "The world is designed to create procrastination problems," says Dan Ariely, PhD, James B. Duke professor of behavioral economics at Duke University and the author of *Predictably Irrational.* "Our emotions get the better of us, and we tend to forsake our long-term goals in favor of short-term desires. It's a major source of human misery."

Ariely surveyed almost 3,000 oprah.commers to explore how procrastination toys with our lives. He found that while people have a general tendency to drag their feet, certain tasks are real "back burners" for pretty much everyone. Of the 12 activities listed (including chores like holiday shopping, paying bills, and scheduling doctors' appointments), exercising and starting a diet are the two people put off the most, topped only by evaluating their retirement plan. Work duties like completing assignments and returning voice mails are attended to much more promptly. Even when people express a willingness to deal with their most avoided to-dos by setting deadlines, the data revealed, they are likely not to follow through. "Just recognizing the problem," says Ariely, "is the first step to overcoming it." Here, a few more strategies.

> **Exercise and diet are two of the top three things people avoid doing.**

Beat Procrastination *Now*

PULL A ULYSSES. "The hero of *The Odyssey* realized that left to his own devices he would succumb to the seduction of the Sirens' song, so he had himself tied to the mast of his ship, limiting his ability to behave badly later," says Ariely. Try to outsmart the temptation of your short-term desires. Don't go grocery shopping when you're hungry, and ask the waiter not to even show you the dessert menu.

BORROW FROM YOUR OWN SUCCESS. If you're good at handling job demands, translate the same tactics to the areas where you procrastinate. "Work seems more urgent because others are depending on you and there are deadlines to meet," Ariely says. "That's what helps make it a priority." Invest in a trainer to give your workouts more structure, or arrange to walk regularly with a friend, whom you'll let down if you don't show up.

GET IN YOUR OWN FACE. Celebrity trainer Jim Karas adds that constant reminders of your mission will help keep you from deferring it. Find a photo of yourself when you last felt happy and confident about your appearance, and make it your screen saver. Put mirrors all over your house and look at yourself constantly, he suggests. "People go around wearing blinders. They don't want to see reality. The more you look at yourself, the more you will want to make a difference—now." —**Tim Jarvis**

Just Give It 10 Minutes...

Pity the poor yo-yo. For something that started as pure fun, it has been keeping grim company of late. First, weight loss researchers coined the term "yo-yo dieting" to describe intermittent weight loss efforts that leave people heavier and heavier. And now there is "yo-yo exercising": Repeatedly starting and stopping a workout routine makes weight gain likely and weight loss more challenging, according to data from the National Runners' Health Study. After a lapse, men had to run at least 16 miles a week before pounds started to come off; women had to log more than 29.

If you can stick to a regular regimen, research suggests that you won't have to spend hours at the gym to gain many of exercise's benefits. With only an hour or so a week—provided you're putting out real effort—you can protect your heart and avoid adding pounds.

So the perfect exercise plan doesn't have to be time consuming, just engaging enough that you'll stay with it. That's the appeal of New York trainer Michael Gonzalez-Wallace's program: All he asks is ten minutes a day, six days a week. He saves you time by combining standard gym classics—doing biceps curls while lunging. And the light weights and high repetitions Gonzalez-Wallace prescribes deliver a strength workout at the same time as an aerobic one. He also incorporates balance challenges such as standing on one leg while extending weights away from your core. But the best part about the plan is that it's fun, keeping you out of the yo-yo trap. Below, and on the following pages, Gonzalez-Wallace shows you how.

Guidelines

● **Start with two- to five-pound weights,** although Gonzalez-Wallace says beginners can use standard full half-liter water bottles. Do one set of the exercises with 30 seconds of rest between each, then repeat. All together this should take about ten minutes.

● **A good measure of your effort is that you're breathing hard but still able to carry on a conversation.** When the moves become easy and you need more of a challenge, you can increase the weight of the dumbbells by a pound or two, do more repetitions per set—25 to 30—or add an extra set of each exercise.

Workout A
Days 1 and 4

② LATERAL ARM RAISES
A: Start with your knees bent, feet splayed, a weight in each hand, and arms hanging. **B:** Raise your arms straight out from your shoulders as you stand up on your toes, your heels about two inches off the ground. Return to starting position for one repetition; repeat 25 times for one set.

① OPPOSITE ARM AND LEG RAISES
With a weight in each hand, arms at your sides, and feet about shoulder-width apart, curl your left arm to your shoulder and then raise it overhead while simultaneously lifting your right leg until your thigh is parallel with the floor. Repeat on the other side. That's one repetition; repeat 20 times for one set.

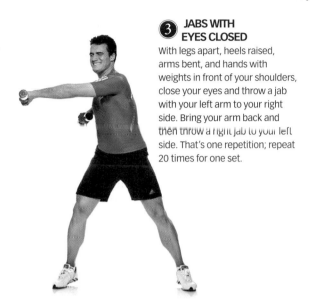

③ JABS WITH EYES CLOSED

With legs apart, heels raised, arms bent, and hands with weights in front of your shoulders, close your eyes and throw a jab with your left arm to your right side. Bring your arm back and then throw a right jab to your left side. That's one repetition; repeat 20 times for one set.

④ FLIES WITH BRIDGES

A: Start on your back, knees bent, feet flat on the floor, and arms with weights straight out from your shoulders. **B:** Raise your hips until your thighs and trunk are aligned while bringing your arms directly over your chest. Return to starting position for one repetition; repeat 25 times for one set.

Workout B
Days 2 and 5

② LUNGES WITH BICEPS CURLS

A: Start in a lunge—left leg back, right leg bent with knee over your toe—with weights at your sides. **B:** Push off with your left toe and raise your left leg until your thigh is parallel with the floor while curling the weights to your shoulders. Return to starting position. Repeat 15 times, then switch legs and do 15 more for one set.

① TRICEPS MOVES WITH KNEE RAISES

With feet shoulder-width apart, arms bent at the elbows, and the weights in front of your shoulders, drop your right hand down and raise your arm back while lifting your left leg until your thigh is parallel with the floor. Return to starting position and then perform the move with your left arm and right leg. That's one repetition; repeat 25 times for one set.

③ BICEPS CURLS, KNEE UP, EYES CLOSED

With feet shoulder-width apart, arms straight, and weights at your sides, close your eyes and lift your thigh until it's parallel with the floor while curling the weights to your shoulders. Hold this position ten seconds. Return to starting position and repeat with opposite leg. That's one set. Repeat.

(continued)

Workout B (*continued*)
Days 2 and 5

④ CHEST PRESSES WITH LEGS IN AIR

Start on your back with both legs up, heels pointing at the ceiling, and arms in a chest press position (at a right angle to your trunk, bent at the elbows). Straighten your arms as you lift the weights over your chest while simultaneously opening your legs to the side slightly. Return to starting position for one repetition; repeat 25 times for one set.

Workout C
Days 3 and 6

② SIDE CRUNCHES WITH WEIGHT

A: Start with one weight held in both hands over your head, feet shoulder-width apart. (To increase difficulty, start in a lunge position with your right leg back.) **B:** Raise your right leg to the side until your thigh is parallel to the floor, while bending at the waist to the right. Return to starting position. Do 15 on the right side, then 15 on the left side for one set.

① LEG AND ARM LIFTS

With weights at your sides and feet shoulder-width apart, perform a curl with the weight in your left hand while lifting your right leg until your thigh is parallel to the floor. Return to starting position and repeat with your right hand and left leg. That's one repetition; repeat 25 times for one set.

③ BICEPS CURLS, KNEE UP, EYES CLOSED

With feet shoulder-width apart, arms with weights at your sides, close your eyes and raise your right knee until your thigh is parallel to the floor. Hold your leg there and do 15 curls with both arms. Return to starting position and, with eyes closed, raise your left leg and do 15 more curls. That's one set.

④ OPPOSITE ARM AND LEG RAISES

Lying facedown with your forehead on a soft surface, arms by your sides, and toes on the ground, raise your right leg six to 24 inches off the ground (only as high as you feel comfortable). At the same time, raise your left arm. Return to starting position and then raise your left leg and right arm. That's one repetition; repeat ten times for one set.

And While You're At It...

The 10-Minute Cardio Plan

Though you can always add more sets to Michael Gonzalez-Wallace's exercises, you can also slip moves into your week with these ten-minute suggestions from Crunch trainers Cindy Lai—in New York—and Wendy Larkin, who is located in San Francisco. Both are certified by the National Academy of Sports Medicine.

● **Boxing combination:** This is good for releasing stress, says Lai. Take a boxing stance—step forward, knees bent slightly, weight on the balls of your feet, arms bent, and hands in a relaxed fist in front of your chin. Throw a punch with your left hand, then your right hand, squat until your legs reach a 90-degree angle, and pop back up. Do this for two minutes, rest for 45 seconds, then do another two minutes. Repeat three times.

● **Slide stepping:** To get your legs more involved, Lai recommends side-to-side boxing moves. Slide step to your right three times and throw a punch to the right with your left hand. Then slide step to the left three times and throw a punch to the left with your right hand. Keep that up for about two minutes—or less if you start to feel exhausted. Rest for 45 seconds, then do another two minutes. Repeat for ten minutes.

● **The commercial-break plan:** Larkin likes breaking up TV time with some quick exercises. When your show goes to the first commercial break, reel off squats until the program returns. At the second break, do lunges; the third, push-ups; and the fourth, planks (see description below). Still watching? Start over with squats.

//

The 10-Minute Yoga Plan

Most yoga classes run an hour or more, but Julie Engsberg, yoga instructor at the Mii Amo Spa in Sedona, Arizona, has developed a ten-minute program that gives you a quick dose of stretching and relaxation. "Focus on your breath to gain some meditation benefits and stress relief," she says. Breathe slowly and deeply throughout this routine, and be careful not to push any of the stretches further than feels comfortable.

● On your hands and knees on a yoga mat, start with the **cat-cow:** Inhale as you drop your belly and raise your chin to the ceiling, then exhale as you slowly lower your head and round your back. Repeat five times.

● Return your back to level, then exhale as you raise both knees off the ground and push your hips high into **downward dog.** Hold for five breaths.

● Inhale and step your right foot forward between your hands to **high lunge,** keeping your left knee straight. Look forward as you lift your chest. Your fingertips should stay on the ground. Hold for a breath,

exhale, and step back to downward dog. Repeat on each side four times.

● The last time, from the high lunge, lower your back knee to the ground **(low lunge)** and, with your shoulders over your hips, raise your arms overhead and hold for five breaths. Lower your hands to the ground, switch legs, and

repeat. Now bring your back leg forward so both feet are together and straighten your knees as far as possible into **standing forward bend;** hinge at the hips with hands stretching toward the floor. Hold for five breaths.

● Bend your knees and place your hands in front of your feet; then exhale and jump or step back into **plank.** Your legs and back should be in a straight line, your arms straight, and your body supported on your hands

and toes. Lower yourself slowly until you're just above the ground, inhale once, and lower to the ground for five breaths.

● With your hands just under your shoulders, press up, arching your back into **cobra,** your legs and hips still on the floor. Hold for a breath, then raise your hips and sit back on your calves, and rest your abdomen between your thighs with your forehead on the floor in **child's pose.** Hold for five breaths. Now you're ready for your day. **O**

The Way to Eat

All it takes is 10 minutes here and there to make a dramatic change for the better in your diet, says David L. Katz, MD.

There are two ways to improve the quality of what you eat: You could study nutrition theory thoroughly, abandon most of what you've been doing until now, and retool your diet from stem to stern. Or you could keep things simple by making just one small change at a time.

Take breakfast, for example. Sitting down to one—if you don't already—can be your first ten-minute intervention. Numerous studies have found that skipping breakfast is linked to overweight and obesity. Women seem to be especially responsive to the benefits: A study of 4,218 adults found that eating breakfast meant that women—but not men—were far more likely to have a body mass index under 25, putting them comfortably in the healthy weight category.

If you do eat breakfast, then the next change is even simpler. When you're at the supermarket, spend some time picking out a whole grain cereal—look for one that delivers about five grams of fiber per serving. (You can save time by going with one of my favorites—cereals by Nature's Path, Kashi, and Barbara's Bakery.) Then buy some skim

milk and fruit. Now you have a meal that takes all of 60 seconds to prepare yet delivers protein, complex carbohydrates, and a hearty dose of fiber, calcium, and antioxidants. A whole grain breakfast seems to have special benefits. Research published earlier this year found that women who got at least one serving of whole grains a day—a cup of whole grain cold cereal, for example, or one slice of whole grain bread—weighed less and had slimmer waists than those who ate none. Remarkably, more than two-thirds of the 2,000-plus women in the study failed to get that crucial serving.

For many people, dinner is the place to cut corners. Cooking a meal at the end of a long day sounds daunting, but it may not be as challenging as you think. A study out of UCLA suggests that putting together a home-cooked dinner on average takes only about ten minutes more of hands-on time than using mainly prepackaged dishes. If you go to the store with a few recipes in mind, you'll have what you need at your fingertips each evening. A dinner of grilled fresh fish with a light citrus marinade (orange juice, olive oil, and dill), steamed green beans, whole grain bread with herb-infused olive oil for dipping, mixed green salad, glass of wine, and a square of dark chocolate for dessert would actually take less time to prepare than a frozen pizza.

Most important, the dishes you make will be much healthier. Processed food, fast food, and takeout often have too much salt and sugar. The fish dinner I described above contains most of the items that make up the "polymeal"—a collection of foods (fish, almonds, wine, dark chocolate, garlic, fruits, and vegetables) that researchers have suggested can lower heart disease risk by 76 percent.

And then there's lunch. To help demonstrate what an impact a ten-minute change can have on your midday meal, I asked six staff members at *O* magazine to track their cafeteria meals and snacks for a couple of days, and then to try bringing their food from home for two days. Although this group tended to make smart choices—and were helped considerably by the healthy fare available in their cafeteria—they still managed to make a big improvement in their diet when they brown-bagged their lunches. While only a couple of volunteers ate fewer calories, they got 25 percent more fiber on average and boosted consumption of healthy fats and vital nutrients like calcium.

"The variety at the cafeteria confuses me," says senior editor Suzan Colón, who was one of the volunteers to cut calories—200—by packing her meal. "And they only have large plates, so it's easy to overdo it. The first morning I brought lunch, I was in a tremendous rush and just grabbed the first few things I saw—some leftover spaghetti and salad. When lunch rolled around, it was really freeing not to have to make any choices." Assistant editor Dorothea Hunter was reluctant to bring her lunch because it seemed like too much hassle. "But it wasn't at

> ## A fish dinner is made up of foods that can lower heart disease risk by as much as 76 percent.

all," she says. She made sandwiches or brought in leftovers. "I love saving the money, and now I'm trying to pack my lunch at least twice a week."

My experience with patients over the past 20 years tells me that if you switch from typical cafeteria fare or fast food to a meal from home or a snack pack (that's what I bring to work), you will derive even greater benefit than the *O* staff. Like Colón and Hunter, you can use leftovers from a delicious dinner you made the evening before. Or make a sandwich of sliced turkey with lettuce, tomato, and mustard on whole wheat bread; it will take at most a few minutes to make, cost less than most fast food, and will likely save you a few hundred calories, many milligrams of sodium, and several grams of saturated and even trans fat. And you'll be getting—as with breakfast—a dose of many valuable nutrients, including lean protein and fiber.

If you're like me and prefer to graze during the day, you can skip the sandwich and go for a snack pack. Mine typically contains some fresh fruit, nuts or seeds, nonfat yogurt, dried fruit, perhaps some whole grain bread, and maybe some fresh veggies like diced peppers or baby carrots—finger food, in other words, that I can munch on whenever I am so inclined. Preparing these kinds of snack packs is an investment of roughly two minutes a day.

Experiment to find what works best for you. My feeling is that you should approach your meals the way you approach the weather. If it looks like rain, take an umbrella; you can defend yourself against an inclement food climate—fast food restaurants, processed food, vending machines—by packing your lunch, preparing your dinner, and eating a smart breakfast. A ten-minute time investment here and there is all it takes. **O**

Take 10 minutes for breakfast

● A whole grain cereal with fruit and skim milk adds up to a healthy dose of fiber, loads of calcium and antioxidants, and protection against weight gain.

 +

Take 10 minutes for lunch

● You'll save not only money by making a sandwich at home but hundreds of calories over the typical fast food fare. And you'll gain a big nutritional boost.

Take an extra 10 minutes for dinner

● Believe it or not, research suggests it takes on average only ten minutes more of hands-on time to prepare an evening meal from scratch compared with using mainly prepackaged dishes.

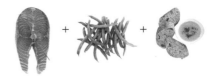

Can You Think Yourself Fat?

You can lose all the weight you like, but until your self-image catches up with your new, thinner body, you're in danger of gaining it right back. **Emily Yoffe** reports on the phenomenon of phantom fat.

Sandra Blakeslee reentered her body one afternoon about 15 years ago. As a young woman in her early 20s, she had gotten heavy and, like many who struggle with weight, thought of her body with loathing and shame. This persisted even after she discovered exercise in her 30s, became slim and fit, and managed to maintain her weight loss. Intellectually, she knew she was in shape; emotionally, she still believed she was plus-sized. "I felt there was an iron plate between my head and my body," she says of those years. Then, when she was 50, she was taking a long, solo bike ride into the wilderness of New Mexico, and as she ascended a trail everything shifted. "Suddenly, it was like I was hit by lightning. My body completely changed." She had an image of herself as a beautiful 16-year-old girl—the girl she had once been and long ago left behind. "I started to cry," she recalls. "It was a sense, all of a sudden, that I was in a body I didn't hate."

What had happened to Blakeslee, a science writer who is now 64, was that her image of her body and her actual body shape dramatically and instantaneously got in sync. Even though she had long ago left her excess weight behind, until that moment in the wilderness, she was still dragging it around with her in her head. Her experience was the basis for a chapter in her latest book, *The Body Has a Mind of Its Own.* (Her son, Matthew, is her coauthor.) Blakeslee describes how for some people with weight problems, the warring maps in their head between what their body really is and their emotion-laden mental image of it can sabotage successful dieting.

Margo Maine, PhD, says she has seen many patients who've lost a lot of weight continue to experience what she calls "phantom fat"—it's analogous to the phantom pain an amputee can have in a missing limb. Maine, a Connecticut psychologist specializing in eating disorders and coauthor of *The Body Myth: Adult Women and the Pressure to Be Perfect,* says she's had patients who continue to wear what they call their "fat clothes"—though everyone tells them they need to go shopping—because they still feel that layer of flesh around themselves. Sometimes after patients lose weight, they have trouble emotionally letting go of their outsize presence because it served as a shield against social interaction. "It's scary to be their new size," Maine says. "They might feel more noticed and be embarrassed by the attention their bodies are getting."

When dieters come to Judith Beck, PhD, a cognitive therapist and the author of *The Beck Diet Solution: Train Your Brain to Think Like a Thin Person,* one of the first things she does is have them work at accepting their bodies—whatever stage they're at. "They may decide keeping the weight off isn't worth it. They've done this hard work and they don't feel any different," she says. Beck tells a client to take advantage of the more objective vision of family and friends by asking them to cut pictures out of magazines of real women who are her size, or to point out in crowds women whose bodies resemble hers. Beck suggests looking at the magazine pictures frequently and saying, "This person is similar to me." Seeing one's body shape reflected in a stranger won't trigger all the emotional associations of seeing a photograph of oneself.

Rosalyn (not her real name), 43, a teacher in New Jersey and a client of Beck's, prides herself on being a logical person. She knows that after more than a year of Weight Watchers, she is, at 170 pounds, 102 pounds lighter than when she started, and she has gone from a size 26 to a size 12. "But I have had to work at thinking of myself as smaller. That when I meet people, the first thing they think is not *Boy, she's huge.*" One night at a family gathering, Rosalyn's sister, who is of average size, came up with an idea. "She made me switch clothes with her," Rosalyn recalls. "She said, 'I know we're the same size.' So I put on her clothes, and they fit. That was mind-blowing." Rosalyn continues to work at knowing she has lost the weight. She sometimes goes out for retail therapy: Even if she doesn't intend to buy anything, she picks size 12s off the rack and tries

them on; she says she's surprised, then reassured, when the pants fit. "There are times that the waistband on a pair of pants looks tiny to me."

Gina Macdonald, a dance movement therapist in Branford, Connecticut, has many techniques for helping her patients banish what she calls the "ghost image" of their heavier bodies. In one, patients get involved in literally redrawing their body map. They stand in front of a large piece of paper while partners trace a precise outline of their bodies. When they step away and look at what their size really is, "they do not believe it," Macdonald says. She also has clients close their eyes, envision their bodies, then place their hands out in front of them at the width they believe their waist is. "I have them open their eyes and look at their hands, and I guide them back to where they should be. They can see the difference in inches. Some start crying."

Sometimes a woman must recalibrate her body image before she can begin to address her weight issues. For years Michele Secaul, 45, an office manager who lives in Boca Raton, Florida, thought of herself as a floating head. She could look in the mirror at her face—how many times had she heard she had a pretty one?—but not below it, at her 288-pound body. Desperate about the shape she was in, she tried a movement therapy class at the Renfrew Center, a facility that treats eating disorders, in Coconut Creek, Florida. It was the "lotion therapy" that finally helped her connect her head to that body. Although she hated to touch herself, the therapists made her go home every day and gently apply lotion to her whole body—"to feel my body, to take care of it, respect it," she says. It was this reconnection that prompted her to want to address her weight issues.

Secaul had a gastric bypass and within a year weighed 150 pounds and was a size 10. "I was on top of the world, but again, I wasn't really dealing with how my body had changed," she says. The weight started coming back on—almost 40 pounds—until she went back to movement therapy and realized she was no longer applying her lotion. Once more, she had lost the connection between her head and her new shape. Now she does lotion therapy every night. Inhabiting her body again has allowed her to be kinder to it—she eats mostly protein, walks three miles a day, and has lost 20 pounds. "It's when I lose touch with how my body feels and how I feel about it that I put on weight. That's the key." ❶

> My sister made me switch clothes with her. I put them on, and they fit. That was mind-blowing.

O

health

25 Burning Health Questions

WE TAKE YOU RIGHT TO THE BOTTOM LINE

Is my microwave emitting death rays? Is bird flu still a threat? I do yoga, but should I also be lifting weights? You don't need to waste another second wondering and worrying. We've got the definitive answers right here.

1 Could my cell phone kill me? It seems unlikely. But if you use your mobile phone a lot, consider getting an earpiece or putting your caller on speaker so you can hold the phone away from your head. The biggest study yet, in which Danish researchers tracked 420,000 cell phone users for up to 21 years, found no cancer risk, but much of the data was collected when cell phones were more of a novelty than a primary form of communication. In a smaller recent Israeli study of 1,726 people, heavy cell phone use raised the risk for salivary gland tumors 50 percent on the side on which the subjects usually held the phone (though the risk overall is still vanishingly small). The biggest threat, however, has nothing to do with cancer: Driving while talking on a cell phone puts you in the same league as a drunk driver. You're four to five times more likely to have an accident.

2 Will vitamin D save my life? Should I really be taking four times the recommended daily dose? A growing body of evidence strongly suggests that vitamin D in high doses not only helps keep bones strong but also reduces the risk of colon, ovarian, and breast cancers, and diseases such as diabetes and multiple sclerosis. And many of us don't get enough because of a lack of exposure to sunlight (the sun triggers D's production in the skin) or diets that omit good sources (fatty fish such as salmon, mackerel, and tuna, and fortified milk and cereal). While the official daily dose for people age 51 to 70 is 400 IUs, most experts agree that they should aim for 800 to 1,000 IUs of supplemental D a day. But if you're under 50 and you consume the recommended 200 IUs (the equivalent of two glasses of milk daily) and get ten to 15 minutes of sun exposure—without sunscreen—a day, a 400 IU supplement should do you fine.

3 Is it okay to cleanse your body by fasting from time to time? As long as you are in good health, a brief liquid fast or cleanse is fine. But don't expect wonders—other than a sense of personal accomplishment, perhaps: Any physiologist will tell you that properly functioning lungs, liver, kidneys, and intestines do a fantastic job of keeping your body free of impurities without the help of fasting. If you decide to pursue a fast, always make sure to drink enough fluids to avoid dehydration.

4 Can I trust my tap water? Sure. Unless you're on a private well, tap water comes from municipal treatment plants that are carefully monitored and better regulated than bottled water. (Some popular brands like Aquafina and Dasani are just that: tap water.) Very strict federal rules now require extensive filtering of the water supply, but minuscule amounts of chemicals and pharmaceuticals may still turn up. If you want to ensure you're drinking the purest water possible, consider adding a filter to your tap. For information on filters, go to nrdc.org/waterfilters.

5 Is my kitchen microwave giving me cancer? No. Microwaving doesn't alter food in any way that could make you sick. All a microwave does is spur the water molecules in your food to move, and the friction of those molecules heats up your meal. The ovens do generate a tiny magnetic field, but there's very little evidence that such a field poses a problem for humans. What's more, there's an easy way to avoid any potential harm—step back when the oven is on.

6 How long am I contagious when I have the flu or a cold? As long as you have symptoms. Your ability to spread these viruses remains until the last sniffle, says Bill Schaffner, MD, a physician and infectious disease expert at Vanderbilt Medical Center in Nashville. And you're contagious 24 hours before you first show symptoms.

7 Is it true that 48 hours after starting antibiotics I can't infect someone else? Yes, that's true in most cases, and provided you really had a bacterial infection, like strep throat, and not a viral one—against which antibiotics are useless, says Schaffner. But the bug may come back if you quit the drugs early; also, if you fail to complete the full prescription, the leftover bacteria could develop antibiotic resistance and the drugs might not work next time.

8 Is bird flu still a danger? Yes. As of this writing, influenza A virus subtype H5N1—bird flu—has not made an appearance in the United States. But it still lurks in many parts of the world, particularly Asia and parts of Africa. What makes the virus so scary is its deadliness—it kills 50 to 80 percent of the people it infects. Currently the virus is primarily passed from an infected bird to a human. "You're not going to get it because you're on the plane with someone who has it," says Richard V. Lee, MD, a physician and infectious disease expert at the State University of New York at Buffalo. Nor does cooked chicken pose a risk, since heat kills the virus. But influenza viruses can evolve rapidly, and despite some promising vaccine developments, if the H5N1 virus develops an ability to spread rapidly between people anytime soon, it could spell disaster.

9 **How often do I really need to have my teeth professionally cleaned?** The answer depends on your habits at home, says periodontist Sally Cram, consumer adviser for the American Dental Association. Studies show it takes about three months for bacteria to take hold in the gums. Daily flossers who brush twice a day can get by with twice a year professional cleanings, but those who let things slide or have prior gum disease may need visits every two or three months. Diabetes, autoimmune diseases, and medications like antidepressants that dry out your mouth can also speed bacterial buildup and create a need for more cleanings, says Cram.

10 **Do the plastic bags from my dry cleaner contain toxic chemicals?** The plastic bag isn't dangerous, but the chemical residues it traps in your clothing might be, says Sarah Janssen, MD, an expert with the Natural Resources Defense Council, an environmental advocacy group. That smell your dry-cleaned clothes give off is perchloroethylene (perc), a chemical the state of California classifies as a potential carcinogen. Reduce your exposure by removing the bag and hanging the clothes outside—or in your bathroom with the window open or the fan on—to air. Don't leave bagged clothes in a hot car: The heat accelerates perc's release, and could make the air in your car toxic, says Janssen.

11 **Are the new birth control pills that eliminate your periods really safe?** Yes. There's no evidence that suppressing your period is dangerous. The periods you get on the regular Pill aren't real anyway, because the hormones prevent your uterus from building up the thick lining that's normally shed during menstruation. One reason the Pill's inventors included the off week was to mimic the normal menstrual cycle in the hope that the Pope might bless the Pill. Needless to say, he didn't.

12 **Will staring at a computer all day make me blind?** No. A marathon computer session is like a long hike. "If you walk long enough, your legs will be tired, but that doesn't mean you've permanently damaged them," says ophthalmologist John C. Hagan III, MD, a spokesperson for the American Academy of Ophthalmology. Focusing on a computer screen—a fixed distance—will leave your eye muscles tired and stiff, he says, plus you tend to blink less. The antidote: Look up from the computer screen every so often and focus on something 20 or more feet away, then blink briskly four or five times.

13 **Can diet soda kill me?** If you mean, could it give you cancer, the answer is probably not. Diabetes? Unlikely. Osteoporosis? Maybe. And it seems possible that the drinks are related to weight gain. Recent research suggests that having several diet drinks a day can weaken bones and is linked to weight gain, though the causes are very murky. Respected nutritionist Marion Nestle, PhD, author of *What to Eat* and *Food Politics,* has this to say: "I so prefer real sugar. The other sweeteners are all chemical and all artificial, and I'm not aware of much real evidence that they help people cut calories." A study published this year indicates just the opposite: In rodents, at least, there's evidence that the substitutes interfere with the body's ability to register how many calories it's taking in—which could lead to overeating.

14 **Flu shots—should I or shouldn't I?** Yes, absolutely. Although the CDC does not say everyone needs a flu shot, it does recommend them for enough people (due to health risks, age-related concerns, and other factors) that about 82 percent of the total U.S. population qualifies. Even if you don't, you'd be best off getting in line. According to flu expert Trish Perl, MD, a professor of medicine at Johns Hopkins University, "it usually prevents you from catching the flu, but even if you do get sick, your symptoms won't be as severe." More important, it prevents you from spreading the flu to others who might be at risk for developing a fatal case. (About 25 percent of people who have the flu don't even realize it.)

15 **Is there any surefire way to stave off Alzheimer's disease?** Unfortunately, no. The closest scientists have come was a vaccine against synapse-destroying beta-amyloid deposits, a hallmark of the disease. But human trials were stopped abruptly a few years ago when some volunteers developed severe brain inflammation. Still, studies suggest that you can take steps to help your brain—from staying intellectually, socially,

and physically active (exercise raises levels of a brain chemical called BDNF that encourages the growth of new brain cells) to eating more fruit, veggies, and salmon.

16 I have to stop eating tuna, swordfish, and salmon, right? Swordfish, yes. But for most other fish, the benefits of wise consumption outweigh the risks, according to a landmark study in the *Journal of the American Medical Association.* Swordfish contains high levels of mercury; canned albacore (white) tuna has more mercury than canned light tuna, which is why the Environmental Protection Agency recommends that women of childbearing age eat no more than six ounces of albacore per week. Though salmon does not pose a mercury risk, it may have PCBs (industrial compounds). Limit servings of farmed salmon to one a month; enjoy wild-caught four or more times a month. To learn which seafood is lowest in contaminants and isn't overfished, visit oceansalive.org.

17 When should I see a doctor about...
...a backache? See a physician immediately if the back pain keeps you from sleeping; you also have numbness in your leg, foot, groin, or rectal area; you also have fever, chills, nausea, vomiting, stomachache, weakness, or sweating; you've also lost control of urination or bowel movements; you've been in a car crash or other accident; you have a history of cancer. Otherwise, try over-the-counter pain relievers, alternating heating pads with ice packs, and a day or two of rest followed by gentle exercise for two to three weeks before making an appointment.
...heartburn? You'll want to call after two weeks of a burning sensation in the middle of your chest or abdomen—or

sooner if you have other signs of gastroesophageal reflux disease such as a dry cough or trouble swallowing despite using an over-the-counter antacid or reflux medicine.
...a fever? Go to the emergency room if you also experience stomach pain, nausea, or vomiting (it could be appendicitis); severe headache, neck stiffness, drowsiness, vomiting, and light sensitivity (possibly meningitis); you feel faint and confused after spending time outdoors in hot weather (signs of heatstroke).

Call your doctor right away if you have one or more of the following: a fever above 103 degrees; bloody diarrhea; a red rash or red streaks on your arm or leg; an earache; painful urination; sore throat; muscle and joint pain; back pain. If two days of an over-the-counter fever reducer (like aspirin or ibuprofen) doesn't bring down your temperature—or if you're also vomiting—it's time for professional help. Call in two weeks if you have a persistent low-grade (101 degrees or less) fever that doesn't go away.
...a sore throat? See a doctor immediately if you have one or more of the following: a fever of 101 degrees or higher; dehydration; difficulty swallowing or breathing; tender or swollen lymph glands in your neck; pus in the back of your throat; a red rash that feels rough, with increased redness in the skin folds; a persistent cough.

Call after three days if you also have body aches, headache, cough or runny nose.
...abdominal pain, diarrhea, vomiting? You'll need emergency treatment if you have one or more of the following: a fever above 102 degrees; tender abdomen; bloody diarrhea or black stools; sudden sharp pain that starts under your ribs and moves to your groin; backache; bloating and severe cramping; or you're pregnant and have abdominal or pelvic pain or vaginal bleeding. Call your physician right

away if you're in constant pain and have vaginal discharge or a burning feeling when you urinate; traveler's diarrhea that doesn't respond to over-the-counter medicines; or are taking a new medicine that seems to be causing diarrhea.

...muscle and joint pain? Get your internist or general practitioner on the phone immediately if you have a fever; red or swollen skin over the muscle; severe pain that has no obvious cause, a tick bite or rash; or if you recently started a new prescription or changed doses of a drug you've been taking. Otherwise, give rest and pain relievers three days to work before making a call.

18 Is liposuction worth it? Yes—but only to resculpt stubborn bulges after weight loss. It won't get rid of cellulite, and it's a bust for keeping you slim: In one study from the University of Texas Southwestern Medical Center, 43 percent of people who'd had lipo put the fat back on, mostly because they didn't adopt a healthy diet or exercise.

19 What's a sure way to stay cancer-free? There isn't one. The ugly truth is, some people who do everything right get cancer anyway. Still, bad habits worsen your odds. Tobacco use causes about one in three cancers overall, and diet, inactivity, and obesity contribute to another third of cases, says Peter Greenwald, MD, PhD, director of the division of cancer prevention at the National Cancer Institute.

20 Do I really need to lift weights? Isn't yoga enough? Yoga can build muscle, exercise physiologists say, as long as your muscles burn a little; poses like downward dog require you to lift and shift your own body weight. It's less clear whether yoga can build or maintain bone density—a benefit weight lifting confers—simply because it hasn't been studied. If your current yoga sessions don't feel challenging, or if your bones are thinning, consider adding strength training to the weight-bearing exercise (walking, for example) that you're already doing for your bones. (You are already doing it, right?)

21 Do self-tanners cause cancer? Nope. The faux glow is delivered by dihydroxyacetone (DHA), which only interacts with dead surface cells on the skin to create a color change that simulates a tan for five to seven days. However: "Although self-tanners do not cause cancer, they generally don't give any protection against UVB or UVA, so it's still important to use sunscreen to prevent aging, sun damage, and skin cancer," says Oanh Lauring, MD, a dermatologist at Mercy Medical Center in Baltimore.

22 Skip exercise when I have a cold, right? Not necessarily. "If the symptoms are above the neck, like a runny or stuffy nose, sneezing, or sore throat, exercising should pose little or no risk," says Cedric X. Bryant, PhD, chief science officer for the American Council on Exercise in San Diego. "In fact, mild to moderate exercise has been shown to help boost immune system function." But if your symptoms include body aches, chest congestion or tightness, and a hacking cough, workouts should be postponed.

23 Shouldn't everyone get the shingles vaccine? Not yet. "The vaccine has been studied only in relatively healthy people over age 60," says Stephen K. Tyring, MD, PhD, clinical professor of dermatology at the University of Texas Medical School at Houston. "There's no problem with healthy people under 60 receiving the vaccine, but insurance companies won't pay for the shot, which usually runs at least $150." People with weak immunity—those with cancer or HIV—should avoid this vaccine. A recent study coauthored by Tyring suggests that if a blood relative has had shingles, you could be at higher risk and may want to consider getting the vaccine.

24 Is it true that aluminum-based antiperspirants are dangerous? There's no evidence, according to the National Cancer Institute, though you wouldn't know it from the persistent Internet and e-mail rumors. Aluminum-based compounds such as those in antiperspirants can be absorbed by the skin and may behave like cancer-promoting estrogen in the body. But no one can say whether antiperspirants lead to a buildup of aluminum in breast tissue, or if that would trigger the breast cell changes that may lead to cancer. Aluminum-free alternatives are out there, though their effectiveness is questionable.

25 What's the best superfood? Sorry; there just isn't one. Forget the latest news stories on those supposedly magical treats like blueberries, chocolate, emu meat, or red wine. Researchers often get their amazing results by isolating a substance in the food and then injecting it into cells in a petri dish or administering amounts to rats that far exceed what you could realistically get in your diet. Yes, these foods are indeed healthy—but only as part of an overall sound diet. Don't let that news dismay you; it should be freeing. You don't have to track the latest food craze making headlines—just eat right and in sensible portions. Phew; that sure makes things easier. ◻

Is Your Medicine Making You Fat?

It's the side effect nobody thinks about until they look down and realize—hello!—they've gained 10, 20, 30 pounds. Yet almost any medication, from antidepressants to antihistamines, has the potential to make you ravenous or sluggish, or meddle with your metabolism. Sara Reistad-Long points to the worst offenders and tells you how to fight back.

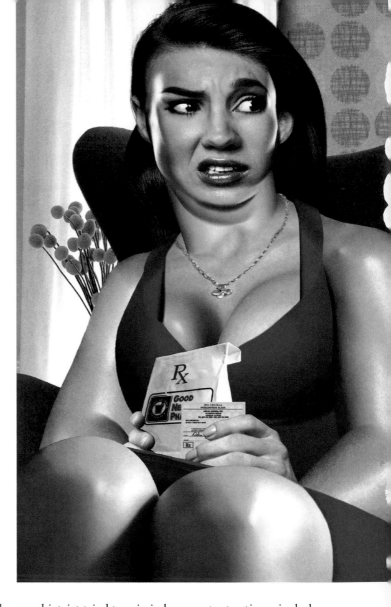

M ired in depression and a vicious work dispute, Barbara Tunstall placed her hopes on the antidepressant Remeron. Her doctor warned that food cravings were a potential side effect of the drug, but the 45-year-old Maryland insurance specialist put such concerns aside—initially. Tunstall felt so much better on Remeron that she soon found the energy to resolve her work troubles. Then she realized that she was gaining weight at an alarming pace: Just six months into her treatment, she had put on 30 pounds.

"I'd eat anything in my way," she says. "I knew I was out of control, but I still couldn't stop." Tunstall and her psychiatrist tried to rein in her constant eating—including adding a course of Topamax, an antiseizure medication known for its ability to suppress appetite—and yet nothing helped. The weight gain was adding a whole new list of frustrations and anxieties. Finally, her doctor weaned her off Remeron in favor of the antidepressant Celexa, a milder drug. Her cravings subsided, and Tunstall gradually shed the weight.

Fewer than 5 percent of Americans who are overweight got that way because of their medications, suggests research by Louis Aronne, MD, director of the Comprehensive Weight Control Program at New York–Presbyterian Hospital/Weill Cornell Medical Center, and a past president of the North American Association for the Study of Obesity. That's not a staggering number, but doctors are concerned nonetheless. Heart disease, diabetes, depression, and cancer are on the rise, and it's the drugs used to treat them that are most likely to pack on the pounds. "I think this is an underrecognized problem," says Aronne. "Most of the people we see aren't aware of the relationship between their weight and the drugs they're taking."

Some drugs drive up weight by making you drowsy or lethargic, which means you'll burn fewer calories throughout the day. Others affect brain chemistry in a way that trips hunger switches. Because everyone reacts differently to these drugs, it's virtually impossible to predict how much you might gain during treatment. What's more, remedies that aren't known for adding pounds still could. "Almost any medication can cause changes in weight," says Lawrence Cheskin, MD, an associate professor at the Johns Hopkins Bloomberg School of Public Health and director of the Johns Hopkins Weight Management Center. "Generally speaking, people who are sick lose their appetite. So when they're successfully treated for an illness, they may begin to eat more. If you're not aware of that consequence, it's easy to go overboard."

The best way to preserve your shape is to monitor yourself closely. "Anytime you start a new therapy, weigh yourself every morning," says George Blackburn, MD, PhD, associate director of the division of nutrition at Harvard Medical School, where he teaches a course that includes a section on drugs and weight gain. "Five pounds is your red flag to check with a physician." Act sooner if you suddenly feel excessively hungry or lethargic because you may be able to change prescriptions. "Increasingly, drugs linked to weight problems are being replaced with second-generation alternatives," Blackburn explains. Some are so new that your physician may not be aware of them, so consider seeing a specialist. A doctor who's trained to treat your specific problem, or at least an internist or an endocrinologist with an interest in obesity issues, will be up on the latest treatments.

In some cases, switching drugs—or readjusting the dosage—isn't an option. But according to Blackburn, eating 100 to 200 fewer calories each day is enough to counteract the kind of weight gain you'd experience on most drugs, especially if you increase your exercise. Below, the drugs most likely to tip the scale and what you can do about it.

ANTIDEPRESSANTS: Tricyclic medicines can add as many as nine pounds a month; lithium-based mood stabilizers, two and a half pounds. Another class of antidepressants, SSRIs, target the mood-and-appetite-related neurochemical serotonin and may also cause weight gain. If you begin to gain on one of these, look into switching to a bupropion drug; these target neurochemicals that don't increase hunger.

ANTIPSYCHOTICS: Haloperidol and clozapine can have a big effect on metabolism and appetite, adding as many as five pounds a week. Usually people on these drugs are already being monitored by a psychiatrist, so if the pounds start to add up, don't hesitate to ask about alternatives such as atypical antipsychotics, which appear to be weight neutral.

ANTIHISTAMINES, SLEEP AIDS: Many over-the-counter allergy remedies and sleeping pills contain diphenhydramine, an ingredient that can leave you drowsy during the day and interfere with your sleep patterns at night, reducing the number of calories you're burning.

BLOOD PRESSURE MEDICATION: Both alpha- and beta-blockers can cause fatigue, which may add pounds in some patients. If your energy fades, look into ACE inhibitors and calcium channel blockers.

CANCER THERAPY: Women with breast cancer are likely to gain weight during chemotherapy. The exact reasons for this are poorly understood, but doctors believe the treatment can slow metabolism. Also, the anti-estrogen drug tamoxifen may increase appetite; Decadron, a steroid used on cancer patients, is another potential culprit. Additionally, chemotherapy often induces early menopause, which can add pounds. Switching drugs isn't an option, so work with your doctors to develop an eating-and-exercise plan.

DIABETES DRUGS: Insulin helps process blood sugar by depositing it into cells. Insulin and drugs known as sulfonylureas can bring on bouts of hypoglycemia (low blood sugar), which stimulates appetite. Some patients report gaining up to 11 pounds during the first three to 12 months. Ask about weight-neutral medications, such as metformin.

MIGRAINE MEDICINES: Those based on valproic acid can stimulate hunger. These days, doctors are more likely to prescribe Topamax or Imitrex. Neither medicine is associated with weight gain, and both are thought to be safer.

STEROIDS: Oral corticosteroids, commonly used to treat rheumatoid arthritis and chronic inflammation, add pounds in multiple ways. They rob calories from your energy stores and send them to fat cells. So not only are you gaining weight but your energy is being compromised, which drives up your cravings. Some people can gain as many as 28 pounds on steroids. Ask about switching to prescription-strength NSAIDs (nonsteroidal anti-inflammatory drugs) such as ibuprofen.

If you gain weight due to medication, the key is patience. "When you go off the drug, you won't lose weight as fast as you gained it," says Aronne. "But by taking control of this aspect of your treatment, you'll start to see results." □

A Month of Living Perfectly

What would happen if instead of just thinking about taking better care of yourself (eat right, get enough sleep, exercise, floss, blah, blah, blah), you went ahead and—*urk*—did it? Would it be awful? Would you feel any better? Carol Mithers reports.

My health habits weren't horrible, but they weren't great, either. No sodas, fast food, or cigarettes, and I ate my share of broccoli...but I also liked heavy cream in my coffee, butter with dinner, and fortifying spoonfuls of ice cream when afternoon hunger hit. If I was stuck on what to have for lunch, the solution invariably included melted cheese. I was too fond of my evening cocktail(s). I exercised hard, but sporadically, and I never stretched. I wore sunscreen...sometimes. I usually forgot to floss. Etc.

I'd always gotten by. Mostly because of dumb genetic luck, I'm thin, with low blood pressure and cholesterol (I know, you hate me already). But I couldn't deny seeing some changes as I hit my 50s: less energy, a growing pot belly, pain that I assumed was early arthritis in my neck whenever I looked over my shoulder. Caring for aged parents and in-laws offered a none-too-gentle reminder that this was just the beginning.

But could it be slowed if I were very, very good? If I really cleaned up my act? What if, for a month, I embraced every health dictate we all know we should follow but blithely ignore? Would I feel rejuvenated, young? Or just like the butt of that old joke: "Eating healthy doesn't make you live longer...it just feels that way"?

With the help of the Internet, I researched a plan for perfect living. I'd follow traditional USDA guidelines for diet: 2,000 weight-maintaining calories a day, no more than 67 grams of fat (only 22 of them saturated fat), and no more than 1,500 milligrams of sodium. Exercise advice came from the government as well: a minimum of 30 minutes at "moderate intensity" most days of the week, though my goal was the more highly recommended 60 minutes of running, jogging, swimming, weight lifting, walking at 4.5 mph, or biking at more than 10 mph. Afterward I'd stretch my major muscle groups.

At some point during the day, I'd also do more personal exercise, aiming for increased sexual pleasure now and protection against urinary leakage later by strengthening

my pelvic floor muscles with Kegels, something I've been meaning to do, oh, since I gave birth 14 years ago. I would sit and stand up straight. Because I'm an osteoporosis poster child (a thin white woman whose grandma had a hump), I'd take a calcium supplement to make sure I got the recommended 1,200 milligrams each and every day. After I learned that as many as 30 percent of adults over 50 may have a reduced ability to absorb vitamin B₁₂ from food, I decided to add a B supplement as well.

Although evidence on the benefits and risks of alcohol is mixed, to be safe I also decided to cut out cocktail hour. I'd get seven hours of shut-eye a night because a six-year, large-scale popula-tion study of sleep done at the University of California, San Diego School of Medicine associated it with the low-est death rate among adults. I would floss every single day. And I would never, ever, *ever* venture out of the house without slathering on UVA/UVB sunscreen 30 minutes prior to exposure.

Sound uplifting? Frankly, the first two weeks were hell. I quickly realized that the peanut butter I always put on my morning toast (while healthy) along with the heavy cream in the coffee and my afternoon ice cream fixes (not so great) added up to about 45 grams of fat a day, almost half of it saturated. One tablespoon of the hot mango rel-ish I use as a condiment was 94 per-

> The temptation to say, *Oh, the hell with it!* hit daily when I craved something sweet and gooey.

cent of my daily salt allowance. And while I was getting too much fat, I wasn't getting nearly enough potassium, calcium, fiber, or variety. (Data from the Centers for Disease Control found that only about a third of Americans consumed fruits twice a day and only a quarter ate vegetables at least three times daily. Oy.)

Figuring out what I could and should eat, via "Dietary Guidelines for Americans," published jointly by the USDA and the Department of Health and Human Services, meant three hours of slogging through an 84-page downloaded file. Put as simply as possible, it advocated eating from all food groups every day—two cups of fruit and two and a half cups of vegetables a day, including veggies both dark green (kale, broccoli) and orange (carrots, squash), starches (potatoes, corn), and "other" (artichokes, green beans). I also needed six-ounce equivalents daily of grain (at least half of it whole grain); about five and a half ounces of meat, fish, or poultry; and three cups of milk or yogurt. I would also include four to five servings a week of legumes (varying from a half cup for beans and peas, one ounce for nuts, and two tablespoons for seeds). I made copious notes, shopping lists, menus.

As I switched, perhaps too quickly, to whole grain rolls with less peanut butter and nonfat milk in my coffee; salads heavy with vegetables, four nutritious ounces of white beans, and virtually no dressing; and yummy snacks of plums and raw carrot sticks, my stomach went noxious with fiber overload. Let's just say it was a good thing I work at home, alone.

The exercise regimen was only slightly better. Since I've worked out in the past, I know that a first-thing-in-the-morning session of lifting weights followed by a stationary bike ride in the later afternoon are the two things I'll do on a regular basis. I even own the equipment—I wasted money maintaining a gym membership for five years after I became a mother before admitting I'd never again find time to use it. Plus, when you work out at home, you can freely sweat, curse, and look like hell. But starting exercise after a lull is never pleasant. The only way to get through it was the fitness equivalent of "lie back and think of England": Outline what to do—today, work on triceps, chest, shoulders—do it, and don't even *think* about having fun. Listening to music with a driving beat made the time endurable. I also did a late afternoon dog walk, but as a work-

What I'd thought was arthritis had simply been unstretched muscles.

out it was utterly useless given my dog's stop, sniff, and pee habits. I missed my enormous yellow Lab; Haskell, may he rest in peace, demanded a daily death march at breakneck speed. Now *there* was a personal trainer.

As the days went by, the combination of workout and diet left me both charley-horsed and starving, longing for the satiation that only sugar and grease provide. The irony: Normally I'm one of maybe ten women in America who *aren't* obsessed with food, but I became fixated on portions, grams, what I had eaten that day, and what I could consume next. "You see what it does to you," said my friend Cathy, who has struggled with weight and diets for decades. "You get to where it's all you think about, and your whole approach to eating becomes distorted."

Other friends became positively indignant when I complained. "If *you* have trouble maintaining this diet, what use is it?" demanded one, her subtext transparent: *Oh, goody. I don't even have to try.*

By the end of the second week, hunger had become a constant companion, and I was in a foul mood about how little fun it was to eat, especially out of the house. I went to a Chinese restaurant with family on my birthday and sat, fuming, while everyone gorged on fried/salty/fatty delights and I got the broccoli garnishes. At my favorite Mexican joint, I exchanged my customary cheese-filled chile relleno for a bowl of sopa con pollo. I baked my daughter a birthday cake and watched as others wolfed it down.

It didn't help that my regimen was a time-consuming royal pain. Shopping became a two-hour ordeal because I constantly had to read labels to check nutritional content; only a tiny percentage of the grocery store bread marked "wheat" is actually *whole* wheat. I always put off flossing until right before bed, sometimes forgot, then had to get back up to do it. Remembering to stop whatever I was doing to tighten my pubic region several dozen times a day was distracting. The temptation to say, *Oh, the hell with it!* hit daily when I craved something sweet and gooey or a drink to ease my way into evening (actually, realizing just how much I missed alcohol was...sobering). But instead I had to worry about meeting my daily quota of orange vegetables. Butternut squash, pumpkin, sweet potatoes—I hated them all.

On the other hand, some things were becoming easier.

Good Is the New Perfect

It's hard as hell to do everything exactly the way the experts tell us to, but anyone can do better. Some painless ways to trick yourself toward health:

■ **Slash sugar and salt intake just by reading.** Labels, that is. You'll be shocked at how many foods—ketchup, spaghetti sauce, peanut butter, juices, cereals—are loaded with hidden sugar (a.k.a. glucose, fructose, sucrose, and the ubiquitous high-fructose corn syrup). The same goes for sodium: Abandon canned chicken noodle soup (a whopping 1,780 milligrams of salt per cup) for low-sodium minestrone or vegetable (a mere 290).

■ **Drink yourself skinnier.** There are about 144 calories in six ounces of white wine, 136 in 12 ounces of soda, 380 in a mocha Frappuccino, and—*caramba!*—as many as 740 in a frozen margarita. Make water or seltzer your beverage of choice.

■ **Don't cut out, cut back.** You can have your cake and eat it, too—on weekends. Two hundred fewer calories a day translates to nearly two pounds a month. So what, you ask? That's around 20 pounds a year, that's what. Enjoy the way weight loss creeps up on you…the same way weight gain did. But increase the amount of fruits and vegetables you eat—without frying, buttering, or drenching them in oil.

■ **Whatever exercise you're doing, do more.** You say you're too out of shape, too busy, too tired, too poor? Sisters, observe your feet. Already attached, always available, and free. Use them to walk to work (and eventually up the stairs), around the block at lunch, and down the hall when you need to talk to a colleague, instead of using the phone or e-mail. Walk from the farthest parking place at the mall, and walk on the weekend with friends and family. Walk around the house while you're on the phone.

■ **Pop a pill.** Take a basic, one-a-day multivitamin (with 400 micrograms of folic acid if you're of childbearing age). Ditto a calcium supplement; we need 1,000 milligrams a day until menopause and 1,200 thereafter (ask your doctor if she thinks it should be more and when to start annual bone density scans). Add B12 if you're over 50.
—**C.M.**

& Order reruns. It was possible for me to work at the computer without slouching—and when I listened to the little voice insisting that I "sit *up!*" my back didn't hurt at the end of the day. My exercise routine was getting easier (and if the music was particularly raucous, even enjoyable). Just ten minutes of stretching afterward—I followed a basic plan from the Mayo Clinic Web site—was loosening me up dramatically; in the car one afternoon, I looked over my shoulder to change lanes, and my neck didn't hurt. What I'd thought was arthritis and something I had to accept as part of getting older had simply been unstretched muscles. And given the pounds of roughage I was consuming, my normally recalcitrant bowels were working properly for the first time in decades. I realized that I'd grown accustomed to a constant feeling of bloat, which had disappeared.

By the end of the third week, something astonishing happened: The hunger went away. I missed the taste of chocolate, but I no longer fixated on it. I found a thick, Greek-style low-fat yogurt that was pretty satisfying if I packed it with fruit. (Okay, I also added some maple syrup.) I ate new vegetables, like Swiss chard and turnip greens. I tried recipes from an Indian cookbook that were high on spice, low on grease, and involved healthy combinations of potatoes, mushrooms, cauliflower, and lentils. Even my 14-year-old daughter liked them.

During the fourth week, I went to the dentist and for once was complimented on my "good oral care." I felt a little internal tightening from the Kegels, though I'd read that measurable results—like a husband shouting "Wow!"—could take months. My skin was rosy, and my thighs and upper arms looked sculpted, in a middle-aged kind of way. And my pants were way loose. Not only had I lost weight, but the roll around my gut was *gone.*

When my month of perfect living ended, I drank a double Scotch on the rocks, slept in instead of rising to pump iron, enjoyed ice cream and a chile relleno burrito that oozed grease. It was lovely not to have to worry about putting on sunscreen just to walk the dog, to let the flossing go (just for tonight), not to have to down a pile of squash.

But I never bought a replacement pint of cream for my morning coffee, so who was I kidding? Clean living hadn't made me young, but I felt and looked pretty freakin' terrific. My refrigerator is filled again with whole wheat muffins, fruit, and vegetables—orange ones, too. I'm giving myself a little leeway, like special occasion permission to indulge. But I'm back on the program. One month down; can't wait to see what happens in six. ◘

Taking calcium and B vitamins and putting on sunscreen every day wasn't hard. I had more energy after dinner now that I wasn't sucking back cocktails. I could realistically get seven hours of sleep a night by just saying no to *Law*

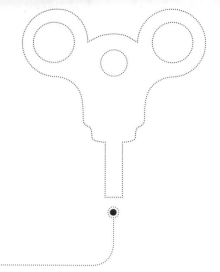

The Energy Makeover

Forget being able to leap tall buildings in a single bound—all **Penny Wrenn** wanted was enough oomph to get through the day. And she needed something more inspiring than "eat right, sleep right, exercise." So she went looking for her very own, very personal wind-up key….

W hen you spend as many hours as I've spent collapsed on the couch in front of the TV, you have a lot of time to think about how bushed you are and what you might do to give yourself more energy. At 30—single, no kids—I suffered not only from exhaustion but also from exhaustion guilt. I knew I was too young and unencumbered to be so tired, but even on my best days, when I started off grooving, the grooving inevitably became chugging, which quickly turned to churning, which eventually sank into grinding.

I'd tried the "exercise, eat right, get a good night's sleep" program—and found it unsustainable. I would run for a week, then run out of steam. My budget did better with $5 Kung Pao chicken dinners than $10 salads from Whole Foods. And my life as a freelance writer was too unpredictable and deadline intensive for a minimum-daily-requirement approach to sleep. There had to be another way.

So I devised an incredibly random and totally unscientific strategy to recharge, based on a few "if, then" theories I'd speculated about during those lethargic hours on the sofa.

1. If sluggishness, like yawning, was contagious (and judging by my family, I'd say the chances were good), then might energy be, too? In which case, would spending time with energetic people pep me up?

2. On the other hand, if one's energy level was the result of genetic predisposition, like big breasts or flawless skin, then, in the spirit of push-up bras and concealing foundation: Would faking energy give me energy?

3. Or maybe low energy was the result of a bad attitude—in my case, expressed by the mantra "I don't feel like it." If so, could I turn things around with a hearty dose of "I think I can"?

I'd conduct my own energy-building experiment, answering these questions and checking in with some experts along the way.

Afraid of losing momentum before I even got started, I quickly made a list of people whose energy I might be able to tap. My first (insane) thought was the fifth graders my friend Maria teaches—if ever a group of people had pep to spare, it would be a bunch of manic kids. But when I talked to Jon Gordon, author of *The Energy Bus,* he encouraged me not to confuse frenetic with

energetic; the former, he warned, is often a sign of being hopped up on what he calls stress energy. "The people who make you feel energized may not be the ones who are bouncing off the walls," Gordon said. My energy-by-osmosis experiment made sense to him; he told me that every social interaction is an exchange of energy. But he urged me to gravitate toward "the right kind of high-energy people"—people whose oomph was enthusiastic but focused, passionate but purposeful.

I immediately thought of my good friend Tracey—an irrepressibly happy, married working mother who lives in Brooklyn. In Tracey's world, everything is always "Great!" and "Yay!" Stop by her house unexpectedly, and she'll whip up a batch of cupcakes. She took up deejaying when her daughter was just 4 months old, and she spends her weekends zipping off to Home Depot with her happy, handsome husband. If my life were an episode of *Extreme Makeover*, Tracey would be my desired "after" picture. And hanging out with her would be more than just a chance to borrow some octane; it would also give me a chance to flex some faking-it muscle. I would match her "Yay!" for "Yay!"—even if it killed me.

But a funny thing happened on the way to Brooklyn. The sun was shining. All my normal clothes were in the laundry, waiting to be washed, so I ended up wearing a sexy summer dress I wouldn't otherwise have chosen. And feeling sexy gave me a spark—a spark so strong that it didn't fizzle out even when I ran into an old boyfriend and his new fiancée (whom I liked more in 20 minutes of chatting than I'd liked the boyfriend in two months of dating). By the time I showed up for brunch with Tracey, I was on an energy roll. I was present. I was engaged. My dress got the attention of an actor sitting one table away. (Flirty glances from handsome actor? Instant energy boost.) Tracey came with her family, and as we laughed and talked, I forgot I was there to wiretap her zest. I simply enjoyed myself.

NEW ATTITUDE: Penny Wrenn found her inner potential for pep.

And then another funny thing happened: On the way to Tracey's house after brunch, she expressed surprise at my low-energy complaints. "I've always seen you as energetic," she said. Then she stunned me with the news that *she* envied *my* energy vibe—specifically, the way I could talk to anyone about anything and become the resident conversation-engager in a room.

I figured that since we were being honest, I might as well tell her that I was jealous of the way she was always "Great!" and always had stuff to "Yay!" about.

Then she compared me to Dorothy's friends in *The Wizard of Oz*—the Scarecrow looking for brains, the Tin Man looking for a heart, the Lion looking for courage, when in fact they'd had these things all along.

I went back to my couch to think about what Tracey had said. She wasn't the only person who was baffled by my energy quest. So maybe I wasn't as low energy as I thought. Or maybe I was defining energy the wrong way.

It was true, as Tracey believed, that I zoomed in the presence of other people. I greeted friends with an excited "Hey!" or "Look at you!" I hugged, kissed, complimented, checked in on the latest news. I smiled a lot. And laughed—loudly—when I got a kick out of someone. It was usually when I was alone that I felt zapped.

Maybe I had two personas—

onstage and backstage. Or maybe I'd been unwittingly faking it all along, at least in some situations.

Judith Orloff, MD, author of *Positive Energy,* doesn't believe in faking it; instead she endorses "acting as if." "You want the energy to be real," she told me when I called her for advice. Faking it, she explained, is merely going through the motions—the product of a "getting it over with" mentality. "Acting as if," on the other hand, requires actually getting into the energy act and telling yourself, *I am energetic* or *I have the energy I want.* It is about trying, and practicing, and it could lead to something positive.

When I told Orloff about my date with Tracey, she zeroed in on the jealousy. "Being envious or comparing yourself all the time binds up energy," she cautioned. Point taken. But why, then, had the "I'm jealous of your ____"; "Well, *I'm* jealous of *your* ____" exchange with Tracey felt so refreshing?

"Expressing yourself clearly and lovingly—while not holding anything back—can be an amazing energy boost," Orloff said. "Honesty can set energy free."

Expressing yourself clearly and lovingly can be an amazing energy boost. I couldn't get those words out of my head; and it dawned on me that maybe this was because I am at my least clear and least loving when I'm *in* my head. When I'm feeling lethargic, I don't give myself a pep talk; I don't recognize the specific things I *have* accomplished, or remind myself of my ability to get things done. Instead I let my inner Mommie Dearest take over, which leads to brutal self-accusations about falling short, underperforming, underproducing, underachieving. The voice in my head turns into a hammer: *Get out of bed! Off the couch! Get it together already! What's wrong with you? Whatever it is, get over it!*

I'd always believed that voice. I believed that lethargy could be cured only with scolding and tough love. Now Orloff was telling me it would rather be killed with kindness. In her eyes, beating up on myself for feeling low only brought me lower. A more effective step toward "setting an energetic tone," she said, would be to practice compassion for myself. If I could be kind to myself, without a "must" or "should" attached, I would be all the more energized.

The real enemies of energy are anxiety and hopelessness.

More than a week had passed since I began my experiment—so was I brimming with vim and vigor? Put it this way: No. But there was a shift that came directly from moments of being nicer to myself. Saying to myself, *I know you're not up for it—and baby, I know you're tired—but let's give it a go anyway, shall we?* made it easier to get up in the morning. Being kinder to myself also helped me become more aware of the places in my daily routine where lethargy liked to lurk but could be cut off at the pass. My desk chair, for instance: I noticed that after three hours, my bum started to hurt; since discomfort can be a downward spiral to exhaustion, I started getting up and walking around a few times a day. My bed: Those snooze-button intervals were a drag. I didn't fall back to sleep—I just lay awake wallowing in "I don't have the juice" self-pity. So I started rising as soon as the alarm first sounded.

When I spoke to Orloff again to report on my progress, she said I was energetically tuning in to my body. Yet even with the slightly higher buzz from all my findings (that a sexy dress can tilt the energy scale in your favor, that confessing your jealousy to a good friend lightens an emotional load, that exhaustion isn't a thing to be beaten into submission), I still didn't have the energy I was hoping for.

But I had one more task to go: overcoming "I don't feel like it." So I called David Burns, MD, author of the cognitive therapy bible, *Feeling Good: The New Mood Therapy.* Cognitive therapy helps people change the self-defeating thoughts that lead to self-defeating behavior; "I don't feel like it" seemed ripe for such a change.

When I told Burns that I was looking for alternatives to the "exercise, eat right, get a good night's sleep" prescription, he had this to say about that advice: "That's garbage." The man was now officially my hero.

"Those solutions offer more of a placebo effect than anything else," he told me. "They don't get at what's really going on with people." Burns said the real enemies of energy are feelings of inadequacy and worthlessness, anxiety, hopelessness. And he was willing to guide me through his method for dealing with those feelings.

When clients complain to Burns that they wish they had more energy, his response is always, "More energy to do what?" It's an obvious question, but when he turned it on me, I was stumped.

What *would* I do with more energy? Shower more often? Floss before bedtime? Hang the framed paintings that had been stashed in the corner of my living room for I'm ashamed to say how long? Scrub the coffee cup rings

off my desk (which would first require digging out the desk itself from under the piles of junk that had accumulated all over it)? Shop for a new pair of ballet flats? Read *The New York Times*? Learn Spanish? Rejoin eHarmony (oh, but the thought of filling out that online questionnaire again—it had to be ten pages long!)?

I floated these ideas to Burns, who insisted that I choose one thing to start with. If I examined a single

Energy Boosters & Busters

■ Boosters

EXERCISE. A University of Georgia analysis of 70 studies on exercise and fatigue overwhelmingly showed that regular workouts increase energy levels.

TYROSINE SUPPLEMENTS. "Tyrosine is an amino acid that acts like caffeine without the downsides," says Hyla Cass, MD, author of *Supplement Your Prescription*. She also recommends coenzyme Q10, a fat-soluble vitaminlike compound that helps convert nutrients into energy.

ACUPUNCTURE. "An unexpected benefit is that it seems to make a person's energy more available to her," says Rosa N. Schnyer, an acupuncturist and investigator at the Osher Institute at Harvard Medical School.

NAP. To recharge from the afternoon dip, lie down for 20 to 30 minutes—no longer, or you'll wake up groggy, says Phyllis C. Zee, MD, director of the Sleep Disorders Center at Northwestern Memorial Hospital in Chicago.

■ Busters

STRESS. When prolonged and unresolved, it can cause the adrenal glands to stop producing as much cortisol. Low levels of cortisol, known as the stress hormone, can leave you feeling lethargic.

WINTER DARKNESS. "Lack of energy is the number one complaint of people with seasonal affective disorder," says SAD expert Kelly Rohan, PhD, an assistant professor of psychology at the University of Vermont in Burlington (more info at healthyminds.org/factsheets/LTF-SAD.pdf and mayoclinic.com/health/seasonal-affective-disorder/DS00195).

BOREDOM. "We know about burnout, from doing too much, but there's also 'boredout,' caused by doing too little," says Carl Mumpower, PhD, a clinical psychologist in Asheville, North Carolina. The longer you're bored, the less energy you have and the more likely that this temporary feeling can become permanent, he says. —**Dana Sullivan**

daunting task, he said, I could uncover what was making me avoid it. Dubious, I chose the desk.

Burns went to work, tossing out diagnostic questions: "Why would you bother cleaning your desk?" (Oh, I don't know—maybe because stuff is starting to stick to the coffee cup rings?) "What negative thoughts come to mind when you consider the task?" (Only disorganized losers, with little hope of ever making sense of their lives, have desks that look like mine.) "On a scale of one to 100, how angry, hopeless, frustrated, inadequate, or guilty do those thoughts make you feel?" (85.)

I could almost feel the dots connecting. No wonder I rarely felt like doing anything: The mere thought of the attempt detonated a smoke bomb of negative self-opinions. Emotionally, it was easier to avoid the tasks altogether.

In his book, Burns talks about a problem that is endemic even to to-do-list makers. He calls it do-nothingism, and says that like its close relative, procrastination, it's rooted in defeatism (the belief that your efforts won't get you anywhere), feeling overwhelmed (*It's all too much*, you think), and fear (of disapproval, of success, of failure, or of not getting it "just right").

I saw, now, that "I don't feel like it" was my version of do-nothingism. Given that so many of the to-dos on my list were ruled by other people's needs or whims, "I don't feel like it" was my attempt at invoking some do-as-I-please autonomy. But if Burns was right in saying that action often leads to motivation and energy—and not the other way around—then my stubborn refusal to engage was only getting in my way.

That insight led me straight to Jim Loehr, coauthor of *The Power of Full Engagement: Managing Energy, Not Time, Is the Key to High Performance and Personal Renewal.* I liked Loehr's definition of engagement: "the ability to bring your full and best energy to whatever one is doing at the moment—right here, right now." And I felt a perverse glee when he told me, "People start getting less efficient at producing and recovering energy around age 25 or 30." (Depressing but validating; maybe I wasn't too young to be exhausted, after all!)

What I didn't like so much about Loehr's ideas, at least at first, was that he's a big "exercise, eat right, get a good night's sleep" guy. But as we talked, I started to see his point. A higher energy dividend, he said, comes with properly earning and spending the get-up-and-go currency that we call oomph, pep, zest, or "the juice." According to Loehr, the energy cycle breaks down this way: Make it, use it, replenish it, repeat. Twenty-minute walks and leafy green vegetables were "make it" endeavors. Six hours of sleep instead of three were replenishment.

And where I usually messed up—as Loehr told me most of us do—was in the "use it" cycle. Loehr blames the *underuse* of energy for much of the world's exhaustion. The biggest underuse culprit: being in a sedentary position for long periods of time. As in, ahem, watching TV.

Yet energy isn't only about what we do to, and with, our bodies, Loehr said. He, like the other experts I spoke with, believes energy must be considered from four angles: physical, mental, emotional, and spiritual. I was starting to understand the first three components, but what about the fourth?

I thought back to the conversation I had with Jon Gordon; he'd asked if I felt spiritually connected to a higher power.

"Like God?" I'd said. "Not really." Don't get me wrong; I believe in something bigger than me. But did I feel the pull of a certain life force lately? No. And now I began to wonder if my lack of vigor was related to a spiritual disconnect.

So I took a final detour in my energy journey: I made a date to see a clergyman.

Sitting across from me in his office at the Convent Avenue Baptist Church in Harlem, Jesse T. Williams Jr., the church's head cleric, shared with me that energy is a spiritual notion—or as he put it, "God has everything to do with it."

As a churchgoer, I'd felt the motivating boost of a booming Sunday morning sermon. But it always wore off. How then, I wondered aloud, to tap into this power on a regular basis? Williams's answer was simple: Ask. "Give us this day our daily bread"—that's his own approach, requesting no less zest, and no more, than he needs.

And maybe sufficiency is the point. Call it "giving it all you've got." Some days my all is a lot; some days it's not. After conferring with the experts and starting to practice what they preach, I've discovered that I can tilt the odds in favor of higher-energy days by being more present, letting go of envy, getting out of bed, eating a vegetable once in a while. Just as important, instead of stressing out about low-energy days—which only adds to the cycle of exhaustion—I now take them in stride. I show myself some compassion. I give myself a break. I say to myself, *Not bad, baby,* and I feel good. Not "Great!" exactly. But pretty damn good. Which, for today, is energy enough for me. ◨

"Why Am I So Tired?"

Sari Harrar reports on four of the most often overlooked causes of fatigue.

The bounce in your step has become a plod. Climbing stairs feels like summiting Mount Everest. Your brain's mired in fog. Whatever your personal energy crisis might be, it's time to act. "Fatigue that's new or dramatic, prolonged or unexplained, can signal a serious medical problem like heart disease or anemia," says Lori Mosca, MD, director of preventive cardiology at New York–Presbyterian Hospital. "A lot of women hesitate to tell their doctors about low energy. But if you're feeling any new kind of tired, speak up." Your physician should check for the usual suspects, like insomnia, stress, sleep apnea, depression, and diabetes. If she rules those out, ask her to probe deeper for these often overlooked causes.

LOW THYROID

Located at the base of your neck—and barely larger than the knot in a bow tie—the thyroid gland controls your body's metabolic speed by producing the hormones T4 and T3. If it churns out too little—as may happen in 12 to 15 percent of women at midlife—"all the processes in your body slow down," says Alan Farwell, MD, chairman of patient education and advocacy for the American Thyroid Association. The result: decreased endurance and a sluggish mind.

WHY IT'S OVERLOOKED: "Some people are very sensitive to small changes in thyroid hormones," Farwell says, "even when their numbers aren't low enough to qualify for treatment. After age 70, 25 percent of women may have subclinical or mild hypothyroidism."

OTHER SYMPTOMS: Weight gain. Feeling cold. Constipation. Dry skin and hair. Depression.

TESTS: You'll get blood checks for levels of T4 and thyroid-stimulating hormone (TSH). High TSH plus low T4 is a sign of full-blown hypothyroidism, but pay attention if your TSH is high and your T4 is normal—you may have mild hypothyroidism, which should still be treated.

TREATMENT: Synthetic thyroxine pills.

HEART TROUBLE

Fatigue is a distinct characteristic of cardiovascular disease in women, according to recent research. In one study of 515 female heart attack survivors, 70 percent reported unusual fatigue in the weeks before; just 57 percent had acute chest pain. In another study, fatigue was a symptom for women with dangerously clogged arteries that escaped notice on heart scans.

WHY IT'S OVERLOOKED: Only one in ten women realizes that heart disease is her biggest health threat. And emergency room doctors are six times more likely to give women with serious heart problems (as opposed to men) a clean bill of health.

OTHER SYMPTOMS: Shortness of breath. Indigestion. Pain in your shoulder, arm, or jaw. But for many women, nothing at all.

TESTS: Your doctor will order an exercise stress test or angiogram if she suspects clogged arteries in your heart. Because that test isn't always accurate in women, she may order a CT scan or echocardiogram as well. She'll also test your cholesterol, blood pressure, and blood sugar—diabetes can quadruple a woman's heart risk.

TREATMENT: You may get a cholesterol-lowering statin and medicines to treat blood pressure, such as diuretics. You'll also be advised to follow a heart-healthy diet and get regular exercise.

TIRED BLOOD

Heavy menstrual periods, pregnancy, avoidance of red meat, or being a vegetarian or a serious distance runner can all drain your body's stores of energizing iron, leaving you anemic. That means underpowered red blood cells can't deliver enough oxygen to every cell in your body, says iron researcher Rebecca J. Stoltzfus, PhD, professor of nutrition at Cornell University. Your muscles may feel weak, your thinking gets cloudy. One in five women and half of all pregnant women may have low iron.

WHY IT'S OVERLOOKED: In a blood test, having numbers at the low end of normal can mean you won't get treatment

even though it could help. Studies show that treating anemia with iron supplements under a doctor's care can relieve fatigue. (Never take iron supplements on your own—about one in 200 people have a genetic condition in which their bodies can't process iron, leaving them vulnerable to overdose.)

OTHER SYMPTOMS: Abnormally pale skin. A fast heartbeat. Irritability.

TESTS: Hemoglobin and hematocrit screens will reveal the levels of iron-rich, oxygen-carrying hemoglobin in your blood and the number of red blood cells. Your doctor should also look at the size and color of your red blood cells (small and pale could mean trouble). Ask about a serum ferritin test, too—it measures a protein that helps store iron.

TREATMENT: Expect to get a short course of iron supplements and advice to follow an iron-rich diet. "Your doctor will retest your blood in one to two months. If your iron levels are rising, you'll continue on the same plan for a few more months to rebuild your reserves," says Matthew Heeney, MD, director of the Hematology Clinic, Children's Hospital Boston. "If levels are still low, your doctor will look for other causes." These can include mild but chronic internal bleeding or compromised blood cell production.

LIVER VIRUS

If you ever experimented with IV drugs (even once), snorted cocaine through a straw, had a blood transfusion before 1992, or have ever received abnormal results on a liver function test, you need a hepatitis C test—whether or not you're feeling tired. "Most of my patients are pillars of the community today—the things they did in their youth are well behind them," says liver disease expert Michael W. Fried, MD, director of hepatology at the University of North Carolina at Chapel Hill. "Once you're feeling persistently tired, liver damage may have begun."

WHY IT'S OVERLOOKED: "Many family doctors won't ask about risky behavior in your distant past—especially if you don't look the part now," Fried says. "If you're feeling tired and know you have risk factors, tell your doctor so you can be tested."

OTHER SYMPTOMS: Jaundice, diminished appetite, fever, aches, and other flulike symptoms may occur soon after infection. But often the only symptom is fatigue 20 or 30 years later.

TESTS: First, a blood check for hepatitis C antibodies. If results are positive, further testing includes a liver enzyme check and possibly a liver biopsy to assess liver health.

TREATMENT: Weekly injections of peginterferon plus daily ribavirin capsules. This combination can cure about 50 percent of hepatitis C, Fried says. ◘

Kelly Corrigan with daughters Claire (*left*) and Georgia, at home in Piedmont, California, 2005, the year after her treatment.

You Can't Possibly Let Cancer Have Its Way

How can you be sick—or worse—when there are two little girls who need you? **Kelly Corrigan** confronts the mother of all fears.

It's clear to you immediately that you can have anything you want when you have cancer. Your doctor called at 1 P.M. and since that moment, your husband has met your every need, even anticipating needs (proving that he has been capable of doing so all along). Word spreads and your doorstep shows it—a cheery bunch of gerbera daisies, a little tin of peanut butter cookies, a calla lily. The phone calls are endless. Everyone treats you like a saint, an elderly disabled saint.

Except two people who still want you to find their bunny—not that one!—and fill up their sippy cup and read them a book. They never say please and they always interrupt and they lean into you even when you are so hot already. And their ignorant self-centeredness is proof that you are still managing to put your children first even when you are in the crisis of your life.

Claire comes toward you with her diaper bulging and her hair stuck to her forehead with the musty sweat that builds up during her morning nap. She knocks over your tall pilsner glass of iced peppermint tea, the one Edward made for you in a moment as romantic as the one in which he proposed. Claire doesn't say she's sorry, she just cries because now her T-shirt is wet on the bottom part and she loves her Elmo and Rosita T-shirt. Georgia cries, too, because the tea went onto her paper where she is scribbling. She is so close to 3. Her party is in five days. You've been talking about it for months—when you cut up her apple, when you push her in the swing, when you put her to bed.

"Guess what's happening in two weeks from today?" you say.

"Ooh, look! The mailman took the party invites!"

Then, between all of the calls to medical centers, long sessions on breastcancer.org, and e-mails to work colleagues, Edward says, "We're not gonna do the party, right? It's too much." But you say, "No! She has to have it!" because you are feeling dramatic and magnanimous and like you can't possibly let cancer have its way with your daughter's first real birthday party. He says, "She'll never even remember it."

"I will," you say.

On Wednesday, you swing into the mammography center to pick up your films to take them over to the national expert you will wait three hours to see, making lists and pretending to sleep and reading old *People* magazines about Jen and Brad and that Angelina Jolie. On the way home, even though you've just been told you will do chemo for five months and then probably have a mastectomy after that, and even though it's dinnertime, you pass Michaels craft store and tell Edward to pull in—"real quick"—so you can get some decorations and grab some balloons, and he looks at you like you've just cut your own hair with a kitchen knife.

But then you're there, at Michaels, and it's so exciting to be in line with people whose great concerns are finding three matching green photo mats and some extra-wide grosgrain ribbon for their fall door wreath. The tired cashier says, "How are you tonight?" and you say, "Good!" and it's the biggest lie you ever told as well as the God's honest truth and you don't really know what you're doing but someone's gonna have a great birthday on Saturday and it'll all be because of you and you aren't irrelevant yet, even if you are defective and are messing up everything for your family.

You are perky coming out of the store, even holding the door for the woman behind you, who is having a bad day, you can tell. Edward is slumped over the steering

wheel like he's been shot from behind, which he kind of has. He sits right up when he feels you coming toward the car. He is "fine, just tired."

Your kids are asleep when you return home and Sophie, the babysitter whose skin breaks out every time she has a pop quiz, looks at you tragically but you divert her by saying, "Look! Look at these great party hats—they go with the plates—see?" You sound like Mrs. Dalloway. Edward hands Sophie a wad of twenties and says, "Thanks, Soph."

You unpack your shopping bag from Michaels and show Edward the candy decorations for the cake you haven't made but will and he says "good" and you can't

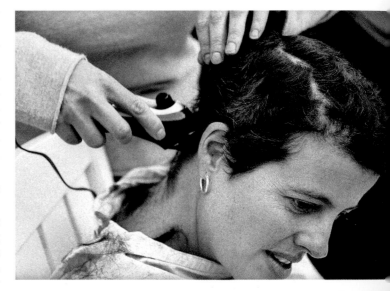

...you realize you will have to have a conversation... You google "talking to children about cancer."

And then you realize your daughters don't know what death is. Because why should they?

bear to ask him how he is again because it might come out this time for real and so you just turn on the stereo and as he heads to the answering machine, you say, "Let's do that tomorrow" because the machine says 14 people called and every one of them wants to tell you that you are in their prayers and that God doesn't give you anything you can't handle and what doesn't kill us makes us stronger but Edward is responsible and levelheaded and says, "It could be about your bone scan." You realize you forgot something in the car, maybe, so you say, "Okay, I gotta go get something in the trunk anyway," and when you come back he says, "The scan is on Friday. I'll call Sophie."

The party is scheduled for Saturday afternoon and when you send out the e-mail about it—yes, it's happening, please no cancer talk—you realize you will have to have a conversation with your children before all these people come over. You google "talking to children about cancer" and you start to worry that some kid will say, "My grandma died of cancer" and then you realize your daughters don't even know what death is. Because why should they?

Then you find this line: "Cancer is like weeds in a garden." That's really good—so tangible, so everyday. You think you should send a thank-you card to the person who came up with that phrase. *See how important words are?* you think.

The bone scan makes you cry. "Stay still, please," says the technician, who has an Irish accent and looks like a guy who loves his pub. It's so big, the machine, it's so Willy Wonka/Mike Teavee and you can tell it is extremely expensive and you know very little but enough to know that if they find it in your bones, you'll probably die before you turn 40. And that's why you cry and that's why the technician asks you again to "stay very still" but when he comes to your side to help you up off the table, he has tears in his eyes and you know that he does this every day so why would he cry?

Friday is a two-Ambien night. Sleep is deep and black and divine.

Saturday! The party. Georgia is at your feet in no time. "Mommy! I'm 3! I'm 3 years old!"

From left: Edward, Georgia, Claire, and Kelly regroup at home after a round of chemo.

"You are. Do you feel any different?"

"No."

"Are you sure?"

"No, I don't feel anything. Everything feels exactly the same." She looks concerned.

"Well, even if you can't feel it, it's real," you say, newly expert in the matter.

Edward comes in and lifts Georgia up and she is so happy and the party will be great.

Everyone will come with a bigger gift than they had planned—at the last minute they will tape something extra on the top: a recorder, a ponytail holder, a My Little Pony. Claire will also get a pile of gifts. In an hour, Georgia will blow out her candles and there will be wrapping paper everywhere and the goody bags that complement the paper plates will be torn through and it'll all be on film and toward the end, after about half the people have left and the afternoon is drifting toward 5 o'clock, you will open a bottle of Chardonnay and the remaining mothers will gather around and fill little polka-dot paper cups and you will all stand in the sun and look at each other and your children and shake your heads and make that little laugh sound you make when you don't know what else to say, the little sound that says "didn't see this coming" and you will lean into one of them and feel that tiny contraction in your throat that means you're going to cry and you will decide to let it come, it's really okay now, because Georgia is running in circles on the back deck with her new butterfly wings on and a hot pink helium balloon tied to each wrist and needs absolutely not one more thing from you.

For now. ⓞ

beauty/style

The Revolution Starts Here!

Everywhere we turn, there are images of gorgeous women, constant reproaches to the reality of *us*, with our real bodies and un-Photoshopped flaws. We're not buying it anymore. We're tackling the critics—from the parents and teachers who favor the prettiest children to look-ist employers to the most hurtful of all, that nasty, catty girl who lives right behind our eyes. By Valerie Monroe

ot long ago, I sat in my office, chatting with a friend. "I want to talk to you about your face," I said. "Oh my God," she said, looking stricken. "Do I need a facelift?" (I forget that people think I have a right to be openly critical of their appearance because I'm a beauty editor.) No, no, I said; I only wanted to know what she saw when she looked in the mirror.

"I like my face now," said this woman, a classically beautiful 38-year-old, very polished and buttoned-up, as neat and perfectly composed as a Modigliani painting. "But I was adopted from Korea when I was 3, and I grew up in a predominantly white community in a small Midwestern city, where there weren't many other people who looked like me. I was teased, called names; I basically spent my entire childhood being made fun of because of my face." She said this calmly and, recollecting, was silent for a moment. I waited for her to go on. But when she tried to speak again, she burst into tears. And there she sat in the chair across from my desk, crying hard for several minutes. I offered her a handful of tissues while she apologized for breaking down. This woman is so self-controlled, I've even seen her yawn. Finally, she said, "I didn't realize how fragile I still am about this.

"I wanted to do anything I could not to look Asian, because it set me apart," said my friend. "You know, I had some really bad perms. But when I got to college, where there were a mix of ethnicities, the stigma of my face just disappeared. There were people who appreciated my beauty, and so I began to see myself the way they did." In other words, she made the liberating discovery that there was nothing wrong with her face, and something wrong with the culture of her hometown.

> Gorgeous is not a good stock to invest in. No matter what you do, how well you take care of yourself, one day you are going to lose everything on your investment.

Though race hadn't been an issue for me, I, too, was teased and called names because of my appearance (suffice it to say I spent several difficult years as a grasshopper before slowly metamorphosing into a normal-looking teenager). And I, too, did everything I could to try to fit in with my peers, including dying my dark hair blonde and tweezing my brows into a shape that might generously be called unnatural. In a way, we're all trying to "pass," minimizing with cosmetics (or, in the extreme, surgery) what deviates from the cultural ideal, playing up what conforms, says Rita Freedman, PhD, a clinical psychologist and author of the 1986 book *Beauty Bound.* "It's what you project onto the reflection in the mirror that determines how you evaluate it," she says.

I spoke to several other women I had assumed—because they are all accomplished and beautiful—felt fine about their face. One, thinking of a photograph of herself as a 13-year-old, teared up as she remembered the depth of her self revulsion. (This time I was ready with the tissues.) Another tried determinedly to convince me that she was a truly ugly person till her 20s, at which point, she said, she was briefly attractive before becoming merely plain in her 30s. A third told me she couldn't wait to get glasses so that she could hide the gigantic bump on her nose (a gigantic bump that was invisible to me). And a fourth—stunning, without a stitch of makeup—said that she knew she wasn't horribly disfigured, but avoided looking at her face in the mirror whenever possible (as if she were...horribly disfigured).

Though the cultural ideal has broadened to include more diversity, it remains an ideal, setting an unrealistic standard by which we all, consciously or not, judge and are judged. The painful truth is that physically attractive people get rewarded in all kinds of ways: As children they're usually disciplined less harshly and favored in the classroom; as adults they tend to have better-paying jobs in higher-level positions than their less attractive counterparts, writes Gordon L. Patzer, PhD, in his recently published book, *Looks: Why They Matter More Than You Ever Imagined.* Which, frankly, stinks.

It stinks even if you're gorgeous, by cultural standards. Valuable as it is, gorgeous is not a good stock to invest in. It has a completely predictable payout. No matter what you do, how well you take care of yourself, how much surgery you submit to, one day you are going to lose everything on your investment. You know this, I know this. Even so, we buy into the beauty rules, colluding with a culture that makes us feel inadequate, whipping ourselves when we come up short. Which makes us—come to think of it—part of the problem.

What if, instead of colluding, we traded cruelty for kindness? What if we started a revolution, if each one of us took a vow to catch ourselves scowling or sneering at our imperfections—and simply stop? If we noticed every time we had a nasty, hostile response to someone else's appearance—and simply stopped? Think about who your inner critic is: She's the mean girl who doesn't want you in her club, the one who takes pleasure in pointing out all the ways you don't measure up. Her trump card is your fear, fear that you will *never* measure up, that you are, bottom line, unlovable. Every moment you spend calculating your imperfections (or anyone else's), you are taking her side.

This is a call to arms. A call to be gentle, to be forgiving, to be generous with yourself. The next time you look into the mirror, try to let go of the story line that says you're too fat or too sallow, too ashy or too old, your eyes are too small or your nose too big; just look into the mirror and see your face. When the criticism drops away, what you will see then is just you, without judgment, and that is the first step toward transforming your experience of the world.

Are you ready to quit the cruelty and take a pledge to be kinder? Sign up today for the beauty revolution. Go to oprah.com/omagazine and click on Val Monroe. **O**

Barbour, *left,*
and *below,*
at age 11,
Indiana, 1974.

"You Look Fine. Sit Up Straight."

Parents say the darnedest things. Two *O* staffers come forward with their own stories, starting with Celia Barbour.

I knew how I was supposed to look, and that I didn't measure up. My sources were, on the one hand, *Charlie's Angels* and, on the other, the hallway mirror, which testified to the inadequacy of my 13-year-old body.

"I'm so fat and ugly no one's ever going to like me," I moaned to my mother.

She was not alarmed. She said, almost scoldingly, "You look fine. You are *not* fat. Sit up straight and finish your breakfast."

Clearly, she was blind. I embarked on a jogging regimen, awakening in the darkness to put on my Adidas, slip-

Instead of helping me overcome my freakishness, my parents pretended not to see it.

ping out of the house. When I returned, my father barely looked up from his oatmeal. "If you want exercise, there's plenty of lawn to be mowed," he said.

My parents' obtuseness antagonized me. Instead of helping me overcome my freakishness, they pretended not to see it. To them, exercise and dieting were frivolous. The whole pursuit of beauty—makeup, blow-dryers, my beloved *Mademoiselle* that explained step-by-step how to create a *smoldering eye*—was a huge, scandalous waste of energy. I longed with the deep hunger of the malnourished to experience prettiness in all its artificially enhanced forms. But I couldn't even walk through the kitchen with blush on my cheeks without drawing their quiet censure.

In those days, my father was a professor at a liberal arts college. His colleagues had shaggy hair and dressed in smocks made by Guatemalan peasants, or bore epaulets of dandruff on the shoulders of their thrift store suits. The only people who dolled up their faces and feathered their hair were the townies, and they were not worth emulating. The prevailing attitude on campus was clear: You worried about your appearance only if you had nothing better to contribute to the world. If you were talented, brilliant, funny, or wise, you were free to ignore superficial things, like beauty.

Eventually I emerged into a kind of quiet prettiness. It suited me fine. I was never drop-dead stunning, but I went out with the boys I had crushes on. It was a happy way to spend my late teens and 20s.

Now I am 44 and once again do not love the mirror. In it I see a body stretched and battered by the birth of three children, a face turning wrinkled and gray. And I think, *Yuck.* But I also think, *Well, okay, I'm 44. Prettiness was mine when it should have been mine. Now I have other things to attend to.*

Sometimes I still wish I were a little more skilled with the eyeliner, but I don't despair. I've realized that my parents' seeming cluelessness was actually great wisdom; they valued my accomplishments more than my looks. And this freed me up to discover a really important secret: The things that make me feel like a superhero—

making love, swimming across a lake, staying up all night to write, giving birth to a baby who holds infinity in his eyes—make me look like tangled, puffy hell. But the mirror can't take away what I know in my heart to be true: At times like these, I'm drop-dead gorgeous. **O**

"You Could Get a Nose Job."

Her model-mother meant well, but **Suzan Colón** never forgot that offer.

Having a mother who was a model had predictable perks and drawbacks. As a child I was the envy of all the other kids when Mom came to pick me up at school; she looked like one of their Barbie dolls come to life. But a few years later, she could send my teenage inferiority complex into overdrive just by existing in all her blonde goddesslike perfection.

At that point, it seemed as if I'd inherited all the wrong genes. I had her height but not her bust size, her myopia but not her beauty; I was this tall, flat-chested kid with features way out of proportion to my face. My huge eyes were positively buggy behind my thick glasses; my already full lips were pushed out by my buckteeth. And then there was my nose—too long, too wide, and, well, too much.

Mom told me all the time that I was beautiful, but she was supposed to say that. Besides, what did she know? Her nose fit her face perfectly. As a teenager, it had been her only imperfect feature, but she'd gotten it "fixed," as people used to call it. So Mom didn't see a problem with interrupting one of my agonized rants about my looks: "Well...you *could* always get a nose job. It wouldn't be major surgery—just this." She gently pinched the sides of my nose, near the end where it tapered out, and tilted it upward.

My mother's offer of a nose job seemed confirmation that I needed one. But I was a rebellious kid, and my answer to every parental suggestion was "*No!*" The idea that there was something unattractive about my nose made me protective of it. I identified with it, sympathized with it—it was me and my nose against the world!

My feelings about that conversation changed as I got older. I understood that my mother didn't really think there was anything wrong with how I looked. She was just offering to help me get past the awkward stage (or just trying to shut me up; I was an expert whiner back then). As my features settled and found harmony, I came to appreciate my strong nose, which balances everything else on my face.

Occasionally I pinch and tilt it the way Mom did that night, imagining what it would be like now if I'd gotten it fixed. I'd look like a weasel. It makes Mom and me laugh, which only makes us prettier. **O**

Colón, *above*, and *left*, at age 5, 1968.

Lisa Kogan Tells All

Life (okay, it was bread and pasta) threw our columnist a few curves, causing her to retreat into a fashion life of oversize schmattes. Enter Adam Glassman, a man with a sleek, chic makeover plan.

It started with an untucked shirt. I mean, you put on a pound or two and you want to be comfortable, right? And maybe hide out in something just a little on the baggy side—that seems perfectly reasonable, doesn't it? And clogs are so easy to slip into—nobody really notices shoes, do they? Besides, the baby needs breakfast and the nanny is running late, and I've got to get to the office and who has time to deal with accessories or makeup...or one's reflection in a full-length mirror? Yep, it started with an untucked shirt, and before anyone could say "Stevie Nicks: the chunky years," the baby was ready for kindergarten and I had taken up residence in Schlumpadinka City.

I tell myself that it's obscene and vain and idiotic to think about personal style when the world is falling apart. This despite my mother's keen observation that "refusing to put on a pair of tailored trousers probably isn't doing all that much for the Iraqi people." Here is the truth:

I allowed myself to gain a lot of weight, and maybe as a punishment, or maybe as a form of denial, or maybe because I just couldn't find plus-size clothes that corresponded to the way I wanted to look (simple, sleek, modern, with just a hint of bling), I gave up on trying to look any way at all. I stopped paying attention to myself and hoped everyone else would have the decency to do the same.

AFTER

SHE'S GOT THE LOOK: Lisa was convinced she could never wear jeans until she tried on this slimming dark-wash denim.

BEFORE

Enter Adam Glassman. One part angel of mercy, one part dictatorial devil, all parts swathed in cashmere, Adam is the creative director of *O*. But his influence doesn't stop there. The man is on a personal crusade to keep America beautiful. He will point out when your hair is too big. He will come to your home and angle your sofa. He will let you know if your hemline dips too low or your heels reach too high. To paraphrase *Monsters Inc.*, he scares because he cares.

We are sitting in his office, reviewing an "O List" layout. "Adam," I begin, "what makes this particular candle so special?" He answers my question with another question, "What the hell kind of bra are you wearing?"

The rest is sort of a blur. All I can tell you is phone calls were placed, clothes were brought in, measurements were taken, and I suddenly find myself in a busy Madison Avenue shop aptly named Intimacy, where Dee (a.k.a. the Miracle Worker) ushers me into a dressing room, looks me up and down, declares me a 36 E (who knew?), and proceeds to fit me in every bra style ever devised. Now it's time for the body shapers. Suddenly Dee is Hattie McDaniel and I am Scarlett O'Hara getting my corset strings pulled till breathing no longer feels like a viable option. "My husband always helps me get into this one," she says with a Herculean tug. "Does your husband live near me?" I ask feebly. We settle on a lightweight little Spanx number called Higher Power. God may be good, but *this* higher power actually flattens my tummy.

The next day I walk into the office (though technically my chest arrives about seven seconds before the rest of me makes it off the elevator) and receive the following news from Polly, my unflappable assistant: "Adam stopped by." I hang up my jacket, grab a bottle of water, and reach for my glasses. "He probably wants to go over the schedule," I murmur as I click on the morning's first e-mail. Polly shakes her head: "He said he just wanted to look at your boobs."

All righty, then.

I walk the girls over to his place and am greeted with instant approval. "Whoa!" he says. "You're narrower and straighter!" I have impressed Adam Glassman, and life is sweet! "Your blouse isn't gaping at the bust anymore, and you've obviously gotten into your Higher Power. You now have a proper foundation. Do you know what this means, Lisa?" I know serving red wine with fish is generally frowned upon. I know Denny McLain pitched for the Detroit Tigers in 1968. I know love means never having to say you're sorry, but where this particular phenomenon is concerned, I'm clueless. "What does it mean, Adam?" "It means we can get down to business."

SERIOUS RESULTS *Left:* Proper fit makes all the difference with the often intimidating jersey dress. *Right:* The decorated neckline draws attention away from a tummy and up to a beautiful face. Pinstriped pants are always a lengthening look.

Business begins with Adam asking me to honestly describe my look. I think for a while. "Well, I guess I'm doing a second-trimester bohemian Greek widow kind of thing." He smiles—we've been friends for a lot of years. "I mean, I know the flowing earth-mother stuff just makes me look bigger...it might even make me look like I'm off to slaughter a goat in some weird religious rite—but I don't know how to fix it." I can feel my eyes welling up and my neck getting blotchy, but I forge ahead. "For starters, it's hard to look polished in these pathetic grandma shoes—where do I find anything even remotely sexy in extra wide? How do I find bracelets that fit my wrists? And clothes are so expensive," I say as my whine climbs the shrillness scale. "I've seen jeans that cost a couple of hundred dollars, not that they'd even fit me, and..." Adam nods in that way people nod when it dawns on them that they're trapped in a confined space with a crumbling crazy lady. "Take a breath, honey." He is calm but definitive as he slips me a Kleenex. "I'm way ahead of you."

He leads me to the fashion closet (which happens to be larger than my living room), where a rack of clothes is ready and waiting. He puts me in a little black dress—

THE HAPPY ENDING: Lisa didn't want to go sleeveless in the shift dress and she didn't have to. A cashmere cardigan, *left*, keeps her chic and covered. She tops it with a tweed coat, *right*, when it's chilly out. Patent leather pumps that fit her wide feet are a match made in makeover heaven.

Adam Says: Tips for Working with Your Curves

- Dress for the size you are—not what you want to be or once were! Work with what you have! *Own it.*
- Dress from the inside out. A well-fitting bra and shapewear will camouflage all lumps and bumps.
- Clothes should skim your body, not cling to it like sausage casing! Think high-waist, wide trousers, and A-line or flared skirts.
- Don't cover your curves! Big clothes on big bodies only make you look bigger.
- Skirts should end just before or under the kneecap. Your legs will look longer.
- Shorter, fitted jackets will also flatter your legs—and your waist.
- Avoid elasticized waistbands. They might be comfortable, but they add bulk to your midsection.
- Keep necklines open. A deep V- or scoop neck lengthens your neck.
- A dress with a belt will cinch you in, focusing attention on your smaller waist.
- Wide feet need to be counterbalanced with wide heels. A thinner heel only draws attention to your wider foot.

but it's sleeveless and I am horrified. "I won't show my upper arms and you can't make me!" I wail. He quells my hysteria with a purple cardigan and prescribes nightly biceps curls. Then he hands me a crystal necklace, black stockings, and a pair of heels he found on the Internet in an extra wide—and it all comes together. "The dress is double knit," he points out, "which holds you in a bit more." I'm wondering which organ I can put up on eBay to buy that dress. "And," he adds, "it's from Old Navy." He throws a tweed car coat with a funnel-neck collar over the dress: "This works with everything." He hands me another Old Navy dress—a jersey wrap. I don't love it, and I say so, but Adam instructs me to hang on, does some pinning to tighten the sleeves, and puts me back in my heels. "Okay, look again," he commands. I'm shocked by the difference. "You see, Lisa, sometimes a little tailoring takes a piece from just okay to fantastic. Notice how the skirt has some fluidity, how gracefully it moves with you; look at the way it hits right at the knee, and the way your underwear is smoothing everything out." I nod in amazement. "Good! Now quit rushing to judgment before we've even got your shoes and jewelry

on." I try gray slacks with an elongating pinstripe and top it with a silky print tunic. "The bejeweled V-neck creates the illusion of a leaner torso and draws attention up to your face. This is perfect for the holidays," he assures me. He puts me in a sharp black suit from Calvin Klein that drapes beautifully, and he insists I can wear the jacket with jeans. "Adam, I can't wear jeans—if they fit in the waist, they're baggy in the thighs and butt." He explains that this is because I'm not a plus size everywhere, that my thighs and bottom are actually pretty slender. It is a quote I plan to have engraved on my tombstone: "Here lies Lisa Kogan and her slender thighs." It gives me the strength to try 17 different jeans until a high-rise skinny-legged pair by a brand called Evans does the trick. Eureka! He pairs them with my new favorite top, a soft cotton jersey tunic with a bead-embellished scoop neckline (built-in jewelry!), and the Calvin jacket. We are both a little giddy with success. If I didn't know better, I'd say I was thin. I do, however, know better—the fact is, I'm not thin. But here's my newfound reality: You don't have to be thin to look great! **O**

BOTOX, ANYONE?
How far will you
go to feel pretty?

The Tipping Point

What is it that finally pushes a woman into *doing* something about her anxious little frown lines, her mousy hair, or whatever she's (more or less) "accepted" about her looks? Three women step up to *O*'s Beauty Challenge and discover what they can and can't live with.

A Shot at Gorgeous

Millions of women are looking remarkably fresh and rested thanks to tiny injections of a botulinum toxin. Why wasn't **Valerie Monroe** one of them? *O*'s beauty director develops a few new worry lines.

It's not like my face is that symmetrical or anything—no more symmetrical than yours, I bet—but the idea of doing something to it that even in the *slightest* way might increase the chance that it could become lopsided? That put the fear of God into me. So I canceled my first appointment with a New York dermatologist who had offered to shoot me up with Botox when I told her I was considering trying it for this story. I called her specifically because I know she has used Botox on herself for years, and she looks fantastic, by which I mean she can smile and frown like a normal person and she has no issues in the facial symmetry department. The day before my rescheduled appointment, I googled Botox, hoping for motivation. I saw before and after photos of men and women who had (purportedly) had it injected into their foreheads to reduce the lines between their eyebrows. A little note underneath the photos read: "Results may vary." And "Chances are, you'll like what you see!" *How much* may the results vary, I wondered, and what, exactly, *are* the chances?

I was late for my appointment (snarled crosstown traffic and...ambivalence). As I sat in the calming, all-beige waiting room, I leafed through a couple of magazines—the way you do in that too-fast, aimless way when you're anxious—thinking about why I had decided to get myself shot. Did I look in the mirror one morning and see something—a wrinkle, a crease, a spot—I couldn't live with? Did I realize that I had lost my youthful demeanor and suddenly wish I could have frozen it in time? No. But it seemed that almost everyone around me—professionally, that is—had tried Botox, and, no doubt about it, many of

them looked way more relaxed and less troubled than they probably should have. Plus, none of them were lopsided, or limping around because their legs had gone numb, and, as far as I could tell, their brain function seemed just fine. So I thought, *What the heck; why not go for it?*

In the treatment room, the doctor, gracious and attractive as ever, sat down with me. She handed me a mirror. "So, what do you see?" she said. I looked into the mirror. I saw a very worried face, and told her about my fears. What if my brow drooped from too much of the stuff? What if it leaked into another part of my body? "The treatment is really safe," said the doctor. She told me that she'd been using Botox for many years, on patients and on herself, and had only had good outcomes. She stared at my forehead for a second. "I could get great results for you," she said, and patiently showed me where she would inject me: between my brows and just above them. Four little shots. She might give me a little under the sides of my mouth, she said, where it was starting to look a bit droopy. She told me that I might be slightly red at the injection sites for about ten minutes, that I should move my forehead muscles for a half hour after the shots to distribute the Botox, and that I probably shouldn't lie down for several hours after the treatment. *Move my muscles to distribute the Botox? Don't lie down?*

Feeling acutely anxious and at the same time oddly curious, I resorted to an impersonal, reporter-like agenda. As if we were talking about some other woman in the room, I asked the doctor, "What else might you suggest?" "A bit of filler under your eyes would soften the bags," she said. "And your upper eyelids are beginning to sag; if you had an eyelid lift, you would look absolutely fantastic."

I picked up the hand mirror and peered into it again. This time, I looked old, frail, and terminally exhausted.

"All right," I said. "I'll do the Botox."

A nurse appeared with a consent form. I ticked off the boxes, agreeing that various unlikely mishaps, should they occur, were my responsibility. Then, feeling sad and vulnerable and somewhat feebleminded—I had given in, given up, I was damaged by the ravages of age and I needed fixing—I signed the form. I put the pen down. And in that moment, it felt as if a switch went off in my brain, or my heart. "No," I said. "No," I said, "no. I don't want it."

"That's okay," said the doctor, kindly. "That's the right decision for you. Would you like something else?" she asked, as if I might find another, less invasive choice from her menu of treatments a little more palatable.

"No, thanks; I'm good," I said. And I fled.

In the cab on the way back to the office, I was both disappointed and happy. Disappointed because I actually would like to see the lines between my brows diminished and I would like to look less tired. And happy because I felt that in a small way I had practiced a kind of acceptance that I believe will be valuable to me as I get older. It's hard to come by, this acceptance, especially in my business, and I refute it often: I'll continue to color my hair as it grays; I'll use a retinoid cream to keep my skin in good condition, and probably have some laser treatments. But for now, I won't be injecting anything into my face. Not Botox. Not fillers. You have my blessing to do it if it makes you happy. Maybe it will make me happy one day, too.

But it isn't what makes me happy today. ⬛

The Laser's Edge

Her friends saw enviably rosy cheeks. She saw 18th-century painted ladies. Her dermatologist saw a skin condition with an unpronounceable name. After a few false starts, Jessica Winter finally stops turning red.

My facial features have never necessarily matched my inner state. My pupils are somewhat dilated most of the time, as if I've just bumped my head or dropped acid. In college I was constantly misplacing my glasses, and I was hopeless when it came to the minimal upkeep required for contact lenses; as a result, I tended to wander around campus squinting at people like the Wicked Witch sizing up Dorothy, even when I was in a Glinda kind of mood. I have a deviated septum—breathing through my nose was a skill I acquired only as a teenager—and a short upper lip, which means that in unguarded moments my mouth hangs open in bovine wonderment, even on days when I feel relatively confident of my three-digit IQ.

Then there are my cheeks. (The ones on my face.) Until recently, they blazed bright red day and night, in every season and emotional climate. I could spend an afternoon curled up on the sofa with a bag of Pirate's Booty and a month's worth of *Us Weeklys* and still look as if I'd just run a marathon in 100-degree heat, given birth at the finish line, and felt *really* embarrassed about it. For most people, a deep blush can signal exertion, coyness, shame, anger. For me, it could additionally indicate boredom, happiness, fatigue, or "What's for lunch?"

All my life, my cheeks were an unsolvable problem, blaring at me from every reflective surface in varying shades of cherry blossom, spiced burgundy, and scarlet fever. I've tried every concealer on the market, matched to my otherwise pale skin. Each would throw a translucent veil over the fire, like a shawl over a lamp; hours later, I'd peer into my compact and see Santa Claus staring back at me again, almost as if those overactive vessels beneath my skin could pump fast and hot enough to vaporize mere titanium dioxide and talc.

When I was 21, I stopped by a cosmetics counter at a mall in New Haven. They told me to exfoliate.

"No, it's not zits or irritation or anything," I said. "It's just blood vessels. See, there's nothing wrong with the actual skin." I patted my cheeks reassuringly.

I might as well have dragged my nails across my face. Cosmetics Girl No. 1 actually shrieked. "No, don't touch it! You'll make it worse."

"No, it's *under* the skin," I said. "It's not *the* skin."

"You're not washing right," said Cosmetics Girl No. 2. "You have to treat your skin better."

"I have *perfect* skin," I said ridiculously.

"Try this scrub," No. 1 said, warming up for a pitch.

I paused. "Would you tell me to scrub a birthmark?" I asked. "Or a mole?"

"Depends," No. 2 said.

I left.

At 24, living in New York City, I visited a dermatologist I'd picked at random off my healthcare provider's Web site. She had a crispy perm and silvery blue eyeshadow up to her brows, and she attacked my cheeks with a sharp, stinging laser encased in a beige plastic wand. A week later, I looked like I had fallen asleep facedown in a hammock with a sunlamp burning beneath me. Those crusty lumps and bumps eventually healed, while the flush both remained and changed—it was more mottled now, more like an archipelago of splotches and blotches than a smoothly continuous crimson tide.

I tried to undo the damage at a day spa in SoHo, where a beautiful Russian-accented woman told me to lie on a table beneath an enormous camera-like device suspended from the ceiling—for all I know, it was discarded parts from a Proton satellite left over from the Soviet space program. The apparatus flashed in my general direction over the course of three serenely pointless sessions, costing about $1,200 in total. (Let's put that figure in perspective: At the time, *I worked at an alternative weekly*.)

After the calamity of the $1,200, I just tried to live with it. The English major in me reached for cultural-historical perspective. I thought of the libertine fops and madams of 18-century France, with their white-powdered faces and crimson-painted cheeks. I thought of John Keats, dead at 25 of tuberculosis, which gave its sufferers a telltale milky pallor with flushed cheeks—a look that actually became fashionable in 19th-century Europe. (Their version of heroin chic, perhaps.) Keats was the bard of the blush: He wrote irresistibly of a cheek "rosy-warm / With the tinge of love, panting in safe alarm," and elsewhere compiled a taxonomy of the versatile blush:

There's a blush for want, and a blush for shan't
And a blush for having done it,
There's a blush for thought, and a blush for naught,
And a blush for just begun it.

I thought of the phrase *apple-cheeked,* so sweet and wholesome. I thought of Marge Simpson's mother, dispensing advice on prom night: "If you pinch your cheeks, they'll glow," she rasped. "Try to break some capillaries."

I thought of my friend Julia, who once told me, "I love your cheeks. They're Victorian." I had no idea what that meant, but she said it with such a quintessentially Julia-esque mix of

> My cheeks blazed bright red day and night, in every season and emotional climate.

kindness and certainty that there was no need for clarification—my self-consciousness had already been bundled away in a confidence-boosting swaddle of crinolines and velvet and Charles Dickens by the fireside.

And there I stayed for six years, until the good people at *O* spirited me off to the renowned dermatologist Roy Geronemus, MD, director of the Laser & Skin Surgery Center of New York. There, at last, the apples in my cheeks get a clinical diagnosis: *telangiectasias,* or dilated blood vessels near the surface of the skin. Over several sessions, the wonderfully calm and steady Geronemus will zap my *telan*-et-ceteras using a pair of lasers with names straight out of a *Buck Rogers* comic: the Gemini and the V-Beam.

"It works like a smart bomb," he says, with a gentle matter-of-factness that strips any violence out of the analogy. "We're selectively injuring the vessels. They aren't critical to the skin's functioning, so you can shrink them down, constrict the blood flow, and as a result, reduce the redness."

The Gemini feels like hot needle pricks; the V-Beam like concentrated blasts of subzero air. When I leave the Laser & Skin Surgery Center after the first round, I look like a windburned skier; a few hours later, irregularly shaped islands and isthmuses of swelling come out in relief on my cheeks. For a couple of days, I look like I'm storing nuts for the winter. By the third session, the post-zap puffing isn't so bad—it creates a honeycomb pattern that reminds me of the syphilis slides from eighth-grade health class. As the swelling recedes, it leaves tiny, angry purple flowers scattered across my face, which disappear within the week.

I make a total of four visits to Geronemus's office, at three-week intervals. Each time I return, the ruddiness I've worn forever has faded by several degrees. It's like watching a Polaroid develop in reverse. One week after my last treatment, my cheeks simply glow, beaming palest petal-pink.

Upkeep may be required: Geronemus tells me that any major hormonal change—a switch-up of birth-control methods, pregnancy, or, eventually, menopause—could put me back in the red. So could time. For now, I go everywhere without makeup—a first. Sometimes I'll give a little start, as if I've just realized that I forgot to wear a bra or my skirt is bunched in the back. Then I remember that only my face is naked, and I can feel myself blushing. ◖

Fair-Haired Girl

She was blonde as a child. What had she missed out on by letting her hair go brown? Stung by strangers' comments, Celia Barbour decides to reclaim her birthright.

I am failing to live up to my hair.

My hair deserves to be taken out to fancy dinners. It should be admired, adored.

I, meanwhile, can't even find a mirror. We (husband, three kids, and I) have just moved from the city to a small town, and me and my freshly colored hair spend our days unpacking boxes (but not, dammit, the one that holds the mirrors), me in a T-shirt, my hair wadded into a clip. When I do happen to catch myself in the rearview on the way to the store, I am startled: Me! With blonde streaks! Check 'em out!

My hair droops in dismay.

I didn't set out to disappoint my hair. On the contrary, I thought my timing was quite clever. A new town seemed like the perfect place to start over with the hair I was always meant to have. When I was a kid, it was blonde—white-blonde, the color of a sugar cookie. But starting at about age 4, it began its long, slow descent into darkness; by high school it was the color of oversteeped tea. "You know what's neat about your hair?" asked a classmate whose gorgeous, honey-colored curls tumbled to her butt. "It's the exact same color as your eyes."

Yeah. Thanks. Brown. Wow.

Still, I would have been fine spending my whole life brunette because being fine was something I was very good at. I'd been working at it for years, thanks to my big sister. Growing up, Elisa saw everything as change-able. Her hair was long, then short; blunt then feathered; straight then frizzy; brown then Cheez Whiz (remember Sun-In?). For her, nothing was fixed. Everything was mutable.

I took the opposite path, probably just because sisters do that—Elisa was scattershot, ergo I would strive to be grounded, steadfast, deep. Instead of incessantly changing the things I didn't like about my appearance, I'd accept them. My hair, which was long and straight in seventh grade, was long and straight in college, and long and straight on my wedding day. If superficial dissatisfactions ever roiled my life, a new hairdo wasn't going to fix them—or so I told myself. I cannot pinpoint the moment when this philosophy crossed over from Zen acceptance into a kind of stern inflexibility—from "I don't need to change my hair" into "I need to *never* change my hair."

Life has a way of playing tricks on people like me; the more self-righteous we are, the better. And so life handed me three kids, all of them blond. Stunning, spectacular blond. Strangers would see us and say, "Where'd they get that fantastic hair?" or "I guess your husband is blond." No, I'd say, sighing. No, it was me. Once. A very long time ago. (I hate strangers. They always stir things up.)

Before long, they had me wondering about the blonde life I never lived, my unfulfilled birthright. And so I decided to try it out, if only to coordinate better with my kids. Mind you, I had no idea what "going blonde" would entail, having never so much as squeezed lemon juice into my hair. I knew that it would be time-consuming and difficult. But when I found out that I would have to strip all the brown from my hair before it could be dyed, I blanched. Covering over my brown was one thing, but erasing 40 years of comfort scared me.

I told Gina Gilbert, the colorist at the Serge Normant at John Frieda Salon in New York City, that I was starting to chicken out. I expected her to be irritated at my spinelessness, and so to rekindle my nerve. Instead she smiled and said, "Thank God. When I heard that you're a mother, I thought, *Blonde is going to be a nightmare.* You'd be in here every three weeks."

"Oh," I said, relieved.

The right kind of change doesn't take you away from yourself; it wakes you up to yourself.

"Besides," said Gina, "I like your hair brown. It's the right color for you."

I nearly laughed out loud. Perhaps the plain, brown rut where I'd spent the last four decades was exactly where I belonged.

I was wrong—not about the brown part, but about the rut. Gina didn't change my color, but somehow made it gorgeous, like a polished tropical wood. It was as if she had noticed in me a prettier, nicer person than I'd ever dared see in myself, and coaxed her out of hiding. For the first time in ages, I felt that my surface matched my core.

As the week wore on, though, my curiosity gradually began to reignite. And so, two weeks later, I was back in the colorists' chair again—this time, Marie Robinson's, at the Sally Hershberger Downtown salon—for brighter, lighter highlights.

I told Marie that I needed to experience life as a blonde—even just a partial, streaks-of-gold-through-a-mane-of-brown blonde.

"I bet you'll like it," she said, as she enfolded segments of my hair in foil envelopes. "But once you've tried it, I think you should go back."

"Why?" I said.

"Brown suits you."

She was right, of course, on both counts. I do like my sunny highlights. And they don't quite suit me. It's fun to have gold-streaked hair, the same way that it's fun to try on gorgeous-but-not-me clothes in the dressing room. In front of the mirror, it's all make-believe, but the moment I step out in public I get insecure, lose my poise. For me to feel pretty, I have to be confident, and for that, I have to feel like myself.

That doesn't mean I'm going back to my plain-Jane hair, however, because that doesn't feel like me anymore. All those years when I thought I was being true to myself, I was just growing numb on monotony. Getting a great new color made me realize that the right kind of change doesn't take you away from yourself; it wakes you up to yourself. So what if the self I discovered doesn't happen to be blonde? I can accept that.

So I'll let my highlights fade. I imagine that will happen about the same time the last box is flattened and sent to recycling. Then I'll head back to the salon and watch the colorist turn the hair color I've simply put up with all my life into the color I now crave—the beautiful, vivid, glossy brown that feels just right for me, a woman who knows a thing or two about change. ◐

balance

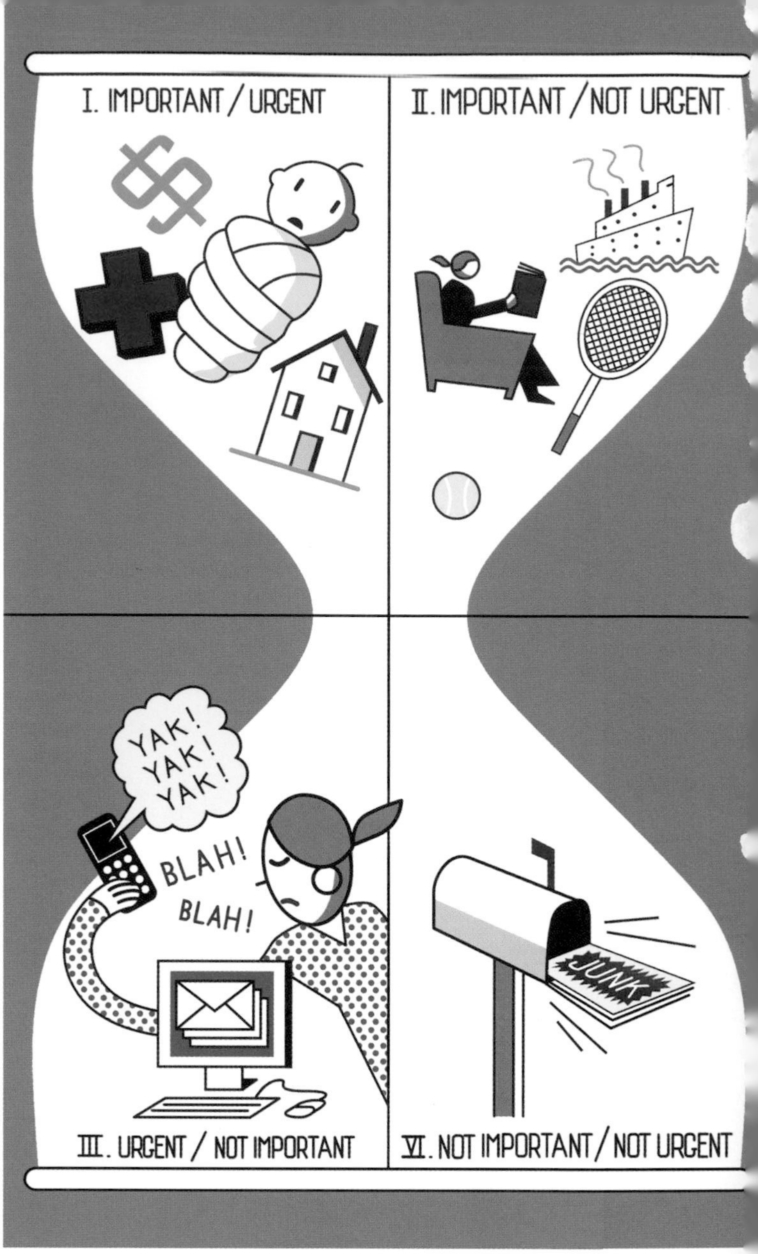

I. IMPORTANT / URGENT

II. IMPORTANT / NOT URGENT

YAK!
YAK!
YAK!

BLAH!
BLAH!

III. URGENT / NOT IMPORTANT

IV. NOT IMPORTANT / NOT URGENT

Urgent! Urgent! (Or Is It?)

If you're spending all your time putting out fires—and never getting to the things that really matter—STOP! Martha Beck shows you the chart that draws a line between must-do-this-minute time killers and "I've always wanted to…" soul satisfiers.

About a year ago, I watched a speech online about time management given in 1998 by Randy Pausch, PhD, a professor at Carnegie Mellon University. Pausch cautioned listeners not to waste energy on activities that seem urgent but aren't important. Choose instead, Pausch suggested, to spend time on activities that are deeply important, even if they don't seem critical.

That was an excellent speech. It would become ex-tremely poignant in 2006, when the then 45-year-old Pausch was diagnosed with pancreatic cancer. Watching another of his speeches online—the famous "Last Lecture" (now a best-selling book), in which he teaches his three young children how to make their dreams come true—I wondered if this time management expert sensed, even back in 1998, that he'd spend less time on earth than anyone wished.

Pausch's work and his personal story drive home a les-son we all know but frequently forget: To live richly and avoid regret, we must give priority to things of real impor-tance. But in a world where everything from your BlackBerry to your car's oil filter to your grandmother is competing for your limited time, this requires deliberate, consistent choice. The good news is that we can develop the habit of choosing what's really important over everything else. Life seems designed to teach us how to do this. Pay attention, and you'll notice that even when you're under "urgent" pressure to do something unimportant, it feels discordant and wrong. Do what really matters, and your life comes into harmonious alignment. Don't believe me? Apply the concepts below, and call me in the morning.

First (and Second) Things First

To me, Stephen Covey will always be the smart, funny guy on my high school debate team who, when it was time to be cross-examined by an opponent, would drop the "c" from the traditional phrase "I'm now open for cross-ex," so that it came out "I'm now open for raw sex." The judges never noticed, and the rest of us debaters thought Steve was hilarious. We also sort of knew that his dad, Stephen Covey Sr., was a renowned management guru. Randy Pausch was quoting Steve's dad when he proposed categorizing all activities on a matrix of apparent urgency and ultimate importance, like this:

As Covey observed, we almost always do the things in Quadrant I (stuff that's both important and urgent, like feeding the kids and paying the rent), and almost never get to Quadrant IV (like reading junk mail). That's good. However, we tend to focus on Quadrant III (urgent but not important things, like talking to a demanding co-worker about her rotten boyfriend) to the detriment of Quadrant II (no-deadline pastimes like writing a book, basking in nature's beauty, or taking time to be still). Covey proposed devoting less time to the dinky tasks, even those that are urgent, and more time to those things that are really important.

Here's an exercise he proposed:
1. Get 20 or 30 notecards. On each card, write down one thing you should do, want to do, hope to do, plan to do, or dream of doing. Include everything, no matter how large or small. Keep this up until your brain runs dry.
2. When you've written down all your goals, plans, and ideas, separate the cards into two piles: things that have to be done right this minute (or feel like it) and those that don't.
3. Now go through both of these

piles, separating each into "important" and "not important" stacks. The four resulting stacks correlate with the Covey Quadrants.
4. Carefully place both of your "not important" card stacks in a safe spot. This, if my experience is any indication, will ensure that you'll never find them again. If you do happen to stumble across them at any time in the future, burn them.
5. Commit to eliminating from your schedule all the activities that didn't make it into the "important" stacks. If you have time after doing your important and urgent things, use it on important but not urgent activities. No matter how pressing something may seem to be, if it's not important, just don't do it.

From Theory to Practice: Living a Quadrant II Life

Planning to live this way is one thing; changing habits of thought and action is another. You're subjected to daily pressure to do things that, while unimportant in the long run, may seem unavoidable in the middle of a PTA meeting. Congratulate yourself every time you drop a Quadrant III activity and replace it with something from Quadrant II. Here are some substitutions I made after doing this exercise:

- Postponed promoting new book to raise money for research on Down syndrome.
- Canceled a client meeting to bake my daughter's birthday cake.
- Blew off e-mail to chat on the phone with dear friend.
- Blew off e-mail to volunteer at local methadone clinic.
- Blew off e-mail to exercise.
- Blew off e-mail to bathe.
  - Blew off e-mail to sleep.
  - Blew off e-mail to sense a theme developing here.

At this point, I'd like to apologize to all of you who didn't receive an e-mail response from me this month. Blame Covey and Pausch. (Actually, thanks, Covey and Pausch!) E-mail may be crucially important to you, in which case it should get your consistent attention. But it amazed me, when I did the Quadrant exercise, how many of my urgent-seeming e-mails felt less important than working for people in need, caring for my health, or being with friends and family. I realized that I could easily

Quadrant I	Quadrant II
Important, Urgent	Important, Not Urgent
_____	_____
_____	_____
_____	_____
Quadrant III	**Quadrant IV**
Urgent, Not Important	Not Important, Not Urgent
_____	_____
_____	_____
_____	_____

spend all my time shoveling out the electronic Augean stables, missing countless small experiences that add up to my life's purpose.

How to Determine What's Important

As powerful as this exercise was for me, it posed a few vexing questions. Highly effective people seem to cut through life's complexities in bold, clean strokes; reading their books or watching their lectures, you can practically hear them telling their secretaries: "No, no, Mabel, can't you see that's *urgent,* but it's not *important?* And cancel my 5 o'clock; I'll be meeting with His Holiness the Pope instead."

By contrast, my prioritization is plagued with ambiguity. Is chasing my beagle round and round the sofa important? Urgent? Many would say it's neither, but Cookie clearly thinks it's both, and who am I to say he's wrong? I might dismiss Cookie's opinion on the grounds that he's small and furry, but what about, say, the authors who'd like me to promote their books? The stack of manuscripts in my office is taller than I am, and every volume is both urgent and important to its author. If you, like me, tend to include other people's priorities in your decision making, the Covey Quadrant exercise requires you to break that pattern. You can't differentiate between "this is due today" and "this is important" when you are (to quote the 15th-century mystic Kabir) "tangled up in others." You must untangle yourself, still all other voices, and go to the deepest place within to know what's important and urgent in your unique and singular life.

This can be difficult at first, but as you focus on it, you'll discover a beautiful surprise: Your life has been waiting for just this opportunity to help you choose what's right for you, even when other people (and the occasional beagle) are telling you that their own code-red desires should take priority. It does this like a good psychological behaviorist, by making things difficult and taxing when they're not important, delicious and relatively effortless when they are.

When I say this to new clients they look at me cynically, as if I've promised them a unicorn. But when they begin paying attention, they soon notice how good life feels when they're doing what thrills them, and how bad it feels when they're not. The bad feeling is most noticeable at first; a sense of awkwardness, like petting a cat from back to front. Tasks go badly. My clients forget things: their keys, their wallets, the way to the office. Conversations are stilted. Energy ebbs without ever flowing. If these clients don't change course, unease may grow into anger, depression, health problems, or total burnout.

This feels awful, but the uncomfortableness is a wonderful incentive to begin finding out how good a life of real significance can feel. Drop what's unimportant and replace it with activities from Covey Quadrant II—things that replenish your physical, emotional, and spiritual well-being—and suddenly, everything becomes much easier. Energy returns, anger disappears, you begin smiling spontaneously. The cat stops generating static electricity, and starts to purr.

To follow your life's guidance, you may have to reassign some seemingly important things to "unimportant." If you believe that pleasing your horrible boss or having a spotless house is a higher priority than playing with your children or sleeping off the flu, be prepared for a long and strenuous battle against destiny. Also, be prepared to lose. And after you've lost, go online and watch Randy Pausch's last lecture. In Pausch, who died on July 25, 2008, you'll see the clarity and joy of a man who chose all along to do what really mattered. That's no consolation prize; that's true victory.

As you start to focus more on what's important to your soul, filling your schedule with the kinds of things that are vital though maybe not due this minute, every day will bring much more enjoyment and refreshment. You'll be fascinated and invigorated, open to everything from artistic creativity to (in the legendary words of Stephen Covey Jr.) "raw sex."

> The good news is that we can develop the habit of choosing what's really important over everything else.

"This is the true joy in life," wrote George Bernard Shaw, "the being used for a purpose recognized by yourself as a mighty one.... Life is no 'brief candle' for me. It is a sort of splendid torch, which I have got hold of for the moment; and I want to make it burn as brightly as possible before handing it on to future generations." This is the credo of Quadrant II. Abide by it, and you'll find a path that illuminates the world for you and others, even after you're gone. No matter what others may think, say, or do, your whole life will become a blaze of glory. ◻

53 Ways to Say...NO!

Dinner companions always bugging you to try a bit of this? See #22 & #23.

If a 2-year-old can do it, why is it so hard for a grown woman? Okay, we know why. But we also know it must be done: If you accepted every invitation, you'd never sleep. If you gave to every worthy cause, you'd go broke. If you went along with everything everyone ever wanted from you, you'd be…as exhausted as you are right now. So for the times when you're truly sorry to decline, and for the times when you'd rather have a root canal than say yes, **Penny Wrenn** found 53 ways to say ixnay, thanks but no thanks, and count me out—courtesy of etiquette maven Anna Post, entertaining expert Donatella Arpaia, international mediator William Ury, and other well-boundaried people who *will* give no for an answer. **Plus One Big YES!**

1 **[SOCIAL LIVES AND LIES]**

...the friend who says, "Do I look okay in this?"
If you can save her from herself right now—i.e., the price tag is still on the dress and you haven't left the dressing room—say, "*You* look great, but that micromini doesn't do you justice."

2 If it's too late to save her but you want to help her avoid repeating the disaster, say, "You look great, as usual—though I have to admit, my favorite style on you has always been...." Then mention a specific outfit that makes her look great.

3

...the not-quite-close-enough friend who asks to borrow your lipstick:
Celebrity makeup artist and sworn germaphobe Mally Roncal says: "I learned my makeup-sharing lesson in high school, when my friend used someone else's mascara and ended up with pinkeye. It's classic: You start passing around the blue eyeliner, and next thing, everyone's wearing eye patches." No need to imply that your friend is a walking virus factory, though; just say, "I didn't feel well this morning, and I'd rather not spread my germs."

...the friend or coworker who wants your help with yet another school bake

sale or project at the office—when you don't have time to deal with your *own* stuff:

4 Tell her, "I'd love to help; but I'm already overextended."

But if you're one of the pathologically accommodating women who can't open their mouths without saying, "Sign me up!": Shake your head and point to your STOP ME BEFORE I VOLUNTEER AGAIN button (12 for $24 at annetaintor.com).

5

stop me before I volunteer again

...the friend or relative whose request to borrow money makes you uncomfortable:

6 "I'm not broke, but I can't afford to lend anything."

...the perfectly nice would-be friend who keeps inviting you to lunch— when you know in your gut that the two of you won't click:

7 "That sounds great, but I just can't put one more thing on my calendar for the next few weeks. Let me call you when

things clear up." Who's to say things will ever clear up?

...the person who always wants to get together in the name of friendship but who you suspect just wants something from you:

8 Put her on the spot, politely: "I'm horribly overbooked right now, but I get the sense there's something in particular you wanted to discuss. What's up?" Any appeal— for your money, advice, contacts, time, whatever—can then be either easily satisfied or dismissed with a simple, kind "I'm sorry, I can't." Which should put an end to the lunch invitations.

...the social hug:

9 Do the preemptive handshake—or try the grab-the-forearms-then-stand-back-and-say-"Look at you!" move, as if you're admiring the would-be hugger's sheer fabulosity.

...the friend who asks if it's okay to bring another guest...

10 ...to your wedding: "I'm so sorry, but the guest list is set. It's a numbers thing—I'm sure you understand."

11 ...to your dinner party: "I'm planning to keep this gathering small and focused. I'd really like to stick to the guest list."

...the friend or relative who asks you to babysit:

You think you have to invent some elaborate excuse. You think it's a big, huge deal to say that you're sorry, you can't. Here's what you say: "I'm sorry, I can't."

...the neighbor who asks you to check in on her cat while she's gone for the weekend:

If you have no pets or plants of your own— or anything else that might ever, under any circumstances, need tending; if you have no trash cans, newspapers, or mail that, in your absence, might ever need to be brought in; if it's guaranteed that no child of yours will ever damage your neighbor's property in a way that might make her think, *Lawsuit?*—then by all means say, "I'm sorry, but it's not a good weekend." Otherwise play by the golden rule. Someday you will thank us.

[DINING DILEMMAS]
...a bad table at a restaurant:

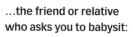

14 Donatella Arpaia, co-owner of New York restaurants David Burke & Donatella, Mia Dona, and Anthos, advises a friendly "We'd be happy to sit at the bar until another table opens up." If you can pull it off (i.e., keep it charming and light), a little wry humor never hurts, either. Arpaia's favorite lines:

15 The too-close-to-the-kitchen table: "We came out tonight so we *wouldn't* have to be in the kitchen."

16 The too-close-to-the-door table: "Unless you think we'll need to make a quick exit?"

17 The rowdy table: "We'd rather not sit next to the party. We didn't bring a gift."

...an ill-prepared dish you're served at a restaurant:

18 Arpaia's all-purpose no: "I'm not happy with this dish. Can I please see the menu so I can pick another one?" Her made-to-order lines (again, keep it light and low-key):

19 The cold dish: "My pasta is temperature challenged. I'd like to send it back for a warm-up."

20 The well-done dish that was supposed to be medium-rare: "I'm glad your cooks are so thorough, but this is a bit overdone."

21 The dish you didn't order: "I've had people send me a drink before, but a steak? This is a first."

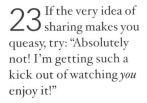

...the dinner companion who's always insisting, "Try a bite of this!"

22 If you have an allergy, or you've never liked the food in question, tell the truth. Anna Post, author of *Emily Post's Wedding Parties,* uses this exit strategy for radishes: "The bite would be wasted on me. I'm just not a fan."

23 If the very idea of sharing makes you queasy, try: "Absolutely not! I'm getting such a kick out of watching *you* enjoy it!"

...ordering dessert—when everyone else at your table is having molten chocolate cake and trying to peer-pressure you into not being the skinny bitch:

Beat your frenemies to the punch. Samantha von Sperling, founder and director of Polished Social Image Consultants, recommends a lighthearted preemptive strike: "I know, I know, I'm that annoying too-full-to-eat-dessert person. What can I say—there's always one."

24

25 "I think I'll drink my dessert tonight. Waiter, one more glass of Pinot, please."

...splitting the check (when you ordered only a salad):

Turn the tables with a request of your own: "May I just take my portion out of the bill instead of contributing to the

26

even split?" "If your friends say no to that," says Post, "you need to get new ones."

[HELP!]

...the cashier who's trying to sell you on a two-for-one deal or a frequent-shopper card ("It's free!") or something else he thinks you'd be crazy not to take advantage of:

27 "No, thanks." Repeat as needed. Repeat as needed.

...the sweet-talking salesperson who's nearly convinced you to buy the season's "hottest" pants (though on a better body-confidence day, you'd recognize the look as cruelly unflattering):

28 Even fashion authority Tim Gunn has purchased a garment he later regretted, simply because he "didn't want to hurt the salesperson's feelings." To avoid pushover-buyer's remorse, he's learned to say, "This is just not for me" or "It's a stunning piece, but it's beyond my budget." Now, if Tim Gunn isn't shy about announcing that an item is out of his price range, why should you be?

29

...in the salon chair, as your hair is being butchered before your eyes:

Scream on the inside, smile on the outside. New York salon owner David Evangelista advises telling the stylist, in your most congenial tone: "I don't see this shaping up to be the look I was going for. Let's stop and talk it over so we can get back on the same page."

30 If, on the other hand, the stylist is doing exactly as you asked but you've realized you were insane to ask it: "I'm sorry, but I don't love where this is going after all. Can we stop and change direction?"

...Girl Scouts selling cookies:

31

Just order the Thin Mints. Seriously. It's for a good cause, resistance is futile, and you know you want them anyway. Do-Si-Dos are excellent, too.

...a bad hotel room:

Don't call, says von Sperling; go downstairs. "Your objection will be taken more seriously if it's made face-to-face." Ask for a manager at the front desk, and in your calmest, most matter-of-fact voice, state the problem (awful smell, awful view, lumpy mattress, lousy plumbing, broken heating or cooling apparatus); express your dismay ("This is not the experience I expect—or am accustomed to—at such a fine hotel"); then say, "Surely this isn't acceptable to you, either. I'm hoping you'll be able to find a solution."

...the customer service representative who says, "Can you hold?"

33 Resist giving in to phone rage. Atiya Morgan, a switchboard operator at the Hudson Hotel in New York City, says that a polite no works wonders.

[IN THE BEDROOM—AND GETTING THERE]

...the nice guy—nice, but not your type—who asks you on a date:

34 "I'm sorry, I can't." If you're feeling weak, you can add, "I'm seeing someone." If you have no spine whatsoever, you can start with "I'm very flattered, but..."

35

...your partner, who's suggesting a far-out sexual act:

Look appalled and shriek, "What is *wrong* with you?!" Just kidding. Spare your partner your horror, says relationship expert Logan Levkoff, author of *Third Base Ain't What It Used to Be.* It's enough to say, "I understand why you're curious, but it's not something I'm ready to do right now."

...a partner's sexual performance that feels all wrong:

36 Say nothing, Levkoff advises. Move your partner's hand or your own body to signal the change in action that you'd prefer.

...sex, period:

37 Use the same body language and tone of voice you'd use if you were saying yes, says sex therapist Joy Davidson, PhD. Instead of immediately shooing away his bedroom advances or wriggling out of his come-up-behind-you-in-the-kitchen embrace, "enjoy it for five seconds," Davidson says. Then give your version of an *Mmm, that's so nice* before explaining your reason for not going any further ("I have a deadline..." or "I'm so exhausted tonight..." or "Damn! I've got 30 seconds to get out the door...").

[AT THE OFFICE]

...the extra task your boss "asks" you to take on:

38 Let her know that if you do what she's asking, something's gotta give: "I'm working on projects X, Y, and Z right now—which one should I put aside to make room in my schedule?" Even if she doesn't take the bait and reconsider, at least you've done your best to keep your workload manageable.

39 Pass the buck: "Really? I would have thought Sally's ____ [insert: talents, skills, experience, current projects] were a better fit."

...your boss's bad idea:

40 Buy in briefly ("That's so interesting..."), then remind her of one of her better brainstorms ("I just wish we were going ahead with your earlier thought; that was such a great idea!").

41 Deliberately misunderstand, while describing your own, better plan ("You mean...? That's brilliant!").

...your underling's bad idea:

42 Be noncommittal in a supportive-sounding way ("Hmm, I hadn't thought of that!"), then steer her back on track ("And it actually gives me another idea...").

...the person who's always tapping on your office door, saying, "May I come in?"

43 "Sorry, this is a bad time."

...pitching in for a gift for a coworker you don't know well or don't like:

"I don't think our relationship has reached the gifting stage."

...an invitation to a work-related social event (when you suspect the higher-ups are taking attendance):

45 R.S.V.P. *immediately,* conveying both your delight at the occasion ("This sounds great!") and your dismay that you'll have to miss it ("Unfortunately, I have something else scheduled that night").

...the person whose request for your professional advice or access to your hard-earned Rolodex feels like an imposition:

46 "Nothing/no one comes to mind right now, but if I think of anything/anyone that might be useful, I'll let you know."

[ANYTIME, ANYWHERE]
..."You wouldn't mind _____, would you?"

47 "Actually, I would."

..."You know what I mean?"

48 "Actually, no I don't."

...unsolicited advice:

49 "Now, there's an idea!"

[ADVANCED "NO"-ING]
...the person you've said yes to in the past:

50 Steer clear of the "three-A trap" (accommodating, attacking, avoiding), says William Ury, PhD, author of *The Power of a Positive No.* Instead, park your no between two yeses. His "Yes! No. Yes?" sandwich:

Yes! (as in, yes to your gut feeling that the right answer is no): "I know I've agreed to _____ in the past, but it only made me feel anxious/uncomfortable/overwhelmed. That's why it's important for me to now say no."

No (the simple, matter-of-fact bottom line): "I'm no longer willing to _____."

Yes? (the positive endnote): "What if we try _____ instead?"

Ury advises coming equipped with an "anchor phrase" that will help you stand your ground. Consider "That doesn't work for me," "I prefer not to," "I'm no longer willing to do that"—and repeat your phrase as needed, knowing you needn't say anymore.

...the person to whom you've said maybe:

51 Ury says, "A quick no is better than a slow maybe." So when you finally do respond—by saying, "I've given it some thought, and my answer is no"—expect the other person's disappointment. And next time you're tempted to say maybe, say this instead: "If you need to know now, the answer is no."

...the person you've been avoiding because you dread saying no:

52 It's been, what, three months now? Time to bite the bullet and say the inevitable: "I know I've been out of touch, but I did get your phone call/e-mail/proposal. I'm going to say no, and I hope my delay in getting back to you hasn't caused you an inconvenience." Kind of painful, isn't it? This is why Ury avoids avoidance.

...someone else's no:

53 If you can't take no for an answer, Ury, who is also an internationally appointed mediator and the author of *Getting Past No,* says the key is negotiation. First, ask: "Can you help me understand why it's difficult for you to say yes to the proposal/loan/offer/promotion?" Next, assess: "As I hear you, your first concern is A and your second concern is B—have I got that right?" Then, answer: "If I were able to address your concerns by doing X and Y, would you be more amenable?" Just keep in mind that a yes isn't guaranteed, and you might need to repeat the steps a few times before you even get close. O

The Year of Saying YES!

What if "no" is no problem for you, but "yes" is scary? What are you missing?
Patricia Volk tries 12 months of accepting all invitations, challenges, and blind
dates, and discovers that sometimes yes is more.

It's short, unequivocal, to the point. I say no at the drop of a hat. I'm good at saying no. I couch it as *knowing what is good for me.*

Then I have dinner with Louisa Ermelino. Louisa works in publishing. Late one afternoon, her editor says: "Louisa, I'm the keynote speaker tonight and I've got a conflict. You have to help me out."

"I found myself on a stage," Louisa reports, "looking down at a sea of faces. I had no idea what I was going to say. Then it occurred to me: *Louisa, you know more about this than they do.* And I started talking. And it was fine."

"I would have said no," I say.

"And wound up at home in bed with a book."

"What's wrong with that?"

"You're not living," Louisa says. "You're in a cocoon. You're not stretching."

Stretching? I have to keep stretching? Haven't I stretched enough? Didn't I support a husband through medical school while going to night school and raising two kids? Haven't I earned reading in bed with a bowl of Grape-Nuts for dinner? Peace, my new drug of choice.

Louisa and I kiss goodnight. Heading uptown, I argue with ME:

ME: "What's so good about a book in bed? Since when don't you take chances?"

I: "I'm *relieved* about what I'm missing."

ME: "But *what* are you missing? How do you know?"

I like arguing with myself. Everyone's a winner. By the time the bus drops me off, I've made a decision. Starting tomorrow, for one year, I'll strike *no* from my vocabulary. Tomorrow morning begins the Year of Saying Yes.

Viridiana

Tim McHenry, an old friend of mine, runs programming at the Rubin Museum of Art. "I'm doing a Friday night movie cabaret," he says. "How would you like to introduce a film?"

I'm not a film scholar. I call films movies.

"Sure," I say. Tim reads his list of esoteric films. None ring a bell till he gets to *Viridiana. Viridiana* was my first art house movie. It was life-changing, freshman year in college. Will it hold up?

It holds up. I research Buñuel, Franco, and fetishism. What's better than exploring what excites you, understanding what makes it work, then sharing that with like-minded people? The audience asks thought-provoking questions, and Tim presents me with the same kind of white silk scarf the Dalai Lama often wears.

Congratulations! It's a Book!

A new book coming out is like having a baby. No stretch marks, but it's

yours to nurture. So yes to the Spencertown book fair in upstate New York even though it costs $210 to rent a car and I only sell one book. And yes to the Caltech Athenaeum High Tea, even though I spend more time flying to Pasadena than in Pasadena. And yes to talking to my friend Patti Rohrlich's book club. "I have a great idea," Patti says. "Since your novel deals with the importance of secrets, let's everybody tell a secret we've never told."

That night Patti asks me to go first. I tell a secret involving my ninth-grade boyfriend, Harry, that once seemed devastating. Tincture of time makes this secret hilarious. Or so I think. But the women sit there frozen. Finally somebody ventures, "Um, how old were you when that happened?" Nobody else will tell their secret. I sell 11 books.

Broadway Debut

Martin Sage coproduces the *Thalia Follies* at Symphony Space. This month the theme is food.

"Would you write something for it?" Martin asks.

I write lyrics to "How About You?":

I miss the fudge at Schrafft's,
How about you?
And Luchow's roasted pork
Ribs at Ruby Foo's...

"Why don't you sing it?" Martin says.

Rehearsals begin with actors I've paid to see. The big night arrives! We share a dressing room! It's time for my Broadway debut! So what if it's Broadway and 95th Street! There are two shows, 6:30 and 8:30. I print the lyrics on a doily in case I forget them. During the second show, I'm so excited that my daughter's in the audience, I forget to look at the doily. I flub my lines. It doesn't matter. I read somewhere that when asked why he chose to spend his life on the stage, Sir Laurence Olivier replied by clapping. I get it.

The Professor

Bennington's low-residency MFA writing program asks me to teach for one semester. I step out of the car into wall-to-wall faculty meetings. The program is beyond intense. It will be complete submersion for ten solid 14-hour days, with five 40-plus-page student packets arriving each month.

That first night I creep into bed. How can I get out of this? Say someone in the family had a heart attack? What am I doing here? I want to go home. I can't go home. In the morning, terror is replaced by raw excitement that doesn't let up for ten days of the most exciting, endorphin-fueled work I've ever done. The students are dazzling. I could easily have missed out on that. Last year I would have.

A Blind Date with a Famous Man

It's been decades since I've been on a blind date. The last one I had, I married. I know and like the Blind Date's work. And I have to say yes, yes?

He picks me up in my lobby. We're both wearing blue and white gingham shirts! He's funny! Cute, too, even if I'm taller and outweigh him. At brunch he gets sad talking about his late wife. He won't eat. Walking me home, he asks, "What are you afraid of?"

"I'm afraid I'll never see a man in his underwear again." Right there in the street, he yanks the tail of his belt and starts to unzip. I scream. He laughs and says, "Now, if you hadn't yelled so loud, you would have seen a man in his underwear."

This, I think, is a man I could like. We take the long way home through Central Park. He raves about his new TV equipment, then offers to come up and check out mine.

Examining the jerry-rigged setup, he says: "Do you have some time?" We walk more miles to a Best Buy, where he discusses my case with a salesman. Then we walk more miles back and he writes it all down.

Three days later, an e-mail arrives. The Blind Date breaks up with me before we hold hands. If I ever upgrade my TV, I'll know just what to get.

Iris Apfel

I'm invited to the final performance of *Grey Gardens*. I loved this musical the first time I saw it. Why would I want to see it again?

Settling into my seat, I look to my left. There is Iris Apfel. I recently spent an afternoon in her closet. Iris Apfel is one of two living people to have a one-woman show of her clothes at the Metropolitan Museum of Art. I'm sitting next to the most creatively dressed woman in the world. Turns out Iris Apfel discount shops, too. We're going to the Woodbury Common outlet mall together, and I am putting myself completely in Iris Apfel's gorgeous, multi-ringed hands.

The Year of Saying Yes isn't over yet. Looming is a kayak trip on the Hudson, cooking for a PEN fundraiser, a hat-making class at FIT, an ashram with my sister, two speeches, and participation in New York City International Pickle Day. When Yes Year is up, will I go back to no and Grape-Nuts? Less. There isn't one thing I said yes to I'm sorry I said yes to. And look what I would have missed. "No" means safety and the numbing stasis that implies. I'm changed. The change has to do with the joy of being available to chance. There is a thrilling difference between being comfortable and being too comfortable. That difference makes you feel—there's no better word for it—radiant. ◗

How to get the e-mail monkey off your back: Only disconnect.

The 30-Day E-mail Detox

Stressed-out from too much sending and replying, **Katie Goodman** did what the rest of us only dream of: Quit e-mail cold turkey. Weeks later, she was a new (and much improved) woman. Take that, in-box!

74

My e-mail was making me sick. No, I'm not paranoid that it was emitting cancer-causing electricity. But whenever I opened my in-box, I noticed a creeping resentment. I had come to hate e-mail, for all the reasons anyone does. It interrupts and overwhelms. It causes stress. It distracts the brain and encourages the fracturing of attention. Because it's devoid of verbal tone and facial expression, it leads to miscommunication, confusion, and hurt feelings. All for the sake of making our lives "easier."

I started thinking about the problem a few months ago, when I was burned out from a year of overwork at the theater company I run. By chance, I found myself with a copy of Carl Honoré's *In Praise of Slowness,* a brilliant criticism of the culture of speed. Honoré is a proponent of the Slow movement, which encourages a deceleration of everything from cooking to business management, driving to talking styles—based on the belief that speed can produce disconnection from daily life. And every time I read the word *speed,* I couldn't help substituting *e-mail.*

Of course, I might never have read his book at all if I hadn't been kindly put on mandatory vacation by everyone in my life. One of my theater partners said, "Why don't you take four weeks? You can't get anything done over the holidays, anyway." Though I burst out laughing, I conceded, kind of: I took three days. And after they passed, I took another. And another. I put up an outgoing message on my e-mail saying I'd be away for an entire week. Then total irrationality struck. I couldn't take vacation for the rest of my life, but I began fantasizing about what would happen if I gave up e-mail for good.

In the end, I decided to do a 30-day e-mail detox. No e-mail, in or out, for one month. Anyone can do a month, right?

A week before I go off e-mail, the reactions from friends and coworkers range from nausea to abject envy and awe. There are those who revel in their "crackberry" addiction and dread the looming disconnection, and those who long to walk on their own without their iron lung. Everyone wants to explain why *they* could never do what I'm about to.

I create a chirpy bounce-back message that people will receive if they e-mail me, and offer my cell phone number as an olive branch.

At a staff meeting, I announce that I will be unreachable by e-mail for 30 days! I enthusiastically outline the plan and the motivation behind it! I am met with dead silence. The staff are neither enthralled nor inspired. They are wondering how this is going to affect them. Oh, dear. I hadn't thought of the impact on these lovely, generous, already overextended people. Now everyone hates me. I am The One Whom No One Can Reach.

Two days to go. There are a million ways to cheat at the abstinence game, and I'm flirting with every one of them. Each time, the idea seems reasonable enough (*I'll just look to make sure I'm not missing a great work opportunity! I'll switch to text messaging!*), until I voice the thought aloud and am met with looks of pity mixed with disgust.

I dream that my girlfriends kick me out of their clubhouse.

Going through my final e-mails, I feel a nervous tingling, imagining myself slipping down the slope of out-of-the-loop-ness. I have pictured this process, imagining the quiet solitude of recovery. The time freed up, the interaction on a human plane. But panic takes over as the click of my mouse sends the final Dear John message out across my world.

Day One

Halfway through the day, my cell phone battery dies from overuse.

By noon, I have four outraged voice mails from my best friend: "If you're going to do this, leave your cell *on*! And *in your pocket*!" I've had a cell for only four years. We've been friends for 12. How did our friendship survive?

I call my mother. "Thank God you're *somewhere*!" she jokes. In fact, the Internet is the most *not*-somewhere you can be. But I see what she means.

I had pictured having some mongoose-like vigor that would send me into a fury of creativity, but it's not happening. I made the horrible, horrible mistake of clearing out the day for this. And now I sit here while everyone else in the theater office is reading e-mail. The desire to cheat is ravenous.

Still Day One

There's a Bermuda Triangle in my life of to-do items that get lost until a significant space of rediscovered time is created, at which point these items reappear like lost pilots who walk toward their loved ones through a mist, wearing 1940s clothes. The pilots are now reappearing.

I need to contact my whole cast to change tomorrow's

rehearsal time. Six actors times two minutes per call equals 12 minutes. The upside: One actor never checks e-mail, another's is down; phone calls assure rehearsal change works. Might hang on to this system after my 30 days are up.

I wish I had someone looking at my in-box for me, to make sure nothing disastrous is happening. Although, really, what could be disastrous in an office setting if you're not, say, a terrorist watch organization? My inflated sense of self-importance is becoming clearer. My Zen teacher would be so proud. Screw her.

Day Three

On vacation. At Disney World, with my mother and 4-year-old son. For a person who has not been on vacation without a laptop or within walking distance of an Internet café in eight years, yesterday was a cruel beginning. I was in old-school mode: rushing to get in as many rides as possible, dashing back to the Fastpass area when what we needed was a break and a snack. So, no surprise to anyone (but me) that by 3 P.M. we were in full 4-year-old meltdown mode.

But today I am *here*. Finally. Disconnected from everything but my son's energy level and my bladder. And if you can believe it, it is a sweet, slow Disney day.

Day Six

Back from vacation. Virtually no voice mails at work. Panic. Did I write the wrong number on that final e-mail? Or are they not calling because (a) it's too annoying, (b) it's too time-consuming, (c) they're lazy, or (d) they've forgotten me? Oy. There goes my career.

Day Ten

I am getting used to this. And liking it. A *lot*. Getting out of the quick-response mode that e-mail fosters has allowed me to slow down mentally and physically.

I call Carl Honoré, author of *In Praise of Slowness*, in London. Though he's made vast changes in his life since researching slowness (talking slowly isn't one of them, I'm amused to note), he admits that he's been unable to curb his e-mail use. I ask what he thinks of the detox idea.

"It's fabulous, though obviously extreme," he says. "I don't think many of us can do without e-mail permanently. The pendulum has swung too far. But a 30-day break could remind you that

you *can* do without it. In this always-on culture, you can be reached anytime—as though that's always a good thing. It's not. We need times to be silent, to be unplugged."

"But where does energy come in?" I ask, relieved to voice a question that's been nagging me. How can we be slow but still enthusiastic, impulsive, spontaneous—all that good stuff that goes along with creativity and engagement?

"The reason that's even a question is that there's such a strong cultural taboo against being slow—which has come to mean being lazy, a slacker," he says. "It's true that doing *everything* slowly would be lamentable, but the Slow philosophy isn't about that. It's about shifting gears to rest, recharge, reflect, tap into the deeper stuff." Thus the Slow movement encourages eating with attention, taking the time to think before you respond, and, in general, practicing the art of stopping to smell the coffee. Well, maybe not coffee. Decaf, perhaps.

"And then when you need to shift into higher gear," Honoré explains, "you have more get-up-and-go, more clarity, more va-va-voom. You have *more* vitality because you're not worn out. Life becomes richer; you develop new rhythms."

Halfway There, and Beyond

I'm starting to have Hawaiian Vacation Syndrome: that urge that grips you midway through a fabulous trip, when you start casually flipping through the local real estate listings, entertaining what seem to be perfectly rational thoughts about moving to a tropical island permanently.

What would happen if I canceled AOL for good? Sent out a final mass e-mail saying I'd found the light? Like all new converts, I would spend my time at cocktail parties proselytizing. And like all new converts, I would quickly stop being asked to cocktail parties. Then I'd become uninformed, reclusive, out of touch, and I'd lose my sense of humor. Maybe not the result I'm looking for.

Surprisingly, the final two weeks go by with no thoughts of e-mail. All that sending and receiving just holds no interest or concern. Extracting myself from e-mail took more effort than existing without it.

The Day After

Nervously, fearing the worst, I go online. How many messages could there be before AOL simply stopped processing them? But the pile is shockingly light. For the first week of my

> I had pictured having some mongoose-like vigor that would send me into a fury of creativity, but it's not happening.

absence, there were about 35 e-mails a day. Then it peters out to ten or so a day (not including several daily offers for penile enhancement); since I wasn't sending any mail, I wasn't generating any communication. Several messages, from friends and coworkers, start out, "I know you're not on e-mail, but..." And by the time I'm reading these, almost everything in them is irrelevant.

I missed nothing.

A Week Later

I've gotten a ton of e-mails saying it's so nice to have me back. The ridiculous thing is that these are from friends I'd been seeing in person all month long.

Some changes may definitely stick. I'm no longer multitasking. No talking on the phone while doing e-mail. I now stop to listen to people with full attention. I respond more thoughtfully, not reacting immediately to demands from coworkers or 4-year-olds. I continue to call actors when I have rehearsal changes. And something fun or interesting always comes out of our chats.

I've noticed that when I begin the morning by checking e-mail, I don't create anything worth a damn all day; by the time I've slogged through my in-box, I'm tapped out. So I've started doing all my writing and brainstorming before I even log on. I can't remember the last time I had so much creative energy.

Surprisingly, I'm a lot less hostile to e-mail than I was before. Having proved that I can ditch it if I want to, I'm now *choosing* to use it. I'm more appreciative of the ways in which it really is useful.

So many of us are addicted to doing and achieving. And e-mail plays into that ego-affirming drive; you can get a powerful sense of leading an army as you send out your marching orders.

An e-mail halt gives you the opportunity to examine that drive to *do*. Every spiritual practice encourages a period of stillness, whether it's prayer, a daily five-minute meditation, or ten days of silence. That retreat offers a way to get perspective on the habitual movement toward achieving. In stepping back, in *single*-tasking, you can hear the calm, still voice that speaks clearly. This is where you find peace, reprioritize, and rejuvenate creative energy.

Three years ago, I wrote my husband a note that I left on his keyboard: "No one on their deathbed ever wished they had spent more time on the computer." It was a way to help him let himself off the hook for not working 24 hours a day. I never imagined it would become his closing gesture at the end of every day to place that note back on his keyboard. And I never imagined I'd believe my own advice. ⬛

Mail Management

To lessen the compulsions of e-mail without doing a complete detox, take these steps:

CONTAIN: Limit e-mail to certain hours. If you must check your in-box frequently, do so at set intervals, perhaps every two hours. Don't just leap every time you hear a new e-mail arrive. Better yet, turn off the alert sound.

EASE OFF: Try dealing with e-mail less and less frequently, and see what happens. Are people truly annoyed? Is work really not getting done?

CREATE FIRST: Establish your day's top priorities before you open your in-box. Try doing some creative work first.

PAUSE: Wait before you respond to e-mails, especially tricky ones. And before sending out mass e-mails, consider: Does *everybody* really need to weigh in? Some companies now have policies that discourage sending interoffice e-mails that will generate more work for everyone. Other companies are scheduling e-mail mini-detoxes, such as U.S. Cellular's e-mail-free Fridays.

SINGLE-TASK: Don't e-mail while you're doing something else. Read incoming and outgoing messages carefully to avoid miscommunication and the extra work it usually creates.

USE YOUR PERSONAL SECRETARY: When you need an e-mail break, create an outgoing message that says you're out of the office and directs people elsewhere (say, to your cell phone) in case of "emergency." This message may make people think twice about bothering you. And many issues resolve themselves simply with the passage of time.

—K.G.

48 Decisions We've Made for You

Paper or plastic? Shave or wax? Stay at this job or go? From pesky little quandaries that ought to be no-brainers…to the mysteries of the universe (should I wash that man right out of my hair? and must it be organic shampoo?), deciding on the best course of action isn't always easy. We made a list of life's vexing questions, then went in search of perspective, reason—and answers. Consider it our gift to agonizers everywhere. By Arianne Cohen

WHAT NOW, MY LOVE?

1 I'm married and exhausted. Sex or sleep? "Both," says Paul Glovinsky, PhD, coauthor of *The Insomnia Answer.* "It's not just a question of sex but of timing. Often women are stimulated by sex and can't sleep afterward." Which, as you know, means he crashes like a mighty oak while you lie awake and fume. "If you can time things to coincide with the time of day when you're at peak energy, your sex life will be significantly more satisfying." (Remember sex in the morning? Weekend naptime?) And speaking of time, Linda Young, PhD, a Washington-based therapist who specializes in helping women foster healthy relationships, adds this: "The average encounter is only around 20 minutes, so ask yourself why you're hesitant. Your resistance might be a reflection of your lack of sat-

isfaction with the sex." Or your fear of intimacy, your performance anxiety, your anger about something else in the relationship—the point being that sexual unhappiness can be a shield for many other types of issues.

2 My clock is ticking. Settle for the guy I care about, or hold out for The One, who may never show up? Do. Not. Settle. "Both of you—not to mention the children you might have—may pay the price of a fractured relationship later," says psychotherapist Ken Page, founder of the dating workshop Deeper Dating. Marrying Mr. Almost The One is, on the other hand, perfectly admissible. "If someone is your match in 75 to 85 percent of the things that are important to you—values, character strengths, how he treats other people, emotional fitness—that's not settling," says Young. "But it's up to you to infuse 'good enough' with energy and passion so that it becomes fantastic. And chemistry counts; you need to be attracted to each other."

3 **I've met a great guy. He never calls. Should I call him?** "It's 2009. You can call," says Steve Santagati, author of *The MANual* and the resident expert at askstevesantagati.com. Still, Santagati urges you not to put the guy on the spot. "Let him initiate plans. You can just say hello to open the lines of communication, and he might hear something in the phone call that he didn't get the first time you met." The way he responds will tell you whether you have a future together.

4 **He's married, but he says he's not happy and it's ending. I should stay away, right?** Run as though you're fleeing a burning house. Which, in fact, you are. "He's already showing you he hasn't put enough distance between himself and his problematic relationship," says Young. "If you get involved, he's going to subject you to all his issues, and you're going to be a wonderful dumping ground."

5 **When, if ever, is it a good idea to try again with a guy whose heart you've already broken?** About as often as pigs fly. "Usually, you can't go backward," says Manhattan-based matchmaker Janis Spindel. "It's a case-by-case scenario, but statistics show that it doesn't usually work." The case where it might work: when the failure was unrelated to your attraction or personalities but caused by outside circumstances—say, one of you was going through a family tragedy, or you were transferred to another city. Absent such extenuating circumstances, analyze what went wrong the first time, assume a similar dynamic will arise again, and then determine whether that dynamic is feasible in your current life.

6 **I love my partner, but the sex is underwhelming. Stay the course or go?** Neither. Instead, you're going to do the hardest thing you've ever done. "Think about the things that turn you on in the deepest ways, the things that make you feel most loved and cared for," says Page. "What kind of touch? What words? What kind of pacing makes you feel the most affection for your partner? Tell each other, no matter how wild or tame your desires might seem. When the two of you are unafraid to be naughty and vulnerable together, the experience can be amazing." Sex thrives on risk and surrender, and you're probably missing one or both.

MONEY MUDDLES

7 **When buying electronics or appliances, should I buy the warranties, too?** You might as well toss your money in the air and wave your hands like you just don't care. Extended product warranties are a multibillion-dollar industry unto themselves, raking in 40 to 80 percent profit margins. "The retailers are making a significant profit on those policies," says Laura Rowley, Yahoo! Finance columnist and author of *Money & Happiness*. Why? Because most products come with a one-year manufacturer's warranty anyway, and according to a recent *Consumer Reports* survey, repairs, on average, cost about the same as the policy. And while we're on the subject, you can skip the extended car warranty, too. A new car is already warrantied, typically with a three-year/36,000-mile bumper-to-bumper warranty, plus a longer power train warranty, which covers the more expensive engine and transmission repairs. The time to consider an extended warranty is when your car is spending a lot of time in the shop as the basic warranty is winding down. "You might consider a contract with the manufacturer or a company you know you can depend on," says John Paul, AAA car doctor. "Skip the small warranty companies. They may be fly-by-night, so when you try to collect, they become very difficult."

8 **Buy a house now or rent for two more years in the hope that prices continue to drop?** If you have a good FICO score (around 720 or above), can afford a standard 15- or 30-year fixed-rate mortgage, can handle a 20 percent down payment, and intend to own for at least five years, then, says *O* columnist and personal finance expert Suze Orman, go ahead and buy. As with stocks, it's too risky to try to time the market at its absolute lowest. Ask

When is it smart to buy a product warranty? Only when you want to throw your money away.

a local real estate agent to show you some comparable sales so you can bargain for the best price.

9 **If I'm saving for a down payment on a house, does it make sense to sock away the maximum IRA contribution?** In time, the house will give you better tax write-offs than the IRA, not to mention a roof over your head. One exception, says Orman: "If your employer offers a 401(k) with matching contributions, I wouldn't pass up the free money."

10 **Is long-term-care insurance worth it?** "Generally, it makes sense only for a very specific group of people: those with liquid assets between $400,000 and $1.5 million," says finance expert Jean Chatzky. The average nursing home stay lasts two and a half years, at an average cost of $78,000 a year—which means that if you have more than $1.5 million in assets, you can pay for your own care, and if you have less than $400,000, you could quickly qualify for Medicaid. "Age 60 is the time to buy insurance if you need to," says Chatzky, "unless you know you're at high risk for a medical condition, in which case buy earlier." For the greatest security, choose a company with a top rating from agencies such as Moody's or A.M. Best.

11 **Do I need life insurance, and if so, how much?** Only if you love your loved ones. (That's a yes.) "It's so cheap that everyone with dependents or debt should have it," says Rowley. Insuring yourself for five to ten times your annual household expenses can cost as little as $1 to $2 a day. "That means if something happens to you, your family has five to ten years to figure out how they're going to go forward."

NOT EASY BEING GREEN

12 **Which produce is it important to buy organic?** "People can decrease the amount of pesticides they ingest by 90 percent by avoiding the 12 most contaminated fruits and vegetables and eating the 12 least contaminated instead," says Lori Bongiorno, author of *Green, Greener, Greenest*. The dirty dozen, according to the Environmetal Working Group: peaches, apples, bell peppers, celery, nectarines, strawberries, cherries, lettuce, imported grapes, pears, spinach, and potatoes. (For the complete list, go to foodnews.org.) "I also buy organic dairy and meats," Bongiorno says, "because that's the only way to guarantee avoiding antibiotics and hormones." In packaged foods, such as cereals and macaroni and cheese, the health benefits of organic versus nonorganic aren't nearly as dramatic.

13 **Should I be buying organic makeup and body products?** You should be buying nontoxic products. "The problem with 'organic' is that there are so many different labeling systems, it's hard to know what you're buying," says Sonya Lunder, senior analyst at the Environmental Working Group. Check your toiletries at cosmeticsdatabase.com, the Environmental Working Group's list of more than 25,000 products rated by toxicity and ingredient safety. When possible, purchase those rated 0 to 2 on their 10-point scale.

14 **Do "green" household cleaners really work?** Yep—because it turns out that our households don't need to be sterilized. "No surface is going to stay sanitized for very long, anyway," says Bongiorno. "Remember, too, that disinfectants can be poisonous—they're regulated as pesticides—and that there are many affordable and worthwhile green options."

15 **Paper or plastic?** Canvas. "The paper versus plastic question is a wash," says New York University professor of nutrition, food studies, and public health Marion Nestle, PhD, author of *What to Eat*. "Plastic pollutes the environment, and paper either cuts down trees or costs a lot of energy to recycle."

WORK WORRIES

16 **Should I stick with a stable job in an office I enjoy or say yes to a new and more lucrative offer?** Option three: "Go to your boss, tell her you've gotten an offer, and ask if she'll match it," says Robin Ryan, career counselor and author of *60 Seconds & You're Hired!* (Of course, there's an art to doing this: You want to make clear that you love your job and aren't just using it as a bargaining chip.) "She may say no, but there's a good chance she'll say yes. Whatever you do, though, do not bluff, because you could end up unemployed."

17 **Is an advanced degree worth the time and money?** Depends on the degree. MSN Money personal finance columnist Liz Pulliam Weston calculated which degrees pay off over time in salary. "Advanced degrees in business, education, engineering, law, and science do," she says. "But the average liberal arts and social sciences master's degrees typically don't." Her advice: Talk to people in the positions you see yourself in someday, and ask what degrees they have and whether they needed those degrees. If you just want to spruce up your résumé, Ryan suggests seeking credentials from professional associations or getting short-term seminar "degrees," which, depending on the field, can provide the desired education, networking opportunities, and salary increases.

18 Which e-mails can I not answer? Those where you are cc'd; messages to more than three people; all one-liner e-mails ("Done," "Perfect," "Sounds great"); messages that start with "FYI"; thank-yous to thank-yous. "If it doesn't bluntly request a comment back, assume it's just for your information and don't reply," says Ryan. Endless discussion chains (Subject: Re: Re: Re: Re:) should be handled by phone or in person after two to three e-mails, says Will Schwalbe, coauthor of *Send: Why People E-mail So Badly and How to Do It Better.* And when higher-ups send answers to a question, give them a break. "You've asked, they've responded, and now you can do them a favor by not cluttering their in-box with 'Thanks' e-mails. But if you're a boss, err on the side of responding; people take it quite personally if you don't."

19 When should I send a handwritten thank-you instead of an e-mail? Ignore your mom on this one: It's an e-mail world now. "People expect such an instant response that an e-mail within 24 hours is often preferred," says author and corporate productivity consultant Julie Morgenstern. It's okay, however, to follow your e-mail with handwritten thanks. "Busy people are getting more than 100 e-mails a day," says Pamela Eyring, owner and director of the Protocol School of Washington. "If you want to stand out, you can showcase appreciation with a good note."

20 What should I give my boss at the holidays? A lovely note showcasing your appreciation. "The most meaningful gifts I get are the thank-you cards from people who work for me, and that's all I ever want," Morgenstern says. But if you feel you simply must buy something, says Penelope Trunk, founder of the Brazen Careerist blog, "your only goal is not to be wrong. So in my book, that leaves food. Wine could be wrong. Art could be wrong. Food can't be. The only thing is, if your boss is overweight, try not to buy really fattening foods."

CLOTHES CALLS

21 I've heard it said that there's one hemline that will always be correct. What is it? The perfect hem hits the top of the knee or an inch above—no higher. Period. If you despise your knees, says *O*'s creative director, Adam Glassman, wear a skirt or dress that grazes the bottom of the kneecap and a higher heel. But odds are your knees look fine.

22 Can I wear brown and black together? Navy and black? There's nothing chicer. And since all three colors function as neutrals, there's not much heavy brain work involved. Especially on the upper half of the body, navy is kinder than black, which tends to draw color out of the face. "A brown or navy shoe, belt, or bag worn with a pair of black pants shows that you possess a certain amount of flair," says Glassman. To make this look no-fail, always match socks or hosiery to your shoe.

WHAT SHOULD A WOMAN NEVER WEAR IF SHE WANTS TO DRESS HER AGE?

23 In your 20s: Matching suits—dressing like a Park Avenue matron just makes a young person look dated.

24 In your 30s and up: Colored tights—too juvenile. Low-slung jeans, shorts, or skirts—no one wants to see muffin top or midriff.

25 In your 40s and up: The schoolgirl look—rounded collars, pleated plaid skirts, and pinafores look wrong on grown women. Short skirts—hems that hit midthigh or higher aren't appropriate no matter how hot your legs look.

26 In your 50s and up: Anything strapless—unless you're wearing a jacket or other shoulder coverage. Innerwear as outerwear—leave the bias-cut slipdress in the bedroom (and, for that matter, the terry cloth hoodie and sweatpants).

Psst! Green cleaning products really do work— without the scary chemicals.

27 **In your 60s and up:** Bikinis—there are gorgeous one-piece swimsuits that don't reveal the whole landscape.

28 **No matter your age:** Nude or white hosiery—better to go barelegged with a spray tan. Shoulder pads—honestly, why? Ankle-length straight skirts—flattering to exactly no one. Retro trends—if you were old enough to wear it the first time, don't revisit it.

29 **Safe at any age:** Heels (two inches and up)—they make every pair of legs look toned. Jeans—there's a modern pair made for every body shape. T-shirts—a soft, fitted cotton tee always gives off an unstudied, contemporary vibe.

BEAUTY: IN THE EYE OF THE BEFUDDLED

30 **Should I let a manicurist cut my cuticles?** **Dermatologists say no, but what an eyesore!** The cuticle protects the nail as it grows; when you cut it, you run the risk of deforming the nail. But we see your point. Loretta Ciraldo, MD, a dermatologist in Miami, suggests having your manicurist push back your cuticles for the first few visits; then, if you feel that she has been very conscientious and careful, ask her to gently trim only the dried-out part of the cuticle.

31 **Should I shave or wax my legs?** Shaving is much less expensive, but you have to do it every two to three days; full leg waxing at a salon can cost anywhere from $40 to $100, but you can typically wait almost a month between repeats. And if your hair is very coarse, shaving may cause razor bumps (a.k.a. *pseudofolliculitis barbae*), which occur when newly cut strands of hair curl in on themselves and grow into the skin. So if you can afford it, wax.

32 **Is it harmful to wash my hair every day?** No. "You wash your face every day, and your hair encounters the same amount of dirt," says trichologist Philip Kingsley, who points out that a clean, flake-free scalp will lead to thicker and stronger hair. If your hair is very dry, try using a conditioner made for dry, damaged hair, along with a leave-in conditioner. One caveat: The combination of washing and then using a blow-dryer or flatiron daily can damage hair, so limit your use of heated tools to every other or every third day. And a clarification: The idea that you need to rotate your hair products for your hair to be its healthiest is a myth. "If you're constantly changing brands, you'll probably just get confused about which ones worked best for you," says Kingsley. "Think of how you would describe your hair [fine, limp, dry, thick, oily], and then find good corresponding products and stick with them."

33 **What's the best kind of blow-dryer?** If you want to dry your hair quickly without damaging it, invest in an ionic dryer that's between 1,500 and 1,800 watts, says New York City hairstylist Patrick Melville. (One of his favorites is the very lightweight FHI Heat Nano Weight Pro 1800, $150.) And buy one that comes with a nozzle attachment, which will prevent you from holding the dryer too close to your hair.

34 **What's the most effective antiaging product I can buy?** A broad-spectrum sunscreen. Avobenzone and Mexoryl (chemical absorbers) are most effective against UVA rays, while zinc oxide and titanium dioxide (physical blockers) will shield against UVA and UVB rays. Try Neutrogena Ultra Sheer Dry-Touch Sunblock SPF 55 or Nia 24 Sun Damage Prevention SPF 30. If you already have sun damage (wrinkles, age spots, thin skin), also buy a serum or cream that contains high levels of scientifically studied ingredients such as retinol; vitamins C, B3, and B5; and glycolic acid. Use it religiously; treating aging skin takes months to years, not days.

TECH: WHAT THE HECK?

35 **Update my computer or buy a new one?** If the keys are falling off, the hard drive is full, and the operating system is molasses slow, it's time to hit the computer store. "But if the idea of waiting another half year doesn't grate on your soul, then wait," says tech writer Daniel Pink, author of *A Whole New Mind*. "Products improve so quickly that you'll get more features and power for the same price in six months."

36 **Should I buy CDs or download music?** "Downloading is easy and cheaper—the savings on not manufacturing a product are passed on to you," says *Popular Mechanics* senior technology editor Glenn Derene. Your best bet is AmazonMP3, which offers songs for as little as 89 cents, and is free of digital rights management software, so you can copy them onto any device—including CDs, if you miss them.

37 **BlackBerry or iPhone?** Depends on your technology needs. If you're an e-mail fanatic, the BlackBerry historically has had the edge, though the iPhone may be closing that gap. If you're a video, music, or gaming junkie, buy an iPhone for its unparalleled entertainment options, suggests Paul Reynolds, electronics editor at *Consumer Reports*.

38 **LCD or plasma TV?** LCD is your best option for screens under 42 inches, but for screens over 50, go for plasma. Between 42 and 50, it's a toss-up; you may want to let your living room make the decision for you. "Plasma has a wider viewing angle, meaning it's good for rooms with seating in corners," says Reynolds. "LCDs do a little better in rooms with lots of lights and windows."

CAR CONFUSION

39 **Should I get all the interior extras that come with my new car?** Just say no. "Paint protection, fabric protection, and alarm systems can often be installed far cheaper after you buy the vehicle," says AAA's John Paul.

40 **Should I pay extra for car insurance when I rent a car?** Not unless you enjoy double paying. If you already have car insurance, and you're charging the rental on your credit card, you're likely covered, says Jean Chatzky. Call your credit card and insurance companies before you go, and ask what your policies cover.

WHAT KIND OF CAR SHOULD I BUY…

41 **If I'm a long-distance commuter?** Three things to consider: gas mileage, comfort, and stereo extras to keep you entertained. "I like the Toyota Prius," says Brian Moody, senior road test editor at car pricing and review Web site edmunds.com. "It's a hybrid and gets over 40 mpg." Nonhybrid options include the Honda Fit or the Ford Focus; the Focus comes with the Sync system, which allows you to control your MP3 player by voice command. Visit fueleconomy.gov to check gas mileage.

42 **If I hate to drive?** Moody goes with the Prius again: "It requires so little effort. The steering is electric, the shift is electric, and it has a certain ease."

43 **If I'm a mom with two kids?** "I would get a sedan, because they're cheap and roomy, and they don't guzzle gas," says Moody. "Unless you live where it's snowy, in which case a compact SUV, like a Honda CR-V with all-wheel drive, would make sense." Before you buy, scour safety ratings at safercar.gov and iihs.org.

44 **If I'm a weekend outdoorsy person?** A Subaru Outback or Land Rover LR2. "They're essentially easy-to-drive station wagons with decent fuel economy, but they slug through mud," says Paul. Visit edmunds.com to see both the dealer cost of the vehicle and typical buyer prices.

45 **If I'm single and want a car as carefree as I am?** The Mazda MX-5 Miata or Saturn Sky. "They're fun, you can put the top down, and they're not an awful lot of money—less than $30,000," says Paul. Note the minimal storage space, though: A small, soft duffel is just about all that fits in the trunk.

THE BIG STUFF

46 **To vote or not to vote? In other words, does my one puny vote actually count?** It does! Think of it as your one big bad vote, which will give your candidate marching orders. "Studies show that officials pay attention to groups that vote and ignore those that don't," says Harvard Kennedy School professor Thomas Patterson, PhD, author of *The Vanishing Voter.* As for choosing which elections to show up for, "never in history has a presidential election been decided by a single vote, but many smaller races have," Patterson says. "The smaller the electorate, the more important the single voter. And if you want to make an even bigger difference, get involved in the campaign, where you have the power to affect dozens or even hundreds of votes."

47 **Is the prestige of a private college really worth the price?** Yes—but only because prestige can come so cheap these days. "Many parents are surprised to learn that some of the most selective private schools in the country are the least expensive to attend," says Jeff Brenzel, PhD, dean of Yale undergraduate admissions. Yale offers a full ride to students with family incomes below $60,000; Harvard, Princeton, and Stanford offer similar packages. But Brenzel—himself the father of one child in private school and another at a state university—adds that state universities often offer some of the best honors programs. "If your child is high-achieving, it would be difficult to do better than some of the prestigious programs at state universities. Your child's future is not going to be determined by which gate she walks through. It's going to depend on every decision she makes once she's through it."

48 **What about all the decisions you haven't addressed here?** If it's a question of fact, you'll almost certainly find an answer online. If it's a matter of figuring out your heart's desire, our best advice is this: Flip a coin. Seriously. Dig up a quarter, toss it in the air, see what turns up. If you're disturbed, dismayed, or disappointed by the result, well, that's your answer. And having figured out what you want to do, we hope you'll do it! ⬛

12 Ways to Unclutter Your Life

He's got organizational superpowers! He can bring order to your kitchen and demystify the reasons you're hanging on to things you don't need (and don't even like) in your closets, drawers, basement.... And he's here to help get your house, and your sanity, back. He's **Andrew Mellen**, a.k.a. VirgoMan.

Think of this scenario: If your house were burning and your family, pets, and purse were already out of harm's way, what else would you want to save? Probably not the blender that only works on one speed, the china you inherited but never use, or the photo in which you're not exactly looking your best. Which begs the question: If those things aren't worth taking, why are they in your home in the first place?

There's no reason to be surrounded by things that don't work, that you don't need, or that you don't even like. As a professional organizer, I help my clients figure out what they should keep and what they should kiss goodbye; then we figure out how to make what they have work for them. You can do it yourself by following the steps I've outlined:

THE GROUND RULES

1. Everything you own should have value, either because it's functional or beautiful or you just love it. Remember the question of what you'd grab if your house were on fire; that's your baseline for determining an object's worth.

2. Every item needs a place where it "lives." Setting things down on the coffee table or kitchen counter creates piles and confusion. My clients mock me when I say, "Where do your keys live? They live in a bowl or on a hook by the front door"—but you never lose anything when you put it where it lives.

3. Focus on one thing at a time. Multitasking is supposed to help you get more things done quickly, but when you try to do 19 things at once, everything ends up incomplete. You're trying to simplify your life, so simplify your approach to getting organized. Now let's get started.

THE CRAMMED KITCHEN

Your kitchen is a food preparation area, not a storage space. The idea here is to weed out what you're not using, then put similar items together and in the best places.

Appliances: Machines that are broken or aren't used are just taking up space. If your Crock-Pot has a missing lid that you say you're going to replace someday, or you're keeping the bread maker just because it was a gift, then get rid of it.

Food containers: All your plastic storage items should have corresponding lids. If you don't have one or the other, it's a recycling item.

Pots and pans: If there isn't a lot of space in your kitchen, use a pot rack. If you have the space, hang them along the wall for fast access.

Knives: If you're short on counter space, consider the type of knife block that fits in a drawer.

Plastic bags: Everybody has a plastic bag full of other plastic bags. Use the ones you have for trash can liners, or take them back to the supermarket for recycling. Keep canvas shopping totes in the car so you don't accumulate more plastic bags. Mesh shopping bags roll up small enough to be kept in your handbag for unexpected trips to the market.

Cookbooks: Unless you're a collector or you have a lot of room, edit them. How often do you use the cookbook? If you've had it for years but it's never gotten a single stain or burn from use, donate it.

THE PILE OF MAIL

If you can't finish the mail, don't even start the mail. You can't slice chicken for dinner and sort your bills at the same time, so when you come in the front door with a stack of mail, put it in the basket, box, or whatever container you have handy for this purpose. You don't have such a container? No wonder there are so many piles of mail around your house.

When you're ready, take your mail basket to wherever you deal with paperwork. First, pull out the circulars and flyers and set them aside; you'll either clip the coupons or put them in the recycling bin—later. Also set aside the catalogs. If you're shopping for something specific, save them. (Caveat: no multiples. The new catalog replaces the old one, which gets recycled.) If you're getting catalogs you never wanted in the first place, pull off the pages with the mailing label and put them aside; that's an action item for later. Then separate the rent bills, personal correspondence, time-sensitive invitations, requests for charitable donations, membership renewals, new credit card offers, and so forth.

Open the bills first because they represent a relationship that must be honored; if you want the services, you have to pay. All the stuffing that says "You've been selected to receive these free gifts" goes into the recycling bin. All you want is the bill and the return envelope.

Put any invitations aside; later on, you'll transfer those into your calendar and send your response.

If there's room in your home office, have small bins in which to stack bills, invitations, and the correspondence you're keeping.

When you're done sorting, then you can read your magazines. Or get those back pages you ripped out, call the companies that sent them, and tell them what you *don't* want—their catalogs. (You can also log on to catalogchoice.org, a free service that will stop these unwanted mailings from being sent to you.)

THE OVERSTUFFED CLOSET

My clients have a lot of "someday" best. *Someday I'm going to fit into these again. Someday this trend might return. Someday I'm going to wear this.* The problem is, "someday" doesn't exist; there's only today. Here's what to do with what's being worn only by your hangers.

Clothes that don't fit: If you've gained weight, keep the smaller-sized clothes that you'll get the most use from and work on fitting into them again. If you've already lost weight, don't keep a whole closetful of big clothes as though one day you're going to suddenly be struck fat; donate them to charity.

Trend items: If you're waiting for something to come back in style, don't. Even if it does return, it will look dated—and so will you.

Special occasion outfits: The old rule that says "If you haven't worn it in a year, donate it" is a perfect guide for

> If you have to clear off the backseat for company, there's a problem.

when to say goodbye to these items.

Sentimental pieces: You say, "I really loved this jacket." I know you did. But if you haven't worn it in ages and it doesn't work with your other clothes, it's time for it to go away. If you're saving your wedding dress, be honest—do you have the space to store it? Do you have a daughter you're saving it for, and is it a timeless classic she won't roll her eyes at? If the answers are yes, keep it. If you're short on storage space, you have only sons, or your dress has puffy sleeves, lace, and buttons up the arms because you did a kind of Linda Ronstadt circa 1974 thing, give it to a thrift store or donatemydress.org, which provides formal wear to girls who can't afford prom or special occasion dresses.

Now that you have a closetful of clothes that you actually wear, organize them—all the short-sleeved shirts together, all the jeans together, etc. Do the same with your shoes. If you have the space, they can be kept on shelves so you can see them immediately. If not, try stacking shelves or hanging shoe racks.

THE DRAWER FULL OF PHOTOS

If you don't have time to put your photos in an album or scrapbook, it's okay to stop pretending you're going to do it. Get clear shoeboxes to store them in instead.

Then get a kitchen timer. Why? Because sorting through photos leads to reminiscing, and suddenly it's three hours later. But you're not looking at photos now—you're organizing them so that looking at them later will be more fun. Decide how long you have and set the timer.

Group the photos by subject—the family reunion, your trip to Istanbul. While you're grouping, you're also sorting: Is it a clear picture? Do you even know who those people are? Throw away any that don't measure up, and any in which you can't stand the sight of yourself. When you're done, label the boxes accordingly: "Family Reunion, February 2009".

THE NEW THINGS THAT HAVEN'T BEEN USED

Do you buy things because they're on sale? If you didn't need them, they weren't a bargain. Here are the three questions to ask before you buy anything:

1. Where would this live? A very practical consideration, especially if you're trying to de-clutter.

2. What am I going to do with it? If it has a purpose or fills a need, fine. If you already have four of them, not fine.

3. What is it replacing? When something is broken or you don't like the old version as much as the new one, then by all means, charge away. But be prepared to get rid of the old item when you get home.

THE INHERITED ITEMS AND MEMENTOS

Your home is not a museum. Many people subscribe to the unwritten rule that you're obligated to keep your great-aunt's dishes, even if you don't like them, just because she used them. But maybe your great-aunt never liked them either and also felt too guilty to let them go. Things don't have to become yours simply because they belonged to a relative. You're not living her life, and you're not a bad person for giving inherited items away.

If the acquired stuff is worth money, you may feel bound to it financially: "It's real silver—I can't give it away." Yes, you can. Donate it, document what it's worth, and take it off your taxes. Or give it to another family member who would really like it. Or sell it on eBay. And if you like something enough to keep it, consider it a replacement, not an addition—keep Grandma's reading lamp, but donate the one you already have.

Mementos from your own life are harder to part with because when you see them, you relive the story: To you, it's the cashmere V-neck you wore on your first date with the man who would become your husband; to anyone else, it's just an old sweater full of holes. The key to parting with items suspended in time is not to replay that story. Leave the room, come back in, and see what you're really holding on to—a sweater that's seen better days. Rule of thumb: If it serves no purpose, let it go.

THE CAR (OR, "THE STORAGE SPACE ON WHEELS")

If you have to clear off the backseat for company, there's a problem.

What shouldn't be in the car: old food wrappers, toys, the dry cleaning or recycling you've been meaning to drop off for a week (just take it out of the car until you're ready to make the trip), out-of-season tools (if it's June, you can remove the ice scraper from the trunk).

What should be in the car: registration, insurance certificate, owner's manual, maps and/or GPS, extra pair of sunglasses in case of glare, small folding umbrella, headset for your cell phone (preferably you're not talking while driving, but if you are, please be hands-free), envelope with supermarket and drive-through restaurant coupons and any gift certificates you've received (it's pointless for them to be in the drawer at home).

What should be in the trunk: tool kit, flashlight, working spare tire. In winter, add ice scraper, bag of kitty litter (for traction in snow), a small blanket.

THE CHAOTIC COMPUTER

You don't want to spend an hour looking for a scone recipe—or your résumé—because you're searching through all the stuff on your desktop. If you can't see the pretty picture on your computer screen because it's full of icons for documents, downloads, and photos, start making folders. Color-code them: The folder for your financial documents can be green, the one for your job search can be blue. Like goes with like—all your résumés in one folder, all photos in another. Label each one clearly. Then put all your folders in "My Documents," a master folder that you have whether you're on a Mac or a PC.

You can save e-mail correspondence, but discard the one that says, "Great, see you at 12 on Thursday!" and save the one with information about what you discussed.

By the way, if you're constantly responding to e-mail, you're being pulled away from the things that you need or want to do. Try checking it hourly.

THE (SHUDDER) BASEMENT OR GARAGE
Where do you start? With the bad, scary corner. First, get rid of unsalvageables. If the basement flooded and a whole bunch of stuff got waterlogged, these are no longer your possessions; they're a mildewfest. Just say goodbye.

Once you've gotten rid of the garbage, start grouping similar items, which makes it easy to see what there's too much of and what's broken. Tackle one category at a time—the holiday decorations, the seasonal clothing, the journals you've been keeping for years. If you have enough room, spread everything out to take stock of it all.

When everything has been sorted, prune: Is this important enough to save? Is it useful? Discard what isn't.

Next, containerize what's left, but don't buy storage bins until you have an understanding of what you're putting into them. It doesn't serve you to come home with two 40-gallon tubs if what you need is 19 shoeboxes. I'm all about clear plastic storage; sure, you can label boxes, but why not be able to see the contents immediately? And if you also use your basement as a play space for your kids or to entertain, get rolling shelves that can be moved to one side of the room and perhaps even covered with drapes.

At the end of this project, you'll have accomplished three goals: There will be less stuff, what's left will be in order, and everything will be in containers that work with your space. Being organized isn't about getting rid of everything you own or trying to become a different person; it's about living the way you want to live, but better. There are enough things in the world that you can't control—but you *can* bring some order into your home and into your life. **◐**

WHAT I KNOW FOR SURE: OPRAH

"Yes, there are many things that need to get done, but in *this* moment I have to do nothing."

Leadership is the key to everything." That's a running mantra for Stedman Graham. I've heard it in so many conversations over the years; no matter what we're talking about, that's his refrain: "It's all about leadership."

I never fully disagreed but always thought he was generalizing a bit. Not long ago, though, I found myself overwhelmed by a lack of leadership in almost every area of my life, and now I willingly admit, even say for sure—you are right, Stedman. (He's probably going to frame this.) Without proper leadership there is always confusion, which eventually leads to crisis and chaos.

I'm still affirming that lesson in the aftermath of the crisis at my school in South Africa. I've been on an inter-

Oprah's retreat, under a canopy of oak trees, at her home in Santa Barbara.

national search for a new Head of School, while also searching for a CEO and president for my TV network, OWN—while also doing two shows a day, banking radio shows to air in the future, trying to read every page in *O* magazine before it goes to print, having preshow meetings with producers, dealing with the business of all the businesses, and hearing from Gayle: "Your 'What I Know for Sure' column is *waaay* overdue. You're holding up the process!"

I had an LOL moment when I was told that with everything else I have going on, I was supposed to write a column about being overwhelmed.

How about this: I AM OVERWHELMED! Too many answers that need to come from me. Trying to do too many things at once. Flying from Africa to Chicago to California to New York. Doing. Doing. Doing.

So I stopped. Everything. For one day I just stopped. Didn't interview anybody. Or take any phone calls. Or return any e-mails. I stopped doing in order to return to the being of myself.

I pulled out my gratitude journal, in which I'd been too tired to write even a sentence for months. I went to my favorite place on earth, the place where 12 oaks form a canopy on the side of my front yard; I call them the apostles. I watched the sunlight filter between the branches and enhance every leaf. I listened to the birds, and tried to decipher how many different ones were singing—or were they just talking at the same time?

I let myself absorb the sacredness and dignity of the oaks. I let those trees remind me how to be: still. I took a few deep breaths. I said "Thank you" out loud. I felt like I'd come home.

And I wrote in my journal: "I am grateful for my breath and the recognition that I am here, alive. Breathing. I am grateful for life. And for this time alone. In this moment I have to do nothing. Yes, there are many things that need to get done, but in *this* moment I have to do nothing."

I sat in silence. I prayed. I meditated. I napped. I filled three more pages with praise and gratitude for all that's gone right. And stopped giving my attention to what wasn't working. I watched the sun move across the sky. I went inside and filled a bowl with lemon sorbet and fresh strawberries purchased at the farmers' market that morning. I savored every spoonful, then licked the spoon.

I went for a run with my dogs. I sat in a tub of bubbles until I got crinkly. I put on a new pair of pj's I'd been saving for a special...what? I read myself to sleep with Mary Oliver poems.

The next day I found the new Head of School. Two days later, a president for OWN.

I no longer have a crisis in leadership. I know for sure that what's best for me is already on its way.

happiness

This Is Your Brain On Happiness

Circuits in your brain light up when you're happy. **Penelope Green** talks to the groundbreaking researcher who's discovered how to *keep* them lit.

There are no dark corners in Madison, Wisconsin, a university town that sparkles with endowment and research dollars—more than $900 million last year—as well as just plain Midwestern niceness. The grants are well earned: It was at the University of Wisconsin–Madison that the first bone marrow transplant was performed and the first synthetic gene was created. It was here that human stem cells were isolated and cultured in a lab for the first time. And for more than a decade, one of the campus's most productive hit makers has been the Laboratory for Affective Neuroscience, run by a 56-year-old neuroscientist and professor of psychology and psychiatry named Richard J. Davidson, PhD, who has been systematically uncovering the architecture of emotion.

Davidson, whose youthful appearance and wide-open smile give him more than a passing resemblance to Jerry Seinfeld, has been studying the brain structures behind not just anxiety, depression, and addiction but also happiness, resilience, and, most recently, compassion. Using brain imaging technologies, in particular a device called a functional magnetic resonance imaging (fMRI) machine, a sort of Hubble telescope for the brain, Davidson and his researchers have observed the areas associated with various emotions and how their function changes as an individual moves through them. His "brain maps" have revealed the neural terrain of so-called normal adults and children, as well as those suffering from mood disorders and autism. Davidson has also studied a now rather famous group of subjects: Tibetan monks with years of Buddhist meditation under their gleaming pates.

Probably his most well-known study mapped the brains of employees at a biotech company, more than half of whom completed about three hours of meditation once a week led by Jon Kabat-Zinn, PhD, founding director of the Stress Reduction Clinic at the University of Massachusetts Medical School. After four months, the meditating subjects noticed a boost in mood and decrease in anxiety, while their immune systems became measurably stronger. What made headlines, though ("The

Science of Happiness" sang a January 2005 *Time* magazine cover), was that Davidson vividly showed that meditation produced a significant increase in activity in the part of the brain responsible for positive emotions and traits like optimism and resilience—the left prefrontal cortex. In meditating monks, he'd separately found, this area lit up like the lights in Times Square, showing activity beyond anything he and his team had ever seen—a neurological circuit board explaining their sunny serenity.

These and other findings of Davidson's have bolstered mounting research suggesting that the adult brain is changeable, or "plastic," as opposed to becoming fixed in adolescence. What this means is that although an individual may be born with a predisposition toward gloominess or anxiety, the emotional floor plan can be altered, the brain's furniture moved to a more felicitous arrangement; with a little training, you can coax a fretful mind toward a happier outlook. It's a new understanding of the brain that represents a paradigm shift of seismic importance, and one that's sent a steady stream of reporters out to Madison like pilgrims on the road to Santiago. Perhaps

just as seismic is Davidson's "coming out of the closet" (his phrase) as a highly regarded, marquee-name brain researcher with a focus on contemplation, and a commitment to putting compassion and spirituality on the scientific map.

The letters on the license plate of Davidson's silvery green Subaru Outback spell out EMOTE, but the man himself does not ooze. Gentle and precise in his speech, he is the consummate scientist, curious, quietly passionate, and utterly on topic. And despite all the buzz about his work, he'll tell you simply that he has been chipping away at the same ideas about consciousness for more than three decades.

Raised in Brooklyn—his father was in the real estate business—Richie, as friends call him, is still married to his college sweetheart, Susan, a perinatologist and director of the perinatal program at St. Mary's Hospital and Dean Medical Center in Madison. They were born nine days and a few blocks apart; both graduated high school at 16 (she from Erasmus, he from Midwood), and both have graduate degrees in psychology from nearby universities: his from Harvard, hers from the University of Massachusetts. "You couldn't have arranged a better match," he says.

When they arrived in Cambridge in the early 1970s, every swami guru and his mother was selling his wares and giving lectures, says the Davidsons' old friend Jon Kabat-Zinn, who had recently completed his own PhD, in molecular biology at MIT: "You could get an alternate education just by going to all the talks." The first spiritual leader to touch Davidson was Richard Alpert, the Harvard professor who'd been fired for his liberal deployment of LSD among his students and was reborn, phoenixlike, as Ram Dass. Through him, Davidson learned "that there was a way to work on yourself to transform your way of being, to make you happier and more compassionate." And that way was meditation.

Another big influence was fellow student Daniel Goleman, who went on to become a psychologist and the author of *Emotional Intelligence,* among other books. In 1973 he had already traveled to India, developed a contemplative practice, and published papers about it. At that time, Goleman remembers, "there was a strong sense of the new, a sense of something that had not been realized or executed before, and that it had some sort of importance for the culture."

Two visuals that distill the period for Davidson are the memory of Goleman's bright red VW van, its dashboard decorated with photographs of lamas and yogis—as enticing and otherworldly as Ken Kesey's psychedelic school bus—and a 1974 snapshot of him and Goleman wearing Harvard T-shirts and sarongs in Sri Lanka, where Goleman was then living, and where Susan and Richie visited before embarking on their first meditation retreat in India.

"My professors were firmly convinced I was going off the deep end," Davidson says. "But I knew I was going to come back. I was committed to a scientific career. Still, I needed to taste more intensive meditation in that setting." And it was the hardest work he's ever done—16-hour days, two weeks of them, in utter silence. "Anyone who says meditation is relaxation doesn't know what they're talking about. It's like trying to change the course of a river."

When he returned from India, he finished his PhD and started to craft a research career around emotions, at the time the backwater of psychology. It was extraordinarily difficult. "The measuring devices were too crude," he says. "You couldn't see, as we can now, what was happening in the brain." And neuroscience barely existed.

"Richie was always kind of eclectic—he wasn't bound by any discipline," says Susan, who became, as her husband likes to say, a "real doctor." His roving interests made him an odd fit, initially, for some universities. "Richie had finished his degree at Harvard, been published in all these journals, but he would go to job interviews and they would say, 'Oh, you're too clinical for our psychology department, or too this for our that,'" Susan says. "People found him interesting, but they didn't want to commit."

What changed the face of his career, according to Davidson, was a meeting in 1992 with Tenzin Gyatso, otherwise known as the 14th Dalai Lama, who urged him to hone in on compassion as the object of serious and rigorous study. "If you look at the index of any scientific textbook, you won't find the word *compassion*," Davidson says. "But it is as worthy a topic of examination as all the negative emotions—fear, anxiety, sadness, anger, disgust—that have long occupied the scientific community."

When I visit Davidson in Madison, where he and Susan have lived since 1985 and raised their children, Amelie, now 26, and Seth, 20, he tells me about his latest research: Reminding me that the Dalai Lama's mandate is to effect change in the world through the power of compassion, Davidson says, "If this is truly possible, then we should be able to discover circuits in the brain that underlie compassion and that are strengthened when it is cultivated."

His new studies on the monks—"the Olympic athletes of meditation," as he calls them—are designed to measure what happens when they engage specifically in compassion practice. So far, he's found that their brains show dramatic changes in two telling areas: increased activity not only in the prefrontal cortex—which floods them with well-being—but also in the areas involved with motor planning. It seems the monks are not just "feeling" good; their brains have primed their bodies to spring up and "do" good. "They are poised to jump into action and do whatever they can to help relieve suffering," Davidson says. (As for his own practice, Judaism is Davidson's "birth religion," but he characterizes his spiritual path as being most similar to a Buddhist one, though he hesitates to describe himself as a card-carrying devotee. Certainly all who know him say that Davidson is a glass-half-full sort of guy—his mother even called him her Joy Boy, while Susan says, "Richie is consistently upbeat." And yes, he has mapped parts of his own brain, and admits it "showed moderately strong left prefrontal activation.")

Whether generosity of spirit rubs off on others is another question Davidson has begun to probe. "We've launched a study with a highly trained, long-term Buddhist practitioner, looking at the impact of his compassionate attitude on ordinary individuals. We bring them into the MRI scanner, we expose them to pictures of suffering—gory accidents and things like that. We do this under two conditions: one where they are in the presence of an experimenter, and one where they are in the presence of the monk." Davidson is curious to see whether the results will bear out anecdotal reports that in the presence of an extremely compassionate person, you feel more relaxed, se-

Although an individual may be born with a predisposition toward gloominess or anxiety, *with a little training* you can coax a fretful mind toward a happier outlook.

cure, loved, and safe. His team is also putting ordinary individuals, first-timers, through a two-week intervention that includes 30 minutes a day of compassion meditation. Davidson predicts changes in the brain regions associated with emotion and empathy as well as the subjects making more altruistic decisions: "They will also have the opportunity to give away some of what they earn for their participation in the study," he says. "We expect that those undergoing compassion training will donate more money."

The idea that compassion can be learned—and that the process can be measured scientifically—is what thrills Davidson. And he envisions compassion training in a variety of settings, from public schools to the corporate world. "Now we mostly have monks and other religious figures preaching about these ideas," he says. "It's quite another thing to have a hard-nosed neuroscientist like me suggest that such training may have beneficial consequences for how we act toward others as well as promoting health. Most people accept the idea that regular physical exercise is something they should do for the remainder of their lives. Imagine how different things might be if we accepted the notion that the regular practice of mental exercises to strengthen compassion is something to incorporate into everyday life."

To what extent can we really brighten our outlook? What is the best way to deflect stress? How can people become more resilient? Are there other ways aside from meditation to boost the brain? Many questions remain to be answered. It is a tantalizing prospect: that even a little more joy might be within everyone's reach. "I've been talking about happiness not as a trait but as a skill, like tennis," says Davidson. "If you want to be a good tennis player, you can't just pick up a racket—you have to practice." **O**

5 Things Happy People Do

Definitely try these at home. Gabrielle LeBlanc on a few simple actions that add up to a formula for joy.

Sages going back to Socrates have offered advice on how to be happy, but only now are scientists beginning to address this question with systematic, controlled research. Although many of the new studies reaffirm time-honored wisdom ("Do what you love," "To thine own self be true"), they also add a number of fresh twists and insights. We canvassed the leading experts on what happy people have in common—and why it's worth trying to become one of them:

They find their most golden self. Picture happiness. What do you see? A peaceful soul sitting in a field of daisies appreciating the moment? That kind of passive, pleasure-oriented—hedonic—contentment is definitely a component of overall happiness. But researchers now believe that eudaimonic well-being may be more important. Cobbled from the Greek *eu* ("good") and *daimon* ("spirit" or "deity"), eudaimonia means striving toward excellence based on one's unique talents and potential—Aristotle considered it to be the noblest goal in life. In his time, the Greeks believed that each child was blessed at birth with a personal daimon embodying the highest possible expression of his or her nature. One way they envisioned the daimon was as a golden figurine that would be revealed by cracking away an outer layer of cheap pottery (the person's baser exterior). The effort to know and realize one's most golden self—"personal growth," in today's lingo—is now the central concept of eudaimonia, which has also come to include continually taking on new challenges and fulfilling one's sense of purpose in life.

"Eudaimonic well-being is much more robust and satisfying than hedonic happiness, and it engages different parts of the brain," says Richard J. Davidson, PhD, of the University of Wisconsin–Madison (see "This Is Your Brain on Happiness," page 90). "The positive emotion accompanying thoughts that are directed toward meaningful goals is one of the most enduring components of well-being." Eudaimonia is also good for the body. Women who scored high on psychological tests for it (they were purposefully engaged in life, pursued self-development) weighed less, slept better, and had fewer stress hormones and markers for heart disease than others—including those reporting hedonic happiness—according to a study led by Carol Ryff, PhD, a professor of psychology at the University of Wisconsin–Madison.

They design their lives to bring in joy. It may seem obvious, but "people don't devote enough time to thinking seriously about how they spend their life and how much of it they actually enjoy," says David Schkade, PhD, a psychologist and professor of management at the University of California San Diego. In a recent study, Schkade and colleagues asked more than 900 working women to write down everything they'd done the day before. Afterward, they reviewed their diaries and evaluated how they felt at each point. When the women saw how much time they spent on activities they didn't like, "some people had tears in their eyes," Schkade says. "They didn't realize their happiness was something they could design and have control over."

Analyzing one's life isn't necessarily easy and may require questioning long-held assumptions. A high-powered career might, in fact, turn out to be unfulfilling; a committed relationship once longed for could end up being

> When the women saw how much time they spent on activities they didn't like, *"some people had tears in their eyes*. They didn't realize their happiness was something they could design and have control over."

irritating with all the compromising that comes with having a partner. Dreams can be hard to abandon, even when they've turned sour.

Fortunately, changes don't have to be big ones to tip the joy in your favor. Schkade says that if you transfer even an hour of your day from an activity you hate (commuting, scrubbing the bathroom) to one you like (reading, spending time with friends), you should see a significant improvement in your overall happiness. Taking action is key. Another recent study, at the University of Missouri, compared college students who made intentional changes (joining a club, upgrading their study habits) with others who passively experienced positive turns in their circumstances (receiving a scholarship, being relieved of a bad roommate). All the students were happier in the short term, but only the group who made deliberate changes stayed that way.

They avoid "if only" fantasies. *If only I get a better job…find a man…lose the weight…life will be perfect.* Happy people don't buy into this kind of thinking.

The latest research shows that we're surprisingly bad at predicting what will make us happy. People also tend to misjudge their contentment when zeroing in on a single aspect of their life—it's called the focusing illusion. In one study, single subjects were asked, "How happy are you with your life in general?" and "How many dates did you have last month?" When the dating question was asked first, their romantic life weighed more heavily into how they rated their overall happiness than when the questions were reversed.

The other argument against "if only" fantasies has to do with "hedonic adaptation"—the brain's natural dimming effect, which guarantees that a new house won't generate the same pleasure a year after its purchase and the thrill of having a boyfriend will ebb as you get used to being part of a couple. Happy people are wise to this, which is why they keep their lives full of novelty, even if it's just trying a new activity (diving, yoga) or putting a new spin on an old favorite (kundalini instead of vinyasa).

They put best friends FIRST. It's no surprise that social engagement is one of the most important contributors to happiness. What's news is that the nature of the relationship counts. Compared with dashing around chatting with acquaintances, you get more joy from spending longer periods of time with a close friend, according to research by Meliksah Demir, PhD, assistant professor of psychology at Northern Arizona University. And the best-friend benefit doesn't necessarily come from delving into heavy discussions. One of the most essential pleasures of close friendship, Demir found, is simple companionship, "just hanging out," as he says, hitting the mall or going to the movies together and eating popcorn in the dark.

They ALLOW themselves to be happy. As much as we all think we want it, many of us are convinced, deep down, that it's wrong to be happy (or too happy). Whether the belief comes from religion, culture, or the family you were raised in, it usually leaves you feeling a little guilty if you're having fun.

"Some people would say that you shouldn't strive for personal happiness until you've taken care of everyone in the world who is starving or doesn't have adequate medical care," says Howard Cutler, MD, coauthor with the Dalai Lama of *The Art of Happiness in a Troubled World.* "The Dalai Lama believes you should pursue both simultaneously. For one thing, there is clear research showing that happy people tend to be more open to helping others. They also make better spouses and parents." And in one famous study, nuns whose autobiographies expressed positive emotions (such as gratitude and optimism) lived seven to ten-and-a-half years longer than other nuns. So, for any of those die-hard pessimists who still needs persuading, just think of how much more you can help the world if you will allow a little happiness into your life. ◘

Angela Bassett's Aha! Moment

Hey, her family didn't *have* average children (or kids who embarked on high-risk careers). Then, in college, the actress made a passion-filled, regret-free, A-plus decision that would transform her identity.

"I wasn't average and I shouldn't settle for being average."

From the time I was in first grade, I knew I was going to college. I didn't even know what college was back then, but my mother made it clear to my sister and me that going to one was a given. She was a single parent who hadn't taken high school seriously. She now knew that emphasizing education was the key to our futures, and she wouldn't allow us to compromise them by settling for less than a college degree.

I always got As and Bs in my classes; then, in seventh grade, I got my first C. It was in physical education, but still I knew that was not going to fly with my mother. I needed to come up with a compelling argument to convince her that the grade was nothing to get upset about. "Getting a C isn't bad," I tried to explain to her. "It's average, the standard." In this one instance, I was the norm; I didn't see any harm in that.

My mother, however, did. She just looked me in the eye and said, "I don't have no *average* kids." In that moment, a sense of pride developed in me. I was not average, nor should I ever settle for being such. I had already shown the potential to excel. If my best happened to be average, then fine. But if my best was excellent and I knowingly gave less, then I was not giving the full measure of my abilities, and that, in my mother's mind and now my own, was unacceptable. I never got another C.

That is, until I got to Yale.

At the university, I wanted to major in theater. But my father's sister, who was the only person in my family to both go to college and graduate school, told me, "Angela, please don't waste your Yale education on theater." She was afraid I wouldn't be able to make a living for myself as an actress. I had nothing but the utmost respect for my aunt, so I listened; I went back to school and chose a different major, administrative science, a business and sociology degree.

But in my junior year, I found myself on the brink of failing one of my classes. I was giving an average effort again, although I realized that now I was doing it because I was forcing myself to do something I didn't love. I wasn't as passionate about business as I was about theater. There was never a time when I wouldn't give myself fully when it came to acting. It was as if the final piece of the puzzle presented itself and everything became clear: If you do what you love to do, then you won't do it in an average way.

From that point on, work became a joy. I made choices based on what I believed in, and I had no regrets. At the end of the day, you have to ask yourself: Of the many different lives that can be lived, which is the one that's going to inspire you? ◑ —*As told to Naomi Barr*

Who's Sorry Now?

"I ate that pound of chocolate." "I lost the love of my life." "I blew the audition on *American Idol*." You can keep dragging your load of coulda-woulda-shoulda's—or you can use **Martha Beck's** six-step plan to regret-proof your life.

So here's the story: After a lifetime of hand-copying ancient texts, an elderly monk became abbot of his monastery. Realizing that for centuries his order had been making copies of copies, he decided to examine some of the monastery's original documents. Days later, the other monks found him in the cellar, weeping over a crumbling manuscript and moaning, "It says 'celebrate,' not 'celibate!'"

Ah, regret. The forehead-slap of hindsight, the woeful fuel of country ballads, the self-recrimination I feel for eating a quart of pudding in a crafty but unsuccessful attempt to avoid writing this column. If you've ever made a bad decision or suffered an accident, regret has been your roommate, if not your conjoined twin. It's a difficult companion, prone to accusatory comments and dark moods, and it changes you, leaving you both tougher and more tender. You get to decide, however, whether your toughness will look like unreachable bitterness or unstoppable resilience; your tenderness the raw vulnerability of a never-healing wound, or a kindness so deep it heals every wound it touches. Regret can be your worst enemy or your best friend. You get to decide which.

There are at least two time zones where you can choose to make regret's powerful energy healing rather than destructive: the past and the future. Both can be transformed by what you decide to do right now, in this moment.

Let's start by changing the past. If you think that can't be done, think again. Literally. The past doesn't exist except as a memory, a mental story, and though past events aren't changeable, your stories about them are. You can act now to transform the way you tell the story of your past, ultimately making it a stalwart protector of your future. Try these steps, more or less in order.

1. Get beyond denial.

As long as you're thinking, *That shouldn't have happened* or *I shouldn't have done that,* you're locked in a struggle against reality. Many people pour years of energy into useless "shouldn't haves." The angry ones endlessly repeat that their ex-spouses shouldn't have left them, their parents shouldn't have overfed them, or their bosses shouldn't have made them wear uncomfortable chipmunk costumes in 90-degree heat. Even drearier are the sad ones, who forever drone some version of "If only." If only they'd married Sebastian, or gotten that promotion, or heeded the label's advice not to operate heavy machinery, they would be happy campers instead of *les misérables.*

I call this unproductive regret. People use it to avoid scary or difficult action; instead of telling the story of the past in a useful way, they use it as their excuse for staying wretched. If you're prone to unproductive regret, please hear this: Everyone agrees with you. That thing you regret? It really, really, really shouldn't have happened. But. It. Did. If you enjoy being miserable, by all means, continue to rail against this fact. If you'd rather be happy, prune the "shouldn't haves" from your mental story, and move on to...

2. Separate regret's basic ingredients.

Of the four basic emotions—sad, mad, glad, and scared—regret is a mixture of the first two. Your particular situation may involve enormous sadness and a little anger ("My father died before I ever met him. Damn cruel fate!") or enormous anger with a side of sadness ("Why, why, why did I get a haircut from a stylist who was actively smoking a bong?"). Whatever the proportions, some regretters feel sadness but resist feeling anger; others acknowledge outrage but not sorrow. Denying either component will get you stuck in bitter, unproductive regret.

Considering anger and sadness separately makes both more useful. Right now, think of something you regret. With that something in mind, finish this sentence: "I'm sad that _____." Repeat until you run out of sad things related to that particular regret. For example, if your regret is contracting Lyme disease, you might say, "I'm sad that I feel awful." "I'm sad I can no longer ride my pogo stick." "I'm sad that the woods don't feel safe to me anymore."

When you've fully itemized your sadness, make another list, beginning each sentence with the phrase, "I'm angry at _____." For example, "I'm angry at my body for being sick." "I'm angry at God for creating ticks." "I'm angry at the entire town of Lyme, Connecticut, for which this $#@* disease was named." Write down all the causes for your rage, even if they're irrational.

Once you have a clear list of your sorrows and outrages, you can move on to step 3, where you'll work both angles to transform unproductive regret into the productive kind. This is extraordinarily useful but also profoundly uncomfortable, because the only way out of painful emotion is through.

> That thing you regret? It really, really, really shouldn't have happened. But. It. Did.

3. Grieve what is irrevocably lost.

Sorrow is a natural reaction to losing anything significant: a dream, a possession, an opportunity. Productive grief passes through you in waves, which feel horrific, but which steadily erode your sadness. The crushing mountain of sorrow eventually becomes a boulder on your back, then a rock in your pocket, then a pebble in your shoe, then nothing at all—not because circumstances change but because you become strong enough to handle reality with ease.

You're finished grieving when you see someone gaining what you regret losing and feel only joy for them—maybe even secret gratitude that circumstances forced you to enlarge your own capacity for joy (this is how I feel about people who don't have a kid with Down syndrome). If your sadness stops evaporating, if a certain amount of it just isn't budging, simply grieving may not be enough. Regret is telling you to seek out a part of whatever you've lost.

4. Reclaim the essence of your dreams.

You can't change the fact that you binged your way up to 300 pounds, or lost a winning lottery ticket, or spent decades in celibacy rather than celebration. But you can reclaim the essential experiences you missed: loving your own healthy body, enjoying abundance, feeling glorious passion. In this moment, resolve that you'll find ways to reclaim the essence of anything you can't stop grieving.

Jenny's big regret was that one disastrous gymnastics meet had tanked her chances to make the Olympic team. When I asked her what she would've gotten from the Olympics, she said, "Pride, excitement, world-class competition, attention." Once she'd articulated these essentials, Jenny found herself gravitating toward a job in television, which provided all of them. Now, she says, her life is so exciting that she virtually never thinks about the Olympics. Instead of sidelining her, regret became just one more springboard.

I've been coaching long enough to brazenly promise that if you decide to reclaim the essence of anything you regret losing, you'll find it—often sooner than you think, in ways you would never have expected.

5. Analyze your anger.

The anger component of regret is every bit as important and useful as your sadness. Anger is a bear, but if you pay attention, you'll hear it roaring useful instructions about how you should steer your future. Don't fear it, run from it, tranquilize it, try to kill it. Just leave the kids with a sitter, team up with a sympathetic friend, spouse, therapist, or journal, and let your angry animal self bellow its messages. There will be a lot of meaningless sound and fury, but there will also be information about exactly what needs to change in your present and future so that you'll stop suffering from old regrets and create new ones. Basically, your anger will roar out this next instruction...

6. Learn to lean loveward.

When I saw *A Chorus Line,* I wondered if it's literally true that "I can't regret what I did for love." So I did a little thought experiment. I recalled all my significant regrets, and sure enough, I found that none of them followed a choice based purely on love. All were the consequence of fear-based decisions. In the cases where my motivations were a mix of love and fear, it was always the fear-based component that left me fretful and regretful.

For example, I'll be up most of tonight, having spent the daylight hours eating pudding in reaction to writer's block, which is a species of fear. I predict that tomorrow I'll regret this—I've spent many, many sleepless nights fearing this or that, and no good ever came of it. But I've also lost a lot of sleep for love. I've stayed up communing with friends, rocking sick babies, avoiding celibacy. And I really can't regret any choice that brought me one moment of love. Do your own thought experiment, and I suspect you'll come to similar conclusions. (Let's face it, a song that catchy just can't be all wrong.)

So the ultimate lesson of regret, the one that will help guide you into a rich and satisfying future, is this: Every time life brings you to a crossroads, from the tiniest to the most immense, go toward love, not away from fear. Think of every choice in terms of "What would thrill and delight me?" rather than "What will keep my fear—or the events, people, and things I fear—at bay?"

Sometimes the choice will be utterly clear. Love steers you forward, and no fear arises. But on many occasions, the path toward what you love may be fraught with uneasiness, anxiety, terror. The pound dog will tug at your heart, but worry about upkeep will push away the sparks of love and leave you without a four-footed friend. You'll long for success but dread the risks necessary to earn it. Your impulse to champion the oppressed might compete with panic for your own sorry hide.

That's when you can call on regret—not as a burden that you still have to bear but as a motivator that can forcefully remind you not to make choices that will feel awful in retrospect. If you've grieved your losses, reclaimed your dreams, and articulated your anger, regret will have made you the right kind of tough-and-tender: dauntless of spirit, soft of heart, convinced by experience that nothing based on fear—but everything based on love—is worth doing. Living this way doesn't guarantee an easy life; in fact, it will probably take you on a wondrously wild ride. But I promise, you won't regret it. ◗

Lisa Kogan Tells All

It's the eternal question: What if? Our columnist on lost jobs, forgotten tutus, the croissant not eaten…and what she got instead.

It took a little time, but my daughter and I have finally got our Sunday mornings down to a system. Just as the light starts inching through our blinds and the pigeons start making those peculiar pigeony noises and the hungover 22-year-olds start cursing whoever invented the Jell-O shot, Julia wakes me with words that come in a rush from her heart: "Did you buy me anything?" And "Are you going to buy me anything?" And my personal favorite: "Would you like a list of things you could buy me?"

We wash our hands and preheat the oven. I get the mixing bowl down from its shelf while she heads for the box of Duncan Hines muffin mix in the cupboard. We hear a dull *thwumph* sound from someplace beyond the dining table, where we've set up our workstation. "What was that?" she asks, and I tell her it was either *The New York Times* being plopped at our doorstep or her great-grandmothers (both accomplished bakers) turning in their graves. I snip the bag of dry ingredients open and she pours it in the bowl. She tells me that her pal Fiona would like to be a pastry chef when she grows up: "She's going to make squillions and squillions of cookies and cover them in rainbow frosting." I ask Jules if she'd like to do that, but she remains committed to a career in the ballerina industry. "I wanted to be a ballerina when I was 5," I say, pirouetting to the refrigerator for a couple of eggs. "So what stopped you?" Leave it to a kindergartner to ask the $64,000 question. There's the short answer: my distinct lack of athleticism and grace coupled with an abiding love of all things potato. And then there's the longer answer, the one about having the confidence and guts and perseverance to go after what you want. The one about the need for approval and the fear of failure and (in my case) the even greater fear of success. I measure three-quarters of a cup of whole milk and reply, "I turned 6."

I like being a writer—you get to wear a lot of black sweaters and claim to be on a deadline when your mother calls—but I do catch myself wondering about the road not taken. Julia and I hunt for the vegetable oil and I talk to her about what might have been. "Your grandfather was a stockbroker with Merrill Lynch for 37 years. He worked very, very hard cold-calling strangers and turning them into loyal clients, creating a career out of thin air and intense ambition. He never came right out and said it, but I know it would have made him really happy if he could have taught me how to be a broker. The thing is..." Julia's interest trails off somewhere around the Merrill Lynch reference, which I suppose is to be expected from a person in oven mitts and a tutu. Fair enough. How can I expect my daughter to make sense of this allergic reaction I have to corporate life? Do I explain that Mommy doesn't take kindly to management seminars and fluorescent lighting? Perhaps I should simply present her with my SAT scores and leave it at that. We open the can of blueberries that Mr. Hines so thoughtfully includes in every box, rinse them in the sink, then begin folding the berries into the batter.

Julia positions pleated paper muffin cups in the tins. "One for Domingo, one for Jai, one for Loic, and two for Luan," she says, rattling off the names of all the doormen on her breakfast distribution list. I ask how come Luan gets an extra and she tells me that Luan lets her try on his doorman hat. "I think he's got a big crunch on me," she confides. "How can you tell?" Julia tastes the batter, pronounces it ready, and returns to my question. "Mommy, when a boy likes you, there are signs," says my tiny dancer/relationship expert: "Like if he punches you in the arm and says he doesn't like you, that means he likes you." Now she tells me! As good advice goes, this is right up there with "Stay in school," "Pack a sweater," and "Get plenty of roughage."

One rainy afternoon, I ran into a long-lost buddy from my days in advertising. It had been almost 25 years since we'd spoken. I'd gained some weight and he'd lost some hair. We

> "I always had a little thing for you," he said. And I actually looked behind me to see who he was talking to.

ducked into a little coffee shop to dry off and catch up. He showed me a picture of his wife and kid and told me that the three of them spend summers in Paris. "We just get completely immersed in the culture." I showed him a picture of Julia and Johannes (that would be my boyfriend for those of you who've managed to miss my last 735,000 columns) and told him that the three of us summer in my bedroom. "We just get completely immersed in the air-conditioning." And then it happened: "I always had a little thing for you," he said.

And, my friends, I'm not proud of what I'm about to tell you, but here it is: I actually looked behind me to see who he was talking to. "Wait, you mean me? *Me?* The woman who helped pick out everything from long-stem tulips to La Perla lingerie for your many, many girlfriends? You had a thing for *me?*" I asked him why he neglected to speak up all those years ago. If this were a movie, here's the part where he'd reveal some incredibly dramatic secret— "The truth is, I was a CIA operative only posing as an account executive. In my heart I knew that you were the one girl I'd be tempted to blow my cover for, and if I did that, my angel, well, we'd all be speaking Chinese right now." But this is not a movie—he thought for a minute, shrugged, and answered, "You know, I honestly can't remember."

Julia plants four or five fresh blueberries in each paper cup of batter—our secret trick to make these muffins taste like the real deal—while I wipe sticky splotches off the table and imagine what might've been. I could've spent August boating on the Seine. I could've been bullish on America. Hell, I could've danced *Swan Lake.* Anyway, that's the fantasy. The reality is I tend to get seasick; I would've pleased my father but lost my mind; and as for becoming the next Dame Margot Fonteyn, there's an excellent chance I'd have jetéed straight into the orchestra pit and crushed a cellist six seconds into the first act.

We put our muffins in the oven and set the timer for 16 minutes. Julia announces she will be using this time "to have three babies and take them swimming." I will use my 16 minutes to shake off all dreams of a road less traveled. You make the choices you make based on what you know about yourself and what you think you know about the world. And sometimes the world will turn around and break your heart, but other times, a 5-year-old will saunter in with three dolls wet from their swim lesson. The five of you will sit down to blueberry muffins, and the reality of what you wound up with will suddenly seem like the only possible choice—it just couldn't have turned out any other way. ◑

confidence

Self-Esteem: The Repair Kit

Janine Latus spent years looking for validation in all the wrong places—until the day she discovered it was hers to give all along.

In high school I was voted "biggest flirt." (Look at me! Value me!) I justified it by saying I was only being fun. When I got older, that clamoring morphed into something more overtly physical. I justified it by saying I was simply expressing my sexuality, which is natural and healthy and right. What I didn't say, and perhaps didn't realize, was that I used sex to confirm that I had something to offer.

As I lured a man in, I knew he was paying attention. And during the sex act itself? Clearly I mattered.

When I was still older, I stopped sleeping around, but I continued making eye contact on the street, in the grocery store, as I passed construction sites. (Look at me! Find me attractive!) I justified it by saying I was being friendly, but the truth was, I needed the people around me to make me feel important.

And not just sexually. If I wasn't told constantly that I was wonderful in all realms of my life, I fell into an I'm-a-failure funk. Then I'd pester the people closest to me— love me, love me, love me—or trumpet my most minor accomplishments, or complain to friends that—poor me!—some man at the grocery store kept following me from aisle to aisle, trying to make conversation. I measured my value by the

The author as a kindergartner in Kalamazoo, Michigan, 1965.

attention I got from others.

"In some ways, that's not un-healthy," says Kathleen Brehony, a clinical psychologist, personal and executive coach, and author. "Everyone likes to have a reflection coming back that's positive," she says. "We're social animals. We want to be liked and approved of. The question is to what extent we will go to get that, and to what extent we need it. Anybody who says they don't care what other people say or think about them is probably not well liked or adjusted. On the other hand, there's a problem if you think that if men aren't looking at you, if you don't get an A on a paper, if you don't accomplish something professionally, then you're worthless."

Logically I knew I wasn't worthless, but there was something inside me that felt like George Jetson, running as fast I could, the treadmill about to sweep me under. No matter how I excelled, the voices in my head told me I was never enough. And I wanted to be enough, just me, without accomplishments, without flat abs, without flirting in the frozen food aisle. I wanted to *feel*—in my bones, my soul, my self—worthy.

So I set out on a quest to find my value on the inside, hoping also to find serenity and, at long last, peace.

I started with books. First I tried the intellectual ones that delved into the female psyche and our traditional/historical role in society. They didn't help. I was already much too cerebral and could understand the heck out of this problem without doing diddly for my self-esteem.

Then there were the perky self-help books that told me all I had to do was open my mind to the beauty inside. That message was all well and good—except I knew what was inside, and it was inadequate. I was sure I had to be perfect to be loved.

The books kept me in my head, but my problem was deep in my gut, and hard to reach. I had done therapy, talk talk talking about this inner chasm, yet there it stayed, needy, gaping. Then I met Kim Forbes, a psychotherapist in Virginia Beach.

"We have to take the problem outside," she said, "where you can address it with all the resources you have as an adult."

Those voices, the ones saying I wasn't pretty or com-

Those voices saying I wasn't pretty or competent or worthy were voices from childhood, echoing, stuck in an endless loop.

petent or worthy, were, Kim told me, voices from childhood, echoing, stuck in an endless loop. To the little girl who heard them, they were inarguable, but not to me as an adult.

Which is how I find myself talking out loud to a photo of a sweet little gap-toothed girl, her bangs cut straight across her forehead, her eyes innocent and wide.

"You are beautiful," I tell the picture.

Kim leans in. "Tell her it's not her fault. Tell her she is lovable."

I struggle not to roll my eyes. I am the anti-woo-woo, the confirmed skeptic. Still, I repeat her words.

"You are lovable," I say, feeling foolish. But then I get mad.

"How can anyone have told her she was stupid, fat, or ugly?" I ask. "Look at her!"

"I know," Kim said. "She's wonderful."

The photo is of me, of course, at age 5, wearing a yellow dress my mom had made. Kim and I are doing an exercise designed to separate my intellectual side from the emotional, and allow the former to comfort the latter. The picture is supposed to represent my emotional side, the one that has been bruised and quashed and never made to feel important. It's Kim's theory that both of those sides have to be acknowledged in order for me to feel mentally well.

"This is the child who needs to be told that she's lovable, that she's enough," she says. "That she's not perfect, and it's okay. She needs to hear it. *You* need to hear it."

In spite of my internal eye-rolling, I do it. I tell the little girl that she is lovable, that she is worthy.

You don't have to be perfect," I say. I say it out loud. And, awkward and artificial as the whole thing seems, tears well up. It feels hokey to be talking to a photograph and to cry, but there it is, a deep swell of feeling spouting up, a realization that it's true, that that little girl is enough, just as she is, without accomplishment, without successes, without even trying. And that little girl is me.

I leave the session somewhat drained.

I grew up in a big Catholic family, my parents scrambling to meet everyone's needs in spite of erratic income and their own parents' stilted parenting. Their expectations were high, in hopes, no doubt, of helping us succeed. But the message I grew up with was "You'll be good enough if...." The "if" was different depending on who was doing the messaging, but it was never just "You'll be good enough" or—even more unlikely—"You *are* good enough."

So the next day I draw my living room blinds, prop the photo on a chair, and clear my throat, feeling utterly goofy.

"I know you're sad. I know you hurt. I know you want to open up and feel joy," I tell the picture. "It's okay. Because I—the grown-up version—am here to protect you. I am here to celebrate and marvel with you. It is okay to feel. It is okay to admit to flaws."

As I speak, I think of my daughter and the effort I have put into making her world a place where it is okay to have fears, to cry over boo-boos, to believe someone else is taking care of the big picture. I think of how I hold her and tuck her in, how I brush back her hair and laugh at her stories. I hope she'll grow up knowing she's enough.

Even as I form the thought, I feel a swelling of hope for myself. Maybe I need to do that for me, silly as it sounds. Tuck myself in, tell myself I'm worthy, laugh at my own jokes. Maybe that little girl with the trusting smile is going to be the one who heals me. I open my eyes and look again at the photo. This time, though, I'm talking to myself, the grown-up version. "I am flawed and I am imperfect," I say, "and I am enough." 🔘

How to Love That Woman in the Mirror

The amount of misery we suffer just from the heft of our thighs, not to mention the misbehavior of our skin, just might—if you could quantify it—inspire a global initiative. The topic has certainly intrigued Nancy Etcoff, PhD, author of *Survival of the Prettiest: The Science of Beauty,* and a Harvard Medical School psychologist whose research concentrates on appearance and happiness. Three years ago she founded the Program in Aesthetics and Well-Being at Massachusetts General Hospital to explore how concepts of beauty relate to satisfaction. Recently she sat down with *O* to tell us what she's learned:

O: **HASN'T THE WHOLE BEAUTY INDUSTRY GOTTEN OUT OF CONTROL? AND AREN'T WOMEN THE WORSE FOR ALL THIS HYPE ON LOOKING YOUNG?**
ETCOFF: If we say, "Just get rid of the advertisements and tell the companies to stop making products, and no one will care about beauty—this is all just a creation that we can wipe away," we are denying who we are. People do care about how they look. They have adorned themselves since Paleolithic times. This is not a vanity issue or a women's issue or a United States issue. It is human nature.

O: **HOW MUCH OF A WOMAN'S HAPPINESS IS BASED ON HER APPEARANCE?**
ETCOFF: That's a hard question to answer, but we know that people who focus a lot on their looks as a major source of their self-esteem tend to be a lot less happy than people who focus on, say, their social life. Why? In general we're social animals, so people without good relationships tend to be less happy; the same is true if you're not doing work or other activities that bring out your strengths. Those are the sources of real happiness, not external things like money or beauty.

O: **CAN A POSITIVE SENSE OF SELF MAKE YOU MORE PHYSICALLY ATTRACTIVE?**
ETCOFF: Watch a woman enter a room with that sense of confidence, that sense of "I matter, I'm worthwhile." The way she walks, her facial expression, everything about her says, "Look at me." Really, why do we care about being beautiful? We care because we don't want to be excluded. We want attention. Right from the start, babies look straight at your face and into your eyes. When you look away, they get upset. There is that little baby in all of us: "The world is so big—how do I get your attention?"

O: **IS THERE ANY WAY— BARRING COSMETIC SURGERY—TO CHANGE YOUR ATTITUDE ABOUT HOW YOU LOOK?**
ETCOFF: Scientists researching body image have done eye-tracking studies, in which people are asked to stare in the mirror. Subjects don't look at anything they think is good; they just stare at their so-called faults. Stop that. Retrain yourself: "Why don't I look at what I like? I like my lips— what lip shade should I wear today?"

O: **ANY OTHER SUGGESTIONS?**
ETCOFF: We tend to think about social support bringing happiness, but it's also very important to give support to other people. There is a lot of evidence that suggests that those who volunteer are happier. Feeling part of something larger than you is very important. When you do something good for someone else, the reward system of your brain lights up. We tend to seek things that actually contribute very minimally to our happiness—like a nicer car and, again, looking perfect. So know where your own joy resides: What are you good at? What do you enjoy? What is meaningful? What is going to keep making you happy for a long time?

—Thea Singer

Great Moments in Self-Esteem

I hereby forgive me. By Valerie Monroe

I used to feel as if I were living in a foreign country. It was as if I were an outsider, never comfortable with the customs, never fully understanding what was expected of me. And so I was always walking on eggshells: Did I do the right thing? Did I somehow unknowingly offend you with my last remark? Was my work not quite good enough? Were my friends, lovers acceptable? I felt as if I were being judged, and most often coming up short, like I was playing a game with a set of rules no one had bothered to explain to me.

The older I got, the more uncomfortable I became. One night I had a vivid, frightening dream. Motivated by the desire to untangle it, I began psychotherapy. In my sessions I talked about the many instances when, as a child, I felt as if I had come up short: showing a marked lack of graciousness, for example, about the arrival of my baby sister; my constant need to know my mother's whereabouts at all times—perhaps suffocating to her. My therapist wondered aloud about how I, by then a mother myself, might feel toward any other child—my son, for instance—who demonstrated that behavior. It was a no-brainer, literally: My heart was instantly awash with compassion. As I remembered more of my childhood shortcomings, and forgave them, it became like a practice—the forgiving—and before long I was doing it with my adult self, too. Forgiving myself for past mistakes in love, in work, in the many daily interactions always open to missteps. I would forgive the mistake, learn from it, and try to do better.

Is all self-esteem nurtured by mastery? I'm not sure. But it was mastering forgiveness that nurtured mine.

My Old Boyfriend By Lisa Wolfe

I was walking in midtown Manhattan a couple of years ago when I ran into Robert, my boyfriend from sophomore year of college. He wasn't just any boyfriend, but a special one—great looking and adorably romantic. We hadn't seen each other in more than 20 years. "Do you have time for a cup of coffee?" he asked. Of course I didn't have time, but of course I did. We ducked into a coffee shop to chat. After we filled each other in on our families and work, Robert became nostalgic. "That was a magical time together," he said. "I've thought about it often. Life gets so complicated, relationships get so complicated. There was an innocence in the way we were with each other. Even the sex. You know what I mean? There was something very pure and direct about it." Impressed by his candor, I was candid back. Robert had been gorgeous, I a little chubby at the time. "To be honest," I said, "I spent a lot of

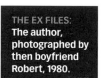

THE EX FILES: The author, photographed by then boyfriend Robert, 1980.

our time in bed worrying about whether you thought my thighs were fat." Robert looked shocked. Then he narrowed his eyes, leaned across the table, and said, "I'm so glad you raised the issue of your thighs. I've been meaning to talk to you about them all these years." At first, I thought he was serious. *I knew it!* I said to myself. *They really* were *as bad as I imagined!* But then I saw the wistful look in Robert's eyes and realized I was being ridiculous. I had been ridiculous then to waste a moment of young love worrying about my thighs, and I was being ridiculous now. Nobody examines, or has ever examined, the shape of my body parts as closely or as critically as I. Have I felt great about my body every day since that coffee? Of course not. But I have certainly felt a lot better.

"A" for Effort By Kelly Corrigan

In the mid-1990s, I went to grad school at night to get my master's degree in literature, assuming it would be like book club without the wine. My first class, the portal course that would prepare me for all seminars to come, was led by a celebrated professor who, in his spare time, hosted a daily show on NPR. My first paper in that first class was about whether or not a reader should consider the author's biography when interpreting a novel. And on this crucial paper, I got my

first C since high school econ. Actually, I believe it was a C minus.

Suddenly it seemed I had no aptitude for the very thing I most wanted to do—write. But I had paid for the semester; I had committed to two years of eating Trader Joe's frozen burritos and shopping exclusively at a brand-new store called Old Navy. So I met with the professor to review the many missteps in my argument, started reading more than what was assigned, and pored over my notes each night after class, jotting down questions, filling in holes.

One night near the end of the semester, I had to give a presentation on Toni Morrison's *Sula.* The Q&A period lasted until the final minute of class, and I left knowing I had defied expectations. I understood something essential about the book. I had a way to talk about it that was meaningful, even compelling. I had thoughtful responses to my classmates' questions.

On the ride home from class that night—after my professor called my presentation "insightful"—it occurred to me that my aptitude was never the problem. It was my work ethic. If I was willing to read slowly, think hard, and rewrite endlessly, I'd always have something worthwhile to contribute.

And this is how I know that self-esteem is less about adding a shiny new bell to your bike or learning how to pop a wheelie than it is about recognizing that you don't always know what to do but, lookee there, you figure it out.

They Said Yes! By Patricia Volk

I was writing in a vacuum. Actually, I was writing in a three-by-four-foot carrel at the Mercantile Library on my lunch hour, but it felt like a vacuum. Would I ever finish this novel? Would anybody read it? Would anybody care that the protagonist, a burned-out copywriter named May Ney Graves (Many Graves, get it?), worried she was losing her survival instincts? Had I lost my survival instincts? What made me think I could be a writer? Eudora Welty was a writer. What if the only person who read me was me? Did that matter if I loved hunting for what Maugham called the gypsy phrase? May Ney Graves wore a braid. I grew a braid.

A friend introduced me to his agent. The agent would get 10 percent of this novel if it sold. A year went by. The agent raised his fee. Now he would get 15 percent of the novel if it sold.

I groused: "The agent raised his fee!"

"What's 15 percent of nothing?" my friend said.

He had a point. I sent *White Light* in. The agent didn't like it. "Rewrite it," he said.

I applied to an artist's community called Yaddo, froze 17 days' worth of meals, lined up babysitters and grandparents, laid out checks, and left for Saratoga Springs with Wite-Out and a typewriter. I was alone with my work for the first time. No kids, no husband, no job, no night school, no in-laws, shopping lists, nothing. Unencumbered, I wrote in a frenzy. Seventeen days later, I mailed in the revise.

"Usually, when people revise a book, they do very little," the agent said. "They think they've changed it, but it's the same book. You've written a new book."

He sent it to publishers. Joyce had 22 rejections on *Dubliners*. I was up to 14 when the phone rang.

"I want you to remember this moment," the agent said. "I want you to remember exactly how you feel because, no matter what happens after this, you will never feel this way again. Your novel has been sold."

He was right. I never felt that way again. I never again felt an all-encompassing, head-to-toe visceral shock that says, *You are not an idiot. You did not waste your time. You wanted to do this and you did.*

I hung up the phone. I imagined someday being on a bus, seeing someone reading *White Light* (that never happened), someone who might be moved or changed as I've been by books. I was no longer a hopeful dreamer. I was something else. ◖

WRITER'S RETREAT:
Patricia Volk
(*above, in blue shirt*) at dinner, Yaddo, 1983.

Oprah and Maria in Oprah's teahouse garden in Santa Barbara, California, March 5, 2008.

THE *O* INTERVIEW

Oprah Talks to Maria Shriver

They've been great friends for 30 years. But in one afternoon, Maria reveals for the first time what's made her run so hard—and Oprah asks a question she never dared ask until now.

I'll never forget the morning I met Maria Shriver. It was 1978, and I was working on a show called *People Are Talking* at WJZ-TV in Baltimore. Maria joined the WJZ team as a producer for *Evening Magazine,* and she had an office just down the hall from my cubicle. For weeks after she started, the office was aflutter with talk of the arrival of a member of the First Family in American politics, the Kennedys. Maria was the only daughter of Robert Sargent Shriver (who was a vice presi-

dential candidate in 1972 and the founding director of the Peace Corps) and Eunice Shriver (founder of the Special Olympics and sister of President John F. Kennedy and Senator Robert Kennedy). There was such an aura surrounding that clan, I didn't know what to expect. But I certainly didn't think I'd walk into the office bathroom one day and see Maria splashing her face in the sink.

Somehow I dredged up the nerve to ask, "What are you doing?"

"I've been at the office for four days, working through the night," she said, laughing. "This is my idea of a bath." That was the beginning of a friendship that has lasted three decades. Neither of us could have predicted how dramatically our lives would shift in the years between that morning at the station and the afternoon we recently spent in my Santa Barbara teahouse garden.

Maria was just 23 when she came to work at WJZ, and one of the first in her family to pursue journalism—an unconventional choice, given the Kennedy legacy. Working her way up the ranks of broadcasting, she became a reporter at CBS News in 1983 and a coanchor on *CBS Morning News* (at the time, I so wanted a gig like that!) in 1985. The following year, she joined NBC News as a correspondent; she would go on to contribute to *Dateline,* interview everyone from Fidel Castro to Ted Turner, and earn a Peabody Award for a 1998 report on welfare reform.

In 1986 she did something even more unconventional for a Kennedy than becoming a newscaster: She married a Republican movie star. Four kids (Katherine Eunice, now 19 years old; Christina Aurelia, 17; Patrick Arnold, 15; and Christopher Sargent, 11) and a couple of *Terminator* films later, Maria and her husband, Arnold Schwarzenegger, settled into family life in a Los Angeles suburb, with occasional visits to the Kennedy compound in Hyannis Port, Massachusetts.

In August 2003 Arnold announced that he would run for governor during California's recall election. Maria was reluctant to return to politics, the landscape that had defined her childhood. But Arnold won, and in November, Maria became the First Lady of California—and found herself out of work as a journalist. The dramatic changes were not what she would have wished for herself. Yet they ultimately led to an important aha! moment, one that inspired *Just Who Will You Be?,* her sixth book, which was published in April.

Last October at the annual Women's Conference, an internationally attended forum she organized in Southern California, Maria summed up that moment in a riveting speech. "You can spend the rest of your life trying to figure out what other people expect from you...or you can make a decision to let that all go," she told the 14,000 women who had gathered at the Long Beach Convention Center. "And for this people-pleasing, legacy-carrying, perfection-seeking good girl, that was a news bulletin."

OPRAH: Let's start by admitting how weird it is to do an interview when we've known each other for 30 years.
MARIA: I'm very proud of having such a long-term friendship. You were the first friend I made outside of my fam-

ily. I was raised in this clan mentality; the only people who could understand what I was experiencing were my siblings and cousins. I went to an all-girls school, and I hung out with classmates there, but before I met you, I had never gone out and made a friend who wasn't steeped in my family's history. You weren't an Irish Catholic from Washington. You were a friend I made on my own, at a job I got on my own, in a city I'd never lived in before.

OPRAH: At the time, I didn't know any of that. I was a little afraid of you when you first came to WJZ-TV.
MARIA: Why afraid?
OPRAH: You were such the talk! I don't know what gave me the courage to engage with a Kennedy, but you turned out to be so friendly.
MARIA: Well, I was always conscious that people would think I got the job because I was a Kennedy and that I wouldn't be one of the team. I had to prove myself at every juncture. I worked hard.
OPRAH: Do you think you overdid it?
MARIA: Looking back, yes. I was so into my work for 25 years. I put on blinders to everything else; if I hadn't, there would always have been something more exciting happening in my family that could pull me away. So once I decided to go into journalism, I just worked all the time. I thought I had to show people that I would get in early, stay late or even all night, work on holidays. I didn't want to be the rich kid who was along for a free ride. And I thought *you* were such a big deal because you had an apartment.
OPRAH: You had an apartment, too....
MARIA: But mine was on the bottom floor of the little complex we both lived in, and it had no furniture!
OPRAH: Oh, that's right. The bottom-floor apartment rented for less. As a single woman, I was always very cautious about the first floor; no matter what it cost, I'd get an apartment on the third floor or above.
MARIA: You had a nice apartment and furniture, and you spoke in churches all the time. You'd say, "I'm going to preach on Sunday," and I was like, *What's up with that?* I didn't know anybody my age who preached, or even had something to say.
OPRAH: Oh, gosh, I was like a preacher woman. I would be invited to speak at churches all around.
MARIA: I know! I'm Catholic—I was used to priests doing the talking. I thought, *Who does she think she is that she can just get up and preach?* I mean, you lived upstairs and you ate with me in a supermarket....
OPRAH: The supermarket in Cross Keys. They had a little dining section.
MARIA: It was pathetic. And you would say, "I don't know

what I'm going to do," and I'd think, *But you're already on TV doing the news and the weather, and you're preaching on Sunday!* To me, all that was big, but you didn't see yourself that way.

OPRAH: No, not at all. I still have journals from those years, and I remember writing, "I understand why they call the show *The Young and the Restless*, because I am so restless." In my 25th year, I just didn't know what I was going to do with my life. I knew there was more than news stories, but I didn't know what that was. I didn't know what the future held. I was very anxious.

MARIA: I've always been that way. I've always thought that the answer was in the next thing. If I worked a little

MARIA: Correct. You must do, and do big. You must change the world. And you must do this 24/7. My mother, who's 86 now, has had several strokes this past year. She's on a pacemaker. But if you try to help her up the steps, she'll slap your hand. There's no rest. I look at my mom and think, *Wow, that's one way of living and accomplishing.* And I admire her for it tremendously. But do I want to duplicate it? No. That's a big revelation for me because I'm my mother's only daughter. Yet I'm different from my mother—and that's okay.

OPRAH: What helped you to get there?

MARIA: A lot of deep digging. Losing my job at NBC News was big. I identified myself with my job. Whenever peo-

1963–1975: Maria, age 7 (*on left*), with cousin Caroline Kennedy and uncle John F. Kennedy; in her room at age 14; the Shriver family (*from left*)—Mark, Bobby, Eunice, Sargent holding Anthony, Maria, and Timmy.

1969

1963

1975

harder, produced an incredible show, wrote a best-selling book, anchored the morning news, won a Peabody Award, worked with the Special Olympics, then I would be less restless. And I kept going and going and going.

OPRAH: After you accomplished these things, then what?

MARIA: I'd have to find another thing. That's what I wrote about in the book *Just Who Will You Be?* I made the mistake of thinking that external accomplishments would bring me peace. I thought it was about the job or a book or making a name for myself. So many people would come up to me and say, "Which Kennedy are you?" At a very young age, I thought, *You're going to know which one I am.* I decided that I was going to be the Kennedy who makes her own name and finds her own job and works like a dog. My comeuppance was when Arnold got elected—I became the Kennedy who was married to the governor.

OPRAH: And you were right back where you started.

MARIA: The 25 years I'd spent trying to make a name for myself seemingly went out the door. I started thinking that I'd taken the wrong road—one that ultimately hadn't curbed that restlessness.

OPRAH: In your new book, you say that the constant doing wasn't just the way you were brought up; it was the doctrine of your life.

1982

1982–1996: Maria and future husband Arnold Schwarzenegger; with *CBS Morning News* coanchor Forrest Sawyer; meeting with then California secretary of state Bill Jones.

1985

ple asked what I was up to, I would talk about covering this or that subject, or traveling to New York. I was Maria Shriver, newswoman. I belonged to WJZ, CBS, or NBC. What I did became who I was. It gave me an identity separate from my family. When people looked at the Kennedys, they just saw us as a mass of good teeth and lots of hair, all smiling together and being very family oriented, sailing, playing games...

OPRAH: Touch football at the Kennedy compound in Massachusetts...

MARIA: Tackling people, throwing them overboard.

That's how we operated. I sometimes knew that such competitiveness wasn't quite normal. When people would come over, they were like, *Whoa.*

OPRAH: I remember being at the compound once, early on in our friendship. As an outsider, I thought, *God, I'm actually here on the lawn with all the Kennedy cousins.* But the games never ended. I'll never forget being in the house and someone saying, "Where is she? Oprah, we're starting another game!" And I ran into a closet and closed the door because I'd already done three games—enough! It was all very intense.

MARIA: It still is! It's competitive when you walk in the door. It's competitive at the table. It's competitive on the playing field. It's competitive in a boat. Even my mother is very competitive at everything—from checkers to Ping-Pong to sailing to politics. When I was a girl, she'd tell my father, "Tackle her as hard as you tackle the boys! Knock her down!" She'd tell him to serve the tennis ball at me as hard as he could. I couldn't even return it—it would knock the racquet out of my hand. I thought that was cool. No other mother I knew was doing that.

OPRAH: One of my favorite stories about your mother was the day I ran into her after the tsunami in Southeast Asia. I was on vacation and going to my boat on the wharf, and she waved me down. She said, "What are you doing out

OPRAH: What was it like at your dinner table every night?

MARIA: "What did you do today?" "What did you read?" "What do you think?"

OPRAH: That obviously had its positive effects.

MARIA: Yes—it drives you. But if you're moving all the time, you're not stopping to be or think or experience nature. A couple of years ago, a friend of mine who'd worked his whole life bought a loft in New York and fixed it up. It was serene and peaceful. He said, "When I go there, I feel like I'm on a honeymoon with myself." I mentioned this to my parents, and they said, "What is the point of that? What are you doing to make the world a better place by going on a honeymoon with yourself?" They didn't get it. After I wrote my second book, I saw my father at the Cape. He said, "What are you doing with yourself?" I said, "I just wrote a book." "But you did the book already," he said. "That's over. You need to do a new thing."

OPRAH: Does that make you feel like it's never enough?

MARIA: Yes. When you come from a family that has achieved so much, you're left with the challenge of either making peace with that or finding some way to do what you want to do. It's impossible to compete with that level of accomplishment.

OPRAH: Yes, how can you compete with a legacy that

1996

2007

2008

2007–2008: Maria with her daughters, Christina and Katherine, and sons, Patrick and Christopher, at Arnold's second inauguration ceremony; at a rally for Barack Obama in Los Angeles.

here on a boat? You and Maria need to call Teddy and form a committee to raise money. We've got to do something!" I said, "Okay, Eunice; it's good to see you." The next morning, she took a little boat out onto the water to find me! I was told, "There's a woman out here who says she needs to talk to you." I said, "Okay, I'll call Maria when I get home."

MARIA: My parents' vacations were working vacations. We visited Special Olympics events, Peace Corps volunteers, prime ministers, and priests. They'd be trying to solve the Israeli-Palestinian conflict on Christmas.

includes the presidency of the United States, the development of the Peace Corps, and the creation of the Special Olympics?

MARIA: You can't. It's unbelievable public service. So I found my own way to contribute in my own area, journalism. It's competitive. It's creative. And no one else in my extended family is a journalist. I was feeling really good about my career in journalism—and then I lost it.

OPRAH: How?

MARIA: It all happened so quickly. NBC felt there could be a perception of a conflict of interest between my news job and Arnold's becoming governor. We were in uncharted water. The producers told me, "If we put you on the air while Arnold's campaigning, it'll look like we're endorsing him." A lot of people were uncomfortable with that, so they took me off the air while he was running for office. I thought I'd return to reporting when the campaign was over. And then he won, and that was that.

OPRAH: Were you surprised?

MARIA: I was surprised by the fact that he was even running. I was surprised that I was suddenly the First Lady of California. I was surprised that I lost my job. This all happened in 60 days. When Arnold decided to run in 2003, we were about to build a new house, and *Terminator 3* was coming out, so Arnold was very involved in that. Also, my brothers and I had been focusing on my father; we'd discovered he had Alzheimer's. Around that time, I went to the Special Olympics in Ireland. When I came home, news of a California recall election was building steam. That's when Arnold told me, "I want to run."

OPRAH: When you married him, you must have felt pretty safe that you were about as far away from politics as you could be.

MARIA: Yes! I married a bodybuilder who became an actor and lived in California. No one thought, *Well, there's somebody who'll go into politics.* I don't think I'd ever even met a Republican before I met Arnold. When he told me he was interested, I said I'd spent my whole life getting away from politics. My experience with politics was one of loss. My father lost his vice presidential bid on the McGovern-Shriver ticket in 1972. Campaigning was a great experience for me because it's where I was introduced to journalism, but the rejection of my father was so painful, so personal; I remember the sting of that defeat. Then my father tried to run for president in 1976, and that didn't go anywhere. People who said they would support him didn't. I'd learned early on that political life was about constant travel and being surrounded by 50 people in the house, and either you lose or you get assassinated. So I wanted nothing to do with that.

OPRAH: What made you change your mind?

MARIA: I realized that if I said no, I'd be stopping my husband from achieving his dream. It was a catch-22. So I told Arnold that he should do what he wanted to do, and I found myself in an intense, tumultuous campaign. Two months later, I was the Democratic First Lady of a Republican administration. Whoa! I was elated about Arnold's win, but I didn't want to be involved; I just wanted to go back to my job. But then NBC decided they were uncomfortable keeping me.

OPRAH: Was that one of the more devastating moments of your life?

MARIA: I had been fired once before, from the *CBS Morning News;* that was really devastating.

OPRAH: I remember when you got that job. It was the dream job we all wanted! I had an agent who told me, "You're never going to get a position like that, because they already have Bryant Gumbel and there's only going to be one black person on network television." I said, "Can you just send my tape in?" I thought I could be a substitute for Joan Lunden. But anyway, you had the dream job....

MARIA: Yes, I took the CBS job three weeks after I got engaged to Arnold, and I moved to New York to start working. I was thrilled. Those coanchor morning-show gigs were among the few on the networks that seemed locked down forever.

OPRAH: So why did you get fired?

MARIA: You know, I'm still unclear about that! [*Laughs.*] I thought I was doing really well. But the morning news show had been troubled. Of the three networks, our ratings at CBS were the lowest.

OPRAH: You didn't care, though, right?

MARIA: Oh, no. I was one of three women on a morning show! That's two hours. Live. I loved it.

OPRAH: Even though you had to get up at dawn?

MARIA: Loved it. I had moved into a hotel. I was working with Forrest Sawyer, whom I liked, and there were no expectations because we were in third place. I could do every conceivable subject: politics, culture, the arts. And I was getting paid more than I'd ever thought possible. Although I was engaged, I was single in New York City, and everything about it was terrific. Then CBS decided to move the *Morning News* from the news division to the entertainment division, and we were canceled. We got the news over a fax while we were in London covering the Sarah Ferguson–Prince Andrew royal wedding. I was shocked. I had assumed incorrectly that this group of colleagues was an extension of my family—they were all my best friends. My whole life revolved around these people.

OPRAH: That's right. People at work do become your family.

MARIA: I remember walking out of CBS and saying to myself, *I am never going back in that building again.* I was so hurt and humiliated. In my mind, I was the first person in my family to fail. I'd gotten married by that point, so I moved back to L.A. and thought, *Now what?*

OPRAH: Is that what you thought when you lost the NBC job, too?

MARIA: Yes, but even more so. When I lost my job at CBS, I was 30 and childless; I felt like I could just start over. But when I lost my job at NBC, I was 48 with four children, and I was a Democrat in a Republican administration. All I kept thinking was, *Where will I go?*

OPRAH: Just who will you be?

MARIA: Exactly. I suddenly found myself lost and yet in a familiar place. When you grow up in a political family, you're trotted out a lot, and you're never exactly clear what you're doing. You're in a political pamphlet, in a commercial, at an event. You're part of a story. You have your role in that story.

OPRAH: Tell me about that role.

MARIA: As a child, it was just to be part of the Kennedy family. I was aware of the importance of having the family in the picture when someone ran for office. Politics is about competition, policy, and inspiration, but it's also about appearances.

OPRAH: Even in our most private conversations, I haven't ever asked you this question: Was that Kennedy picture as happy as it appeared to be?

MARIA: Oh, yes. Absolutely. We're a bonded family. Even though it was tumultuous at times, there is a very tight relationship between all of us. My cousins are like siblings and best friends. Not only do I talk to my brothers almost daily but I talk to several of my cousins weekly. We're very connected. Yet there was not a lot of talking among us about how we were feeling. We just kept going.

OPRAH: Were you aware of what you all looked like to the rest of the world?

MARIA: Not when I was a child. Growing up, there was a definite division between the parents and the children — to the point where many of us who are now grown think of ourselves as children when we go to the Cape. The adults ran the whole thing. My grandmother Rose was the matriarch. And even though he'd had a stroke, my grandfather Joe was an imposing figure. They lived in the big house, and when we went there, we wore our best clothes. My grandmother was always immaculately dressed, and she'd correct our grammar and quiz us. She was intellectual. She was revered by the entire family. So I was conscious of being in a large family with a hierarchy. Even now, when my parents walk into the room, I stand up. Our family is old-fashioned in that way.

OPRAH: Were you aware of your family's legacy?

MARIA: Yes. I don't think you could have lived through my uncle's assassination in 1963 and not been aware.

OPRAH: But did you know what that meant to the rest of the world?

MARIA: Yes, but only because others told me. To this day, people still come up to me and talk about how my family impacted their lives. They tell me that they've gotten involved in public service or joined the Peace Corps be-

cause of one of my uncles. When I became First Lady of California, people came up to me and said, "I hope you're going to be like your aunt Jackie." Others were angry because they thought I'd brought the Kennedy legacy to a Republican: "Shame on you," they'd say. "You should be mortified."

OPRAH: And then there's the image: Camelot.

MARIA: Right.

OPRAH: I was at Tina Turner's house over Christmas, talking to her about Barack Obama. She paid no attention to me. But when Caroline Kennedy came out for Barack Obama, I got a phone call from Tina. She said, "Oprah, I heard everything you said to me. But if Caroline says it—and because of what her whole family represents—then I'm for Barack." I thought, *I was sitting at your dinner table, and you don't even know Caroline!* [Laughs.]

MARIA: Yes, I'm aware that my family has that image. I'm also aware that people are sometimes reluctant to talk to me when they first meet me—like you were.

OPRAH: Do you accept that?

MARIA: I've spent a lot of my life trying to make people comfortable, even though I'm not exactly sure why they aren't.

OPRAH: It's the difference they perceive between themselves and the image of your family that they've come to believe in. It's about measuring up.

MARIA: I don't work anymore at trying to make sure others like me. I've given up on that. This is who I am.

OPRAH: It took me 30 years to tell you that I didn't know if I was good enough to be your friend.

MARIA: You're going to make me cry!

OPRAH: I remember being in the bathroom at the Kennedy compound and seeing framed letters from Nikita Khrushchev on the wall. I'm just sitting on the toilet, trying to act like it's normal to have the First Secretary of the Soviet Union's Communist Party in there with me. So I made a decision: I'm just going to be myself.

MARIA: You know, this teaches me that so many of us go through life not communicating. If I'd been more confident, I could have said to you, "This might feel a little awkward, but it's going to be okay." I didn't know how to articulate that. I was always wondering whether a person was coming over because they were curious to see all that stuff and to meet famous people, or if they were coming there for me. And I didn't know whether you would accept me into your circle. *Am I enough?* That's a scary question to ask yourself. I've spent years looking for an answer outside myself.

OPRAH: Maya Angelou once said to me, "You alone are enough. You have nothing to prove to anybody." She gave me a necklace with those words on it.

MARIA: We are all worthy—and not because we've accomplished something or because we're part of a famous family. You're worthy if you don't make the team, if you get Ds and Fs, if you don't get into the best college. That belief is the greatest gift any parent can give his or her child. You and I don't have to do an interview or talk about a project or save the world. We can just sit and be with each other and with ourselves. For me, that was a revelation. An awakening.

OPRAH: **That's what you write about in your new book.**

MARIA: That's right. I'm not the person I was four years ago, so here's the question: *Who am I?* The answer is that I can feel myself evolving into a different person. For the first time, I can actually say that I'm right where I want to be.

OPRAH: **As a friend who has observed you, I can say that you've become more of who you really are. In all the years I've known you, you've been running so fast. You never took a breath. It was so exhausting to watch.**

MARIA: Was it? I'm sorry. I exhausted everyone. I'm still working on that.

OPRAH: **You've come a long way. The fact that you could come to Hawaii with me last summer and just *be* was big.**

MARIA: Huge. And I was so happy. Years ago, I would've been too embarrassed to tell my family that there was no point to the trip other than just sheer friendship.

OPRAH: **Remember when I was trying to get you to go to a spa years ago? You said, "I haven't been to that spa, but I once stopped by and looked in." For you back then, three days at a spa was out of the question.**

MARIA: That used to be true. My mother was not the kind of person who had her hair and nails done, went to lunch, and looked out at the scenery. That wasn't the example I grew up with.

OPRAH: **Well, I'm not just looking at the scenery all the time, but I started to realize you were *never* looking at it.**

MARIA: And I regret that. I thought being a workaholic was good; it isn't. I regret that I didn't take time to stop and enjoy my friends or to have intimate experiences with people in my life, to talk to them and be quiet with them. I was too busy running against my restlessness. Maybe it was a combination of being thrown back into a political life, losing my job, and my parents getting old that prompted my change.

OPRAH: **Otherwise, you might have kept plowing through.**

MARIA: Yes. The transition gave me an incredible opportunity I never would've had if I'd stayed at NBC. There, I would still be running; instead, I've taken all my reporting skills and applied them to my own journey. I've tried to craft the job of First Lady of California into a role that reflects me. That's about connecting people, empowering and inspiring them. I focused on parenting my children—I was determined that they would stay front and center in my life, and I wanted the house I created to be all about them. And in the past two years, I've tried to spend time with my parents, my cousins, and my friends in a way that I never have. I'm mothering my mother. I'm trying to live my life from my heart, being authentic to who I am. I'm trying to feel my way to my truth. I do things now that feel real to me.

OPRAH: **That's amazing.**

MARIA: A friend once told me, "As long as you keep playing the game of trying to be 'the right Maria' for everyone, you're never going to deliver the real Maria. You don't even know who the real Maria is." She was right. So I took a long, hard look at myself and began to strip away a lot of the stuff that kept me running. The most terrifying thing of all for me was to just sit with myself; I didn't know how to be alone. When you grow up in a huge family, you're never alone.

OPRAH: **When I'm alone, I'm so happy I'm dancing the hula!**

MARIA: Being able to be by myself is part of knowing that I'm enough. When I talked about that in the speech, women were sobbing by the thousands; that's their story, too. I thought my journey was about keeping my family's legacy going—and that is still part of my job. I'm very proud of my family and what it stands for. But I'm also trying to create a legacy as a mother, a wife, and a woman, and as Maria, separate from all those things.

OPRAH: **So what do you know for sure about who you are?**

MARIA: I'm a good-hearted person. I think I'm a kind woman. I'm a loyal friend. I'm also funny and a little mischievous! I've learned that it's okay for me to show up in a gypsy skirt with my hair somewhat askew. I'm comfortable with that now. I don't need to change people's minds about me. For me, letting go of that is just huge. I know that I'm a deeply spiritual person. I know that I need to surround myself with people who see me, nourish me, and love me for me, and I can even have the courage to ask for that. I know that I've learned how to be a mother and a daughter differently. After my mother got sick, I tried to get her out of the hospital and back on her feet as fast as possible. Then I began to consider: What if I try something completely different? What if I acknowledge that perhaps my mother doesn't like having a nurse and feeling dependent? That maybe she's afraid, that this is scary to her? And what if I hold her hand? So sometimes I just sit and paint her nails or hold her hand. These little acts of nurturing have led me to be not only more kind to her but more gentle with myself.

OPRAH: **That's right—because you are enough.**

MARIA: Even if I never accomplish another thing. **O**

"You're not your body, and for sure you're not your body image"

After spending weeks in class with Eckhart Tolle, studying his book *A New Earth*, I know for sure that I am *not* my body. I feel more connected to consciousness, or soul, or inner spirit—whatever you choose to name the formless being that is the essence of who we are. I think of all the years I've wasted hating myself fat, wanting myself thin. Feeling guilty about every croissant, then giving up carbs, then fasting, then dieting, then worrying when I wasn't dieting, then eating *everything* I wanted until the next diet (on Monday or after the holidays or the next big event). Wasted time, abhorring the thought of trying on clothes, wondering what was going to fit, what number the scale would say. All that energy I could have spent loving what is.

Sixteen years ago, when spiritual teacher Marianne Williamson was first on my show to talk about her book *A Return to Love*, I asked her why she thought I was having such struggles with my weight. She wrote me a letter saying this: "Until you accept the magnitude of your function, your unconscious mind will sabotage any attempt to show your full magnificence. In fact, if you diet and lose weight, your mind will either put the weight back on or trip up in some other area. In order to lose weight on a permanent basis, you want a shift in your belief about who and what you are. This is the miracle you seek."

I used to carry that letter around in my purse and pull it out when I felt like overeating. I had the words printed on a card and framed on my desk. And yet I still didn't *get it* until recently. Who I am, who you are...we're not our bodies or the image we hold of them. But because what you give your attention to looms larger—in this case literally—all my focus on weight actually made me fatter. Wasted time.

I can look at a picture from any period of my life, and the first thing that comes to mind is not the event or experience, but my weight and size, because that is how I've viewed (and judged) myself—through the prism of numbers.

But I've given up scale-watching—letting a number determine how I see myself and whether I'm worthy of a good day. Part of my awakening through the *New Earth* classes has been to recognize how shallow and small that made me. Aha! So that's what Marianne meant when she wrote 16 years ago about "the magnitude of your function." She was right: It is indeed a miracle when you realize the fullness of who you are. You're not your body, and for sure you're not your body image.

That's a *free at last* kind of recognition. No more wasted time.

spirituality

The Doubter's Dilemma

To pray or not to pray? To believe or not to believe? And how to explain the things that look suspiciously like miracles? **Kelly Corrigan** speaks for a generation of people "pulsing with thankfulness" but not sure they can give it up to God.

My mother is fond of telling me I'm over-thinking it—"it" being anything from the virtues of organic mulch for my flower beds to which booster seats to buy for my daughters—so you can imagine how she feels about my religious ambivalence. While it's not quite true to say she was 30 with three kids before she met someone who wasn't Catholic, it's close enough.

Perhaps as a consequence, she is not a woman who has frittered away her days critiquing her religion. Instead she prays, mostly for her children, who she so hoped would inherit her bulletproof faith but who are more likely to drive away with her navy blue Buick and a left-over case of Chardonnay she bought at a discount in Delaware. Both my parents shudder over our discerning, noncommittal generation that has something to say about everything but nowhere to go on Sunday mornings.

I envy my parents' faith. Supplication, I've often thought, must be easier on the body than Tums and Ambien. And how contenting it must be to believe that someday everyone you love will be in one place and will stay there forever. Who wouldn't want that destiny? But for all its comforting appeal, I rarely go to church and have read only a few chapters of the Bible. Even when disaster struck four years ago, I did not fall to my knees and petition the God of my childhood.

In autumn 2004, both my father and I were diagnosed with late-stage cancer. I was 36, and the seven-centimeter tumor behind my nipple was technically my second cancer. (In my mid-20s, I'd had a melanoma as big as a pencil eraser removed from my calf, leaving a little divot and a long scar that reminds me to use sunblock and stay in the shade at midday.) My dad was 74, and the scattered tumors around his bladder marked round three for him.

The day my doctor called with the diagnosis, I hung up the phone, looked over the heads of my kids, and mouthed to my husband, "It's cancer." Then, after a long hug, a cold Corona, and a cigarette (I had squirreled away a half-smoked pack after a party the year before and for reasons I can't explain, I couldn't wait to suck down a Merit Ultra Light that afternoon), we went to the computer and started searching for information on "invasive ductal carcinoma." My father got his diagnosis in person; after thanking the doctor and scheduling a slew of tests, he and my mother slid into the Buick and drove down to St. Colman's, their favorite little church, for noon Mass. They gave it to God; we gave it to Google.

Over the course of a year, my dad and I both got better, and, especially in his case, people said it was miraculous. At the very least, it was unexpected. Perhaps even unexplainable, though not to Mom, who summed it up in one word: *prayer*. "People around the world were praying for your father," she explained ("around the world" referring primarily to a high school friend of mine who lived in Moscow and had always been fond of my dad).

I had both always prayed and never prayed, which is to say that I often found myself in bed at the end of a day saying to no one in particular, "Thank you for this good man beside me and those girls in the other room." But I had not beseeched God to make me well, had not begged God for my father's life. Among other things, I didn't want to be—to borrow from sixth-grade parlance—a *user*, a phony who thought she could get what she wanted by conveniently nuzzling up to someone she usually snubbed.

After my dad recovered, I talked to an old friend about my parents' confidence in prayer and their belief that God had intervened. Rather than praise the inexplicable glory of God, my friend thought we should exalt the devotion and ingenuity of man. Or, as she put it: *It just bugs me how people want to give all the credit away, as if we were all*

just useless sinners who didn't know how to take care of ourselves or each other. In other words, maybe it wasn't prayer that made my dad better—maybe it was all that chemo. Or the scope with tiny scissors that removed nine moldy tumors from his bladder without his even having to check in to the OR. Or the meticulous doctor who managed his case with such vigilance.

I liked my friend's take on things: Up with people and their hard work and cool inventions. But I kept thinking back to my father's initial prognosis. The urologist to whom I attributed my dad's stunning recovery had told us to brace for the worst. Ten months later, when he declared my father a healthy man, that same doctor said he couldn't explain "how on earth" my dad was disease-free. Could I really give all the credit to a doctor who shrugged his shoulders and said it was anybody's guess how George Corrigan survived?

Part of growing up is coming to terms with the disturbing fact that even the very smartest people don't always have the answers. Let us remember that it was only a generation or so ago when new mothers smoked cigarettes on the maternity ward while nurses fed the infants nice big bottles of formula. Only a few years ago, children were still being taught to believe that poor Pluto was a planet. If history teaches us anything, it's that the truth is subject to change. This means that what is standard practice now may someday be eschewed, in the same way that no health-conscious person puts plastic in the microwave anymore. It also means that notions we now consider dubious may, somewhere down the road, become widely accepted. So might we eventually say, "Can you believe that people used to doubt the power of prayer?"

In fact, the federal government has underwritten elaborate studies asking this very question. Online, I've found a pile of research suggesting a measurable, therapeutic benefit to prayer and prayerful meditation. Sure, the link can be explained away; like any type of quiet meditation, prayer is relaxing, and relaxation has proven physiological benefits. But a click away from the reports was a survey of physicians—a clear majority of whom pray for their patients. So prayer isn't just for my gullible parents. And if doctors can get to belief, might I?

If there is a God, he knows how much I want there to be more to human existence than a series of discrete physical experiences that start with birth and end with death. I want all of us—and all our lives—to be meaningful. But small. I'd be elated to learn that this go-round is only part one of something that has a thousand parts. I'd love to laugh at this life from a distance. As it is, I relish the fact that I am one of six billion people the way my mother revels in Pavarotti's recording of the *Ave Maria*. Being one in six billion means my life can't possibly matter to anyone but me and my little flock—which means that all my mistakes and failures and anxieties are utterly inconsequential. When I forget this, when things begin to matter too much and I find it hard to get a good, deep breath, I close my eyes and imagine flying over houses, lifting off the roofs and seeing all the people whose existence is concurrent with mine. I imagine them arguing, cooking, hugging, suffering and laughing, living and dying. Each of us a little bitty fish in an inconceivably large pond, swimming in circles, nothing to do but enjoy the water.

But maybe that's an incomplete picture. Maybe there's something between and around and inside all six billion of us, and maybe that something knows every hair on each of our heads. Maybe we are not anonymous. Wouldn't that be outrageous? And beautiful?

Faith is the tallest order, the toughest nut: the humbling of yourself before purposes you don't—and cannot ever—comprehend. Let's face it, believing that there is a God who might get involved in your tiny little life is beyond anti-intellectual. And this is why I doubt. But when I'm honest with myself, I have to admit that there's doubt within my doubt. And every time I remind myself of that, I think of Voltaire's confounding line: "Doubt is not a pleasant condition, but certainty is an absurd one."

So I let my parents share their faith with our children. When we visit Philadelphia, where my parents live, I let them take our daughters to church. At night, my mom gets the girls on their knees and shows them how to cross themselves and position their hands and bow their heads. It is a lovely sight, and I would never discourage it. Of course, when we get back home to California, the girls are loaded with new ideas and questions they're counting on me to answer.

Claire, who is a senior in preschool, recently asked what lights are made of. After I told her something about electricity and filaments and Thomas Edison, she said, "In church, they said Jesus is a light." Georgia, a first grader, reprimanded me for saying "Oh my God." "*God* is a bad word," she said. To which I heard myself say, "Oh no, honey. *God* is not a bad word. *God* is a very good word." Both girls have asked

if they could be the Holy Ghost for Halloween.

Regardless of where I am on the spectrum from atheism to theism, I'd rather my girls be grounded in something, even something that seems too good or crazy to be true. This is why, when the girls ask me about God, I say that people believe all kinds of things and no one really knows, including me, but that I *hope*. Then I tell them what my husband, with tears in his eyes, recently told me: I say being with them is the most spiritual experience of my life—the highest high, the deepest yes, the most staggering gift—and that gift must have come from somewhere.

And what about all the little gifts, the everyday stuff like a good cantaloupe or a great public school teacher or the rebate check coming just in time? For that, I've taken to saying grace. At the dinner table we all hold hands while I talk about our friends, our family, our health. Then my husband, generally prompted by my raised eyebrow, says a prayer for the people we know who are having trouble. The girls mostly tolerate all this (sometimes adding a thank-you for a Popsicle or a playdate) and look forward to saying "amen," after which we take turns rising from our seats to do a family wave, as if the home team had just scored.

It feels good, saying grace. But for now, that's as far as I've gotten—just another person pulsing with thankfulness, wondering what will happen next. Someday—despite all medications and all prayers—people in our lives will get sick and will not get better. Georgia and Claire will ask me where they went, and I'll probably be wondering the same thing. Have they gone to a paradise, a separate plane of existence where God holds them in the palm of his hand? Are they internalized in the people who are left behind? Do they become part of the earth and therefore an endless part of the cycle of life?

If you asked my dad, he'd assure you that heaven exists and *boy are you gonna love it*. Just like if you asked him why I got better, he'd say something about how God wants me to be here. I tell him I got better because of four chemotherapies, each an impressive creation of man. But that just makes him laugh, shake his head, and flash his big knowing smile. "Aw, Lovey," he says, "don't you see? What do you think makes a man spend his days trying to cure cancer?" ◖

> Believing in a God who might get involved in my tiny little life is beyond anti-intellectual. And this is why I doubt. But there's doubt within my doubt.

What's a Moment That Defined Spirituality for You?

A window opening. A glimpse of the ungraspable. A sudden surge of love… or hope…or awe. **Ten artists, writers, thinkers, and doers** recall the flashes of understanding that took their breath away.

Julian Bond
CHAIRMAN OF NAACP

I experienced transcendent spirituality at a mass meeting in Selma in 1965. The church was packed, state troopers loomed outside, and the Selma Youth Choir were singing with their hearts as well as their lungs. I knew with clarity and certainty that I had become a part of something much, much bigger than myself and the physical confines of the building. A transforming feeling of fellowship and community and the rightness of our common cause suffused me, and it has carried me ever since.

Laws—and lives—were transformed during the civil rights marches of 1965.

Jane Goodall, PhD
FOUNDER OF THE JANE GOODALL INSTITUTE, UN MESSENGER OF PEACE

I don't think there was a single moment. It grew with me as I grew, this sense of the other world, a world as real as the physical one we're in now. After my husband died, there was this very strong, extraordinary experience that he was in the room talking to me. I wasn't able to remember what he said. I don't know that that *defined* spirituality; perhaps *confirmed* would be a better word. There were also moments when I was out in the forest when I felt that I almost understood concepts like eternity but didn't. Or, if I did, then I didn't remember it. It reminds me of a book I loved as a child, *The Wind in the Willows,* and the part when the little otter cub got lost and Mole and Water Rat went to find him, and they met the great god Pan. Afterward they couldn't remember the tune he played because to remember it in this life would have destroyed them. These amazing moments—when you seem to know something beyond what you know and to understand things you don't understand—can't be understood in this life.

Cornel West, PhD

PROFESSOR IN THE CENTER OF AFRICAN-AMERICAN STUDIES, PRINCETON UNIVERSITY, AND AUTHOR OF *DEMOCRACY MATTERS*

The surgeon was rolling me into the operating room for a seven-hour procedure on an aggressive form of cancer that was in the last stage. He said, "I don't understand; how is your blood pressure normal?" I said, "I've made my peace." My response to the cancer was that I was full of gratitude that I had been invited to the banquet of life for 48 years and experienced an abundance of blessings, especially in the form of family and friends. It just turned out that I've been spared for a while.

Kate Braestrup

MINISTER AND AUTHOR OF *HERE IF YOU NEED ME*

When he was a little boy, my son Peter spent hours filling sheets of paper with detailed drawings of human conflict. His soldiers carried fearsome weapons. They were borne into battle clinging to the gun turrets of enormous tanks while flocks of fighter planes wheeled across a Magic Marker sky.

The ordnance in these drawings were neatly labeled in accordance with Peter's understanding of human good and human evil: An American flag fluttered proudly above the good guys, and, in case the point was missed, Peter would write "U.S." across the flanks of their fighter jets and tanks. The bad guys fought under red flags inscribed with swastikas. Peter labeled their tanks and airplanes, too. They were the "NOT-SEES." It was so perfect, I couldn't bring myself to correct his spelling.

Vision as a metaphor for human spiritual insight has a history so broad, deep, and obvious that it doesn't require much elucidation. "I was blind, but now I see" is just one familiar variation on the theme of an opened eye meeting light for the first time.

As a 6- or 7-year-old, Peter named evil as a failure of vi-

sion. I believe he coined the term "Not-See" not only because the phonetics worked but also because it made sense to him spiritually. The Nazis refused to see the human reality of their victims, and those who might have helped the Jews refused even to bear them witness. The Holocaust began with a denial of human commonality, a rejection of that human "us." This, Peter sensed, is the prerequisite for all violence, all enslavement and bigotry, all genocide, and for all the small and crummy cruelties we human beings busily and blindly inflict on one another.

Mine is a simple spirituality: I am called to love my neighbor. Sometimes, despite an extensive and expensive theological education and few obvious hardships or dangers to distract me, I fail to do this very simple thing. I am brusque with a salesclerk or scowl at another driver in the parking lot, or I might just lose my temper and scream at my beloved son.

Oh yes, I have screamed at Peter. Why? Well, sometimes because, let's face it, the kid was bad. But mostly it was because I was tired, or afraid, or pissed off at the world or at myself. I am not so melodramatic as to compare myself with Hitler when remembering these failures (though Peter, now a teen, might do so), but I wince. So it becomes part of my spiritual practice to confess it: Forgive me, God, for I have at times been the Not-See, squinting, blinkered, foolishly resisting the light of love as it stubbornly, by grace, keeps shining.

Kate Braestrup with her son Peter, then 5, in 1994.

Tobias Wolff
AUTHOR OF *THIS BOY'S LIFE*

It's hard for me to imagine coming to an understanding of *spirituality* in a single moment. Does it mean a politician competing with other politicians over who is more born-again? A novice taking her final vows? A Buddhist monk setting himself on fire to protest government oppression? Or could it refer to the determination of an immigrant couple to sacrifice their lives in grinding, minimum-wage work so that their children might have something better? Perhaps the greatest problem with this word is the line it seems to imply between spirit and flesh, between some exalted, superior state and the experience of everyday life, when in fact they are all mixed up together. We define ourselves and our deepest values by the choices we make, day by day, hour by hour, over a lifetime.

Geoffrey Canada
PRESIDENT AND CEO OF HARLEM CHILDREN'S ZONE

My grandmother was a very spiritual person. She tried to save me because she knew that I, as a young boy growing up very poor in the South Bronx, believed that money was the key to everything. She tried to convince me that there was a God, but all I could do was look around and ask, *How could God let people like us, who don't do anything wrong, live in these conditions?*

During my sophomore year in college, my grandmother, who was the most righteous, perfect, spiritual person I ever met, got a very virulent form of cancer. One day it was just us in the room. She was in a lot of pain and dying. I had to ask her: "Grandma, do you still believe in God?" And she looked at me and said, "I believe in God more strongly than ever." That moment crystallized spirituality for me. Her faith and belief is something that has guided me from that point on. There's so much of the belief system that says that things happen to you because of something you've done, or you think there couldn't possibly be a higher order of things. But that's all part of the gift of life. It was something my grandmother knew; even at the end she understood that it was all a gift.

Patti Smith with her daughter, Jesse, then 5, and son, Jackson, then 10, in 1992.

Patti Smith
SINGER AND POET

When you look at the face of your child for the first time and you're immediately in love. That moment is total clarity—all of the 37 hours of labor, or that you had a lot of strife and you're going to have more strife tomorrow—there are no questions, nothing. Just love. And that moment happens over and over again.

James McBride
AUTHOR OF *THE COLOR OF WATER* AND *SONG YET SUNG*

When I was a boy, my godmother, Rachel McNair, used to sit me down in her living room and make me pray with her—which I did with great reluctance. She'd always pray, "Lord, let me be a blessing to somebody." She would preach God's word to anyone she saw in the Red Hook, Brooklyn, housing projects where I was born. She lived there more than 50 years.

McBride with his godmother, "Mother" Rachel McNair, 1989.

She could walk around the projects at any hour. Even the most hardened junkies respected her. When she died at home, peacefully, last year, I saw her just before the funeral home took her away. Her children had cleaned her face, washed and combed her hair. She looked beautiful. And even through my tears, I thought, *She has been such a blessing to me.*

I still dream about her now. I see her smiling. I know she's happy. And her prayer is the one that leaves my lips every night before I go to sleep: "Lord, let me be a blessing to somebody."

Francesco Clemente

ARTIST

When I paint, there is no thought of "I" and "mine." There is no thought of gain or loss. There is no hope for immortality, but rather hope to reach a timeless place. If I could live as I paint and keep a sense of humor too, only then could I claim to know what spirituality is.

Francesco Clemente's *The Ship of Time*, 2006.

Elaine Sexton

AUTHOR OF *CAUSEWAY*

HEAVEN

When my sister lifted the World War II
Army-green flight suit
from a bag, our dead mother,

as WAC, stepped into her empty
pant legs, returned to us
quiet as dust. We carried her up

from the basement. Mice, nesting
in waves of wrinkled wool, left
teeth marks in fabric. Her wartime

wedding band's vines
curled in my palm with an old rosary
blessed by Pope Pius VI

for my mother, a pregnant
believer, in Rome.
Still, I refuse to pray

on dead wood. Some days,
I confess, I caress a circle
of painted orange beads

with a coconut cross I bought
in a zócalo market. Sometimes
I find them to finger

in secret, walking home
from work in Manhattan. Once
I found them in a winter coat pocket

on a plane as the workers de-
iced the wings. You might call this
a prayer, a return to that moment,

that year I believed God
lived in Mexico's mountains.
Trees rushed the sky

as the sky, itself,
gathered thousands of migrating
monarchs. I saw them lift off,

saw the shape of my body, leaving
my body, on a ridge. My body
as air. Not one I'd known,

or had ever known. Not one
I'd seen, or had ever seen
before this. ◑

Beverly Donofrio outside her cabin, Nada Hermitage, Colorado, 2008.

Looking for Stillness

Life: mushy-gray. Spirit: empty. Solution: Get back in touch with God. **Beverly Donofrio** took off six months to go monastery-hopping, and discovered peace, clarity, connection, grace, and, finally, a kind of hush all over her world.

Two winters ago the world turned flat and tuneless on me, and it made no sense. Home was a lively, supportive expat community in an old colonial town in Mexico. I soaked in hot springs, hiked, practiced tai chi, wrote during the day, and spent most of my nights with friends. There were dinners, concerts, readings, margaritas watching the sunset, but it had all gone gray.

Not too long before, I could tap into a presence, a feeling of love—some would call it spirit, I called it God. I'd become one of those lucky people who knew as sure as the moon gets full that God exists and is in me and everyone else. But I couldn't sense the presence anymore. I meditated three times a day and felt no peace. I wasn't bored, exactly; it went deeper than that. I needed a God infusion. And so, while visiting my 8-month-old grandson in Brooklyn and needing to be alone to meet a deadline on a book, I had an inspiration. I wrote to the Abbey of Regina Laudis in Connecticut, a monastery of 40

Benedictine nuns who run a working farm on 400 acres, and requested a retreat. They wrote back immediately, offering two days.

Turning into the driveway, I spotted my first nun, speeding by in a pickup, a sweatband over her wimple, and something about that incongruity, about observing ancient practices in a speeding world, about working the land, praying with song, practicing silence, living on a commune and never leaving, quickened a longing in me.

For three services a day I sat in the chapel and observed the nuns behind a wrought-iron grill, chanting the hours in Latin. I felt the envy I used to feel in junior high school when I pored over the pictures in my brother's high school yearbook. I wanted to skip from layperson and observer to contemplative singing praises to God with my sisters.

Between chapel visits, I did manage to almost finish my book draft and to plant 200 lilies in the forest. The carpet of leaves soaked my knees, and birds twittered above me, as I buried each bulb thinking about stasis and new life, stagnation and transformation, dark nights and how they too can bloom—into holy joy.

I was aware of how I tend to imagine the future through rosy-colored glasses; high school, after all, had turned out to be closer to hell than heaven. Still, to test the waters once I was back in Brooklyn, I told my son how attracted I'd been to the monastery, and wondered what he thought about the possibility of my joining a place where I'd be cloistered—where he could visit me but I'd rarely be able to visit him. He put his hand on the counter to steady himself. "You know I'll feel abandoned," he said. "You won't see Zach graduate. You won't come to his wedding."

Most sadhus, or holy men, in India have had careers and families, but toward the end of their lives they leave it all to walk the path of enlightenment. Christ said a few times in a few different ways that you must be willing to give up everything, not only your riches but your family, too. You must lose your life to gain it. I understood how one must make God the focus, the ground zero of your being. But I also understood that God is love and doubted that he would ask me to abandon my grandson and my only child, who had no other parent.

I went back home and was distraught to find how lonely I felt despite my busy social world. The contemplative nun fantasies began to bombard me nonstop. Wearing a habit definitely factored in, which probably had something to do with my brother winning a nun doll at a local TV clown show when I was 8 and his refusing to give it to me. (I can still picture the little pearly beads on her rosary belt.) Plus, if I never had to sit for another expensive hair-cut in my life I'd be ecstatic. Did I really want to pick up another *Vogue* to gauge the length of hemlines this season—ever again?

I was 55 and my priorities had changed. The prospect of being freed from small conversations, maybe from all conversations, filled me with awe. I pictured myself walking down a hushed hallway, passing another nun and merely nodding. I craved silence and realized that I probably always had.

I decided to take six months to sample the life—and, in case I really was being called, see if I'd be led to a monastery that would have me.

An obsessive search on the Internet yielded a few discouraging facts. The monasteries all seemed to have age ceilings, by whose standards I was a dinosaur. And the contemplative orders were cloistered, which would mean, basically, no visits to my family. But since a rock-solid faith was what I aspired to, I tried to believe, and often succeeded, that if God wanted me in a monastery, God would work it out.

I can't re-create exactly the process by which I came to choose the places I did because logic was not much applied. For example, in Snowmass, the first place I visited, there was a Trappist monastery for men, which surely would not invite me to join. I stayed at Nada, a hermitage in the Carmelite tradition with women and men. I visited my friend Estrella—a hermit nun in an order of one. I wanted to try at least one place run by Catholics who were not in community, that was more a house of prayer, catering to retreatants. And I went to a monastery of Benedictine women who incorporate Eastern practices into their worship.

At Snowmass the snow fell and it fell. I covered my face with my scarf and dug my hands deep into my pockets as I walked to Lauds and Mass, to Vespers and Compline, down the mountain to the chapel whose lights beckoned in the dark. The Psalms were in English and I sang along with the monks and other visitors from a songbook, trying to blend my voice with theirs so well it disappeared. I cooked meals in my little octagonal hermitage and resumed my practice of meditating three times a day. But every time I sat on the cushion, my teeth began to ache. I thought it might be because my ego was threatened and trying to distract me, or maybe toxins were being released. I observed how the pain did make it harder to sit on the cushion, but the pain also took me deeper and made me more tender. I'd read somewhere that Christ's beginning point was not sin but suffering, that God didn't prevent pain but stood with you. I'd also read that one should try to talk to God as an intimate, as a friend, to bare your soul, to tell the secrets of your heart. I avoided this conversation. It was too hard; I had no idea why.

In the silence of Snowmass, my own silence shouted so loudly I heard the echo of all the words left unspoken in every relationship of my life. This realization made me so sad my body fisted into a ball as I wept. When I finally stopped, I wept all over again—from relief, because I remembered how deeply I did believe that anything is possible with God. Even intimacy. And I was not alone.

The night I arrived at Nada Hermitage was moonless and pitch-dark, but luckily Sister Kay, a radiant young woman in jeans, was waiting to show me the way. She said I'd find all the information I needed in a notebook in my hermitage, but she wanted to make sure that I understood that the monks were in the middle of hermit week, and if people didn't say hello it was not personal. She said that there were also hermit days during each week, and, in fact, if I wanted to be a hermit the entire time and never speak to a soul, I was welcome to do this.

In the light of morning I discovered that my little cabin—with a desk, chair, bed, two-burner stove, and tiny refrigerator—was backed into a sand dune. Immediately to the east was a 14,000-foot big-shouldered mountain and to the west the vast San Luis Valley, where the deer and the antelope play, just like in the song, only there are elk there, too.

I began to read spiritual classics with a hunger I hadn't experienced since I'd been a stuck young mother at 17 and literature lit up my life. Back then at the public library I'd found Dickens and Austen, then Tolstoy, Dostoyevsky, Virginia Woolf. Now I read contemplatives and mystics I found in Nada's library: Thomas Merton, Saint Teresa of Avila, Saint John of the Cross, Evelyn Underhill, and Brother Lawrence. One of the ancients said, "If you wish to attain God, there are two things you must know. The first is that all efforts to attain God are of no avail. And the second is that you must act as if you did not know the first." I believed that if I made room in my life for a practice of meditation, prayer, walking, reading, listening in the silence, one day the spiritual life would become real. As Plotinus said back in the third century about the experience of unity, "We ought not to question whence [it comes]; there is no whence, no coming or going in place; now it is seen and now not seen. We must not run after it,

> "Knowing God through intellect is like someone telling you all about her friend, but you don't know the friend."

but fit ourselves for the vision and then wait tranquilly for its appearance, as the eye waits on the rising of the sun, which in its own time appears above the horizon...and gives itself to our sight."

And so I listened in the silence and heard my own breath, a bird, a whisper of wind. I tried to remember to be grateful and send up little prayers of thanks all the day long, to look deeply at things, and to see the sacred in the every day. Then one afternoon it began to snow. I stood at my window, and all of a sudden everything slowed so that I could see flake behind flake for miles as though in a freeze-frame, but all of them moving ever so slowly, distinct and separate, together falling. Snow.

It was just as the mystic Bede Griffiths described these breakthrough moments, "...a veil has been lifted and we see...behind the facade the world has built round us.... It is impossible to put...into words; it is something beyond all words...in the language of theology they are moments of grace."

I wept for the gift of it, for the sight of a bunny darting by, a deer up on the hill nibbling on a weed. When it came time to leave Nada, I didn't want to. But I'd been told that the community was in no position to consider a new member—of any stripe. Their founder had been ousted and removed from the priesthood a few years before. The community was still reeling from it and trying to reimagine itself, a task that the nine members, five in Colorado and four in Ireland, would gather to carry out in the coming year.

I moved on to Missouri to visit Estrella, the hermit nun in an order of one, whom I'd met a few years before in Mexico, where she helped organize a hospital and midwifery school.

Our first evening, after Estrella lit candles and served and blessed our thick steaming vegetable soup, she prayed that my stay would give me clarity, and hoped I would talk as much as I wanted about all that was happening inside, about dreams, about anything, so she could help me with my spiritual discernment. I had a dream about caring for a baby I'd neglected. "It's God," Estrella said. I had another dream in which there was a stick in my salad. I poked it with my fork to bat it away, but it turned into a beautiful, regal bug, bedecked in jewels, wearing a crown. "That's you," Estrella said. "God made you a peacock. Somehow you will use that."

Now I grilled her about her nunhood, and she explained how after her three daughters were grown, she had visited 30 monasteries and convents looking for the one that was right for her and never found it. So she wrote her own vows, and with the blessing of her spiritual director, a Trappist hermit priest, she founded her own order. No bishop or pope has recognized her, but Estrella is the holiest person I know. Her altar is lit by candles that are never extinguished, and lined with pictures of those who have asked for her prayers. The phone rang with prayer requests every day. She counsels mothers, and while I was there she gathered food and clothes to bring to a single mother in need. Like the simple Brother Lawrence, she is in a constant dialogue with God. We practiced yoga together, prayed over our meals, sent up prayers of gratefulness for the littlest things: the honey in our tea, the warmth of her house, the car starting in the morning.

On Estrella's holy land, I began taking my lead from Julian of Norwich, a 14th-century woman mystic who said, "God wants us to allow ourselves to see God continually. For God wants to be seen and wants to be sought. God wants to be awaited and wants to be trusted."

One morning I awoke knowing what I had to do: make a commitment to God as I was never able to make to any other love in my life except my child. I wrote down three vows—Chastity, Silence, Constant Prayer then read them to Estrella, who took my hands in hers and said, "I am so happy for you!" We drove to Estrella's spiritual director, who blessed the vows in a Mass in his living room. No church official would recognize me as one, but that didn't matter, I was a nun.

At the Desert House of Prayer near Tucson I continued my study, my meditating, my silence. It was cold in January, and after Lauds and Mass in the morning the retreatants, sometimes as many as 20 of us, gathered silently to take our own breakfasts. There is a fire in the living room one can sit in front of, but in the kitchen if you sit at the table you can watch the birds at the feeders hanging from a big old paloverde tree.

The king of the birds was a cardinal, magnificently large and regally red. One day I spotted him sitting in another tree, yards away, minus his tail. He could still fly, and balance, but he was clearly diminished and waited till the crowd of birds dispersed before he came around to scavenge for seeds. I was sad for the bird, and concerned that he would die. I wondered if this diminishment of his abilities was a prelude, a preparation for death. And I wondered, too, if my own aging, the imminent diminishment of my own abilities, had at bottom been what fueled my desire to leave the world and draw closer to God. I also wondered if God had been calling me all along and I'd never heard. I'll never know. But I do know that by the time I left a month later, that big old cardinal had begun growing another tail. And I was thinking that instead of embarking on a Prelude to the end, I was beginning Book Two, in which God was my coauthor.

At Osage, in Oklahoma, the last monastery I visited, I grew fond of Father John. He was old himself and had once left the priesthood to teach 3-year-olds at a Montessori school. There was still much of the 3-year-old in Father John, who during Mass would give his homily, then open it up to the crowd, saying, "I'm not the expert here; I'm sure you all have things you want to say." And we did.

Father John told me that "knowing God through the intellect is like someone telling you all about her friend, but you don't know the friend until you meet him and experience him." This seemed to describe precisely how I was different at the end of my pilgrimage than I'd been at the beginning. God was here and God was somehow communicating to me that if I had faith the size of a mustard seed I could move mountains and learn to love, to be loved, to give and to receive, to be, as Mother Teresa said, Christ's representative in this world.

Still, I was in a bit of a panic, thinking about ending my extended retreat and going back to my life. I had no invitation from anywhere, although it did seem to me that I could continue to be a nomad, moving from monastery to monastery. But Nada, where I'd had the moment of grace in the midst of the snow, seemed to beckon me. So I wrote to the monks and proposed that I pay a little money every month, work a bit, gardening and running errands, and see how it plays out.

The community responded that they thought it was a very good idea. I rented my house and have now been in residence for eight months.

A mountain lion was recently spotted sleeping in a tree near my hermitage. I have climbed up to an alpine lake alone, and observe silence one week every month and four days of every week. I have no doubt that God, whom I sometimes call Pumpkin Pie and Bundle of Love, is here, just as he/she/it always was. But in a place where you can hear your own bare feet on the floor, where the stars touch the horizon all around, and hail can fall at any moment, in a place where the spirit becomes the reason and the focus, God is so much easier to know. **O**

Author Rick Moody takes a breather with his godson Clement.

The Godfather

Sure, it may be an old-fashioned role, but novelist **Rick Moody**, who is spiritual guide to four wild-haired moppets, takes his job seriously: no-nonsense truth-telling, baring his heart, backyard swordplay, and a willingness to turn pieties upside down.

It's a strange and archaic word, *godparent*. And maybe it's just as archaic a concept. That's what I was thinking about one day recently after spending an afternoon with my godson Clement, who is 8. It was the first time I'd seen him since his baptism, a baptism his parents had delayed quite a while. For years. They weren't certain into which particular brand of Christianity they wanted to baptize him, if any. Clement, upon getting

a good look at me, proffered an invitation, "Want to see my stuffed animals?" This easygoing Clement was soon supplanted by the Clement who wanted to stage a mock sword fight out on the lawn, one in which I had to use the *floppy* sword and agree to be symbolically run through. With his mop of long blond hair, Clement struck me, in all his paradoxes, as a perfectly sweet, modern kid. What on earth could I give to him that he didn't already have?

He lives in a beautiful home up in the country with deer on the lawn and a pond at the far end. He can walk outside at night and see a sky spilling over with constellations. He has gentle, brilliant parents who've made innumerable sacrifices on his behalf and who are more than capable of instilling in him a spiritual life if that's what they want to do.

Besides Clement, I'm godparent to three other youngsters. I have become a utility infielder in the area of godparenting. I married late in life, don't have any children of my own, and am thus *always* available. Go with the person who is willing and able to serve! So: There's my brother's oldest boy, Dylan; there's Lucinda, the second daughter of a friend who lives in New York's Hudson Valley; there's the aforementioned Clement; and then there's Wolfie, son of a high school friend who lives in northern Vermont.

Besides availability, one of the reasons I imagine that I am often asked to be a godparent is that I go to church. Alas, I don't go every Sunday, because I travel for work. And I like to change parishes and to visit other congregations. But I *do* subscribe to the greater part of Christian doctrine. I'm guessing that a dogmatic godparent looks a little bit like a meddler to many contemporary parents. Wolfie's mom—my friend Laura—made clear that even attendance at his baptism was not essential. In her view of godparenting, and it's one that I find admirably pragmatic, I am simply available in case Wolfie, when older, has questions about the spiritual life.

If going to church or temple or to the mosque is, arguably, the second most important quality for a godparent, the more important quality is a facility with *instruction,* with teaching a thing or two when needed. Is the godparent up to this? Personally, I have a long history of teaching. The mentoring and instructing part is not a stretch for me. But exactly what variety of instructing are we talking about? The sort of teaching I always disliked back when I was a student myself is the sort that involved lecturing and unyielding certainty about the material under scrutiny. Teaching that knows too well what it is meant to teach falls on deaf ears. Teaching does a better job when it's about listening. While none of my godchildren has so far *asked* to be instructed in his or her spiritual life, I remain ready to address the questions when the time is right. And it's likely I will begin by listening. Listening, as I understand it, is about letting Clement go through his entire retinue of stuffed animals, allowing him to take as long as he needs to take. Listening is about letting my nephew Dylan explain to me at great length his understanding of the world of *Star Wars*.

But I think there's yet another quality that makes for a good godparent in these times. More important than evangelizing. I think it has something to do with telling the truth.

And the particular truth I would like to share with my godchildren has to do with spiritual uncertainty. For me, spirituality inevitably entails a healthy dose of uncertainty about my religious life. In fact, uncertainty is as reliable a part of my practice as church on Sundays.

Perhaps a little history is in order. Despite my mother's interest in church and things spiritual, I was completely indifferent to religious education in early childhood. I went to church, as young people did in the suburbs, but I often felt that the insular, coffee-hour Christianity of Connecticut, the inwardly directed instead of outwardly directed faith, left me *out* rather than *in.* I never had many friends at church; I never served as an altar boy. I even found praying mystifying. What was it people were doing when they pressed their palms together? To me church seemed more about show than substance. Sometimes I thought I understood church and wanted to be part of it. But more often I had little interest at all. I'd never been baptized and neither was I confirmed. Like many kids my own age, I guess, I thought of the whole church experience as a bit sentimental. The tales of Jesus' birth and resurrection were lovely *stories,* but were they more than that?

This skeptical approach was fine for my early life, at least until I started experimenting with drugs and alcohol. After a number of teenage experiments with LSD in the mid '70s, I had what is often called a bad trip. In the grip of this drug, I suffered a lot of florid hallucinations, nightmares that became too real. In the aftermath of the experience, feeling unsturdy and fragile, I decided I needed to get baptized. I needed, I thought, the framework of churchgoing. I needed the security of it, and in this fraught and uncomfortable time, all the simplistic pieties of the church of my childhood seemed suddenly generous, bighearted, and welcoming. This is the kind of conversion experience that I can recommend to my godchildren, I think, the kind that has little to do with the herd mentality of churchgoing. I can recommend a spiritual life that is about wanting a direct experience of whatever God is, and which finds its origins in spiritual need.

It would be great if I could report that baptism changed everything, that my spiritual life ran in a straight line thereafter. But in my later teens and early 20s, I merely supplanted the drugs that made me think with drugs that prevented thinking, alcohol first among equals. Drinking has a long tradition among writers, and I wanted to write, and so I felt encouraged to apply myself ambitiously to the goal of having a drinking problem. And the first thing that got in the way of this was a spiritual life.

In local bars I spent a good eight or nine years feeling proud of militant atheism. Atheism, especially as articulated by thinkers like Marx and Freud in their astringent criticism of everything God-related, now seems to me a particularly fervent kind of spiritual belief. Atheism, I suspect, is just as certain as fundamentalism. But also favors nihilists. At the time, nihilism was the best I could do. Upon achieving a bankruptcy of the heart in my mid-20s, of the sort that alcoholism seemed uniquely equipped to deliver, I put aside the bottle, whereupon I finally came to feel, in earnest, that what was happening inside churches was something that I couldn't afford to avoid. I couldn't avoid the seriousness of it, I couldn't avoid the generosity of it, I couldn't avoid the sobriety of it. It wasn't much later that, as a more upright citizen, I acquired my first godson, Dylan.

Since then, my life in and out of church has been disorderly, intuitive, haphazard. Since quitting drinking, I have engaged in any number of spiritual disciplines. I have investigated going to seminary, I have declared myself a Buddhist, I have declared myself a Taoist, I have gone to Quaker services and admired the grace and simplicity of their plain speech, I have pursued some of the rigors of yoga, and I have visited a half dozen Episcopal parishes. I have been full of doubt about God and Christianity, I have been embarrassed, occasionally, by Christianity. And I have been happy, moved, even transported.

This brief catalog of spiritual successes and failures feels very American to me, maybe even very contemporary. My understanding of American life is that it takes place in a frankly religious country, but that our nation treats religious feeling the same way it treats fresh produce: "I'll take one of those, and one of those, and a half dozen of those." Maybe I have been guilty of this myself, the rootless supermarket approach to spiritual research that is more about search-

Vanquished! Godfather and godson in New York City, 2008.

ing than finding. In the consumer-oriented spiritual or religious world, revelations are not hard to come by, but do they last? You can always be *reborn,* that is, but accepting the profound and troubling consequences of your birth in the first place is much harder to do.

These days, I am trying to sit still in one spot, one parish, one faith. From this vantage point, I have a bird's-eye view of all that is troubling about contemporary faith. My church, the Episcopal Church, seems to be falling into division in newer and more violent ways every day—over such questions as the ordination of gay persons and gay marriage. I know what I think about these questions (I believe the church belongs to *everyone*), but that's about the only place in my spiritual life I *don't* have doubt.

If this is, finally, the kind of godparent I can be most truthfully, the one who is *uncertain,* the one who is full of doubt, can I still serve with confidence and with my whole heart? To this question I can respond with a resounding yes. I would like to offer Clem, for example, the kind of godfather who is perfectly willing to be run through with the floppy sword, without complaint, or to teach him the lyrics to "Highway to Hell," by AC/DC, and who believes that embodying a fragile, quixotic approach to spiritual life *is* pursuing the *god* part of godparenting at the same time that it's pursuing the parenting part. Not knowing is the beginning of learning, as they say, and being teachable is the beginning of wisdom. Uncertainty, and the patience that comes with uncertainty—the patience required to investigate and await results where spiritual life is concerned, perhaps even the patience, on occasion, to learn from my godchildren as much as they are meant to learn from me—these ambitions make, I suppose, for a rather flawed and very human godparent, but also one who is willing to live life as it is instead of lobbying on behalf of dogmas and a Manichaean fight between good and evil. This is exactly what I hope to pass along to my spiritual charges whenever required: contentment, uncertainty, and an open-mindedness about the spiritual life. ❶

Teaching does a better job when it's about listening.

Oprah Talks to Eckhart Tolle

The remarkable spiritual leader whose recent book Oprah calls the most important she's ever chosen for her book club explains how to free yourself from the tyranny of the past, live more fully in the present, and come to the calm, joyful place where intuition, creativity, and wisdom live and breathe.

Eckhart Tolle outside his home in Vancouver, British Columbia.

When I interviewed Meg Ryan eight years ago, she told me about *The Power of Now: A Guide to Spiritual Enlightenment,* by Eckhart Tolle. It's one of the most transformative books I've ever read; I keep a copy with me wherever I go, flipping through its highlighted pages time and time again. For anyone seeking to lead a more connected, vibrant life, *The Power of Now* is essential reading, and Eckhart's follow-up books—*Still-*

ness Speaks and *A New Earth*—explain the core principle that has resonated so deeply with me and many others: The only moment we ever really have is this one. Happiness isn't in the future or the past but in mindful awareness of the present.

Eckhart should know. By 29, the German-born author had become an eminent research scholar in comparative literature at the University of Cambridge in England, but success wasn't enough to halt his descent into a depression so severe that he considered ending his life. In what could have been his final hour, Eckhart stumbled upon an insight that started him on the path to becoming a spiritual teacher: We are not our thoughts. The very fact that we can objectively observe our thinking, he reasoned, suggests that the constant and often negative dialogue in our heads is separate from who we really are. Realizing this can bring us closer to the kind of fearlessness and peace that Eckhart has experienced since his dark night of the soul.

It was one of the great joys of my career to talk to Eckhart on *Oprah & Friends* on XM Satellite Radio as part of my Soul Series. He gave a kind of course on conscious living: trading our autopilot existence for intentional awareness; recognizing how we create our own suffering through obsessing over our past history; and learning how to be present, for ourselves and for the people around us, in a compassionate, nonjudgmental way. His encouraging inspiration has allowed me and many other people to see the possibility of an awakened consciousness. I think he is a prophet for our time.

OPRAH: In the beginning of *The Power of Now,* **you describe how, at 29 years old and considering suicide, you thought, "I cannot live with myself any longer.... Then suddenly I became aware of what a peculiar thought it was. Am I one or two? If I cannot live with myself, there must be two of me: the 'I' and the 'self' that 'I' cannot live with. Maybe... only one of them is real." I love this because it's the first time I thought,** *When I say I'm going to tell myself something, who is the "I" and who is the "self" I'm telling?* **That's the fundamental question, isn't it?**

ECKHART: That's right. Most people are not aware that they have a little man or woman in their heads that keeps talking and talking and whom they are completely identified with. In my case, and in many people's cases, the voice in the head is a predominantly unhappy one, so there's an enormous amount of negativity that is continuously generated by this unconscious internal dialogue.

OPRAH: What happened that enabled you to realize this?

ECKHART: One night, at the moment you were referring to, a separation occurred between the voice that was the incessant stream of thinking and the sense of self that identified with that voice, and a deeper sense of self that I later recognized as consciousness itself, rather than something that consciousness had become through thinking.

OPRAH: When you realized that the voice in your head was separate from the awareness, did it blow your mind?

ECKHART: Yes, it did. I didn't understand it; I just realized the next day that I was suddenly at peace. There was a deep sense of inner calm, although externally nothing had changed, so I knew something drastic had happened. A while after this transformation, I was talking to a Buddhist monk who said that Zen is very simple: You don't rely on thought anymore; you go beyond thinking. Then I realized that's what had happened. All that unhappy, repetitive thinking wasn't there anymore.

OPRAH: Where does our identification with these thoughts and this voice in our heads come from?

ECKHART: That identification that is derived from our thinking—which includes all of one's memories, one's conditioning, and one's sense of self—is a conceptual one that is derived from the past. It's essential for people to recognize that this voice is going on inside them incessantly, and it's always a breakthrough when people realize, *Here are all my habitual, repetitive, negative thoughts, and here I am, knowing that these thoughts are going through my head.* The identification is suddenly broken. That, for many people, is the first real spiritual breakthrough.

OPRAH: How is it spiritual?

ECKHART: I see it as not believing in this or that, but as stepping out of identification with a stream of thinking. You suddenly find there's another dimension deeper than thought inside you.

OPRAH: And what is that?

ECKHART: I call it stillness. It's an aware presence, nothing to do with past or future. We can also call it waking up. That's why many spiritual traditions use the term *awakening.* You wake up out of this dream of thinking. You become present.

OPRAH: Your book *Stillness Speaks* **is all about that awareness. I love this line: "When you notice that voice, you realize that who you are is not the voice—the thinker—but the one who is aware of it."**

ECKHART: That's right. The stream of thinking is connected with the past. All your memories, reactive patterns, old emotions, and so on, they're all part of that, but it is not who you are. That's an amazing realization. Of course, the mind may then say, *Well then, who am I?*

OPRAH: That's the big question. So what is the answer?

ECKHART: The answer is, who you are cannot be defined

through thinking or mental labels or definitions, because it's beyond that. It is the very sense of being, or presence, that is there when you become conscious of the present moment. In essence, you and what we call the present moment are, at the deepest level, one. You are the consciousness out of which everything comes; every thought comes out of that consciousness, and every thought disappears back into it. You are a conscious, aware space, and all your sense perceptions, thinking, and emotions come and go in that aware space.

OPRAH: You've often characterized thinking as a terrible affliction, even a disease, that is the greatest barrier to the power of now. But isn't to think to be human? Isn't that how we differ from other animals?

ECKHART: Yes, and thinking can be a powerful and wonderful tool. It only becomes an affliction if we derive our sense of who we are from this dream of thought. In that case, you're continuously telling yourself what I call "the story of me." For many people, it's an unhappy story, so they're always dwelling on the past. That's a dysfunctional and unhappy state.

OPRAH: We live in a world where most people believe they are their story. "I was born in this family, this is where I was raised, these are the things that happened to me, and this is what I did." If you are not your story, then who are you?

ECKHART: That's a very good question. You cannot deny, of course, that these events exist; one's personal history has its place, and it needs to be honored. It's not problematic unless you become totally lost in that dimension. How do you experience your past? As memories. And what are memories? Thoughts in your head. If you're totally identified with these thoughts in your head, then you're trapped in your past history. So, is that all there is to who you are? Or are you more than your personal history? When you step out of identification with that and realize for the first time that you're actually the presence behind the thinking, then you're able to use thought when it's helpful and necessary. But you are no longer possessed by the thinking mind, which then becomes a helpful, useful servant. If you never go beyond the thinking mind and there is no sense of space, it creates continuous conflict in relationships.

OPRAH: Tell me more about that space.

ECKHART: It's that spacious, aware presence that you can bring to any relationship. For example, when you listen to your partner or a friend or even an acquaintance, can you be there as the aware space that is listening? Or, while the other person is speaking, are you constantly thinking, preparing the next thing you're going to say? Are you judging and evaluating what you're hearing, or can you be there as the space for the other per-

As a student at the University of Cambridge, 1979.

son? I would say that's the greatest gift you can give someone. It's especially important for parents and children, but also in intimate relationships. Can you listen to the other person in that simple state of alertness in which you're not judging what you're listening to? If you can, then you're there as a presence rather than as a person. You're not imposing mental labels, judgments, or definitions on the other person. There's a deeper level of awareness.

OPRAH: For those of us who are still working with this idea of separating ourselves from that voice in our heads, how do we become a nonjudgmental space?

ECKHART: You can invite it by bringing more awareness of the present moment into your life. For example, I recommend that people bring a conscious presence to the everyday activities that they do unconsciously. When you wash your hands, when you make a cup of coffee, when you're waiting for the elevator—instead of indulging in thinking, these are all opportunities for being there as a still, alert presence.

OPRAH: Yes. Like when people take showers in the morning, they're not in the shower; they're thinking about getting to the office, what they have to do that day, and making lists instead of feeling the water, staying in the moment.

ECKHART: That's right. Bring those spaces into your everyday life, as many as possible. When you get into your car, shut the door and be there for just half a minute. Breathe, feel the energy inside your body, look around at the sky, the trees. The mind might tell you, *I don't have time.* But that's the mind talking to you. Even the busiest person has time for 30 seconds of space.

OPRAH: *The Power of Now* has saved me many, many times. As a matter of fact, this has been one of the most hectic days. I just got back from Africa. I'm sleep deprived, and I woke up this morning thinking, *Oh my God, I'm going to be so stressed*. But I let that go and just thought, *I will be present now*. I taped four television shows today, and I was very excited about being able to talk to you, but I kept saying to myself, *Don't think about how many other things you have to do. Just be present now*. And that is what has gotten me to the end of the day, in this moment.

ECKHART: That's a continuous refocusing on what really matters—what matters most in anybody's life, which is the present moment. People don't realize that now is all there ever is; there is no past or future except as memory or anticipation in your mind.

OPRAH: But that's what throws me: In *The Power of Now*, you say nothing ever happened in the past. But there has to be a past, because there are all our memories, all these ways we have defined ourselves.

ECKHART: Nobody can argue with the fact that there is such a thing as time. We used time to meet here—otherwise it would have been difficult.

OPRAH: Right. We agreed on this time, and we are here, because this is now.

ECKHART: Yes. So time is something that we cannot do without. We could even say time is what dominates this entire life that we experience here, the surface level of reality. It's completely dominated by time, which is the past and future in the continuous stream. People look to time in expectation that it will eventually make them happy, but you cannot find true happiness by looking toward the future. It's been said there are two ways of being unhappy: One is not getting what you want, and the other is getting what you want. If you think this, that, or the other thing will make you happy, when you get what you wanted, you will again be focusing on the next moment—never being in this moment, which is all we have.

OPRAH: That's another thing that changed me when I read *The Power of Now*: You wrote that all our stress is based on thinking about what happened in the past or what should be happening in the future, and that, no matter what crisis is going on in your life, if you're able to take a deep breath and look at what is happening now, in this moment, you're okay.

ECKHART: That's right. Many people identify their sense of self with the problems they have, or think they have. As a reality test, I ask people, "What problem do you have *at this moment*? Not in an hour or tomorrow, but what problem do

> "Even the busiest person has time for 30 seconds of space."

you have now?" Sometimes they'll suddenly wake up when they hear that question, because they realize that at that moment, they don't have a problem.

OPRAH: Maybe at that moment, during a lecture with you—but what if you're in a dangerous situation in the present moment? That's a problem! What then?

ECKHART: If danger arises in the present moment, there may be an emotion. There may even be pain. But that's a challenge, not a problem. For a problem to exist, you need time and repetitive mind activity. In a dangerous situation, you don't have time to turn it into a problem. So when people ask how they can get over their problems, I suggest that they go into the present moment and see what the problem is now. They always have to admit, "Well, right now I don't actually have a problem." Even people serving life sentences in prison have written to me to say, "I understood your message, and I have become free." They're free inside.

OPRAH: Okay, what if you're not in a dangerous situation but have normal, everyday problems? I have a lot of those swirling around right now.

ECKHART: Start by entering the present moment so you find that space in which problems cannot survive. In that moment, you contact a deeper intelligence than the conditioned thinking mind. That is the place where intuition, creative action, knowledge, and wisdom come from. Make sure you're not in a state of negativity with the present moment, because you can take action on the basis of negativity—for example, you might feel angry about not having much money. You work extremely hard and after some years you become wealthy. But all that action is contaminated by negativity if it comes out of anger, and it will create further suffering for yourself and others.

OPRAH: How can you change that?

ECKHART: See how you relate to this moment. When you do that, what you're really asking is, *What is my relationship with life?* The present moment is your life. It's nowhere else—never, ever. So no matter what the situation is when you align yourself with the present moment, find something to be grateful for. Gratitude is an essential part of being present. When you go deeply into the present, gratitude arises spontaneously, even if it's just gratitude for breathing, gratitude for the aliveness that you feel in your body. Gratitude is there when you acknowledge the aliveness of the present moment; that's the foundation for successful living. Once you've made the present moment into your friend through openness and acceptance, your actions will be inspired, intelligent, and empowered, because the power of life itself will be flowing through you.

OPRAH: Even if what's going on in that moment is making you uncomfortable.

ECKHART: Yes, even if the mind judges the moment as negative. Sometimes the mind will tell you there's no point in even trying. But you don't have to believe every thought that comes into your mind.

OPRAH: Do you practice this all the time? Are you always in the now?

ECKHART: Yes. Occasionally if, for example, I see somebody inflicting pain on somebody else, anger may arise briefly and pass through. But it doesn't link into the brain and create an enormous amount of useless thinking. Emotions can come and go, but I'm in a state of surrender to what is, because what is happening is already the case. You can't really argue internally with what is; if you do, you suffer.

OPRAH: But does accepting whatever is happening leave you passionless for life?

ECKHART: No. In fact, you are more passionately alive when you're internally aligned with the present moment. You let go of this inner resistance, which on an emotional level is negativity and on a mental level is judgment and complaining. People have an enormous amount of complaining going on in their minds. Some even do it out loud.

OPRAH: And usually they're complaining about what happened in the past.

ECKHART: Or what should be happening but isn't. These are ways of denying the present moment. That's a very dysfunctional state because you're basically denying life itself. There is no life outside of now.

OPRAH: All right, but then how do we plan for the future? We're all told that we should do that, not be passive about it.

ECKHART: Yes, and by planning for the future, you won't need to lose yourself in the future. The question is, are you using time on a practical level, or are you losing yourself in the future? If you think that when you take a vacation, or find the ideal partner, or get a better job or a nicer place to live or whatever it is, then you will finally be happy, that's when you lose yourself in the future. It's a continuous mental projection away from the now. That's the difference between clock time, which has its place in this world, and psychological time, which is the continuous obsession with the past and the future. There needs to be a balance between dealing with things in this world, which involves time and thinking, and not being trapped here. There is a deeper dimension in you that is outside that stream of time and thinking, and that's the inner stillness, peace, a deep, vibrant sense of aliveness. You're very passionate about life in that state.

OPRAH: Wow. That's what we're looking for here! *The Power of Now* is one of the most enlightening books I've ever had the privilege to read. Why did you feel the need to write a follow-up, *Stillness Speaks*?

ECKHART: The teaching evolved in the years after the book came out; I had some new perspectives on the basic truth. Also, there was more to be said about that which blocks the new consciousness in most of us; one way to describe it is the human ego.

OPRAH: This is my favorite thing to talk about. How does the ego block consciousness?

ECKHART: Well, first we need to see clearly what the ego is. It's not just being selfish or arrogant or thinking yourself superior; ego is identification with the stream of thinking. The beginning of ego is described in the Old Testament with the famous story of the apple: Adam and Eve ate the fruit of the tree of the knowledge, and they lost that state that is externalized in the Bible and called Paradise; they lost a deeper state of connectedness. I don't think it was as immediate as it's described in the Bible. To me, that story is about the rise of the ability to think, to make judgments: This is good, this is bad. And I believe it took a long, long time of increased thinking until people reached a point where they derived their entire sense of who they are from the stream of thinking, the mind-made entity composed of memories, past conditioning, and mental concepts. This is the ego that people identify with.

OPRAH: Your latest book, *A New Earth*, was my most recent book club pick and the subject of my first-ever Webcast course on oprah.com. In it you write that the ego is no more than identification with forms—physical forms, thought forms, emotional forms—and that if evil has any reality, this is also its definition: complete identification with form.

ECKHART: That's right.

OPRAH: And that it results in a total unawareness of connection with every other being, as well as with the source, and this forgetfulness is the original sin. When I read that, I thought, *You're right*. Every evil act or sinful thing we've heard described is due to a complete disconnection, a lack of understanding that I am the person or being that I am attempting to violate.

ECKHART: Yes. By living through mental definitions of who you are, you desensitize yourself to the deeper aliveness of who you truly are beyond your thoughts. What arises then is a conceptual identity: I'm this or that. Once you're trapped in your own conceptual identity, which is based on thinking and image-making by the mind, then you do the same to others. This is the beginning of pronouncing judgments on others, and then you believe that judgment to be the truth. It's the beginning of desensitizing yourself to who that human being truly is.

OPRAH: You also wrote that we identify with labels in *A*

With partner and associate Kim Eng in England, 2004.

New Earth, and that the more exclusive the label is, the more we identify with it.

ECKHART: Every ego wants to be special. If it can't be special by being superior to others, it's also quite happy with being especially miserable. Someone will say, "I have a headache," and another says, "I've had a headache for weeks." People actually compete to see who is more miserable! The ego doing that is just as big as the one that thinks it's superior to someone else. If you see in yourself that unconscious need to be special, then you are already free, because when you recognize all the patterns of the ego—

OPRAH: **What are the other patterns?**

ECKHART: The ego wants to be right all the time. And it loves conflict with others. It needs enemies, because it defines itself through emphasizing others as different. Nations do it, religions do it. If you identify with one particular religion, you need the nonbeliever—the other—to feel your own sense of identity more strongly.

OPRAH: **You've explained this by saying that it starts when a baby first reaches for a toy, and if the toy is taken away or not given to them, they say, "No, that's mine."**

ECKHART: That's the beginning of identification with things.

OPRAH: **And what happens is, we all grow up and just get** bigger toys.

ECKHART: Yes. Ego is always identification with one form or another, which could be a possession—my house, my car, and so on. Your sense of who you are is in that thing. If that thing is then criticized by somebody else, you become extremely defensive or aggressive because your sense of self is being threatened. There are other forms of identification; opinions are mind forms. "I am right" implies, of course, that somebody else has to be wrong.

OPRAH: **But tell me this: As long as we are in this human form, we must need the ego; otherwise we would have evolved out of it.**

ECKHART: We're evolving out of it now. The ego has been here for thousands of years, and that means it has its place in the evolution of humanity. But our ability to think more and more, so that gradually we became identified with thinking, was how we lost a deeper connectedness with life—with Paradise. I believe we are now at an evolutionary transition where far more human beings than ever before are able to go beyond ego into a new state of consciousness.

OPRAH: **You've said that we face a very stark and daunting choice—evolve or die.**

ECKHART: This is the point where the evolution of consciousness, the awakening of humanity, is no longer a luxury. The effects of the dysfunctional ego are now being amplified by technology. What we are doing to ourselves, to our fellow human beings, and to the planet is becoming more and more destructive and devastating.

OPRAH: Yes. I was speaking with Elie Wiesel, and he was saying that this will be known as the Sick Century because of our ability to do the sickest, most evil things to one another. And you're right: Because of technology, there are even greater bombs, ammunition that can kill from farther distances.

ECKHART: Sometimes people ask me if things are getting better or worse, and my answer is, at the moment, both; things are getting better and worse. There are two streams in existence now: One stream is the old, unenlightened, egoic consciousness, which is still continuing. You see it when you watch the news. The other stream is us sitting here now, talking. I'm not saying we're special, but the fact that we're addressing this and that many, many people are reading it and it's meaningful to them means there is another stream here, which is the stream of humanity awakening. Both are present at this time.

OPRAH: How can we not allow ourselves to be dominated by the ego? I know it's a lifelong process, but what can we begin to do today?

ECKHART: The ego cannot survive in stillness, so invite stillness into your life. It doesn't mean that stillness is something you get from outside; it's realizing that underneath the stream of thinking, everybody already has the stillness.

OPRAH: So you don't have to go to Hawaii and sit on a mountaintop.

ECKHART: No, and you don't have to do anything to create it because it's already there. Look very deeply into yourself and see your sense of "I-ness"—your sense of self. This "I" is bound up with the stillness. You're never more essentially yourself than when you are still. You can invite stillness into your life by taking a few conscious breaths many times during the day. Just observe your breath flowing in and out. Another way is to feel the aliveness of your body from within. Ask, Is there life in my hands? And then you feel it. It's subtle, but it's there. Is there life in my feet, my legs, my arms? You can feel that your entire inner body is pervaded by a sense of aliveness, and that can serve as an anchor for stillness. It doesn't mean you turn completely away from the external world. It brings balance into your life between being still and being able to deal with things out here.

OPRAH: It's finding the space in between.

> "Underneath the stream of thinking everybody already has the stillness."

ECKHART: That's right. And you may also become aware of a short silent space between two thoughts. When you become conscious of that, then it becomes a little longer, so you have a longer gap of stillness.

OPRAH: But if you become aware for so long that you start thinking about it, then you lose it.

ECKHART: The moment you say, "Oh, look, I'm not thinking!" you're thinking again.

OPRAH: What did you mean when you wrote in *Stillness Speaks*, "Look at a tree, a flower, a plant. How still they are, how deeply rooted in Being. Allow nature to teach you stillness"?

ECKHART: When you watch a tree, just be there as the aware presence perceives the tree. Nature is very helpful for people who want to connect with the stillness. Man-made things generate more thinking because they are made through thinking. Go to nature. Eventually you can sustain the state of stillness even in the midst of a city. I enjoy walking along busy streets with infernal noise and people rushing about and feeling the deep sense of stillness in the background.

OPRAH: So it's like being in the world, but not of it.

ECKHART: That's exactly what it is.

OPRAH: You've said that spirituality has nothing to do with what you believe but everything to do with your state of consciousness.

ECKHART: It's the stillness that's the spiritual dimension.

OPRAH: And beliefs are not spiritual?

ECKHART: No, because beliefs are thoughts. Thought in itself is not spiritual, though it can sometimes be helpful because it can be a pointer. If we say, "Find the stillness that's already inside you," that's a thought, but the thought is pointing beyond itself.

OPRAH: At the end of *A New Earth* you say that the foundation for a new earth is a new heaven, the awakened consciousness.

ECKHART: Yes, and that's a wonderful thing. Jesus said, Heaven does not come with signs to be observed. It is already within you.

OPRAH: The stillness.

ECKHART: Yes.

OPRAH: Do you think it will ever be possible to live peacefully in the now, or is that too much of a lofty goal?

ECKHART: Rather than asking if you can ever be free, because "ever" is a huge amount of future time, ask if you can be free at this moment. The only place where you can or need to be free is this moment. Not the rest of your life. Just now. ⬛

DATING, MATING, RELATING

couples

The Snail Whisperer

Can a woman who's always trying to get closer find happiness
with a man who's happily curled up in his shell? Catherine Newman
takes a step back—and a leap forward.

Last summer, in the low-tide shallows of Cape Cod, my young son and his best friend hummed a sea snail out of its shell. It's a trick they'd learned from a visiting marine biologist at their school: The children held the shell up to their peachy, softly droning faces and the snail craned its shy neck out to listen. The snail stretched up its tentative little horns and the children smiled back.

Oh, to be humming and gentle! Me? I'd more likely rap on his shell with restless knuckles: *Anybody home in there? Hel-lo?* I'd nag after his soft, hidden self: *Are you even listening to me? Hel-lo?* Perhaps I'd chide the snail for acting so withdrawn or accuse him of passive aggression. And I'd wonder, hurt, why he didn't reveal more of himself to me. There may be much to recommend fierceness as a style of devotion— what with its hunger and bared teeth, its con-

FAR AWAY, SO CLOSE: Catherine and her husband, Michael Millner, 2007.

stant crescendo of connecting—but patience is a virtue, and I am not virtuous. Silence is golden, and I am not golden. Fools rush in, and, oh, I can be such a fool.

The surest way to intimacy is to turn myself into a kind of whining, boring power tool. I trust I'm correct in my approach here. *What are you thinking? Why did you say that? What did you really mean? Then why did you put your fingers to your forehead like that? Yes, you did.* The trick is to locate tiny, remote pockets of privacy and then drill at them— *zjh zjh zjhhhh*—like they're abscesses. The trick is to express love the way a cuckoo clock expresses time.

I have lived with him for 17 years. For 17 years, his dark hair has fallen into his dark eyes. Even now I might catch sight of him at a party and catch my breath because for a second I'm not even sure who he is. *Who is that gorgeous hunk of... Oh! It's my husband!* He's the kind of person who picks you up from the airport, makes you a cup of tea, and listens while you talk about your feelings, his eyebrows raised in baffled alarm. He's the kind of person whose affection is a wide and bottomless sea, only the water's maybe not as salty as you thought it was going to be. When he cares daily for our children and me—lunch, bad dreams, the to-and-fro of car trips and conversation—I remember the relationship between *tend* and *tender.* His heart is a string of mild, sunny days.

And I have loved him like a hurricane. I have loved him like a scalpel. I have loved him like poison ivy on the dog's paws, like a rock in his shoe, like chewing gum stuck under the table of his heart. Every day for 17 years I have been Columbus sailing up to the continent of his being, and every day for 17 years I have tried to plant my flag on its beach. Some days the gentle people living there have grinned, turned their hands palm up, and offered me unspeakable treasures. Other days, when it seems clear that what I'm spreading is nonnative vegetation and disease, they've chased me away with canoe paddles; they've even suggested to me, through gestures and grimacing, that colonizing might be a funny way to express one's love. Indeed, it might be.

He is pressed flat up against the wall of our marriage, and still I'm saying, "Come closer, my darling." But there's no room for him to move, and I'm actually crushing his rib cage a little bit. It's not a Venus/Mars situation as much as an astronaut/moon one. "What's with your whacked-out gravitational field?" I'm asking. "Why are you so far away?"

I want to look at the photo albums from when we were young, from when we were first in love, from when the children were babies. I want him to say, "These photographs fill my heart with a thousand white and flying doves of nostalgia." And he does, in a way, but the words are about a lamp we once had or a canyon we camped near or the grunting baritone goose impersonation I did while I labored with our firstborn. He does not talk much about his mother's catastrophically short life, but he might remember suddenly the way she cooked zucchini. He is no fountain spraying silver arcs of feelings into the air, but he's a cupful of snow, and if I'm thirsty, I'd do better to thaw it with my breath than continue to curse the cold.

But sometimes I rail against his otherness as if it were a cage or the tiger in it or one of those wedding sheets with a hole sliced into it for intercourse. When really

> Sometimes I rail against his otherness as if it were a cage or the tiger in it. When really what I know is this: To chip away at difference is to make the mistake of a lifetime.

what I know is this: To chip away at difference is to make the mistake of a lifetime. You think you want him to serenade you with all your favorite songs—and you do, of course—but what you really want is to lie in bed and listen to the love of your life strumming the guitar, singing softly to himself when he thinks everybody's asleep. You think you want the topiary trimmed neatly into the shape of a husband, when what you really want is that wild and sheltering maple, all dappled starlight, its helicopter-seedpods fluttering down in the breeze.

Two identical flints lying side by side in the dark are not exactly going to make a spark now, are they?

For some reason, I am best able to value this—the difference and distance between two minds—when the person I'm talking to is a child. In the car, with K.D. Lang on, for example, I say aloud, "Her voice always sounds like something liquid and smooth—it makes me picture a river of heavy cream rippling down a mountain," and my son says, "I know exactly what you mean. Whenever you talk about time? About this o'clock or that o'clock? I think about lemons." I turn my face to look at him, and he smiles, all mystery and light. Who knew? Another person is like a geode lined with hidden glittering. On a clear day, I understand this: The crystals wink out at me here and there, and I am filled with gratitude for the unseen. On a foggy day, I wonder about taking a hammer to it, cracking it into a million pieces to get a better look.

Come New Year's Eve, I lie with an ear to his bare chest, talking. I'm talking about my resolution to talk less. I want to listen, accept, and cherish. I'm not a child on the beach, as sweet and sparkling with sand as a sugared pastry, but I'm thinking about the kids with their snail and I'm vowing patience. "What about you?" I say, when I am nearly done talking, "What's your resolution?" There's a moment of silence, his strong arms around my back, before he says, "You know when you tear off a piece of floss that's really too short to use but you don't want to waste it so you use it anyways? I'm just going to throw it away and start with a fresh piece. I'm not even going to struggle with it." I lift my face to look at him, and he smiles and winks. Then he ducks his inscrutable head to kiss me on the mouth. ◖

Amy Bloom with her husband, Brian Ameche, at home in Connecticut, August 2008.

Eyes Wide Open

How do you know what you're getting into with another person? How can you tell what you really need? Novelist and therapist **Amy Bloom** offers an intensive session in cultivating insight and understanding. Lesson 1: Know Yourself.

I t's a good and bad thing to be considered an expert in love. I don't think there's any point in pretending that you get to be an expert by meeting your soul mate early on, going through a few meaningful ups and downs, marrying in a cloud of good taste or even in a meteor shower of funk and crunk, and then dying, 50 or 60 years later, having had a faithful and fulfilling love life. We don't call those people experts. We call them lucky.

People like me, who write about lust and love in fiction and nonfiction, who have clearly made several important and completely necessary detours in their private life, people who have more than one wedding ring in their jewelry box, these people we call experts.

Go figure.

Here's the heart and the head of it: Know yourself, know the other, and face the truth about yourselves.

What "Know Yourself" Means

Here's what I noticed after 25 years of being a psychotherapist and 55 years of being a person: There is just about no point in complaining about another person. Not because other people aren't annoying. (My God, there are people who've been put on this earth just to make me roll my eyes and mutter disapprovingly. In my family, as a matter of fact, "other people" is the standard explanation for almost all misfortune.) But because—especially in intimate relationships—the complaint about Him or Her will, unfortunately and inevitably, wind its way around to You.

He's often late, which is inconsiderate = I fear not being sufficiently appreciated. Thanks, Dad.

He thinks about his needs first, and mine second = If you express your needs, no one will love you. Thanks, Mom.

Your partner's faults are real (I'm on *your* side here) and various and even grievous, but those are their faults and, frankly, we're here to talk about you...and me.

I went to see my former therapist, for a tune-up, shortly after I remarried. I wanted, on the one hand, to tell him how blissfully happy I was, because I knew that he'd be happy for me, and because I was in that stage of love where I would have paid people to listen to me talk about my wonderful husband. (I had already exhausted my friends, my family, my cleaning lady, and the mailman, who was nice enough to say, regularly, "Sounds like a great guy.") On the other hand, I wanted to complain. My husband was wonderful—but not perfect. This was very upsetting.

Dr. Shrink: So let me make sure I understand—on two occasions, in the course of the last year, he had too much to drink and at least once a week he comes home from work later than he said he would, and although he usually calls about being late, he doesn't always, and sometimes you have to poke him to get him to acknowledge that you've been kept waiting.

Amy: Yes. (The implication of my "yes" is: Feel free to sympathize; also, anytime you'd like to discuss his imperfections and their likely source, go right ahead.)

Dr. Shrink: I want to make sure I understand—

Amy: Yes. (Meaning: Let's get started—he's selfish, possibly unreliable, and impulsive....)

Dr. Shrink: You came to see an expensive psychoanalyst to tell me that the man you married has faults of which you've been aware since you've known him? *This* is why you're here?

Amy: Yes.

(*So not what I was hoping for.*)

We then spend some time on how terrifying I find it to love someone so much and how difficult I find the possibility and the likelihood of disappointment. We do get somewhere, and when Dr. Shrink stops, my best friend takes over. She says to me basically: No one's perfect. It's time you stopped being surprised by this. The question is, do you take this bundle of faults over some other bundle of faults?

I do.

But it's not enough for me to choose this bundle of faults; if I want a love that lasts, I better know why this bundle suits me so well. At first, one loves the faults because they are part of the whole adorable love package. She is a sweet and tenderhearted creature, and her inability to ask for a raise, hail a cab, or defend herself from her unpleasant mother are all part of her sweetness. Of course, someday when you're standing in the rain with your armful of packages and ask her to flag that cab across the street and she says, winsomely, "Oh, darling, I just couldn't—it's so...aggressive"—it will be less adorable. He is determined and unswerving, which is great; he is also hardheaded and heedless. As much as you like the former, you better be comfortable with the latter as well. Understanding why is worthwhile, and usually involves a quick review of parents. Whether or not they had a wonderful marriage you hope to emulate or a disaster you hope to avoid, it's helpful to know which parent you identified with and which parent's part you want to play. (Don't even bother trying to escape both of them entirely; to do that, you'd have to be born into another species.) I think the biggest mistake I've seen in clients and friends and myself is acting on half an understanding: "I don't want to marry my selfish father; look how unhappy he made my sweet mother," sounds like a reasonable, even psychologically astute position, and an awful lot of people (including me) marry their nice mothers (or their nice fathers; bullies come in both genders) and think they've protected themselves. All I can say is: Not so fast, Shorty.

I was always saddened by the lack of intimacy in my parents' marriage, which was a burden for my mother and none at all for my father.

Consider: Marrying your sweet parent may mean that *you* end up playing the bully's role (someone's got to handle the rough stuff). Alternatively, marrying your dear and gentle dad may mean that you get someone with not just Dad's gentleness but his passivity, avoidance of conflict, and fear of public disapproval as well. The man who comforts you quietly after a battle with your mother is a good father—do you have any idea what he was like as a husband? And another thing you ought to wonder about—why didn't your nice parent get what they wanted from the marriage? I was always saddened by the lack of intimacy in my parents' marriage, which was a burden for my mother and none at all for my father, until I suddenly thought: *Why did she marry him?* My mother was good enough, and honest enough, to tell me: I married him because he was tough and ambitious, so I wouldn't have to be. I married him because he was more interesting than the dentists and accountants who asked me. And although I love getting flowers and hearing sweet nothings, and there have been damn few of those, I'm not like you, honey, I don't want intimacy—I just want companionship and romantic gestures. As my mother said to me on another occasion: I like the roses, but not if I have to put up with the thorns. Everyone should be so honest with themselves, and her honesty made me aware that I would accept an awful lot of thorns to be with someone who craves intimacy the way I do. (And I got that someone, which is why I now have a very close and often tumultuous marriage, with a degree of attachment that people find either very sweet or very peculiar.)

So know yourself and know your family. For me that means knowing that, as much as I appreciated my mother's sweetness and practical ways, I need a slightly reckless lion more than I need a sensible lamb in my life. (In the dictionary, right next to a number of hard-charging mammals—including the weasel, famous for attacking animals larger than itself for no reason—you will see my husband's picture.) So, finally, I married a lion, and although I never pictured myself being the person hanging on to the "oh shit" bar on the passenger side, saying, "For God's sake, honey, slow down!" I do prefer that to being the person who says, regularly, "It's okay, honey, if you're scared, we can turn around."

What "Knowing the Other Person" Means

When you look at another person's behavior (and please, do look at what he does, not just how he explains what he does. A man with a good and different explanation for each of the five times he's stood you up is a really good…explainer. Did you want to marry a world-class explainer?), the question will arise: Is it character or circumstance? Did he do what he did because of who he is, at his core, or was he pushed to that behavior by circumstance? Guess what? Pretty much, after 18, it's character, every time. It's true that under extraordinary circumstances—baby trapped under car, grandmother stuck in burning building—you might see some hitherto unsuspected heroism emerge in someone you thought had not a drop, and even so, what you learn from that is: He had a drop of heroism in him, after all. But it is also true that even a man pushed to robbing a bakery for bread for his starving child will show who he is by how he conducts himself during the robbery.

It's not true, despite what the advice columnists often write, that a man who leaves his wife for you will eventually leave you. It is true that a man who leaves his wife for you is capable of leaving you, and you would be smart to look at how he conducted himself during his divorce because no matter how crazy, bitter, unreasonable his ex was or is, his behavior reveals his character. You cannot behave cruelly without having some cruelty in your nature (and most of us do). An angry man who honors his obligations gracefully, a man who shows up on time to see his kids, even when their mother behaves badly—that man is a good bet.

I've also discovered that the Virtuous have their downside. A man who cannot face his own flaws or acknowledge the ugliness (not horrors—just normal human flaws: envy, jealousy, pettiness) in his nature, a man who will patiently explain, for days on end, that you should not be hurt by his behavior because he's a good guy who didn't mean to hurt you—may actually prove to be worse company, in the long run, than a guy who behaves badly from time to time and admits it. (Or at least, that's how it is for me. Deeply, Determinedly Virtuous people scare me.) As it turns out, I prefer the full boil to the long simmer and I wish I'd known it sooner.

When I met my future husband (well, not exactly when I met him; then I thought he was arrogant and needed a haircut), he reminded me just a little of someone. It wasn't my mother (we've been through that, and let me tell you, a lot of women, gay and straight, do marry their mothers) and it wasn't my father (there isn't enough therapy in the world to get me to that point). It wasn't a previous beau or spouse (in fact, at the Cocktail Party of Life, you'd find my husband at one punch bowl with a platter of spareribs, pouring a bourbon into the bowl, flirting with old ladies, amusing babies, encouraging dancing, and conspicuously enjoying himself, and my previous partners, all fine people, would be at a different punch bowl altogether).

Here's how I knew this guy was the right guy, and here's why I married him—despite all the very good reasons that no one should ever marry for a third time: He reminded me of the best father figure of my life, my ninth-grade English teacher. My own father was a responsible, hardworking, self-centered guy who occasionally enjoyed a game of tennis and was devoted to good newspapers and good cigars. He had no friends, not much joie de vivre, no sentimentality, and the romantic soul of a doorstop. (Let me say: His curiosity, his intelligence, his perseverance, his utter indifference to public opinion, and his straightforward analysis of most things were wonderful qualities and make me a better person.) When my surrogate father died, his large circle of friends (80-year-old poker buddies, pals from his teaching days, devoted former students ages 20 to 60) wept. He was old, fat, diabetic, and often short-tempered. Women desired him and children adored him and most men liked his company a great deal. He was loyal, imperious, needy, charming, bighearted, and just about the most pigheaded, interesting, and fearless person I had ever known. And then I met my husband. And from the big heart to the soulful brown eyes, I couldn't shake the feeling that I had come home at last.

Know Yourselves

Be real and be unashamed, even of your faults. I do truly know what he's made of and vice versa. We are both people who want cutmen and foxhole buddies; we see life as wonderful and difficult and requiring energy and stamina and, occasionally, guile. We don't mind any of that. We are both bossy and demanding and largely unrepentant. We don't mind any of that. We yell. We apologize profusely. We are idiosyncratic in our tastes, and we are both quite confident that our taste is better than most people's (including each other's). We take sex and family and food seriously and organized religion not at all. We are hard to embarrass and we cry like babies. We are each what the other hoped for.

> Be real and be unashamed, even of your faults. I do truly know what my husband is made of and vice versa.

Would You Marry Him Again?

If you want the perfect marriage, go to a Doris Day movie. Actress **Rita Wilson** learns a big fat Greek secret from her mother.

I t's a sunny, Sunday California morning. My husband is driving my mother, father, and two of our four children to church. This is the same church where I was baptized with my brother (two for the price of one!), where my sister was married and I was her maid of honor, and where my husband and I were married 20 years ago and both our youngest children were christened in the same baptismal font where, lo those many years ago, my brother's and my cries were applauded and celebrated.

Driving on the freeway, my mother, who is vibrantly curious after 86 years of life and 56 years of marriage, tells us about something she heard on the radio. She had been pondering this question, thanks to the airwaves: If you knew at 25 what you know today about your spouse, would you still marry the same person?

Since it is already a beautiful day, my husband and I add to its beauty by responding instantly, that, yes, we would marry each other knowing what we know now. My father, although not usually available to this sort of dis-

cussion, generously engages and answers that, yes, he would marry my mother all over again. My mother, always interested in good discussion, responds delightfully in her thick Greek accent as if she knows the question to the "Double Jeopardy" answer: "Not me!"

Now, please understand that my parents are Greek and Bulgarian. The idea that this is a subject that one would only discuss after five years of therapy never enters anyone's mind. (When you are Mediterranean, you just speak now, argue later...or maybe you eat now, argue later.) Certainly, these two people, who are sitting with their arms brushing against each other, are not about to announce they are splitting up. I'm pretty sure that after nearly six decades, three children, and six grandchildren, they have the marriage thing down. But I have no idea where my mom is going with this.

Before we go anywhere, though, let's start at the beginning. In 1946 my Bulgarian dad "jumped ship" in Philadelphia, making his way to New York City, eagerly learning English while working at the St. Regis Hotel. My Greek mother had escaped from her ethnically Greek but geographically Albanian village during the war, arriving in New York via Athens with her mother, sister, and two brothers.

My parents met in 1950 in New York City at a Greek-Bulgarian dance. My dad eyed my mom across a crowded room and asked her to dance. He wooed her briefly and then asked her to marry him. My mother, still new to the United States, thought maybe she should wait a bit before she got married— sow some oats, or sew some coats, really, because that was her job at a factory. After a few dates, and no acceptance of my dad's proposal, they amicably parted ways.

Rita with her mother, Dorothy, and her father, Al, in Los Angeles, 2004.

A year later, they met again. A friend of my mother's saw my handsome dad across the dance floor and declared, "If you don't want him, I do. He's nice." There is nothing like someone else's recognition of a good catch to wake you up. My mom, now another year older, realized that she missed my dad, and that she'd only sewn coats, and had sown no oats. So she pushed her friend aside like some desperate contestant on *Dancing with the Stars* and box-stepped the night away.

My parents didn't have a sweep-you-off-your-feet sort of romance. They were both too practical for that. But they loved each other and saw the goodness each possessed. Soon they found themselves planning their wedding, their lives, and their future. About three weeks before the wedding, my dad had some concerns. He worried he might not be able to live up to my mom's expectations. My dad and she spent a few days apart and then talked about their expectations, which weren't major. My mom asked him to be baptized Greek Orthodox. No problem. My mom knew Dad wasn't the most romantic person in the world. Fine. Once they realized that they did want the same thing, they had a double wedding with my mom's brother and his wife on June 10, 1951.

After a few years in New York City, they got a call from my mom's sister and her husband, who'd moved to Los Angeles. So they loaded up the truck and they moved to Beverly...I mean, Hollywood. Swimming pools, movie stars, and the beginnings of a family. My mom was pregnant with my sister soon after arriving. Three and a half years after that, I was born (so I could spill the beans on my parents in a national publication), and then, two years later, my brother.

On the weekends, my dad would pile us all into the Batmobile, a 1950-something black Plymouth convertible with a push-button transmission, which resembled Bruce Wayne's very car, and take us to Griffith Park, in the shade of the Griffith Observatory, for his weekly volleyball game. My mom would wrangle us to fill jugs of water from a spout emerging from a stone wall that was supposedly "spring" water. Hey, in Greece water came out of a spring, why not in Hollywood? At home after the game, my dad would barbecue, Greek-style (no Southern barbecue sauce for us, only oregano, garlic, and lemon), and as the sun set, we kids would watch TV as my parents cleaned up.

I never remember my parents complaining. I never heard either of them say they were tired, or bored, or mad. I remember my dad saying, "God bless America" practically every day of my life. I remember my dad and his brother building an addition to our house one summer while we decamped to Oceanside to be near the beach and away from the dusty construction. I remember my mom sewing our bedspreads, curtains, and clothes and cooking Greek food but also making peanut butter and jelly sandwiches in an attempt to assimilate. I remember my parents laughing together.

Not only did my parents laugh, they cracked us up, too. Get this: My mom would do impersonations of all the kids in the neighborhood. You haven't lived until you've heard a Greek immigrant lady say "bitchin'." My dad had his own special talents, as well. On one outing to the zoo, as we came upon the hyena cage, my dad started howling like a wolf and made the hyenas howl back at him. We could not believe that there, in the middle of Los Angeles, my dad was making hyenas talk to him. So, my mom could impersonate kids and my dad could impersonate animals. Go figure. We were like a Disney movie with an accent.

And now I'm here in the car on a Sunday thinking, *Who knew? My mom not only impersonates teens but can also pretend she has been happy all these years. Because now she is saying maybe she made a mistake?* I remember something else she recently said about relationships. She announced, in her imitable Greek accent: "You know how they say, 'Opposites attract'? Well, later on, opposites attack!" I'm about to find out either that after 56 years of marriage my mom has been the Best Actress Ever or that the "opposition" has been attacking for some time unbeknownst to me. I tell my husband to make a left, not follow the car in front too closely (not that I'm bossy), and ask my mom what exactly she means.

She says, "Don't get me wrong. I love your dad. I always have. We created a beautiful life together and I wouldn't change a thing, but now I know that I like to talk. When I was younger, I didn't know how much I needed that. Back then, people married for life. I didn't really think about things like *Will he watch* The Ed Sullivan Show *with me?* We both just wanted to have a good life and healthy kids. Do I wish we had long, soulful talks? Sure. If I had known then that I needed that, I may have chosen a different kind of person, but I also knew he was a very good man."

My parents didn't demand from each other what we seem to demand today from our relationships. My dad loved sports but didn't insist she be on the golf course handing him his driver. Instead, he taught my sister and

> My parents knew it was all right if not every single one of their needs were being met by the other, because commitment to the life they shared and created was a bigger reward than anything else.

brother to play. My mom didn't complain about his lack of conversation; she found other outlets. She had us kids, her friends, and her extended family.

My parents knew it was all right if not every single one of their needs were being met by the other, because commitment to the life they shared and created was a bigger reward than anything else. So what if my dad wasn't clued in on the latest gossip? Or that my mom was perfectly okay never learning to ride a bike or swim? (A side note: I venture to say that my mom never exercised because she had to escape from her village during the war by hiking—at night, by herself—over some seriously steep mountains. I think she just thought, *That's pretty much it for exercise for the rest of my life.*)

As we pull up to church, my parents are laughing and humorously harassing each other. My dad is helping my mom out of the car. The boys are helping my dad help my mom. I let my parents walk ahead, and, as Dad guides Mom toward the church, ask myself, *Would I ever want two other people as my parents?* The answer is immediate: *Not me!*

I start to understand that as my siblings and I grew up, so did my mom. And my dad. Their new country allowed them the choices they may not have had in their homelands, where my mom would have likely married a preselected groom, as her older sister had, and my dad probably would have married the local girl from his village because she was there. My parents were able to choose each other. God knows, a lot of women have made some foolish choices in their past (stop staring at me!). What if my mom had gotten what she now thinks she wanted, a talker? What if that "talker" was also a gambler, a drunk, or a cheater? I doubt that guy would still be in the car going to church with his kids and grandkids. So I look at these two "opposites" and think, *They're still attracting each other.* The magnet of their lives still has a pretty strong pull. I turn to look back at my husband, who is locking the car, and take his hand. As we head toward church, I hear the bells tolling, something stops me. I turn to my husband and ask him, "Did I just hear hyenas?" ◑

Lisa Kogan Tells All

Perhaps mixing 18 different nasal decongestants had simply gone to her head, but being sofa-bound got our columnist thinking: What makes a working relationship work, what makes it crash and burn, and the big question—what in the world did she do with her vaporizer?

I had the flu. But not just any flu. No, this was the kind of bug that forces a normally rational human being to dial information and beg the operator for Jack Kevorkian's home phone number. This was the kind that leaves a generally well-groomed woman crumpled on the sofa in her rattiest flannel nightgown, the one that her 79-year-old aunt from Detroit presented with the keen observation: "Magenta puppies always make things look zanier." Such was my state when Johannes (in those days my boyfriend, in these days my boyfriend and the father of my child) walked in. "Man," he called out while hanging his coat in the front hall closet, "I've never seen so many beautiful women in one city...." The love of my life continued from the foyer, "I mean, it's like a convention of supermodels out there—" He rounded the corner just in time to watch me sneeze cherry Jell-O over the Arts & Leisure section. "But," he stammered, "none as beautiful as you, my darling."

"Avert your eyes, for I am hideous," I whimpered à la the Elephant Man.

"No, seriously, you look...not horrible," which was true, provided you're drawn to individuals who appear to have combed peanut butter through their hair. Finally, in what can only be described as a genuinely pathetic effort to change the subject, he added, "So, I'm just curious. When was the last time you, uh, you know...showered?" I gathered up my Sudafed, my Tylenol, my Mucinex, my Puffs, my honey-and-lemon cough drops, my lip balm, my thermometer, my blanket, my *TV Guide*, my diet ginger ale, my wonton soup, my cordless phone, and my few remaining shards of dignity, and with all the icy élan a woman dressed in a soup-stained frolicking-puppy print can muster, I replied, "Good day, sir!" He tried for a last-minute save: "Are you losing weight?" But I cut him off. "I said good day!" and flounced gracefully (okay, I tripped over the vaporizer) to our bedroom, where I proceeded to lapse in and out of seven back-to-back episodes of *Law & Order*.

When I was extremely young and shockingly stupid, I thought you weren't supposed to ever get angry at anybody you cared about (lest you suspect I'm exaggerating the "shockingly stupid" part, I also thought Mount Rushmore was a natural phenomenon). I honestly believed that people who were truly in love would never dream of having a good, old-fashioned, knock-down, drag-out fight. I guess when you're the type of girl who walks around thinking that the wind just sort of sculpted Teddy Roosevelt into the side of a mountain, the concept of a fairy-tale relationship makes total sense. Johannes and I don't have one of those relationships. The life we've designed isn't perfect, but I've never been a big fan of perfection—it's a bitch to achieve and impossible to maintain. Instead we argue on a semi-regular basis. Sometimes we look back at the tougher moments and laugh—the influenza incident of 2001, the what the f%#@k do you mean you never want to get married? episode of last Tuesday—and sometimes we get mad all over again. But when Johannes fights, he fights like a grown-up. He isn't mean, he isn't sarcastic, he isn't out to annihilate. He just wants us to order in Thai food, watch MSNBC, and be friends again.

Loving somebody and then having the guts to let them love you back doesn't always come easy. For the first three years of our life together I kept waiting for him to rip off his Mr. Nice Guy mask and turn into every boy who ever broke my heart. I poked, I prodded, I harangued, I guilted, I entrapped, I tested, I stopped just short of waterboarding. But Johannes refused to take the bait. Instead, he maintained his calm, retained his benevolence, and developed migraines.

He made sure I understood that he was in it for the long haul; that I would never again have to sit on a blind date listening to some guy tell me what Pink Floyd was really trying to say on *Dark Side of the Moon*. The man makes me feel loved—even when he hates me. And that, I've come to realize, is no small thing.

Loving somebody and then having the guts to let them love you back doesn't always come easy.

I have a friend, we'll call her Jane because Jane is a lovely, classic name. Jane is married to this guy, let's call him Dick because, well, suffice it to say the name suits him perfectly. I've had fun with Dick and Jane; we've gone to the theater and dinner and a couple of Knicks games together. With Johannes frequently in Europe, I became like a little dinghy tied to the boat of their marriage, just kind of bobbing along behind them in case of an emergency. One Sunday a few years ago, we were brunching in SoHo—because before there were kids and cartoons and Honey Nut Cheerios, there was sleep and sex and brunches in SoHo. Anyway, Jane knocked over her water glass, prompting Dick to spend the rest of the meal excoriating her for every single misstep she'd ever made. He opened his rant with "Christ, it's excruciating to sit next to you at a table," and closed with a reference to her "fat idiot sister." Check please!

Jane called the next morning to apologize for making me part of their *Who's Afraid of Virginia Woolf?* production. I wanted to say, "You're not the one who should be sorry." I wanted to say, "Your only mistake was in not lobbing the basket of stale sweet rolls at his head"—hell, the cheese danish alone was heavy enough to stun him into silence. I wanted to say, "Janey, Janey, Janey, what's become of your self-respect?" I wanted to say, "It's not whether somebody loves you (I mean, for all I know O.J. loved Nicole), it's how he treats you that counts." I found myself wondering: Is Jane afraid to be alone? Is it a money thing? Maybe she's an unindicted coconspirator, provoking him in some way that I'm just not seeing? Or maybe she woke up one morning and 22 years and two sons had simply come and gone—right along with her energy and confidence. Maybe she just forgot who she'd wanted to be when she grew up. In the end all I managed was, "I'm here if you need me."

"What's the matter? Are you coming down with something?" Johannes asks as I crawl into bed. I assure him that I'm fine. His eyes narrow suspiciously. "Then why are you wearing the magenta puppy nightgown of death?" I explain that I'm working on a column and it's got me thinking about him and me and Dick and Jane and love and homicide and that point when a working relationship becomes more work than relationship. I admit there are moments when I'm not sure if it's luck or love or fear of failure that keeps us going, and I ask Johannes if he knows what I mean. There is a very long pause. He is contemplative. He is introspective. He is sound asleep. [0]

RAY SKETTINI AND DONNA MERTRUD-SKETTINI **Through nearly 25 years of marriage, Donna didn't know why Ray kept pushing her away. Now that the abuse is finally out, they have become closer.**

Love Among the Ruins

It was long ago and it was far away, but for the one out of six American men who were sexually abused as children, the results are always present, deeply corrosive, and wildly contagious. **David France** talks to a few brave men—and the women who married them—who have shattered their silence, faced their traumas, and taken their first steps toward healing.

1 Ray Skettini at age 12, when he was abused by his priest, James Hanley. **2** Ray repressed the memory so deeply he asked Hanley to marry him and Donna in 1978 and **3** to baptize their daughter, Sarah, two years later. **4** In 2007 Hanley, who admitted to molesting about a dozen boys, was jailed for a separate incident.

Donna Mertrud fell for Ray Skettini when she was only 17. A year older and the class clown at their Pequannock, New Jersey, high school, he had a chip on his shoulder, some people said. But he made Donna laugh. Three years later, when she agreed to marry him, Ray asked his family priest, Father James Hanley, to officiate.

From early on, Donna felt something was wrong. Among the "red flags" that kept popping up, she says, were Ray's irritability and his tendency to pace. And then there was his subtle but growing detachment from her. "When we got married, we really explored each other. We had fun," says Donna, now 50. "Getting to know each other, forming as a married couple and as a family, we bonded closer. But as weird as this sounds, the more we did that, the more he pulled away, emotionally and physically." Slowly their sex life dwindled. Sometimes she had merely to touch his shoulder when he'd freeze and draw back. Donna wondered if he was having an affair. Mostly, though, she just felt rejected, and this broke her heart.

"I knew he loved me. There are so many ways to show love other than sex—endearing things he would do," she says. "But my self-esteem really was depleting, because I thought, *What's wrong with me?* It was something that I was very persistent about, trying to get to 'why.' There was a thorn in our marriage, and I needed to find out what it was." The more she challenged him about it,

> "Ray knows I'm goddamned sorry for what I did to him, too; right, Ray?"

however, the worse things got. Ray, a surveyor and park ranger who often worked two jobs, would say he was tired or too busy to talk. "There was always an answer," she says, "but it never added up." Uncertain and lonely, she began to overeat—a groping attempt to feed her longing for intimacy, as her therapist would later explain. "So many people said to me, 'Donna, go have an affair!' But I didn't want that. I never wanted that. I wanted my husband back." Little changed through nearly 25 years of marriage. Then in the fall of 2001, Donna returned to college to finish her degree in education. One course in particular, on the psychology of human relations, spoke directly to her. "I started realizing, *Oh my God, there are names for the things I've been going through!*" Poring over her textbooks, she came to believe that her husband had been sexually abused. His behavior fit the pattern.

Confirmation, however, didn't come until one afternoon that spring. While Ray busied himself in the kitchen, Donna turned on *Oprah* and found several young men talking about having been abused by their priests. She stood in stunned silence when she recognized one of the offenders: Father James Hanley—the same priest who had performed their marriage and two years later baptized their first child.

"Then I heard this tiny voice coming from the kitchen," she says.

It was Ray, barely in a whisper: "I guess I'm not the only one."

The shock was so great it capsized Donna, and she dropped to her knees in the living room. "The pieces of my puzzle started falling together," she says.

It took another few days before

CURTIS ST. JOHN AND ILENE LIEBERMAN-ST. JOHN: When Curtis suddenly turned cold to their 10-year-old son, Ilene urged him to face the truth of what had happened to him at the same age.

1 Curtis St. John was 10 when he started going for tutoring with Albert Fentress. 2 The Poughkeepsie, New York, former home of Fentress, where Curtis was subjected to oral sex. 3 Fentress, who was arrested for the murder of another boy, petitioned for release in 2002 but was denied largely due to Curtis's testimony.

Ray told her what had happened when he was 12, how Hanley had pretended to give him an education in sex, demonstrating each lesson on the boy's body.

What came next was a long journey to recovery. Both the Skettinis became activists and members of the national Survivors Network of those Abused by Priests (SNAP). Ray joined nearly two dozen of Hanley's other victims to demand that the priest be defrocked, and lent his name to a civil lawsuit filed to learn what the church had known about Hanley's crimes and how it had dealt with that information. Ultimately Hanley admitted to sexually abusing some 12 child parishioners (although a statute of limitations kept him out of jail), and the diocese paid out a multimillion-dollar settlement to 21 of his victims, including Ray. Because Hanley wasn't required to register as a sex offender when he moved to a new neighborhood, Ray and Donna agreed to help leaflet the streets with warnings. One surprising morning, Hanley appeared and shouted at the protesters.

In a fit of anger, Donna grabbed him by the sleeve and demanded he account for what he had done.

"Did you abuse this man right here?"

"Ray Skettini? Yes, I did," he answered hotly.

"He's my husband.... You married us.... You baptized our daughter."

"Yes, I did," he said, "and Ray knows

A survey suggests that about one in six men is sexually abused before age 16.

I'm goddamned sorry for what I did to him, too; right, Ray?"

After a brief exchange, Ray responded, "Jim Hanley, you still never got all the help you needed."

Hanley agreed: "I love you, Ray, and I hope you forgive me, babe."

"Oh, I don't know if I can forgive anything anymore," Ray answered calmly.

Today Donna and Ray are still digging themselves out from the past, attending individual and couples therapy sessions twice a week (which the church pays for as part of a legal settlement) and making an effort to be frank with each other. They have not yet solved their troubles with physical intimacy, a fact that upsets them both—"but we're working on it," Donna says. In Ray's mind, this could take a lifetime of therapy. "I'm still trying to get back to being close to my wife," he says. "I never had an explanation for 'Why was I not wanting to have sex with her?' I never understood it myself till all this broke. I would like to believe we're moving in a more positive direction. I was scared she was going to leave me."

But Donna is still committed to making the marriage work. A major breakthrough in therapy for her, she says, has been discovering that she wasn't the one who turned her husband off. "I have since realized it was a third person in my marriage—Jim Hanley," she says. Last year Donna wrote the priest a seven-page letter. "I told him it wasn't just Ray he destroyed. He destroyed our marriage, our healthy, normal relationship. And I wasn't going to let him win."

It's hard to know how common sexual abuse is among boys. A survey by researchers at the University of Massachusetts–Boston suggests that approximately one in six men is sexually abused before the age of 16. If correct, that means more than 17 million American men share this ugly history. But many never disclose their victimization. Some may not recognize their early sexual encounters with older men or women as abuse; others blame themselves. In one study, 75 percent of male survivors reported being ashamed that they had failed to fend off the perpetrator. Another reason for keeping their abuse a secret is that they don't want people to think of them as easily coerced or forced, according to Gail B. Slap, MD, professor of pediatrics and medicine at the University of Pennsylvania School of Medicine, who has studied the issue.

Research over the past three decades points to the tremendous difficulty these survivors have in their relationships—the anger, fear, and isolation that typically result from childhood sexual abuse is particularly corrosive to healthy love. As for how their women fare, that's less clear. Very little research has been done on the wives and girlfriends of male abuse victims. "This is really a shame, because they have so many needs," says Richard B. Gartner, PhD, a psychoanalyst and leading expert in the field, who practices in New York City. "The bigger the betrayal, the more the boy reacts as though relationships themselves are traumatic. He becomes kind of allergic to being in relationships. It's very hard for a wife or partner to deal with that." Such relationships can be emotional—and physical—battlefields. Or the men seem coldly remote and "zone out" at home. Many also turn to drugs and alcohol, or become obsessive about food, exercise, or work, devoting so much energy to a career that their families are neglected. Experts call this a hypermasculine response. "We use the phrase *the ripple effect*," says Janice Palm, a Seattle therapist and executive director of Shepherd's Counseling Services, which runs one of the few support groups for the partners of adult survivors of childhood sexual abuse. "This isn't just in the life of the person who was abused, but in the life of anyone in their relationship sphere."

> "It takes a strong woman to deal with male abuse survivors. They can be nasty and abusive because they don't want anyone close to them."

One common ripple, as the Skettinis discovered, is a disruption of sex. Julie and Craig Martin have struggled with this in a different way. Craig, 52, first disclosed his abuse by a family priest when he began dating Julie more than 20 years ago. At the time, he owned a bar in Waite Park, Minnesota. "I told him," Julie says, "'Whenever you are ready to deal with it, I'm there for you.'" But Craig dealt with it by binge drinking and having an affair, at one point fathering a child with another woman. "I didn't cause him to cheat on me, [but] you go through terrible feelings of *What could I have done? What did I do wrong?*" Julie, now 47, explains. Thanks to rehab and therapy, including counseling for sexual compulsion, they are still married and in love. Craig has been sober for eight years, and attends monthly sessions for victims of childhood sexual abuse at the University of Minnesota. He sold the bar to attend graduate school and is now a social worker helping troubled boys. Not that all their problems have been solved. "I don't believe we've had any intercourse for several years—it's awful," says Julie. "It's almost like we're married singles, or best friends living in the same house and raising kids together. I can laugh, but I cry inside. It hurts. It's very sad."

In his book *Abused Boys*, therapist Mic Hunter details the many reasons why sexual intimacy is complicated for male survivors: Some withhold or avoid physical intimacy because they come to think of sex as a disgusting act that people inflict on one another. In a complex effort to show respect, some victims seek out prostitutes or strangers instead of venting their desires on their loved one. Others may come to define sexuality as always involving a perpetrator and a victim. "Often this association is so powerful that the victim becomes physically nauseated even when someone initiates respectful, mutual, consensual sex with him," Hunter writes.

On the other hand, many adult survivors compulsively seek out sex: More than one-third of the men in Sex Addicts Anonymous said they'd been sexually abused as children, according to a study Hunter conducted. Some sort of sexual dysfunction affects one in four abuse survivors, he reports—including inhibited drive and erectile problems.

Healing, for these men, is possible, but experts say that the process they go through can be one of the more

MARILYN STEVENS AND DOMINIC CARTER: Marilyn, a college administrator, and Dominic, a television journalist, grew increasingly distant. Even therapy didn't help. Only when he started writing about his abuse did they begin to repair their relationship.

1 Dominic Carter in 1968 at the Central Park Zoo in New York City, with his mother, Laverne, who suffered from mental illness. 2 Dominic, at age 10, when he'd already been abused. 3 A family vacation in 1997 with wife, Marilyn, and children, Courtney and Dominic Jr.

difficult junctures in their lives. It often involves confronting the one thing they never wanted revealed. And it often makes things worse for their partners. "Recovery is hell on relationships. Many couples don't stay together," says Mike Lew, a Boston psychotherapist who wrote *Victims No Longer: Men Recovering from Incest and Other Sexual Child Abuse.* "And if the couple makes it through, the relationship is different. It's healthier, it's stronger, but it's not the same. The old relationship is dead."

The Martins are living proof of that. Julie says Craig's recovery process has caused them to grow apart. So far therapy hasn't bridged the divide. "I love him. He's gained my trust back," she says. "I admire everything he's done. I give him credit. But he's not the man I married."

It really takes a strong woman to deal with male abuse survivors," says Curtis St. John, president of MaleSurvivor, a national support group for men who have been sexually victimized. "They can be nasty and abusive, kicking everybody in their shins, because they don't want anyone close to them. But I tell women, 'If you make it through with them, they're going to be happier and cooler and more in love than the person you fell in love with in the first place.'"

St. John, 40, should know. He made it through with his wife, Ilene Lieberman-St. John, at his side. "Before Ilene, I wasn't even worth working on. I had no reason to bother helping myself," he says.

When they met in 1996 at Purchase College, where they both worked, he was 28 years old and just divorced, and she was a 40-year-old mother of two young children whose husband had died of cancer. She was nervous about the age difference at first, but they started dating, hitting it off as equals. She loved his exuberance, as did her kids.

One night just before they got married, they were lying in bed watching television when Curtis turned to Ilene and said, "I have to tell you something. I was abused when I was a child."

The man, he told her, was a neighbor and well-regarded history teacher named Albert Fentress, who under the pretense of tutoring Curtis molested him, eventually subjecting him to oral sex—up to 20 times during the spring and summer of 1979.

"Did he hurt you?" Ilene asked.

"No," Curtis answered, and then added, matter-of-factly, "Well, he went on to murder and cannibalize another kid."

It was as though Curtis were recapping a movie plot: Fentress was arrested that August for abusing a second boy, whom he killed—and whose remains he subsequently cooked and ate. At first the story staggered Ilene. Then she asked Curtis how he'd handled it all.

"I'm fine," he told her. "It hasn't affected me."

Ilene, having moved on from her own trauma, was willing to believe him. "I did the widow thing for a while, and then I was done—I didn't identify with widows anymore. So I put what he was saying into the context of my own life."

Curtis recognizes today that the abuse did affect him as a young man. "Here's an award-winning teacher that my parents trust. He said, 'This is okay to do; in fact, it makes you special and mature.' And—people don't like to hear this—it feels good," Curtis says now. "But it causes confusion, at the very least with sexual preference. So here I am, I've got no other sexual experience. And I'm wondering, *Is this who I am? Am I gay?*" He knew he wasn't, but the question would nag him whenever a relationship with a woman failed.

Within a year of their wedding, other issues arose. Ilene started worrying about Curtis's drinking. There were just isolated instances, but one night when he came home drunk and denied he'd even had any alcohol, she put her foot down. "I can't live like this. You either do something about this or you're out," she told him. Curtis entered a 12-week outpatient rehabilitation program and hasn't had a drink since. In all the rehab and attendant therapy, however, he never once mentioned Fentress. And if not for Ilene, he might have gone on living in denial. But when her son Justin turned 10, she noticed her husband was behaving terribly to the boy. "Their relationship was awful," she says. "Curtis was being cold to him and pushing him away." Ilene ushered the whole family into counseling; even then, however, the battles between husband and son continued. "Finally I said, 'Don't you think you should tell Doctor Chris [the therapist] about your story? You've got to say something.'"

For the first time Curtis began to untangle his past. In an odd coincidence, that same week headlines reported that Fentress, who had been incarcerated in a hospital for the criminally insane, was petitioning for release. Curtis called the district attorney to give his story, and when he didn't hear right back, he reverted to the scared, mistrustful child Fentress had left behind. "I thought, *He's not going to believe me, he's not going to listen to me*," Curtis says.

Ultimately, however, he made contact, swore out a deposition, and helped ensure that Fentress stayed locked up in a mental institution. In the aftermath, he joined MaleSurvivor, which he credits with changing his life. The big turnaround, he says, came during one of the organization's weekends of recovery in May 2004. As part of an exercise, he composed a letter from the boy he was to the man he is now. While he wrote, using his nondominant hand as instructed, a vision popped into his head of himself walking over a big, beautiful bridge, Fentress below, unable to reach him. Slowly he came upon a small figure sitting down. It was himself as a child and he was neither sad nor hurt. "There you are," said the boy. "I've been waiting for you."

"Cool," Curtis said, taking him by the hand. "Let's go."

> Some survivors withhold or avoid physical intimacy because they come to think of sex as a disgusting act that people inflict on one another.

Finding the part of himself that was healthy and whole, he says, opened the floodgates. "All of a sudden, the emotions bottled up for 30-some years came flying out. It just turned me around.... Seven years ago, if you said to me I was going to be happy, I would have said, 'No way.' But I did it."

"I am so proud to be your wife," Ilene interrupts. "It's wonderful to see what has emerged."

Many women take longer to reach the happiness Ilene describes. "I've always thought of myself as 'collateral damage,'" says Dawn Haslanger, who is 54 and the wife of a childhood sexual abuse survivor in Seattle. Over the years, her husband, Bob, 58, has regularly suffered bouts of post-traumatic stress, which she says kept him out of work for a period of time and triggered outbursts of rage. In 2006, when the Episcopal diocese decided finally to begin an ecclesiastical case against his abuser—an emotionally trying process for Bob—Dawn realized she was suffering from her own version of PTSD. She feared that the battle would unhinge her husband and undermine her marriage.

"I started having anxiety attacks," she says. "I started not sleeping well. And sometimes during the day—a routine day—my heart would race, my blood pressure would go up, I'd get dizzy." After working for 28 years as a dental assistant, she was fired from her most recent job. "I think I probably was just tightly wound," she says. "I've been really struggling with depression for the last year and a half."

Feeling lonely and rejected is common among women in relationships with men who have been sexually abused as children, according to Mike Lew, the Boston psychotherapist. "The female partner may feel like she is the target of his anger. That might increase her frustration," he says. In a workshop he led for partners of survivors, the women also had a lot of anger. "They were angry because of what was done to someone they love. They were angry because they had to deal with the fallout. They were angry at the lack of resources and lack of help. They were angry because this isn't what they signed on for when they got into this relationship, and they had to deal with it or leave."

Not all women react this way, however, according to Mary Gail Frawley-O'Dea, PhD, a North Carolina therapist and researcher specializing in sexual abuse survivors.

Some spouses and girlfriends adopt an attitude of *Toughen up; aren't you over this yet? When are you going to get over this?* "You don't think of women having this lack of empathy," says Frawley-O'Dea, "which is why I hypothesize that some are embarrassed and ashamed about their husband's lack of quote-unquote manliness. I think they wonder what he did to get this to happen—more often than guys wonder how a little girl got it to happen." And some wives, weighed down by their own problems, are simply unable to deal with such painful baggage brought into the relationship by their men.

Twenty-six years ago, there were a number of things Marilyn Stevens found unusual about Dominic Carter, an 18-year-old fresh off the bus to attend a rural State University of New York college-prep summer program for promising students from disadvantaged backgrounds. For one, he looked entirely out of place in upstate apple country—understandable given his childhood in a run-down Bronx tenement overlooking a gritty expressway. For another, he had an unnerving clarity about where he was going in life, and with whom. He was on campus for only a few days before approaching Marilyn, the 25-year-old program coordinator, to improbably declare: "You're going to be my wife and the mother of my children."

Are you crazy? she remembers thinking. "It was like, 'Me Tarzan, you Jane,'" she says. Over the summer, she did everything she could to redirect Dominic's affections toward women his own age, but he never faltered. He stayed at SUNY and earned his degree in just three years. Two months after graduation, he and Marilyn married. "I guess I got beaten down by the chase," she says. It turned out, however, that they had much in common. Marilyn came from similarly disadvantaged roots in Harlem, where seven of her ten siblings have died, most from heroin and AIDS. Her first step out of poverty was the same summer program that recruited Dominic. Like him, she harbored intense ambition—hers was to work in higher education, while he hung his hopes on a career in journalism.

Somewhere during those early years, he mentioned—only once, and without any details—that he'd been sexually abused by his mother, whom he referred to as Laverne. "We were sitting and watching TV and he just blurted it out," Marilyn remembers. "I was really in shock, because I couldn't imagine that a mother could do such a horrendous act to her child. So I just put it in the back of my head and never revisited

it. He never spoke about it, and I never brought it up again."

But the silence barely masked the issue. Today both Dominic and Marilyn say his abuse has been the single most defining element of their long marriage, which has produced two children, now 20 and 16. Tensions started to mount after the couple conceived their first baby, Courtney. They had moved in with Marilyn's mother in Harlem, close enough to the Bronx so that Laverne could call or drop by unannounced to visit. Over Dominic's objections, Marilyn always let Laverne in. "How do you tell a person, 'I can't have a relationship with you?' That was not within my personality, or my mother's," she says. "We would let her come in, let her eat and break bread, and try to get her out the door before he got home."

They weren't always successful. If Dominic arrived and saw his mother, he would spin back through the door and disappear for hours—sometimes hitting the clubs with friends till daylight, once staying out all weekend.

With Dominic increasingly absent, Laverne came around even more often. She would ask Marilyn or her mother to have him call her for one reason or another, but when they passed along the messages, he would explode: "Stay away from Laverne! She's using the both of you!"

"I felt so trapped," Marilyn says about her relationship with Laverne. "You start to have heart palpitations—*how do I handle this? I don't want to be mean and nasty to her. I don't have all the facts, but I feel like I'm betraying my husband.*"

And the more betrayed Dominic felt, the more angry and remote he became. Rage seemed to gnaw away at him. "He was extremely moody," Marilyn says. "There was all this erratic behavior that was turned inward." She would find him sitting alone in the kitchen, chewing absently on his knuckles till they bled.

Marilyn concedes she didn't handle her frustrations in the wisest manner. Too frequently she defaulted to sarcasm. "Do you want hot sauce for those knuckles?" she'd ask derisively. She never once suspected his childhood experiences had anything to do with the way he was acting. Besides, it was hard for her to accept that the entertaining woman who showed up at her door—a woman she'd come to love—could have done anything remotely like what her husband had once intimated. "She was always put together very nicely, not a hair out of place, and would talk, talk, talk—very funny, very comical sometimes. So in your mind you say,

> "I said,
> 'Dominic, we
> have got to deal
> with this. You
> just can't
> keep running.'"

This didn't happen."

It wasn't a doubt she voiced to her husband. But he sensed it nonetheless. "She didn't want to believe what happened," Dominic, 44, says now. When he once confided Laverne's crimes to Marilyn's mother, she was just as skeptical. "This is so deep," he says, "the natural instinct is to not believe it."

Instead of investing in his homelife, Dominic devoted more and more time to his career, which took off like a rocket—going from a reporter for WLIB, a New York–area radio station geared to the African-American community, to senior political reporter for NY1News, where he has raked in awards and interviewed world leaders from Nelson Mandela to Bill Clinton. Today he is one of New York's best-known local political journalists and a frequent guest on national programs like *Hardball with Chris Matthews.* "He was always on the go, nonstop," says Marilyn, 51, a senior administrator at Manhattan College. But as the years wore on, she realized he was running not only toward a high-flying career but away from her and their children—away from any intimacy whatsoever.

Finally, after a decade of tumultuous marriage, she'd had enough. "'I said, 'Dominic, we have got to deal with this. You just can't keep running and running and running.'" They enrolled in couples therapy. Each also saw a counselor privately. Week in and week out, they talked about their problems and frustrations. She worked to modulate her sarcasm, while he tried opening up more—but their relationship was still rocky. She faulted him for not participating fully in therapy, and felt excluded from his interior life. During all these sessions, Dominic never once mentioned his history of abuse. Not wanting to betray a confidence, Marilyn didn't bring it up either. At this point, she just wanted him to be a better husband, and she was losing hope. "It got to be too much," she says. "It was like we were both locked in the same room with no exit."

About eight years ago, she confronted him one last time. "If you don't want to talk to me, if you don't want to talk to your therapist, write it down," she remembers saying to him. "You have *got* to do *something.* I hate to use the old cliché, but—set yourself free."

Dominic didn't start writing until 2001, shortly after his mother's death. Resolved to unload his secrets about what she had done to him, he quickly realized he knew very little about the woman he refused to call Mother—a term of respect he reserved for his maternal grandmother,

"Recovery is hell on relationships. Many couples don't stay together."

who shared parenting responsibilities. He knew there were times when Laverne would disappear for months on end, sometimes longer than a year. These were periods of joy for him, spent safely with "Mother." But each time Laverne returned, he was passed right back to her.

What he remembered most was how she treated him. When they were alone, her cruelty was severe. There was a blur of beatings. And then, when he was 7, one night he heard her calling "Do-mi-nic" in the singsong way that meant he had no choice but to go to her. He found her in bed, naked, and when he climbed in, as she demanded, she asked him to touch her breasts. Then her thighs, and between her legs where he was surprised to find coarse hair. Her breath was hot as she put her mouth on his tiny lips—she'd never even kissed him on the cheek. He became more and more frightened, he later recalled, when she touched his undeveloped penis and "rubbed it until I feared it was going to fall off." Then, "she lifted my whole body, all 70 pounds of me, and she kept moaning and mumbling and caressing." He knew it was wrong—and feared it would turn him into "a freak of nature" or worse. It never happened again, but his terror "became almost devastating at times," he says. Much as he tried, he could never forget that night. "I would literally wave my hand in front of my face, as an 11- or 12-year-old kid, and go 'Boop.' That would mean: Put it out of your mind." The spell never worked.

Dominic approached the task of retracing his childhood as if he were investigating a news story. Relatives told him that Laverne's many absences were due to mental illness—she had been hospitalized repeatedly at Mount Sinai Hospital in Manhattan. He sent away for her records. The first bundle arrived in 2003. Marilyn was with him at the post office when he opened the large package and poured out an astonishing stack of medical charts, 620 pages tall.

"You want me to step outside and give you your own private moment?" she asked.

"No," he said.

The pages revealed that Laverne had been diagnosed with paranoid schizophrenia. There were notes about straitjackets, long lists of her medications, and judges' orders regarding her detention. She received her first shock-therapy treatment when she was barely 15. The files also contained details of Dominic's life. Once, when he was 2, she folded her fingers around his throat and choked him until his cries snapped her out of her "dreamlike state"; another time, a voice suggested she throw him from the window—"Do it," the voice commanded. She told her doctors that she was afraid one day she might. Meanwhile, she beat him violently. His battered body was a familiar presence in the local emergency room, where he once arrived with swollen testicles after an especially severe spanking.

Twice Dominic was placed in foster care. When he was 12, Laverne petitioned for his return, and a family court judge was about to grant it, when Dominic asked to speak to him alone. In the judge's chambers, he described in detail the night his mother molested him. "It was the first time I had ever mentioned it," he explains. The judge gave his grandmother full custody, and Dominic never lived with Laverne again.

"That ended the abuse right there," he says.

For Marilyn, the stark records finally helped her understand her husband. She no longer harbored any doubts about his story. And for Dominic, the evidence of his mother's hellish existence allowed him to begin resolving his own past. "She was a tortured soul in ways he had no idea," Marilyn says. "She had no control over her life. [Realizing] that was his salvation."

With the documents at his elbow, Dominic began to write a chronicle of his abuse and redemption, which he self-published in 2007 as a book titled *No Momma's Boy*. A chapter at a time, he revealed the secrets he'd guarded all his life. Turning them over to his wife to read and edit marked the beginning of the conversation she had craved for decades—and the end of his life on the run. "She felt that [writing this book] would help me, and it really has," he says. "I can tell you this: I have forgiven my mother and now I would love nothing more than to give her a hug and tell her, 'I love you, you're my mother, and we can move forward together.' It took me a long time to understand this. I feel for the first time in my life that I can breathe the fresh air.

"I'm enjoying my children, my wife," he adds. "And I'm happy. For the first time in my life, I'm happy."

"We have turned a corner in our relationship," Marilyn says. "Everybody in the family has been touched by this. And we're finally seeing our way through it together." ●

Was a Man in Your Life Abused?

"It's very hard to be a partner with someone who has been sexually abused as a child," says Janice Palm, executive director of Shepherd's Counseling Services in Seattle. Especially when the person doesn't talk about it. And many men never do.

Are there clues? Palm, whose center runs one of the few therapy groups in the country for partners of sexual abuse survivors, describes a pattern of behavior whose telltale sign is a pervasive unavailability. Victims are often…

■ EMOTIONALLY DISTANT: When a child is abused by a person he trusts, Palm says, he learns that intimacy is dangerous, that attachment will hurt. Based on this early lesson, he may instinctively avoid closeness as an adult.

■ SEXUALLY ABSENT: Many survivors lose interest in sex completely. Others emotionally withdraw during the act. (Partners will complain, "He's very loving and attentive, but when we start to get sexual, he just goes blank. It's as if he's not there.") Often, young victims learn to disconnect emotionally to get through the abuse.

■ SEXUALLY COMPULSIVE: The fallout from abuse may manifest as promiscuity or sexual addictions like looking at pornography. Another red flag is discomfort at being touched.

■ HYPERVIGILANT: A man who is unusually overprotective of a son or daughter may be expressing what he wishes a parent had done for him as a boy. This behavior may intensify when the child reaches the age at which the father was abused.

Once the abuse is out in the open, Palm says, let your partner take the lead about how much he wants to talk. As a victim, he had no control. Typically there is such shame and inadequacy attached to the abuse—it's the child logic of "I feel bad, I am bad," "I feel dirty, I am dirty"—he likely doesn't want you to see him that way. Or he may be hesitant to expose you to the horror of what happened to him.

The best thing you can do is encourage him to get help. Individual and group therapy are effective (check out malesurvivor.org for a directory of specialists). If he doesn't want to attend, remind him that when he's ready, you'll support him. Finally, be compassionate but truthful ("You know, honey, this is really interrupting our relationship, and I don't think I can live this way anymore").

When you see someone you love suffer and become vulnerable, it's very hard to take care of yourself—but it's crucial for both of you. That may mean finding your own therapist for support.

Greetings from **HOME**

HAVING A GREAT TIME!
GLAD YOU'RE *Not* HERE!

I Love You, You're Perfect, Now Scram

Having her adored husband around: comforting, engaging, fun. Having him away for a few days: pure euphoria. **Cathleen Medwick** on the fine art of staying together while staying yourself.

The taxi is just pulling out the driveway. He is on his way to Indonesia, a five-day business trip. Gone! I don't know what to do first. Take a walk outside with just a noisy bunch of tree frogs for company? Throw a highly objectionable CD (that would be *Carousel* or *Show Boat*) into the Bose and raise the volume to deafening? Turn out the lights, peel off some clothing, and dance? Or sing! I'm great on the choruses, even the solos, I've been listening to this music since I was 10.

Let me catch my breath for a moment. My husband has left the building. And I'm exultant; it's the way you'd feel if you landed alone on the moon and everything was cool and silvery and you knew you could go home to Earth again—just not quite yet. Because I'm crazy about Jeff, my husband of 32 years. We've had coffee together practically every morning all that time. We've bought dinged and battered antiques that nobody else would look at twice. We've lived congenially, for the most part, in a one-bedroom apartment, a rambling prewar classic six, and two drafty, centuries-old exurban farmhouses with sodden basements (doesn't *every* house have water seeping through its limestone foundation?). I've handed him a glass of vodka as he's obsessed about his dozens of orchids, his acres of flax, and shrieked at him as he's uprooted the tender shoots of our 50-year-old peony bushes with the rake of his tractor. I've seen his eyes close in rapture as he's played his guitar, watched him gaze with boundless admiration at our sweet, manic quasi-Labrador, and even at me. I've seen him accumulate a world-class collection of ties—enough to outfit a small company—and a pile of laundry so steep it finally collapses into the bathroom doorway, where he nimbly climbs over it, scattering clothing like rose petals in his wake. I've watched him sleep propped up on his elbow, head resting in his hand and blankets merrily twisted around his legs, as the eternal light from the blaring television flicks hectic patterns onto his face. I've listened to him snore so resoundingly that our neighbor's peacocks honk in solidarity. And I've tiptoed out of the bedroom, slippers in hand, to slide beneath the covers of our daughter's bed (she's long been out of the house), where the velvety night envelops me and I can hear the humming of my own reclusive mind.

In truth I have always been a loner. I love tiny, singular spaces where a body can sit quietly and contemplate. I was never happier than when I lived in my quirky basement apartment in a Manhattan brownstone, and Jeff, a stranger to me, moved into the parlor-floor apartment right above it. We began to meet for coffee, and at night after he got home from his corporate job at a major New York–based textile firm and I finished reading for my graduate courses in Renaissance poetry, I'd clamber upstairs and sip wine with him. I might stay over—or I might go downstairs to sleep alone. It wasn't exactly Jean-Paul Sartre and Simone de Beauvoir, maintaining separate apartments and perfectly calibrated minds. I have no idea what Jeff and I talked about in those early days, but it was probably nothing more complicated than how I could prep for my orals without falling asleep and whether or not he should paint contrasting trim around his ceiling. It didn't matter. What mattered was that we never stopped talking.

Then we moved in together, into his apartment. I had to get rid of my spindly Victorian furniture; it looked ridiculous with his chunky brown sofa and pragmatic oak table and chairs. The shag rug was a bone of contention; luckily, it didn't survive a sheepdog with digestive issues. Crammed in a claustrophobic space, we began to battle, one of us slamming the door and retreating into the narrow bedroom. We built a sleeping loft to escape to. Still, we not only survived the merger but married. We tried to become a "we," traveling for our honeymoon to the Paris I loved (and he hated), always seeing friends together, dragging each other to movies that bored one of us to death. His eyes glazed over when I tried to fascinate him with *Middlemarch*. I rubbed my temples while he replayed a Hendrix album into the wee hours or puzzled over some intricate business deal. We survived corporate dinners and foreign films, poetry readings and rock concerts. My role models were artists, his were entrepreneurs. We tugged persistently at each other's psyches and prayed for continental shifts.

As the decades passed, though, the tugging became less strenuous, more habitual. We perfected the fine art of needling. Our children, Lucy and Peter, grew up exasperated but also oddly liberated by our differences, which at the very least gave them options; one eventually became an editor, the other a musician, and both are avid readers who seriously love rock music. Gradually, it dawned on us that we, too, had grown up. Or we had aged out of social insecurity. We no longer had to prove anything to others or, for that matter, to ourselves. We knew we could trust each other. We could say goodbye when we went to work in the morning, maybe stay in town to meet a friend (someone the other could live happily never seeing), and reconvene at home later to compare notes. It was never boring. It's still not. Yet I have friends who tell me they do everything with their husbands. They push a cart together at the supermarket. (Jeff: "I'd rather be dead. Just let me do the shopping.") They never travel separately. If I ask a childhood pal (now married) out to dinner in hopes of some intimate conversation, she invariably answers, "We'd love to!" Calling a friend in California, I learn that "we" are dazzled by the new exhibition at the Getty; we're vegan now; we saw that movie and we were not amused. I relate more easily to my ex-roommate Ginger, who rolls her eyes in mock gratitude when her stay-at-home husband sallies out alone, to my grad-school friend Jane, who has a heady and deeply satisfying relationship with a man who lives in another state, but worries about what will happen to their blissful independence if the two of them ever move in together. I can see her point. Sartre and de Beauvoir lived apart until their deaths, after which some enterprising soul decided to plant them under a single headstone. They've got to be turning in their grave.

I walk out the door with a suitcase, on my way to speak at a weekend writers' conference in Texas, as Jeff, guitar pick in hand, laptop softly whirring in the next room, gives me the warm, sweet glance I fell for decades ago, and a parting kiss. He tells me to have a wonderful time as he gently and firmly closes the door. I know he's about to celebrate—three days in which the television never goes off, the dog sprawls on the bed, the lights stay on till 3 a.m. No one greets him at daybreak with a list of ancient grievances and a furrowed brow. No one smashes his concentration as he's putting the finishing touches on a complex lecture or presentation. No one gloomily reports to him about diseases he doesn't have and dangers he's too sanguine to fear. He's in paradise, and he's got it all to himself. When I finally return, exhilarated by the readings, the company of other writers, he will be delighted to see me. He will have already opened a bottle of wine, the porch chairs will be ready and waiting. We will have so much to say. ◘

Dr. Phil: "The question is not *if* you are going to leave this cheater but *when*"

• Finding the courage to dump an adulterer • Stopping a teenager from calling the shots • Carving out alone time as part of a couple.

Q In the last three years, my husband cheated on me four times (that I know about). We're both miserable, but we need each other financially. My self-esteem is lower than ever, and I can't help bringing up these other women every day; my husband says that's the reason he treats me badly. All I want is a family for my son, but I don't know how much longer I can stand this. Is it better to stay financially afloat and be unhappy or to leave and struggle?

Dr. Phil: You don't need me to tell you that four affairs in three years isn't a good sign, and it seems you're smart enough to realize that you probably don't know all there is to know about your husband's indiscretions. Even if you don't consider him to be much of a Romeo, there are people out there who might.

Let's take a closer look at what you'll be signing up for if you decide to stay with

him. Since the best predictor of future behavior is relevant past behavior, he's inclined to commit adultery again. So if you have any dignity at all, the question is not *if* you are going to leave this cheater but *when*. The longer you stay, the more damage you will do to your self-esteem, and the more your son is going to be exposed to an emotionally barren home environment. You may also be signing yourself up for mental or even physical abuse. I think I've made my point—you're with a guy who isn't nice, and staying with him means more misery.

Now let's take a look at your other option: leaving. I realize that being a single mother and raising a child in a very expensive world is no easy task. Are you likely to have to compromise on housing, clothing, your car, and other necessities and luxuries? Yes, you will need to adjust, but with planning you can make this work. Assistance is available through more options than you might think, not least of which is court-ordered child support. You probably also have family, counseling resources, or a spiritual community that can help with both financial and emotional support. I've always believed that children fare bet-

166

ter when you invest more time than money in their lives.

Obviously, it's up to you, but for me it isn't even a close call. I would get a lawyer, line up my available resources, file for divorce, and ask the lawyer to file an emergency order for temporary support. If your husband won't respect you, it's time for you to teach your son about self-respect—starting with your own good example.

Q | I have been dating my boyfriend for years; we are both divorced. My daughter lives with me, and he has a 16-year-old son who just moved in with him. In the past, my boyfriend would stay at our house whenever he didn't have his son, which was most of the month. Now he spends the night only occasionally, and we go to his place several times a week. The other day, my boyfriend suggested that we start splitting our time between houses, but his son said he would stay only at his dad's. I don't want to force his son to spend time with us, but I miss being with my boyfriend. His child's demands trump our relationship, which makes me feel frustrated and lonely. Do we have to live our lives around what his son dictates?

Dr. Phil: Simply put, *you* don't. Your boyfriend may feel guilt or shame over his marriage falling apart, which may compel him to cave in to his son's wishes, but you certainly don't have to—nor should you.

But while the 16-year-old has no right to dictate what happens with your families, I think he has a point. Let's look at the situation from his perspective. You fell in love; he didn't. The adults seem to want to play house rather than make a serious commitment to merging the two families, and splitting time between residences only complicates the matter. The kid wants to know, "What's in it for me?" The answer is, nothing.

A teenager shouldn't have to bear the burden of making these kinds of big decisions. You have to recognize that what you and your boyfriend do affects more than just the two of you. Blended families and second marriages aren't for the faint of heart. If you're ready to move your relationship to the next level, there's a lot of hard work that needs to happen first. Get some counseling for all the players involved. Come up with goals, set a date to get married, and keep refining your plans. Chapter 2 in my book *Family First* talks about the challenges people face in the situation you're in, so you may want to read that as well.

Q | My boyfriend of a year and a half doesn't get why I need "me" time. Occasionally I like to do things alone—go to the park, see a movie—because it helps me focus on myself for a while. If I don't get this downtime from my relationship every so often, I go stir-crazy. My boyfriend believes that a person who's dating shouldn't do these things; he thinks it's bad for us and that it must mean I long for the single life. How do I convince him otherwise?

Dr. Phil: You have two separate issues here. First, examine whether your restlessness has greater significance. Don't get me wrong: It's normal to spend time solo and with friends to maintain your sense of self, but I suggest you take a closer look at what this guy really means to you.

The more serious problem is that your boyfriend is insecure and feels the need to be validated by you all the time. A healthy individual would go off and do things in his part of the world while you went off and did things in yours. You need to create boundaries in your relationship. If you start to allow your boyfriend to control and contain you, then you're teaching him to do that going forward. Unless you can figure out an arrangement that gives you both what you need, you shouldn't keep seeing him. There will be a point at which you have to say, "I can't go any further. You're going to have to meet me halfway."

I suggest that you sit down with your boyfriend and let him know that being with you doesn't mean that he gets to possess you. You might have a conversation that goes something like the following.

Script of the Month:
Preserving some personal space

You need to understand that I love and care about you, but I will not stop being all of me to be half of us, and I won't ask you for permission to be who I am. If you have insecurities and need reassurance, I'll help you get over them—but I will not enable those feelings. I've always needed to spend some time by myself to get centered; I expect that will always be the case. Please know I'm not blowing you off, and I wouldn't tell you I loved you if I didn't. If you feel my desire for alone time doesn't leave enough room for you, I understand and respect that. I want our relationship to grow, but if you can't be supportive of what's normal for me, then we need to part ways.

This may seem harsh, but you need to stand up for yourself now, or you'll be sorry for a very long time. Besides, it would be unfair if you didn't let him know exactly what you're thinking so that he can make an important decision about his future, too.

> You need to stand up for yourself now, or you'll be sorry for a very long time.

From how important is sex, really, to a simple trick for getting men to do stuff around the house, *Esquire* editor in chief **David Granger** tackles the basics.

"Why Don't You Notice My Hair?" & *Other*
Frequently Asked Questions

Why do you get so angry when some jamoke cuts you off in traffic? Two things. Testosterone is one. The automobile is the other. See, we have this fight-or-flight thing programmed into our DNA, and when another male of the species challenges us, we are coded to get our hackles up. Add to that the fact that from the moment we got our driver's license, the automobile has been the extension of our sense of both power and freedom, and you have a perfect storm of nature and nurture creating a hostile response to a challenge to the things that make us a man.

That said, we know we need to just calm down. One thing that would help is if you would just rub the back of our head and mutter "bastard" under your breath in sympathy.

You know when you just sit there with a scowl on your face, not saying anything? What is that about? Generally, it's not about you. We tend to take everything personally, and we tend to anticipate not what can go right but what will inevitably go wrong. So, whether it's something complicated at work or getting that stinking sliding door to roll right, we're consumed with the obstacles in our path toward success.

Is everything really about sex? Well, no. I mean, yes. Sex is one of the reasons we're together, you and us. There was something about you the first time we saw you that made our heart sing. If we're lucky, it's still there every time we see you. Plus, is there anything more affirming, more life affirming and satisfying than sex? Essentially, we don't see the downside. So the answer is no, not everything. And the answer is yes, a part of everything is, if we're both lucky, about sex.

What do men talk about?
Usually, we talk about what we're engaged in at that mo-
ment. Or we're telling each other stories of embarrassment or triumph. We grew up telling each other stories, and we'll never stop. We don't tell each other jokes. The topic of our conversation rarely matters, and we probably won't remember what we were talking about later when you ask. The only time we really talk seriously with each other is when we fear we might be failing. But that's rare, and it usually passes quickly. Which is why we didn't mention it.

We can't believe you didn't notice our hair. Yeah, well. That might just be something you will have to learn to live with.

You don't seem to like it when we tell you what to do. Oh, you noticed. Look, we tend to see ourselves as the initiators of action. If we know what needs to be done, usually we'll get it done. In fact, we take joy in accomplishing things. Let's compromise. Just stick a list somewhere of things that need to be done. Don't put our name on it. It's just a list of tasks. We like tasks. We like doing them. We like finishing them. But we like it best when it was our idea to do them.

What do you like most about us? Oh, Jesus. We love it when you sit down on the side of the bed and kiss us for no reason. We can't get over that. We love it when you ask us for advice on something that really matters to you. We love the way you smell. We love the way you smell right after you finish exercising. We love the way you look just before you wake up in the morning. We love it when you argue with us about something—movies, sports, politics—that really doesn't matter. We love the way you will fill a silence at a dinner party and we love the way you give us guidance when it comes to our mothers. We love the way you look when you're half-dressed or half-undressed. We love your certainty, even when you're sure we're wrong. And we love your hair. ◖

Strong and silent is only half true. Chris Abani reveals…

What Men Aren't Telling Us

That women are mysterious and unknowable is something every young man grows up believing. Men, on the other hand, never think of themselves as mysterious or confusing, and we are often at a loss as to why women want to figure us out. But since you asked:

When you say we don't really talk to you, or reveal ourselves to you, we wish you knew just how much we have had to suppress about our desires, pains, fears, and vulnerability over the years to conform to the script of masculinity that we are given. Sometimes we don't open up because we are afraid of what we will find. We are also afraid that if you see who we really are, in all our flawed humanity (and not the flaws that annoy you, like being untidy or driving fast), you won't like us.

Men do communicate, often very directly, but women sometimes cannot accept how simple what we have to say is. We seldom play games—we aren't that sophisticated. If we don't call you for a couple of days after a date, it is because either we are afraid you will think we are stalkers (and we will call on day three) or we aren't into you. That's all there is.

We are as nervous as you are about sex; I don't care what you've heard. Your anatomy is a mystery that nobody bothers explaining to us. Even when we think we have mastered one woman's body, every body is different. We feel inadequate if we can't satisfy you in bed, and since no one has told us what to do with feelings of inadequacy, we project them onto you. Sad but true.

We are very insecure about how we look and what you really think about us, and we are excited when you do small, nice things for us like make coffee or come with us to the barber or just buy us a good book. We've been trained never to show this side to you, but it is there.

We are not subtle creatures. You might think that when you play with your hair in our presence, we know that means you like us. We don't know for sure. Men who do are bad men (sorry, guys!). And anything you've been told about playing hard to get is wrong.

We crave cuddling and hand-holding, maybe even more than you do.

We are desperate to please you because we know you are far sexier and more beautiful than you will ever admit to yourself, and we're confused (but extremely happy) as to why you like us.

Here's the thing: You rescue us every day in small, quiet ways, so why not in this way? Let us into your mystery, tell us how you would like to be loved, show us how to see you, really see you. ◐

> We are as nervous as you are about sex; I don't care what you've heard.

La différence—it has something to do with which duck carries the walking stick.
George Saunders on…

Men and Women...
How to Tell Them Apart

Much has been made of the whole "what do women want/what do men want" thing. I think it's actually pretty simple: Women want men to know what women want. And men want women not to want anything.

If women must want something, men want them to want something easy to get. On the other hand, women want their men to go to great lengths for them. If a man gives a woman something he got with little effort—say, a bowling trophy he's had since he was 20—his woman may feel taken for granted. And he will have to buy her flowers to make up for it. The more egregious the offense, the less pedestrian his flowers can afford to be. For something like this, I recommend the man genetically engineer a species of rare lily not seen on the face of the Earth since Cleopatra's time. That should just about do it. And deliver them in a gold vase. (Note: A bowling trophy does not qualify as a "gold vase," even if spray-painted. Trust me on this.)

Men, in contrast, have very simple desires. What men want is for their woman to love them so much that, when they are doing nothing at all, or are even doing something slightly "wrong"—flirting with the college girl at the Gap, say, invading the wrong country, eating leftover Indian food from the container, with their fingers, in their underwear—their woman just stands there going: *Isn't he something? Wow, look at that fine ass.*

And yet all relationship problems can be solved with a little creativity.

Women: When your husband is eating Indian food with his fingers, in his underwear—join the party by taking your pants off, too!

Men: When your wife looks askance at the rare Egyptian lilies you cloned for her—agree with her that the lilies are inadequate, toss them into the yard, run out in your underwear and give them a vicious kick, to indicate how deeply repentant you are.

Women: If your man keeps calling you by another woman's name—change your name!

Men: If your wife has an affair with her Pilates instructor, make a latex mask of his face, then wear it to bed!

Women: If your husband is thoughtful enough to wear a latex mask of your hot Pilates instructor to bed, reward him with his favorite meal of pot roast, steak, bacon, lard cubes, bourbon, and Snickers bars.

Personally, I'm glad men and women are different. Otherwise how would I know which restroom to enter in a fancy restaurant where the bathrooms do not say men or women, but MSSR or MMSLLE, or just have drawings of a male and female duck, which to me look pretty much identical, except one of the ducks is holding a walking stick, and I am like: I have no idea—maybe female ducks carry the walking stick? Because honestly, I have never seen a duck, of either gender, use a walking stick.

But because men and women are different, I can just lurk nearby, waiting for the next man to come along, then follow him into the appropriate restroom. Or I can wait for the next woman to come along, and go into the opposite restroom from her. Or I can wait for a duck to come along, see which restroom it goes into, then follow it in, turn it over, and see if it's carrying a walking stick.

Anyway, as the French say, *Vive la différence!* Which means: Live the difference! Or, in some translations: What is so different?

I find that so true. What is so different, really, between men and women? Our sexual organs, our breasts, our girth, our life philosophies, the extent to which we consider "mopping" part of "cleaning the kitchen," whether we tend to leap up and pretend to shoot an imaginary basketball right in the middle of a wake? Yes, yes, but other than these few, trivial differences, we are—thank goodness—very much the same. ◨

Divorce Dreams

She's not the only (more or less) happily married woman who fantasizes about freedom, alone-time, and a room clear of somebody's big clunky shoes. **Ellen Tien** on the phenomenon she calls the Mid-Wife Crisis.

I contemplate divorce every day. It tugs on my sleeve each morning when my husband, Will, greets me in his chipper, smug morning-person voice, because after 16 years of waking up together, he still hasn't quite pieced out that I'm not viable before 10 A.M. It puts two hands on my forehead and mercilessly presses when he blurts out the exact wrong thing ("Are you excited for your surprise party next Tuesday?"); when he lies to avoid the fight ("What do you mean I left our apartment door open? I never even knew our apartment *had* a door!"); when he buttons his shirt and jacket into the wrong buttonholes, collars and seams unaligned like a vertical game of dominoes, with possibly a scrap of shirttail zippered into his fly. It flicks me, hard, just under the eye when, during a parent-teacher conference, he raises his arm high in the air, scratches his armpit, and then—*then!*—absently smells his fingers.

It slammed into me like a 4,000-pound Volvo station wagon one spring evening four years ago, although I remember it as if it were last year. He had dropped me off in front of a restaurant, prior to finding a parking spot. As I crossed in front of the car, he pulled forward, happily smiling back over his left shoulder at some random fascinating bit (a sign with an interesting font, a new scaffolding, a diner that he may or may not have eaten at the week after he graduated from college), and plowed into me. The impact, while not wondrous enough to break bodies 12 ways, was sufficient enough to bounce me sidewise onto the hood, legs waving in the air like antennae, and skirt flung somewhere up around my ears.

For one whole second, New York City stood stock-still and looked at my underwear.

As I pounded the windshield with my fist and shouted—"Will, Will, stop the car!"—he finally faced forward, blink, blink, blink, trying, yes, truly trying to take it all in. And I heard him ask with mild astonishment, very faintly because windshield glass is surprisingly thick, "What are you doing here?"

In retrospect, it was an excellent question, a question that I've asked myself from altar to present, both incessantly and occasionally.

What am I doing here?

Don't misunderstand: I would not, could not disparage my marriage (not on a train, not in the rain, not in a house, not with a mouse). After 192 months, Will and I remain if not happily married, then steadily so. Our marital state is Indiana, say, or Connecticut—some red areas, more blue. Less than bliss, better than disaster. We are arguably, to my wide-ish range of reference, Everycouple.

Nor is Will the Very Bad Man that I have made him out to be. Rather, like every other male I know, he is merely a Moderately Bad Man, you know, the kind of man who will leave his longboat-sized shoes directly in the flow of our home's traffic so that one day I'll trip over them, break my neck, and die, after which he'll walk home from the morgue, grief-stricken, take off his shoes with a heavy heart, and then leave them in the center of the room until they kill the housekeeper. Everyman.

Still, beneath the thumpingly ordinary nature of our marriage—Everymarriage—runs the silent chyron of divorce. It's the scarlet concept, the closely held contemplation of nearly every woman I know who has children who have been out of diapers for at least two years and a husband who won't be in them for another 30. It's the secret reverie of a demographic that freely discusses postpartum depression, eating disorders, and Ambien dependence (often all in the same sentence) with the plain candor of golden brown toast. In a let-it-all-hang-out culture, this is the given that stays tucked in.

This is the Mid-Wife Crisis.

Mind you, when I say Mid-Wife Crisis, I mean the middle-of-married-life kind, not the kind where you go to Yale to learn how to legally brandish a birthing stool. As one girlfriend remarked, it's the age of rage—a period of high irritation that lasts roughly one to two decades. As a colleague e-mailed me, it's the simmering underbelly of resentment, the 600-pound mosquito in the room. At a juncture where we thought we should have unearthed some modicum of certainty, we are turning into the Clash. If I go will there be trouble? If I stay will it be double? Should I stay or should I go?

Our mothers knew better than to ponder such questions, at least not out loud in front of God and the hairdresser. They deliberately waited to reach the last straw until their children were grown and the house was paid for. At 25, they were ladies with lady clothes and lady hairdos—bona fide adults, the astronauts' wives. By 40, they were relics.

But we, we with our 21st-century access to youth captured in a gleaming Mason jar with a pinked square of gingham rubber-banded over the top, we are still visually tolerable if not downright irresistible when we're 30 or 35 or 40. If you believe the fashion magazines—which I devoutly do—even 50- and 60-year-olds are (lick finger, touch to imaginary surface, make sizzle noise) pretty hot tickets.

We are also tickets with jobs and disposable income. If we jump ship now, we're still attractive prospects who may have another shot at happiness. There's just that tricky wicket of determining whether eternal comfort resides in the tried-and-true or whether the untried will be truer.

Our mothers, so old too young, believed that marriage was the best they could get. We, the children of mothers who settled (or were punished for not settling), wonder: Is this as good as it gets?

Our mothers feared being left alone. We crave time alone. Alone-time is the new heroin.

What are we doing here?

We were groomed to think bigger and better—achievement was our birthright—so it's small surprise that our marriages are more freighted. Marriage and its cruel cohort, fidelity, are a lot to expect from anyone, much less from swift-flying us. Would we agree to wear the same eyeshadow or eat in the same restaurant every day for a lifetime? Nay, cry the villagers, the echo answers nay. We believe in our superhood. We count on it.

So, did our feminist foremothers set us up for failure? Or were they just trying to empower us so that we wouldn't buy into the notion of having to be a better better half?

Either way, many of us semi–bought into it. As the tail end of the baby boomers/mavericks of Gen X, we still had one foot in the Good Girl pond, or at least the wet footprints leading out of it. In the beginning, we felt obliged to join the race to have it all; being married was an integral part of the contest and heaven forfend we should be disqualified.

Flash-forward to ten years later, when we discover that we can get it all but whose harebrained scheme was this anyway? We can get jobs, get pregnant, get it done. We can try—with varying levels of success—to get sleep, get fit, get control, and get those important Me-moments where one keeps a journal with thought-provoking lists that go "I'm a woman first, a mother second, a laundress third." We get upset, we get over it. What we don't always get is: Why.

My high-powered, high-earning friend discovers that her magnificently indolent husband has been having an affair with a coworker; she threatens to give him the heave-ho, demurs when he demands that she pay the rent on his new apartment, and decides to work it out. For now.

Why?

A woman I know, the stay-at-home wife of a mogul—a really nice mogul with multiple houses, a jet, a chef, the whole pizza pie—throws it all over, packs up her two young children, and leaves him in search of greater satisfaction.

Why?

I watch in frustration as my son desperately tries to talk to Will through a newspaper or computer screen or whatever other large, flat surfaces fathers place between themselves and filial communication, and yet I know in my heart that I would be mightily hard-pressed to remove this father from his son's house.

Why?

> We crave
> time alone.
> Alone-time
> is the
> new heroin.

Reasons and rationalizations abound and rebound. It doesn't matter whether the infractions are big or small. At a certain point, we stop asking why and start asking how. How did it come to this? How much longer can I go on? When there are no hows left, the jig is up.

I recently stood by as a clothing designer, a mother in her 40s, announced to a group of women that she was divorcing her husband. The women's faces flickered with curiosity, support, recognition, and—could it be?—yearning. Not a one of us suggested that she try harder to make it work. No voice murmured, "What a shame."

Because it isn't a shame. Divorce is no longer the shame that spits stain upon womanly merit. Conventional wisdom decrees that marriage takes work, but it doesn't take work, it *is* work. It's a job—intermittently fulfilling and annoying, with not enough vacation days. Divorce is a job, too (with even fewer vacation days). It's a matter of weighing your options.

A friend once compared the prospect of leaving her husband to leaving her child's private school: The school wasn't entirely to her liking, but her daughter was happy there; it wasn't what she'd expected, but applying to other schools involved a lot of costly, complicated paperwork and the nagging uncertainty of whether another school would accept her and/or really be that much better.

Another friend viewed divorce as being akin to an extended juice fast: You're intrigued but skeptical, admiring yet apprehensive. Is it dangerous? Does it work? You're not completely sold, but then again, you could envision yourself attempting it down the road.

What this says to me (other than: my friends sure do come up with awfully good metaphors!) is that women don't view divorce as a scary, shadowy behemoth. It's an unpalatable yet manageable task—like changing schools or extreme dieting—that may or may not yield a better result.

To be sure, there will be throngs of angry women who will decry me for plunging a stake into the heart of holy matrimony. "My husband is my lifeline," I've heard said (and that's bad news for the aorta). "My husband and I never fight" is another marital chestnut—again, bad news (not to mention a big fat lie), since according to the experts, the strongest relationships are the ones in which people can continually agree to disagree. "My husband is my best friend," others will aver.

No. Your husband is not your best friend. Your best friend is your best friend. If your husband were your best friend, what would that make your best friend—the dog? When a woman tells me that her husband is her best friend, what I hear is: I don't really have any friends.

But if self-delusion is your particular poison, well, then that's fine, too. Just make sure that when you phone your life-order in, you say, "One self-delusion, please," as opposed to "One perfect marriage." Fantasy, as we all know, doesn't deliver.

Because in the end, that's basically what it's all about: getting your order right. Our day comes down to choices—and it's finally dawning on the long-term wives of the world that divorce may be the last-standing woman's right to choose. We can admit that our marriages aren't lambent, lyrical ice-dancing routines and still decide to push on together to the final flying sit spin. We also realize that divorce is an alternative that's fully within reach, be it now or later or never. The more readily we acknowledge the solid utility of marriage (as one friend's husband put it, "I'm essentially a checkbook and a sperm bank—but I'm okay with that!"), the more ably we can splinter the box of marital fantasy that makes us feel stuck, trapped, obliged. One eloquent swing of the ax and happiness is thrust firmly back into our own hands.

This is not to say that dismantling one's marriage will automatically bring happiness; it's the idealization of marriage that needs to be shredded, along with its accompanying bumper sticker WIVES MAKE BETTER WOMEN. If we stay, we stay because we decide to, not because our ankles and wrists have been locked into societal expectations. If, after various efforts, we finally leave, we have the confidence to be the leavers and not the left.

Having choices is a cornerstone of strength: Choosers won't be beggars. "Thinking about divorce is kind of like living in New York City with its museums and theater and culture," a doctor friend of mine said. "You may never actually go to any of these places, but for some reason, just the idea that you could if you wanted to makes you feel better."

Maybe one day, marriage—like the human appendix, male nipples, or your pinky toes—will become a vestigial structure that will, in a millennium or two, be obsolete. Our great-great-great-grandchildren's grandchildren will ask each other in passing, "Remember marriage? What was its function again? Was it that maladaptive organ that intermittently produced gastrointestinal antigens and sometimes got so inflamed that it painfully erupted?"

Yes. Yes it was.

Until that day of obsolescence, we can confront the dilemma and consider the choice a privilege. Once upon a time is the stuff of fairy tales. As for happily ever after—see appendix. ▣

talking and listening

It's Showdown Time!

No simmering fuses. No verbal bombshells. **Judith Stone** discovers
a three-step plan that takes the fear (and the fight) out of confrontations.

You say you hate confrontation, that you'd rather have oral surgery without anesthesia than a tough, cards-on-the-table talk with a colleague, spouse, or good friend? Have we got a plan for you.

What's that? You say you love confrontation, that you may even be a little too eager to open up a can of weapons-grade whup-ass—but that, come to think of it, these big blow-ups are getting you approximately nowhere? Have we got a plan for you.

And it's the same one. Developed by corporate coach Esther Jeles, this fresh approach to conflict resolution has been road-tested by hundreds of participants in the workshops she holds for businesses interested in improving communication and increasing productivity. "Confrontation isn't about telling someone off or setting them straight," says Jeles, founder and CEO of Aylet, a Chicago-based consulting firm. "Confrontation is looking at issues and solving problems." You can participate, or you can let things happen to you, Jeles notes. "You can only affect the outcome directly if you speak up," she says. "Nothing ever changes for the better unless opposing parties come together and discuss the situation and solutions." Most important, a healthy confrontation can be a chance for you to help people feel better about themselves, she says. "And to be proud of your own behavior."

Confrontation? A mental health tool, a community builder, a force for kindness? The word definitely has developed

> ## A healthy confrontation can be a chance for you to help people feel better about themselves.

a bad rep, even though it emerged from the mildest of roots, the Latin for "together" and "forehead"; initially it meant simply "to come face-to-face." Jeles urges a return to the collaborative image conjured by the word's origins—putting our heads together to reach a common goal.

The term she uses for this kind of encounter is carefrontation. Reframing the definition creates an instant attitude shift in her clients, Jeles says, especially after she helps them realize that they're already champs at healthy confrontations. "We've all had hundreds of them!" Jeles says. "But we tend to remember only the confrontations that got ugly, and to call the successful ones something else."

What did we intuitively do right in the non-ugly encounters? Some version, Jeles says, of the three core steps that she recommends:

1. Prepare with care.

Before you confront another person, have a long talk with yourself and try the following.

■ Define the problem, separating the practical issues ("I stayed up all night finishing a report because a colleague didn't turn in her share of the research") from the emotions they evoke ("I'm furious with her for sticking me with extra work!").

■ Engage in what Jeles likes to call self-witnessing. "That means asking yourself: 'What does this situation remind me of? How have I handled such issues in the past? What's my pattern?'" For example, the woman stuck writing the report might realize that what she does, over and over, is bite her tongue even when she sees disaster looming, because she dreads conflict. "Maybe she'll notice that the situation reminds her of her relationship with her sister," Jeles says. "Maybe the family pattern was that she was always stuck holding the bag. When she sees the pattern, then she can change it."

■ Practice expressing the problem in a clear, calm way, without blaming the other person. "Don't throw in everything you've held in for a year," she says. "That wouldn't be a carefrontation; it would be an assault."

2. Offer an invitation to talk.

■ There's no single surefire opener, Jeles says. "But a couple I've seen work well are 'I sense there's something you want to talk to me about. If now isn't the time, I'm ready whenever you are,' or 'I've got some suggestions that I think can really help you.'" People might feel suspicious at first, interpreting "I think I can help" as code for "I'm preparing to attack." Eventually, though, Jeles says, "they're grateful, because they're floundering."

3. Practice no-blame talking and listening.

■ Present the thoughts you collected in the preparation stage, being careful not to blame or accuse. "I might say, 'I know I may not have all the information, but here's what I think is happening.' After that, you can ask, 'What do you think is happening?' And then you listen." You're not listening, Jeles points out, if you're preparing your next verbal volley—"reloading," she calls it. One time-honored way of keeping yourself from reloading is reflecting back to the other person: "So let me make sure I understand what you said...."

■ If the confrontation is taking place at work, Jeles stresses, leave your emotions out of the discussion. Suggest solutions that focus on tasks and goals instead of the person's faults. "Get right to what I call www.com:

Who does What by When Communication. That's 99 percent of the communication required in corporate America," says Jeles. "Focusing on productivity instead of blame—fixing the plan, not the person—shifts the mood from threatening to uplifting." Set a time for meeting again to check in with each other about how the new plan is working.

If the confrontation is taking place off the job—friend to friend, spouse to spouse, or parent to child—then you do need to express your emotions clearly, but calmly. "So you might say to a teenager, 'Last night when you didn't come home when you said you would, I felt disappointed and angry, but mostly I was afraid something bad had happened to you. Have you ever had that feeling?' Then ask what was going on with her." The focus should be on understanding each other's feelings and thought processes.

A common cause of conflict both at work and at home, according to Jeles, is not discussing a problem as soon as it comes up. "I don't leave it for a month, I don't leave it for a week, I don't let 15 things go by—I confront every issue one at a time, as it comes up, or as soon as I notice a pattern. Then I find out what the other person is thinking." And if the relationship is one fraught with conflict? "I tell all my clients, it doesn't matter what the history is, you've got to start new somewhere." Begin using carefrontation steps every time the smallest thing comes up, Jeles says. "That creates very different results than waiting until you're just about ready to pop your balloon."

Once you redefine confrontation and learn to do it better, Jeles promises, you'll no longer be tortured by the rule-flouting teen, the shirking colleague, the belittling boss, the secret-spilling friend, or the Man Who Mistook His Wife for a Doormat. The more you practice, she says, the easier it gets to give good carefrontation, and to receive it. ◘

The Friendship Test

Who gives, who takes? Who listens, who rants? Who stays in touch, who calls only when she needs something? Friends don't let friends do all the work. **Martha Beck** tells you how to get the two of you back in balance (and when not to bother).

When my friend Riley and I met for coffee, I was feeling somewhat gloomy, looking forward to a little emotional support. As I sat down, however, Riley recounted a harrowing tale. Only hours before, as she was chomping happily on some caramel corn, one of her front teeth had snapped off, right at the gum line! Her dentist glued it back in, but I mean... The horror! The horror!

My bad mood disappeared as I grilled Riley about every detail, told her it was perfectly normal that the incident upset her more than global warming, and affirmed that her teeth looked great (they did). After a while, Riley drew a deep breath, exhaled, and relaxed.

"Now," she said, "what's going on with you?"

Immediately, my previous unhappiness resurfaced. Riley did some heavy therapy on my private psychological issues, which was no doubt recorded and posted on YouTube by the bored baristas. No matter—I felt worlds better by the time we parted. So, she said through her totally normal-looking teeth, did Riley.

To me, this was friendship at its best. Riley and I spontaneously and easily switched roles, taking care and being taken care of. But not all relationships (certainly not all of mine) flow this smoothly. Many friends have unspoken but ironclad rules about which person will do what share of the emotional and logistical work.

Right now, scan your mental files for friendships where the roles never change: She's the talker, you're the listener; she's the star, you're the screwup; she never calls you, you always call her. Imagine what this friend's response would be if you stopped playing your part or stepped into hers. Would she be shocked or angry? Would she ice you, scold you, or drop off your social calendar? If so, I'm afraid that particular connection isn't exactly a

friendship. Rigid roles enforced by social pressure add up to something else—something I call a naiad dyad.

What the Hell's a Naiad Dyad?

Naiads are mythological nymphs who ruled the rivers and springs of ancient Greece. One of these watery demi-goddesses had a famously handsome son named Narcissus, who attracted many admirers, none more admiring than himself. He fell so madly in love with his own reflection that he did nothing but stare at it. Narcissus's friends found this daunting—all, that is, except for another nymph named Echo, whose curse (naiads were highly curse prone) was that she couldn't voice her own thoughts, only repeat words spoken by others.

In their twisted way, Narcissus and Echo were ideal companions. Both were obsessed with the same person (him) and both expressed the same thoughts, ideas, and opinions (his). I'm sure the next-door satyrs thought their relationship was perfect. Not so much. In one version of the story, Narcissus, unable to work out the logistics of being in love with himself, plunged a dagger into his heart and was transformed into a flower. Echo, devastated, wandered off to haunt canyons and glens, repeating random sentiments shouted by strangers.

Question: Do you see any similarities between your rigid-role "friendships" and the Narcissus-Echo relationship, or do I have to bash you over the head with them? Answer: Too late. Brace yourself.

To paraphrase Tolstoy, unhappy friendships are all different, but those inflexible relationships almost universally signal the psychological dynamics of narcissists and their echoes. On the surface, these friendships look idyllic—as Jennifer Coolidge's dim character says of such a relationship in the film *A Mighty Wind,* "It's almost as like we have one brain that we share between us." Since no two individuals are identical, such unanimity is always an illusion; the "one brain," or at least the dominant will, belongs to the person both friends implicitly agree is more important. The echo voluntarily surrenders personal needs, ideas, and even rights in exchange for the narcissist's "love," which is actually directed at her own reflection. "Enough about me; let's talk about you," she says with words and actions. "What do you think about me?"

> I'm haunted by the fact that I never had a conversation with a college buddy who later committed suicide. Maybe I could have helped by insisting she learn to receive.

Such relationships exist because narcissism is a basic factor of human consciousness, beginning in infancy. Tiny babies literally can't focus on anyone but themselves. As children grow, however, they realize that others have feelings, needs, and rights. They learn to share and care.

Usually.

There are some individuals who apparently never outgrow infantile self-obsession. Throughout life, they take without giving and expect others to give without taking. Even when they have their own children, they can't focus on anyone but themselves. One woman told me quite seriously that her 3-day-old son was "a selfish brat" because "he cries when he knows I'm trying to sleep." Extremely narcissistic parents often have echo spouses, who limply accept unfair treatment from everyone, including their children. "Don't mind me, sweetheart," sighs the echo parent. "Here's money for cocaine—I'll stay here, knitting you a sweater from my hair."

Children raised by such parents grow up unconsciously assuming there are only two possible relationship modes: Some become thoroughgoing narcissists, others eternal echoes. (Some bounce between these two states, acting oppressively in some of their relationships but groveling in others, like the middle manager who trashes subordinates but toadies up to the boss.)

When two people who fall into this kind of dyad meet, they bond instantly, like Krazy Glue. "I feel as if I've known you all my life," they say, basking in the familiar narcissist-echo energy. There are no arguments, no awkward uncertainty about who should do what, because the echo immediately begins reflecting the narcissist. She stops listening to rap, catching her new friend's polka fever.

Even more important, the echo assumes all the subtle work of friendship: initiating contact, arranging activities, offering compliments and other forms of nurturing. She doesn't mind things being one-sided; she's just grateful—ecstatic—that she's being adored by a replica of the parent who couldn't love her. And the narcissistic friend really is adoring—not of the echo, as they both mistakenly believe, but of her reflection in her new friend's eyes. It's all fun and games, right up until someone gets stabbed.

The Bitter End

"I'm devastated," whispered my echo-y client Naomi. "My best friend just...dumped me. I don't understand; we're so close. We went to each other's weddings. We talked every day. Then out of the blue, she tells me I've changed, I'm getting selfish, she's done with me. I don't think she'll ever speak to me again." Baffling as it may seem if you don't understand narcissism, Naomi is probably right. Her long-standing friendship is likely over.

This is how naiad dyads often end. For instance, when Naomi the echo finally became so unhappy she hired a coach, she began to see herself as worthy of reciprocal friendship. She started drawing boundaries and making small, gentle requests. Her supposed friend, a true narcissist, saw this as a selfish betrayal of their implicit arrangement.

Even if Naomi had kept echoing like an empty cistern, this naiad dyad would probably have ended. Because narcissists don't give love, which is half the equation of a genuine emotional connection, they always become increasingly unhappy over time (remember Narcissus's suicide). Many blame their echoes: "You're not making me happy anymore!" Whether the echo gets better or the narcissist gets worse, the relationship may suddenly and completely fracture, the Krazy Glue bond breaking as quickly and completely as it formed.

Real friendship never does this, because it's extremely flexible. Friends take turns performing and receiving "friendship maintenance" tasks, from making phone calls to buying presents. When Riley's tooth broke, she got my immediate attention: I "echoed" her. Then we switched roles, and we discussed my problems. This simple turn-taking is what naiad dyads lack, and it leads to catastrophic failure. Take the quiz (next page) if you suspect that one of your friendships is actually a naiad dyad. If it is, try one of the following fixes.

Let's say your quiz score reveals you're in a rigid friendship where you call all the shots and do none of the work. You might be a narcissist. Which probably means you don't care and won't change. My only advice? Avoid daggers.

On the other hand, if you're disturbed by receiving one-sided VIP treatment, you might want to talk to her and explain that her excessive selflessness is troubling, that you need to give as well as receive to feel like her friend. I'm haunted by the fact that I never had this conversation with a college buddy who years later committed suicide. Maybe I could have helped by insisting she learn to receive as well as give. You can't force a confirmed echo out of her role, but it's worth trying.

And what if your quiz score reveals that you're playing the echo role? You could ask your friend to do something that's usually "your" job: "You know, I'd love it if you'd drive over to my place today, since I always drive over to yours." A normal friend may be surprised, but she'll comply. A narcissist will go cold, angry, or passive-aggressive. This won't immediately end your inner child's adulation for her, but it will horrify you enough to begin seeing reality and disengaging.

If you can't just end a naiad dyad—say your friend is also a coworker—there's another option. You can train her like a sea mammal, as author Amy Sutherland reported in her *New York Times* article "What Shamu Taught Me About a Happy Marriage." Narcissists hate being ignored—and crave praise. A combination of indifference and adulation can powerfully shape their behavior. When your coworker shouts that the coffee you made is too hot, don't react at all. Later, when she's calm, spontaneously exclaim, "You're projecting so much authority!" or "You look great!" The narcissist will react like a junkie inhaling opium, and probably increase the behavior you're rewarding. Is this healthy? God, no. But it's better than helpless echoism.

Making Friendship Blossom

These methods can get you out of truly sick naiad dyads and improve marginal cases, moving them away from strict role division toward reciprocity and flexibility. The more fluid and balanced your relationships become, the more you'll see that friendship, unlike Narcissus, can flower without anyone's getting hurt. As someone who's been blessed with marvelous friends, I can assure you this is worth the effort. But enough about me. What do you think about...you?

> Scan your mental files for friendships where the roles never change. Imagine what your friend's response would be if you stopped playing your part or stepped into hers.

Good Friend, Bad Friend?

There's an unspoken contract in friendship: You be there for me, I'll be there for you. But what if one of you isn't living up to her end of the deal? (What if it's *you*?) Sometimes it's okay to keep score, says **Martha Beck**. Just go through this who-does-what-for-whom list, and add up your points at the end.

1 Initiate contact between the two of you (by calling, e-mailing, dropping by for a visit, sending an invitation to an event, etc.).

	1	2	3	4	5
I do this for my friend:	never	rarely	sometimes	often	always

SCORE_____

My friend does this for me:	never	rarely	sometimes	often	always

SCORE_____

2 Create a supportive atmosphere, making a point of being cheerful, encouraging, and caring enough to make the other person feel good.

	1	2	3	4	5
I do this for my friend:	never	rarely	sometimes	often	always

SCORE_____

My friend does this for me:	never	rarely	sometimes	often	always

SCORE_____

3 Prepare a special event (a dinner, birthday party, fun activity) for both of you to do together.

	1	2	3	4	5
I do this for my friend:	never	rarely	sometimes	often	always

SCORE_____

My friend does this for me:	never	rarely	sometimes	often	always

SCORE_____

4 Stand up for the friend with other people; defend or support her when people aren't treating her well.

	1	2	3	4	5
I do this for my friend:	never	rarely	sometimes	often	always

SCORE_____

My friend does this for me:	never	rarely	sometimes	often	always

SCORE_____

5 Focus on the other person's problems; offer empathy, understanding, kindness, comfort, and verbal reassurance.

	1	2	3	4	5
I do this for my friend:	never	rarely	sometimes	often	always

SCORE_____

My friend does this for me:	never	rarely	sometimes	often	always

SCORE_____

6 Physically help out with the other person's life: show up to take care of things when the other is ill; take care of pets, plants, children while friend is out of town.

	1	2	3	4	5
I do this for my friend:	never	rarely	sometimes	often	always

SCORE_____

| My friend does this for me: | never | rarely | sometimes | often | always |

SCORE_____

7 Give small (or large) presents that will mean a lot to the other person. Remember birthdays and other occasions that are personally significant to that person.

	1	2	3	4	5
I do this for my friend:	never	rarely	sometimes	often	always

SCORE_____

| My friend does this for me: | never | rarely | sometimes | often | always |

SCORE_____

8 Compliment the person's looks, intelligence, talent, importance, fashion sense, magnanimity, and other sterling qualities.

	1	2	3	4	5
I do this for my friend:	never	rarely	sometimes	often	always

SCORE_____

| My friend does this for me: | never | rarely | sometimes | often | always |

SCORE_____

9 Help the other feel better after unpleasant interactions with others (issues at the office, family-of-origin drama, and the processing of romantic relationship dynamics).

	1	2	3	4	5
I do this for my friend:	never	rarely	sometimes	often	always

SCORE_____

| My friend does this for me: | never | rarely | sometimes | often | always |

SCORE_____

10 Make a point of being punctual for appointments, keeping promises no matter what, and remembering and honoring all commitments.

	1	2	3	4	5
I do this for my friend:	never	rarely	sometimes	often	always

SCORE_____

| My friend does this for me: | never | rarely | sometimes | often | always |

SCORE_____

MY TOTAL SCORE _____

MY FRIEND'S TOTAL SCORE _____

Now subtract your friend's score from yours. This may be a negative number. _____
(See score results below.)

Scoring

■ **Between +40 and +25:**
Hello-o-o-o! You are an echo-o-o-o! Seriously, in this relationship, you're doing way too much of the work and allowing yourself to be devalued. At some level, you know this. If you begin standing up for yourself, expecting fair treatment and reciprocity, you may lose the relationship. But if you don't, you'll lose your soul. Time to step up.

■ **Between +24 and +9:**
You're allowing your friend to call most of the shots while she does little to merit it. You probably feel an undercurrent of resentment and disappointment. Begin asking for the things you give but don't get—emotional support, phone calls, gifts—or drop your own level of giving to match your friend's. The friendship may look weaker to you, but actually, this will eliminate resentment and strengthen the relationship.

■ **Between +8 and -8:**
You have a balanced relationship with this person, and that's the starting place for all really beautiful friendships. If the relationship is relatively new, pay attention to maintaining the balance that allows you and your friend to both care for and be cared for by each other. If the relationship is a long-standing one, thank Zeus and give yourself a libation. Few things in life are as precious as a balanced friendship, and you've got one.

■ **Between -9 and -24:**
You may not have realized it, but you're a bit of the diva in this friendship, and the other party might not be as contented as you assume. She's doing the heavy lifting that preserves your bond. Start paying attention to this and expressing gratitude. Then start reciprocating. She may have trouble receiving, in which case you might be reduced to a sort of master-servant relationship, though this is kind of icky. However, you may well find that your relationship blossoms into something new, and that it feels very good to give.

■ **Between -25 and -40:**
You're using this person like a wad of facial tissue. If you see no problem with this, you're on the narcissistic side, and nothing I say will convince you things aren't perfect. If the imbalance in the friendship does trouble you but your friend won't accept care or attention, she's probably a hard-core echo with a seething mother lode of hidden anger and resentment. Talk to her about the imbalance, then start sharing more of the relationship tasks. If this strikes you as unnecessary, impossible, or intolerable, the odds of this friendship surviving long-term are very low. ◘

Dr. Phil: "Just put it all on the line and see what happens"

• Regretting a missed opportunity for love • Managing an unforgiving parent • Salvaging a friendship.

Q I'm afraid I've made a terrible mistake. About two years ago, a man I've known since childhood tried to turn our platonic relationship into something more. At the time, I wasn't interested, but he continued to pursue me. Not wanting to hurt him, I probably gave him false hope. Of course, I ended up hurting him when I started seeing someone else, and we hadn't spoken until we ran into each other at a wedding recently. I was overcome with feelings; he seemed intrigued as well. Weeks later, I can't stop thinking about how great we could be together. He's now with someone else, and I just became single. Have I finally seen what I want my future to be like, or am I looking for some security after a breakup?

Dr. Phil: I have to be honest: It seems like you're a bit of a game player. You chose delicate words to describe what you did ("gave him false hope"), but it sounds like you were blatantly dishonest with this guy, leading him on until you didn't need him, then cutting him loose.

You weren't into him before, so what turned a prior reject into the light of your life? Did he get a personality? Did he get better looking? I'm guessing he hasn't changed—*you* have. He's just as handy as a pocket on a shirt because you have the comfort of knowing that he liked you before. Especially in light of your recent breakup, your interest in him sure seems more convenient than legitimate.

But let's assume for a moment that I'm wrong. Perhaps you've had some revelation, and you're determined to go after him this time. You don't mention whether his current relationship is serious or casual. If he's married, forget about him. If he's dating without a major commitment, I would suggest two things: First, think about what caused your last relationship to fail, and figure out whether you have any unfinished emotional business. Second, communicate your feelings to him by telling him exactly what you've written to me. Say that you think you made a serious mistake, that you have very different feelings for him now, and that you've been doing some thinking to make sure you're not just rebounding. Ask for an opportunity to spend some time together and see if this romance can develop. No more game playing. No more acting one way when you feel another. Just put it all on the

line and see what happens. By taking the time to be certain of your feelings for him, you ensure that any relationship will have a chance.

Q | I've always been reluctant to hurt my mother's feelings, because she has a tendency to be overly sensitive and vindictive. For example, she vowed never to speak to her sisters again when they neglected to invite her on an annual trip she's turned down for the past 30 years. Now I've become the object of her wrath: When I announced my engagement, she couldn't have been happier—but when I told her that my fiancé and I planned to move in together, she was furious. She withdrew financial support for our wedding, which I don't fault her for; I know my living arrangement contrasts with her beliefs. My problem is that she never *told* me; she just stopped speaking to me. I've tried contacting her a few times, with no response. I'm not sure whether I should continue reaching out to her. Can we end this standoff?

Dr. Phil: It will probably sound bizarre for me to tell you not to take your mother's rejection personally, but that's exactly my advice. Because her behavior isn't unique to your relationship with her, you know that this isn't about you. This is entirely about your mother, who I suspect gets an emotional payoff from always playing the martyr. It sounds as though your mother has a mind-set that says, *If you don't do what I want, I'll just go sit over there and eat worms*. Well, I'm suggesting that you essentially tell her to go get herself a big helping. You shouldn't put your life on hold because she doesn't approve of it.

Offer to discuss this maturely, with the goal of finding a way to accept each other's differences. You can say something to the effect of, "You don't have to like everything I do in order to love me. I hope the day comes when you will see things that way. If it doesn't, I understand, and I'm sorry that we can't still be close." Tell her that your door is always open if at any point she chooses to renew your relationship.

In the meantime, don't beat yourself up over what you can't control. I'm guessing your mother is unlikely to respond until it becomes beneficial to her, so give yourself permission to be at peace with your decisions.

Q | I have a great friend who has been through thick and thin with me. We were married the same week, we had babies within hours of each other, and we got divorced around the same time. She's now married to a man who abuses drugs and alcohol and has been in and out of rehab and jail. She keeps kicking him out and taking him back. When we're together, all she talks about is her husband. I want to stay friends, but she's not the same person anymore. How do I handle my disappointment?

You're going to lose this relationship if you don't say anything.

Dr. Phil: You've probably heard me say that there are very few deal breakers in a marriage or friendship, but one of them is substance abuse. Even though your girlfriend isn't the one doing drugs, addiction becomes toxic for everyone who knows the user. The fact that she engages in this dysfunctional pattern of kicking out her husband and taking him back shows that she's succumbing to the unhealthy lifestyle. His issues have taken over her personality and invaded your friendship.

Here's the deal: You're going to lose this relationship if you don't say anything and just start to withdraw. If you talk to her candidly, she may tell you to mind your own business—but at least your friendship could survive. Perhaps your words will give her a reality check and serve as a compass during this difficult time. Even if she doesn't hear you right now, the conversation will echo in her mind and allow her to return to you when she finally wakes up and kicks this guy to the curb if he doesn't get some help. In my opinion, it's worth having a discussion along the following lines.

Script of the Month:
Confronting a friend
We're close enough, and I value you enough, to say some things I don't think you're going to want to hear. I accept that risk because I have faith that we can preserve our friendship. Your husband's substance abuse is dragging you down and changing who you are. I really miss the mutual relationship we had that's now being crowded out by this all-consuming problem. I'd like to support you in taking a stand, getting him into treatment, or helping you get free of him if that's what you want, but I can no longer be involved unless I'm pitching in constructively. Do you want me to help you explore treatment centers? Go with you to a therapist or pastor? Please tell me what I can do. As a friend, I can't let you go into this abyss without saying something, and I won't go down with you.

You have to be prepared for her to get angry and call you a fair-weather friend. Disappointment is a part of life. We become close to people because we have shared interests and similar worldviews, but those factors are subject to change. Would you grieve the loss of an old, dear friend? Of course. But people come and go, and you have to move on. ◻

Just Say What You Want, Dammit!

Hanging back, dropping hints, and generally mousing around gets you nowhere and drives other people—**Ellen Tien**, most vociferously—nuts. Here's what she wants you to do instead.

I want my husband to have more sex with me," a girlfriend remarks at lunch. "I feel like he rarely initiates it, and I want to do it more often."

"Did you tell him how you feel?" I ask, after the waiters have administered strong smelling salts and propped me back in my chair. "Don't you think that the first step might be saying that to him instead of me?"

"Honestly, I could never," she responds. "He would assume I was dissatisfied or accuse me of being a nag. But I've been buying lots of silk lingerie and sheer little nighties and making sure I look my best at bedtime, hoping to pique his interest. Besides, it's not like I necessarily want to have more sex per se, I just want him to want me to."

Right. So, she wants sex, but she doesn't want it. She merely wants her husband to want it so she can get what she wants—which, perversely, is something she doesn't particularly want. Wouldn't it cost less, both in mental and actual currency, if she were to sit out the dance, look him plain in the eye, and speak her mind? Why can't she say what she wants?

She's afraid that people will label her needy, bitchy, clingy, whiny. In other words, wanty. Wanty (known in Italy as *volere,* on New York's shrink-saturated Upper West Side as the id) is the hobgoblin who scrambles the signals so that wanting becomes a bad thing instead of a way to move forward. His cohorts are guilt and denial; his ace up the sleeve is fear of rejection.

What if I look stupid?

What if the answer is no?

What if, what if? So goes Wanty's refrain.

Wanty should not be confused with pure Want. Pure Want is the essence of living. It's the human condition, the slender quill that pricks the sectors of the soul, stimulating yearning or envy, desire or desperation. Nor should Wanty be mistaken for his cousin, Wishy, who pines for a more unattainable horizon and subsists on fountains glutted with coins, birthday candles, and the sternum bones of most poultry. Incidentally—spoiler alert—whoever grasps the wishbone higher up toward the joint will always win.

Wanty looks daggers at Wish and Want and shames them into silence. He flicks open the refrigerator door and slams it shut, thumbs through your credit card statements reproachfully, reaches out and shakes up your mind, juddering friendly old desires into unrecognizable enemies.

Do we even allow ourselves to know what we want?

"Where should we go for dinner?" I ask my husband.

"Wherever you want," he says.

I suggest a nice barbecue place around the corner. No, he says, he doesn't feel like barbecue. Chinese? No, he had Chinese food for lunch. Italian? No, too heavy. Thai? Too much like Chinese. Where, then, I repeat, does he want to go for dinner?

"I dunno. Wherever you want."

Kill me now.

It wasn't always this way.

In pioneer days, when times were hard and the average life span was 37 years, saying what you wanted was good. It was a requisite for survival. Settlers had to be focused, decisive, and make the right choices, just like the contestants on *American Idol,* except there was no video recap of your "journey" and the grand prize was a contract for 160 acres of Osage land.

Nowadays, with life expectancy exceeding 75, our lifestyle expectancy has soared as well. Higher expectations translate into serious want-flation. And with that, for some people—many of them women—comes guilt-flation. Certainly guilt-flation is a learned behavior. Small children have no compunctions about saying, even shrieking, what they want. At a critical point, though—third grade, fourth grade, fifth—the shame of wanting sets in.

An unusually wise friend with a teenager and a grade-schooler ponders the different want styles of her kids. "When we go shopping, my younger child knows exactly what he wants and is extremely vocal about it. But my older one can never say what she wants. How do I make her realize that you have to say what you want in order to receive it? When a person can articulate what she wants, it motivates others to give it to her."

Somewhere between the Homestead Act and *Extreme Makeover Home Edition,* articulating your wants went from being a wardrobe basic to an embarrassing accessory, like control-top underwear or Odor-Eaters. Plain Want evolved into Wanty.

Hence, we stifle yawp and dissent, ensuring unstirred pots, unsplintered peace. When a friend makes a plan to see a movie that conceivably patented the gag reflex, we decide not to make heavy weather of it. In candor's stead, we coax, cozen, and imply; we cloak our language in e-mail and conversation so we don't appear too blunt, too aggressive, too demanding. We either submerge our wants or present them in such a veiled, indirect fashion they confuse and annoy.

"Just for fun," says my visiting mother-in-law, a mid-century minimalist before she hit her mid-70s, that magical age when pastel birdhouses and gilt frames suddenly seem like a good idea, "let's throw out all your pa-

> **Freedom to want is your trump card. It's what enables us to scan new constellations, fall in love or resolve to leave, find our way home.**

perback books."

Wow, that doesn't sound very fun to me. We actually read our paperback books. It also sounds like a lot of work. Still, one would be prudent not to fly in the face of the *filio mater* too hastily. "Do you dislike the way they look?" I ask her. "Do you want me to throw them out?"

"No, no—let's just see what happens," she replies. "I thought it would be a nice thing to do for you."

"So, does that mean you don't want me to throw them out?"

"No." And now the conversation takes a flinty turn. "As I said, I thought we could throw them out, just [*pause*] for [*pause*] fun."

Wanty.

If only she could come right out and exclaim, "Those shabby paperbacks are an embarrassment to the family name!" If only she would flatly state, "This isn't about you, it's about me and my aesthetic values and my desire to regulate my surroundings." If only she could chisel through the shale sheets of Anglo-Saxon breeding and skip the Cheever-ized buck-and-wing so we could have a straightforward conversation.

Wishy.

But who can blame her? Women who say what they want—generally successful, high-achieving people—are considered difficult. Divas. Witches. Sluts. Heaven forbid we should be seen as termagants. Nobody likes a troublemaker.

Last year my son's progressive private school in Greenwich Village held an election for a parent liaison to the board. Two mothers vied for the spot. The first, whom we'll call Helen, was the parent of three children, one of them in my son's class; the second, now dubbed Daphne, was a newer parent.

Helen campaigned aggressively; she sent out e-mails explaining why she was the more qualified candidate, she stood by the ballot box and importuned passersby to vote for her. Daphne took a far less vigorous approach. So unvigorous that one year later, I have yet to figure out who she is. It was a tight race; the vote tally was nearly too close to call. For a moment, it looked as though Helen would emerge the victor.

Until.

Complaints began rolling in that Helen had illegally

tainted the process by standing by the ballot box and making doe eyes. She had strong-armed the parent body. She was competitive, pushy, undeserving. There was an elaborate revote and Daphne was declared the winner.

Understand: Helen is not an intimate of mine. We are like night and day, close only in the way that opposing poles on a horseshoe magnet acquire proximity through a random bend. As for Daphne, well, since I have no earthly idea who she is, I can only wish her well. I couldn't help noticing, however, that Helen's main transgression, the crime that stripped her of her post, was publicly wanting too much. She committed to wanting something and went after it.

In an ideal world, this approach should have been fine, admirable even. In a pink-sky world where kindergarten tuition costs $20,000, it was particularly wrong, naughty, bad. Consequently, Helen was punished by the Wanty mothers around her.

"I guess I learned a lesson from this," she said afterward. I didn't ask what the lesson was, nor did she elaborate. Yet my heart broke a little because I suspected that the lesson was to not want too much. To not try too hard. To not commit to a desire. How ironic that we women, so famous for craving commitment, bar ourselves from committing to self-fulfillment. "Anyway, it's not a big deal," Helen observed. "It's just a medium deal."

The logy middle ground is Wanty's wheelhouse. Certainly, there are times when you can instantly pinpoint what you want. You want health and happiness. You want a ham sandwich. Simple. Between the incredible and edible, though, somewhere between vast and speck, is where Wanty manufactures his dissolute brand of perfidy. Those medium deals are the ones that can break you. It's too tempting to fold up medium-size wants into neat little packets and tuck them away on a high shelf. Left unattended, they can go from hiccup to Hecate before you realize what boiled you alive.

"I wanted my husband to stop drinking, but I was afraid to confront him," an older female friend confides. Rather than risk fussing with the home fires, she had a baby in the hopes that he would sober up. He did—for a little while. Then he resumed drinking. She had another baby. Four children later, she was divorced. Her second husband was a devout philanderer. Obviously, the best way to restore his fidelity

would be to get pregnant. Three more times. He continued to tomcat his way around town until he left her.

Perhaps she has a few tips for my friend whose husband won't initiate sex.

When the concept of standing up to your husband is more painful than the prospect of giving birth seven times, we're knee-deep in hot water and rags. Is it really worse to say, "Honey, you've had enough to drink" than to hear, a decade later, "It's a girl—again!" The whip of rejection leaves a deep lash; the fear it instills can cause us to drink too much, eat too little, stay too long. But better to sprain your sensibilities early than to find your life irrevocably fractured down the road. Speak now or forever sacrifice your peace.

This, I imagine, would be the perfect moment to provide a tidy formula for how to say what you want. No such formula exists. There's no script, no secret recipe for banishing Wanty and embracing Want. Just as wanting comes from within, so must the ability to convey it to the people around you. You might begin trying within your immediate circle, with a husband or sister or best friend, someone who's guaranteed not to belittle your requests. You might try having enough faith in others to have faith in yourself.

In any event, do try. Keep trying. Freedom to want is power steering, your trump card. It's what enables us to scan new constellations, fall in love or resolve to leave, find our way home. What you want isn't merely what you get. It's where you'll be. It's who you'll be.

"My wife is constantly attacking me," laments a former colleague who is having trouble at work. "She's constantly on me, tearing me apart. Everything is my fault. A lot of the time, she's probably right, but I can't take the misery. I'm afraid we're going to have to split up. I just want her to say, 'It's okay, I love you and no matter what happens, we'll be okay. No matter what happens, we'll still be standing.' If she only said that, I could endure anything."

"Why don't you tell her that?" I ask. "Isn't it better to be honest than to get a divorce? How could you not tell her?"

"It's too humiliating," he groans. "It sounds so weak. She would just think I'm pathetic. I can't just come out and say, 'Look, this is what I want.'"

Oh, but you can. You must. ◐

Women who say what they want—generally successful, high-achieving people—are considered difficult. Divas. Witches. Sluts.

A Little Empathy, Please

She thought she was a true-blue pal—loyal, closemouthed, cheerleading. Little did she know she had the emotional understanding of a cranberry. Amanda Robb finally learns what makes the wheels of friendship go round.

I swear on the *Thelma & Louise* video we watched into a scratchy oblivion: I didn't mean to be the worst friend ever. When Lisa—my roommate and boon companion of three years—stepped into our apartment, sank to the floor, and clutched our cocker spaniel, I asked, "What's wrong?" with sympathy.

"I got fired," Lisa told me.

"Wow." I pulled her to her feet. "You'll have an amazing story for Jim's party tonight!"

Lisa's eyes went round and wet as the dog's when we left her at the vet. She said, "Come on, Maya" (who gave me a reproachful glance before obeying), disappeared into her bedroom (for three days), and never discussed career matters with me again.

Boy, was I annoyed. At age 26, I was a sublime friend. Lisa, also 26, was blessed to have an ally so honest about dates and hairstyles, so fiercely supportive of her dreams, and willing to defend her choices (the dates, hairstyles, and dreams) to her habitually nettling mom and dad. Never once in our relationship, I was proud to think, had I ever even been tempted to commit a single mortal friendship sin: being competitive, gossiping, or backstabbing. To me, Lisa's job loss was no big deal. She had complained about the position. Her parents were rich and gave her money. She had nothing to worry about. I

thought that reminding her we had something fun to do that night was an appropriate and kind response.

Psychologist Douglas LaBier, PhD, director and founder of the Center for Adult Development in Washington, D.C., disagrees. He explained to me that my dearest friend was humiliated by receiving a pink slip, feared she might be incompetent at everything she tried, and, because of me, felt utterly alone. I was, LaBier tells me, "catastrophically unempathetic" to Lisa.

Today, 15 years later, I know why my attempt at consoling my friend was so ham-fisted. As LaBier explains, virtually everyone learns the basics of empathy in childhood (from our parents comforting us when we're in distress), but my father died when I was 4, and afterward my mother had to be very can-do, juggling three jobs, graduate school, and two kids. When I was upset, she never said, "Oh, I'm sorry. It must be hard to have me away so much after losing your dad." Instead, on good days, she'd say, "Why are you crying? Nothing is wrong." And on bad days: "You'd better toughen up, because life can get a lot worse." Looking back at my twenty-something self, I realize that if, as LaBier says, empathy is "the ability or the willingness to experience the world from someone else's point of view," I wasn't brought up to be able to do that.

At least my lack of empathy was not unusual. Having practiced as a psychotherapist for 35 years, LaBier believes that what he calls empathy deficit disorder (EDD) is rampant among Americans. LaBier says we unlearn whatever empathy skills we've picked up while coming of age in a culture that focuses on acquisition and status more than cooperation, and values "moving on" over thoughtful reflection. LaBier is convinced that EDD is at the heart of modernity's most common problems, macro (war) and micro (divorce).

When Lisa crept into her bedroom, I couldn't have articulated any of this. She might have felt abandoned, but all I knew was that I felt alone. My roommate had her dog, and they were both shunning me, and my boyfriend of four years wouldn't rescue me from the loneliness I in-

creasingly felt by agreeing to get married. I went into psychotherapy.

I thought my therapist would help me break up with my commitment-phobic lover, figure out how to choose less sensitive friends, and, of course, let me rant about my mother's shortcomings. I did get to rant—about my mom, Lisa, and my boyfriend.

What surprised me was my therapist's response to these tirades. She never said, "Leave that rotten bastard." Or "Your roommate is a big baby." Instead she said, "Gosh, that sounds really hard." And "That must have felt terrible." And "How did you feel after that happened?" My reaction to those spectacularly bland comments was even more astonishing. I loved them.

"These very simple responses make you feel understood," says New York psychologist Frank M. Lachmann, PhD, author of *Transforming Narcissism: Reflections on Empathy, Humor, and Expectations*. He points out that many of the common responses—"It could be worse"; "You should do X"; "Let's talk about something else"—appear to be kind and aimed at soothing. But no matter how well-intentioned, Lachmann says, these remarks are a rejection, a denial, of what the other person is going through. "They are code for 'Don't confront me with things that are unpleasant,'" he says. "Or 'Don't bother me with your pain.'"

About six months into psychotherapy, I started using what I thought of as my therapist's "lines." When Lisa was offered a job at an organization she did not want to work at, I said, "Oh, that's a tough spot to be in." When my boyfriend was invited to study abroad, I said, "How do you feel about that?" But the way I really felt was: "Lisa, that job pays a ton of money, but I guess you can turn it down because your parents are loaded." And, "You selfish bastard, I'll kill you if you go to Europe without me."

Still, Lachmann says, I had taken the first step to becoming empathetic—which is faking it. If you want to act more empathetic, you follow certain steps: Instead of telling people what they ought to do, or becoming tyrannically optimistic, you offer sympathy, inquire about feelings, and validate those feelings. You'll be giving comfort to the other person, even if you yourself can't feel what they're going through.

It's true that for a long time, while I could say the appropriate thing, I could

> Still, I had taken the first step to becoming empathetic—which is faking it. Instead of telling people what they ought to do, or becoming tyrannically optimistic, I offer sympathy.

not relate to their struggles. Still, I took satisfaction in the fact that my relationships were improving. Then a year after starting therapy, I began feeling something intensely when comforting friends: terror.

This turned out to be a signal, Lachmann says, that I was actually feeling empathy. I didn't recognize it because I'd always run from emotional discomfort—and, at least in the beginning, I found trying to be empathetic profoundly uncomfortable. Most of the time I managed to avoid blurting out unhelpful suggestions to my friends—*Happy hour, anyone?* Or *Here's the number for a credit consolidator*—and instead say the appropriate thing. But for years and years, I could stand genuine empathy only five minutes at a time.

For those five minutes, though, I was not alone. And once I had experienced the wonder of that feeling, I was willing to stumble out of my comfort zone to try to be not alone again.

Virtually everything I have ever tried to improve about myself—my weight, my sleep habits, my housecleaning—has resulted in an endless seesaw of improvement. But empathy, I've learned, is not like dieting. (Or, at least, how I diet, which involves ending up back at square one.) Cultivating empathy has its own rewards: The more you do it, the better your relationships are, and the more you want to continue.

Feeling understood in that therapist's office taught me that human beings are not doomed to be alone—and empathy is life's connective tissue. If you have a romantic partner, he or she will someday believe that you are entirely wrong about something, and if you can see the problem from your partner's point of view, you'll be able to get through that conflict without smoldering in the corner or splitting up. If you work with someone you despise (and who despises you back), and you try to understand why that person dislikes you, then you stand a chance of not hating every minute with her at the office. If you live in a world that you would like to see less divided by ethnic, economic, and religious strife, you'll find that your attempting to comprehend the needs of your sworn enemies is a prerequisite to any meaningful action you can take.

Empathy will also require you to get past rationalizations and admit wrongdoing. For about a decade after I started working to be more empathetic, I told myself that I hadn't hurt Lisa too badly, because she never told me I had. But Lachmann points out that the final insult of being treated with a lack of empathy is that the hurt person usually can't complain. "If you say, 'That was such an unempathetic thing to say,' it can easily be heard as, 'Feel sorry for me.' And no one wants to be pathetic." So most people don't say anything, Lachmann says, and relationships "are often ruptured and ruined."

Lisa and I are no longer close. We live on opposite coasts. We have very different lives. But still, I couldn't bear the idea of us being "ruptured and ruined." I recently called her and said I was sorry for being selfish when she lost her job. I said I had eventually learned that it must have been a terrible time for her and that I had made it worse by leaving her so alone with all her confusion. Lisa was gracious ("You did your best"), forgiving ("Really, you were a wonderful friend to me overall"), and honest ("It was 15 years ago, and I'm over it now"). She changed the subject, and we caught up on our summer plans.

Her family—along with the cocker spaniel, Maya, who was still alive and giving reproachful looks—was planning a camping trip. Packing up, Lisa realized none of her jeans fit. Her pregnancies had stripped every curve from her body. She was skinny as a post. I began to wail, "Oh my God, you lucky rat! I gained ten pounds...."

But then I stopped myself.

"Um. So how does it feel to have to buy new jeans?" I said.

There was a silence on the line. Then Lisa started laughing. "Wonderful," she said. "Absolutely wonderful." 🄾

> Cultivating empathy has its own rewards: The more you do it, the better your relationships are, and the more you want to continue.

I DON'T CARE WHAT PEOPLE SAY, YOU DO NOT LOOK YOUR AGE.

Crouching Tiger, Hidden Dragon Lady

Cutting remarks, "helpful" suggestions, subtle (or not-so-subtle) stabs—how to handle these verbal ambushes? You can slink away, lose your cool…or employ Martha Beck's cleverly adapted martial arts techniques to turn your attackers' words against them. *Hiiiiii-yaa!*

Don't worry, hon," said Theresa's husband, Guy, when she failed to extinguish all her birthday candles in one breath. "A woman your age has to be in shape to make wishes come true. You just don't have the lung capacity." Guy chortled. Theresa's face turned scarlet. The rest of us chuckled nervously. We were used to Guy, to the jocular way he planted and twisted stilettos between his wife's ribs. Like most of

Theresa's friends, I'd always found him just charming enough to be tolerable. But as I watched him serve Theresa's cake, something dawned on me: Guy was a mean person. He'd intentionally humiliated his wife, and he did such things often. It was like that moment in a horror movie when you understand that the rogue car, rather than simply straying off course, is actively pursuing children and puppies.

I recall an urge to kick Guy in the throat, which I controlled by reminding myself that it was both illegal and difficult to pull off in heels. I was studying karate at the time, and though it didn't occur to me then, I would eventually realize that the basic principles taught at my dojo could be used to fight evil not just in action but in conversation as well. I think of it as martial arts of the mind, and if you're subject to subtle stabs, deliberate snubs, or cutting remarks, you might find these techniques an effective defense against the Guys of your world.

■ Principle One: Find Your Fighting Stance

Every form of martial arts requires a fighting stance that's fluid, flexible, and centered. Standing this way makes you much less likely to lose your balance, and if someone jumps you, you can quickly duck or dodge in any direction without falling.

Physical fighting stances involve balance, alignment, weight distribution, and posture. A psychological fighting stance is all about emotional balance: self-acceptance, abiding by your own moral code (something you're probably doing anyway), forgiving yourself for failing to reach perfection (this is rarer), and, finally, offering yourself as much compassion as you'd give a beloved friend (I suspect some of us need work in this department). Simply put, you must never be mean to yourself.

This works because cruelty, to be effective, has to land on a welcoming spot in the victim's belief system. Guy mocked Theresa's age and lack of physical fitness because he knew she hated those things about herself. If she hadn't already believed his insults, they would have left her feeling puzzled but not devastated—the way I was when I learned that calling someone a "turtle's egg" is a horrific insult in China. She would have seen Guy as the pathetic head case he was. And that may have led her to our second principle.

■ Principle Two: Practice the Art of Invisibility

I once purchased a book that promised to teach the ninja's fabled "art of invisibility." I was crestfallen to read that the first step in a technique called vanishing was "Wait until your opponent is asleep." The whole book was like that: Get your enemy drunk, throw dust in his eyes, thump him on the head with a wok, then tiptoe away, forever. Well, I could've told you that.

Nevertheless, I recommend these ninja techniques for dealing with mean people. Get away from them, full stop. Sound extreme? It's not. Cruelty, whether physical or emotional, isn't normal. It may signal what psychologists call the dark triad of psychopathic, narcissistic, and Machiavellian personality disorders. One out of about

I recommend these ninja techniques for dealing with mean people. Get away from them, full stop. Sound extreme? It's not.

every 25 individuals has an antisocial personality disorder. Their prognosis for recovery is zero, their potential for hurting you about 100 percent. So don't assume that a vicious person just had a difficult childhood or a terrible day; most people with awful childhoods end up being empathetic, and most people, even on their worst days, don't seek satisfaction by inflicting pain. When you witness evil, if only the tawdry evil of a conversational stiletto twist, use your *ninjutsu*. Wait for a distraction, then disappear.

But, you may be thinking, *what if you're stuck with a mean family member, coworker, or neighbor? What's poor Theresa supposed to do?* Well, Grasshopper, that's when the martial arts of the mind really come in handy.

■ Principle Three: Master Defensive Techniques

All martial arts teach strategies to deflect different attacks. For instance, I was taught to defend against a lapel grab with a punching combination called Crouching Falcon, follow that with a multiple-kick series known as Returning Viper, and finish with the charmingly titled technique Die Forever (I prefer my own techniques, such as Silent Sea Slug, which entails lying down and hoping things improve, or Disgruntled Panda, which is mostly curling up and refusing to mate.)

I also learned this closely guarded martial arts secret: Although there are countless techniques, most fighters need only a few. For instance, judo star Ronda Rousey has clobbered numberless opponents using the Arm Bar technique. Her opponents know she's going to do it, but that doesn't keep her from snapping their elbows like dry spaghetti. Each good technique goes a long, long way. The following are a few that I highly recommend, in order of degree of difficulty.

YELLOW BELT TECHNIQUE: TRUMPET MELODIOUSLY

I'm a lifelong fan of "Japlish," English prose translated from the Japanese by someone whose sole qualification is owning a Japanese-to-English dictionary. One classic Japlish instruction, which I picked up from a car rental company, advised: "When passenger of foot heave in sight, tootle the horn. Trumpet him melodiously at first, but if he still obstacles your passage then tootle him with vigor."

I borrowed the phrase "trumpet him melodiously" for your first anti-meanness technique. It's meant to nip hurtful behavior in the bud. Use it when someone—say a small child or an engineer—makes a remark that may or may not be intentionally cruel: "You smell like medicine," "I can see through your pants," "Why don't you have a neck?"… You can trumpet him melodiously by saying, "Hey, dude, that's kind of mean. Back off, okay?" If the behavior continues, tootle him with vigor by saying, "I'm serious. You're out of line. Stop it."

Practice these lines until you're saying them in your sleep, with clear delivery, calm energy. Then, when you use them in real life, a normal person will react by immediately ceasing all hurtful behavior, and even mean people will be taken aback by your directness. They may even begin to behave themselves. Mission accomplished.

BROWN BELT TECHNIQUE: ZIG-ZIG

As a martial artist, you'll need to get used to doing the opposite of whatever your enemies expect. For example, if someone were to push you backward, you might push back for a few seconds, then abruptly reverse, and pull your assailant in the direction he's pushing. He'd be toppled by his own momentum.

This is zig-zigging. It works beautifully on mean people. They expect a fight-or-flight reaction from their victims—either angry pushback or slinking away. The one thing they don't anticipate is relaxed discernment. Scuttle their plans by zigging instead of zagging, cheerfully accepting any accurate statement they might make while ignoring their malicious energy.

You can observe this technique in the movie *Spanglish,* when a young wife, played by Téa Leoni, lashes out at her

SO…YOU'RE *STILL* NOT SEEING ANYONE?

mother, "You were an alcoholic and wildly promiscuous woman during my formative years, so I'm in this fix because of you!" As the mother, Cloris Leachman nods and says pleasantly, "You have a solid point, dear. But right now the lessons of my life are coming in handy for you." This response stops the daughter cold, partly because it's true and partly because it contains not a whiff of pushback. The mother zigs when the daughter expects her to zag. The result is peace.

BLACK BELT ANTI-MEANNESS TECHNIQUE: WICKED-KIND PARENT

If you keep a balanced stance and surround yourself with normal people, you'll eventually master the black belt skill I've named Wicked-Kind Parent. Mean people are adept at adopting the tone of a critical parent, making others unconsciously regress into weak, worried children. To use this defense, refuse to be infantilized. Instead, use the only thing that trumps the emotional power of a bad parent: the emotional power of a good one.

This is what happened at Theresa's birthday party. As Guy served cake and cruelty, Theresa's older sister Wendy spoke up.

"Now, Guy," she said, in precisely the tone Supernanny uses with kids on TV, "that kind of petty meanness doesn't become you. Show us all you can do better." Guy tried to laugh, but a glance around the room silenced him. Wendy had called on her good-parent energy to tap a great resource: normal people. Kind people. Outplayed and outnumbered, Guy slunk away, leaving Theresa to enjoy her birthday. This is virtually always the outcome when a mental martial artist encounters a Mean Guy. If you choose the way of the warrior, it will happen for you.

■ Principle Four: Walk the Way of the Warrior

Being a martial artist is a way of life. You can't use your skills in an emergency unless you practice them every day. And such daily practice may lead to unexpected adventures. You'll no longer watch helplessly as some Mean Guy emotionally abuses his wife—even if you happen to be the wife in question. Where your prewarrior self would've simply wilted, your warrior self will speak up or, if you're the wife, walk away.

This may require drastic changes in your life. Are you ready for that? Well, you are if meanness has pushed you to the point of anger or despair. You are if you want to be the change you wish to see in the world. You can begin today. Adopt the stance of dauntless self-acceptance, avoid combat when possible, and practice your techniques until they become second nature. Though it might be helpful to remember that it really does help to wait until your opponent is asleep. ▣

family

His wife is sleeping with someone else. It looks like love. What's a fellow to do?
Rodes Fishburne deals with…

The Other Man

A couple of weeks ago, at 3 in the morning, I woke up to find my wife in bed with another man. She likes tall men; he was short. She likes broad shoulders; his were narrow. I don't think I'm offending the parties involved when I say that at 37 pounds he was a bit of a lightweight. If it came right down to it, and it might, I was pretty sure I could take him.

Sadly, this wasn't the first time I'd caught them together. For the past month, it had been happening two or three nights a week, including weekends. Had they any shame? Nope, came the answer, clear as the blinking alarm clock next to the bed, they did not. So with mixed feelings, I kissed my son's forehead and left to go sleep in his room.

As I curled around the cat-size warm spot he had left behind in his small bed, I felt the plastic knights lurking in the sheets running sorties against my kneecaps. It was not going to be a great night's sleep.

And so my mind turned. And turned. This was just perfect. You fall in love with your dream girl, move to San Francisco, marry her, have a child together, and then, at the age of 3, the boy—sleepwalking through his Oedipal debut—displaces you from your rightful position in bed. It was tragedy. It was farce. It was fatherhood. And there would be no intermission.

As I lay there, another fearsome truth revealed itself: The love my wife and I shared with each other had created something that *literally* got between us. It was like having a fire hydrant bolted in the middle of your bed. Resistance would be futile. And feudal.

This shift in family dynamics is disorienting to even the most stable of male psyches. What father hasn't walked up at the end of a long day to his house/grass hut/igloo and been greeted at the front door by a little feller whose first response is:

"Where's Mom?"

The mature thing to do would be to register a jolt of sympathy for the fact that the other male in my household was struggling—just like me!—with a strong urge to be with Mom. And there was a tiny jolt allocated on his behalf. On the other hand, only a fool fails to recognize true competition.

I tossed in my son's bed. What else was in my blind spot? The mind reeled: "First a blind spot, then a bald spot. Then you're dead." It sounded like a fortune cookie written by Samuel Beckett.

How do men get themselves into this situation? Very slowly. For starters, no alien takes over our bodies for nine months, our feet don't swell, we never stand naked in front of a floor-length mirror howling, "*I. Look. Huge!*" in order to signal to our (admittedly) sluggish, (admittedly) reptilian brains that something is coming. Men are selfish, and selfishness is best preserved in a cocoon of ignorance. Preferably one made of beer and pork ribs. So we hang on to the coattails of someone else's biology, winking and cooing supportively, without the foggiest idea of what is about to happen.

Only later do we realize that, in addition to all the other things fatherhood requires—patience, sacrifice, the ability to change diapers with one hand while eating a piece of pizza—we must add the notion of second place. Silver medals all around.

I asked a female friend about this. I wanted a woman's perspective. If I'd asked my wife, she would have told me everything was going to be all right. She would straddle the fault line with more finesse than a Swiss diplomat. My friend wouldn't be so gentle. She had children. She could provide feminine insight that transcended my own beer-'n'-pork-rib cocoon.

"Oh yeah," she said when I brought up the subject of silver medals, "that's a totally real thing."

Oh, boy.

"And I have to tell you, I loved it."

Oh, no.

"The snuggling and the nuzzling. To be honest, there's a part of me that really enjoyed my son's attention. It's not sexual; it's not even sensual. It's animal." Her eyes drifted a bit, as if recalling a particularly faraway cosmic mother-son snuggle that a father wouldn't understand. "And... there's a little part of me that also enjoyed the hunger in my husband's eyes. For my attention, but also for my son's."

Oh, dear God.

"You know, before my son was born, I would have nightmares about my husband drowning and I would dive in to save him. But about a week after our son was born, I started to have nightmares about my son instead. Funny, huh?"

Hilarious.

> The mature thing would be to sympathize with the other male struggling—just like me!—with a strong urge to be with Mom.

It's 4 A.M. now. If I hurry up, I can get just enough sleep to make the day bearable. Hurry up and sleep—the motto of new parents everywhere.

I reach for the shrinking ball of warmth, now the size of a quarter. The paranoid part of my mind is tired. In fact, it's selfishly asleep. Which is good, because the words that come are my father's, who offered them whenever I did something that amused him, or bewitched him, or caused him, I see now, to contemplate *his* perch in the cosmos and the ineffable mystery of why fathers even have sons in the first place. He would quote a bit of old poetry:

"The child is father to the man...."

Which, when you are the child, sounds like a ridiculous adult riddle unworthy of unraveling. But when you are the man, it doesn't need to be unraveled, because the answer is lying right in front of you, next to the woman you love. The dead-of-night idea comes slowly, but it comes: This curious earthly rotation we all take turns on is made real—is made indelible—by the appearance of the next generation.

This same epiphany must have dawned on my father, and his father, and your father, on and on, back through the family tree of sleepless nights.

I wish I could remember the rest of the poem, but it is getting very late now. Finally time to rest. Reason and memory both fading. Led into the darkness by the last of the plastic knights. ❶

Catherine Newman and her father, Ted Newman, New York City, March 2008, and (*right, from top*) in 1969, in the late '70s, and in Florence, Italy, 1989.

The Father's Day Card You Can't Find

Catherine Newman cares enough to write her own.

On a legal pad next to my father's armchair, I see my name in his handwriting. It's between "Atlanta tickets" and "taxes," on a list that also includes such excellent questions as "Sicily?" and "wine?"—and it's crossed off.

And sitting in the half dark, with my own two children asleep in the next room, it occurs to me that the details of parental devotion are nothing you can quite put into words. You could stand all day in an aisle of Hallmark cards, reading four-line stanzas about paternal strength and character, and plenty would be true enough. "I was an ungrateful louse, but you still sent me to college—thanks," they assert in various rhyming couplets, with maybe something about ice fishing and neckties. "You taught me to throw a football; you gave me away at the altar; you left our house with a briefcase every day and we never knew where you were actually going." Sure. But where's the part about the flush of care you feel when you see your own grown-up self on your dad's to-do list?

You worry, you call me, you cross me out.
Because as a father there's none more devout
Than you, Dad.

I would buy that card. Or the one about perching your little-girl self on the closed lid of the toilet to watch your handsome father shave—his lips pressed together in the mirror while foam disappeared in wide stripes like a mown lawn. Although I would want the card to skip the part about how, years later, your future husband would also use Old Spice, and the clovey smoothness of his cheek against your neck would fan the flames of passion into something more like a bonfire of heebie-jeebies. The same way you felt when you realized that Fleetwood Mac's "Oh Daddy" was actually about somebody's *lover*—not their dad, like you'd always imagined. Not really about somebody's *father*.

And yet I was exactly the kind of kid who imagined that you grew up and married your own actual dad. (Did he still walk you down the aisle? What did your mom wear? I hadn't worked out the details.) I wandered the house to be wherever he was: on the carpet at his feet while he rattled ice in a glass and shared pretzel Goldfish with me; on a kitchen stool while he soft-boiled eggs; flung across the bed with my chin in my palms while he emptied the pockets of his suit—subway tokens, handfuls of change, a clacking box of mints. He seemed like a cross between a magician and a billionaire philanthropist. ("Would you like a Tic Tac?" "*Would* I!") Plus, there was the omniscience.

Even now, if we're heading downtown, he cheerfully shakes open the subway map to show us the L train, to remind us to get off the N before it zooms into Queens. I watch his finger point here and there along the colored veins of the city, and I feel like we'll never be lost; I feel like if we were ever lost he'd come out to Far Rockaway and get us; I'm knocking on 40's door and I have two children of my own and what I feel like is somebody's kid. "There's a great sushi place near there," he might recommend, or "I would take the Major Deegan," and his confidence always fills me with something like relief crossed with something that can only be described as a kind of preemptive grief. I want to always feel like somebody's kid.

Explain the IRT
To me
Again, Dad.

If he was in the shower when we left for school, he drew a circle and a dot on the fogged-up glass of the door for "goodbye." If we flew somewhere without him, he met us at the airport, always wearing the same red-and-blue-checked cotton shirt that jellied my knees with the gladness of seeing him again. "Who do you love most?" I asked, "Robert or me?" And he said, "Don't be silly—your mother, of course." He was not exactly kidding, and we screamed with indignation and glee: Our beautiful mother! We felt the same way! Years later, though, our father would fall unpredictably and somewhat dottily in love with a brown Standard poodle. What a relief to raise a dog after the worry and complexity of children! Or so I imagine. Opinions did not need to be proffered about the dog's tone of voice, length of shorts, or sulky posture at her grandmother's dinner table—or about how close to her eyeball the dog penciled in a smudge of black liner. The dog needed to be on a leash, sure, but not to keep her from growing up too quickly. And the dog was able to spend her whole life just wagging around our father in her needy way—"Look at me! Look at me! I'm your dog! Aren't I great?"—without even pretending to mature and make adult conversation.

You didn't want me to grow up too quickly
Only now I'm not sure I can at all.
Uh-oh, Dad!

These days I watch my own young children with their father. Our daughter rubs her cheek on his and complains dotingly about its roughness; our son curls up in his lap, big-kid legs folded up like a giraffe's. They reach sleepy arms from late-night car seats, and their dad lifts them, carries them, whispers "I've got you" and means it in every possible way. Years later, maybe they'll roll their eyes when he counts the holes in their earlobes or frets over their berserk finances; maybe they'll rage and rebel and grow more independent than I ever have. But one day these kids, too, will scan the drugstore aisle for the right card that won't be there—the one that says,

I know it's a pain in the neck,
Dad,
But it means the world to me—
Your agreeing to live
Forever. ◗

Look! Up in the sky! It's a bird! It's a plane! It's Supermom!

She phones daily, e-mails constantly, ghostwrites term papers, drives hundreds of miles to do her kids' laundry, negotiates with their prospective employers, and occasionally kneecaps their competition. She's one of the new "helicopter" parents, always hovering, on alert. Is she helping her children or crippling them? **Amanda Robb** reports.

Three summers ago, Christine Buckles, 38, was thrilled when a young family moved into the brick-fronted ranch house next door to hers on Waterford Crystal Drive in Dardenne Prairie, Missouri. But shortly after, Christine was unsettled when the mother, Lori, began to bad-mouth her daughter's best friend, Megan, blaming her for problems between the girls. Both tweens were slightly overweight, and when they started dieting, Lori broadcast the news, saying her daughter would lose more weight than Megan, even though it was obvious to Christine that Megan was slimming down faster. Christine didn't blame Megan at all when, during the summer of 2006, she stopped wanting to spend much time with Lori's daughter.

Christine's new neighbor Lori—Lori Drew—was the Missouri woman who allegedly would go on to create a fictitious 16-year-old boy named Josh Evans on myspace.com to cyber-torment Megan. As readers of mommy blogs know, for about a month "Josh" said he really, really liked Megan. Then, with little warning, on October 16, 2006, he reportedly wrote, "Everybody...knows how you are. You are a bad person and everybody hates you. Have a shitty rest of your life. The world would be a better place without you."

Within hours, Megan hanged herself, and she died the next day.

Lori Drew, her husband, and two children continue to live next door to the Buckles, four houses away from Megan's father (he and his wife are in the process of getting a divorce after nearly 20 years of marriage).

Parental overinvolvement is nothing new: Queen Victoria's mother slept in the same room as her daughter until Victoria, at age 18, moved out in one of her first acts as England's sovereign. The mothers of President Franklin Delano Roosevelt and General Douglas MacArthur moved to live near them when they went to college. (MacArthur's mother took a hotel room close enough to her son's dorm room so she could see if the lamp was lit, which made her feel certain he was doing his homework.) But such behavior was unusual in an era when most Americans worked six days a week, virtually no one had paid vacations to use for extended parent weekends, and speedy communication was limited mostly to telegrams.

Today parents can go online and track their children's grades, attendance, and missed assignments in real time with software like PowerSchool, which is used in more than 10,000 schools in 49 states and serves the parents of nearly 4.7 million children. In addition, a survey of 4,800 parents across the country conducted by College Parents of America, an advocacy group of more than 100,000 parents of college students, found that 30 percent talk or e-mail with their university-age children every day. Former school principal Jim Fay and psychiatrist Foster Cline, MD, who in 1977 cofounded the Love and Logic Institute, a parent education center based in Golden, Colorado, coined the term "helicopter parents" to describe mothers and fathers who "hover over their children." Since then an entire military-based vocabulary has evolved to describe specific styles of hyperparenting. "Black Hawks" attack teachers, coaches, and even bosses who upset their children. "Stealth fighters" are constantly surveying their children.

Patricia Somers, PhD, University of Texas at Austin associate professor of higher education, is among the first academics to specifically research helicopter parents. She was stunned to discover how involved many of them are: In a study she conducted at 60 public universities and colleges, she found that 40 to 60 percent of parents engage in some type of helicoptering, such as helping with academic assignments, and as many as 10 percent actually write their children's papers for them.

Neither figure surprises Jim Settle, PhD, vice president of student affairs at Shawnee State University in Portsmouth, Ohio. At a seminar on campus issues a few years ago, a young woman raised her hand and said, "My mom has a question." She held up her cell phone and explained her mother had been listening in. Then her mom asked a question about campus security on the speaker.

Even after their children have graduated from college (and are, in theory, on their own), many parents continue to advocate for them. They often contact their adult children's employers. "Over the last three or four years, we've started getting all kinds of calls," says a recruiter for a Fortune 500 company. "Parents want to discuss offer let-

ters and benefits, or information about 'work-life balance.' Or ask, 'Is Johnny going to be able to come home at Christmastime, because we take two weeks as a family at that time?' We had one call last summer because it was little Ginny's birthday and Mom wanted to know if we could have a cake delivered to her and sing 'Happy Birthday.'" The recruiter pauses. "[This is] Wall Street. We don't really do that around here."

Another mother called her late one night. After brief pleasantries, the woman said, "A few years ago, you interviewed my daughter, and you loved her. She turned your company down, but I have another daughter. She's a junior and she's fantastic.... So I was thinking it would be fantastic if you could hire her for the summer."

The recruiter explained that all the positions had been filled. The mother responded: "That doesn't work for me." To get the mother off the phone, the recruiter said she would talk with the daughter but assumed that the young woman would be too embarrassed by her parent's behavior to call. "But at 8:30 the next morning, the phone rang," says the recruiter. "It was the daughter, saying, 'Hi. I know you talked to my mom, so I wanted to get in touch with you right away!'" The young woman, who didn't know anything about the business, did not get the job.

Signs of superparenting surfaced in the 1980s, when mid to late boomers started putting the first BABY ON BOARD signs in minivan windows, says Donald Pollock, PhD, associate professor of anthropology at the State University of New York at Buffalo. That was around the time terrorism first began touching American lives — Iranian students backed by radical clerics held American hostages between 1979 and 1981; a suicide bomber blew himself up outside U.S. Marine barracks in Beirut, killing 241 servicemen in 1983. Starting in the 1990s, many Americans' fears moved from the big and the vague (Communism, the bomb, bad things happening "over there")

THE TOTAL MOTHER: Robyn Lewis with her sons, Brendan (left) and Ethan.

to the specific horrors that began encroaching here, in places we can't help being: school (Columbine), home (Elizabeth Smart), and the office (9/11).

At about the same time, members of the most neglected generation in American history—Generation Xers—began to have children, says Helen Johnson, an adviser to dozens of universities on parent relations and author of *Don't Tell Me What to Do, Just Send Money: The Essential Parenting Guide to the College Years.* "They were latchkey kids, whose parents divorced in huge numbers and whose mothers often worked two full-time jobs—one outside the home and one running it. This generation tends to have children later, when they feel they have ample financial and emotional resources for parenting. Many of the mothers leave or cut back on their careers when they start families. Parenting becomes the vital enterprise of their lives."

The most notorious helicopter parents are those who become overinvested in their children's athletic pursuits, such as Jeff Doyal Robertson, who in 2005 shot his son's Canton, Texas, high school football coach, allegedly because the boy had been suspended from playing, and Thomas Junta, who in 2000 beat to death the father of one of his son's hockey teammates because he didn't like the way the man had supervised a game. Even when they refrain from homicidal impulses, parents of athletes can make stupendously bad choices. Take Terrell Mackey, a Lincoln, Nebraska, mother. Last spring, when her 15-year-old daughter failed to perform to Mackey's expectations in a YWCA soccer game, she forced the girl to repeat mantras about bettering her performance in the car on the way home from the game. "Every time the child messed up a sentence, the mother would slap the daughter," says Public Information Officer Katie Flood of the Lincoln Police Department. According to the police report, the mother hit her daughter on the face or head as many as 15 times, until she stopped the car and had the child get out on Interstate 80. The girl, still in her YWCA uniform, was picked up by a teammate's family as she trudged toward an exit ramp. Mackey was charged with child neglect.

A story like Mackey's sounds crazy—and it is—but parents who think they need to prepare their children for a very competitive world are responding to very real challenges, says Johnson. "It starts with the whole 'getting in' thing. You used to just sign up for preschool. Now you have to apply." And preschool is only the beginning. Public universities—such as the State University of New York at Purchase, Delta State University in Mississippi, and the University of Puerto Rico at Arecibo—all currently accept about one in three applicants. For the class of 1950, Harvard University accepted about 52 percent of those who applied; for the class of 2009, Harvard accepted 9.1 percent of applicants—a record low.

Parents also know that life doesn't get easier after children finish their education: Entry-level wages for college graduates fell steadily from 2001 to 2005, and have only barely risen since then. During the past ten years, a university graduate's average student loan debt has increased about 58 percent.

Those are a few of the reasons that Robin Childress Witherspoon, 44, does everything she can to help her four children get the best possible jobs. She prepares résumés and cover letters for them, advises on appropriate hairstyles for interviews, and makes them practice shaking hands. An elementary school principal in Ferguson, Missouri, Witherspoon also tries to make professional contacts for her children.

"We're not affluent," Witherspoon says. She was a stay-at-home mom when her children were young, and her husband was a fireman. When she'd talk to people who were wealthier, she says, "I found that they were always getting their name out there and meeting people so they could call on them later. I think that being a member of the African-American community, that's not something we necessarily have—an understanding of networking."

Her children complain that she gets on their nerves sometimes, but Witherspoon thinks her involvement has helped their transition to independent adulthood. Her oldest daughter just graduated from Tennessee State University with a degree in electrical engineering and got a job with Boeing. "On her own," Witherspoon says.

Lynn Yale, 55, works as a special ed teacher with high school students in Santa Clarita, California. She acknowledges she might be spoiling her sons by traveling an hour and a half to do their laundry, but she feels college has become such a pressure cooker that "everything needs to be done in a certain amount of time at a certain level." So doing their wash is a small way she can help her two sons, who both take 15 to 18 credits a semester. Her efforts aren't entirely for the boys, she admits. "I really enjoy their company," she says. "I miss them." She's agreed to pay her youngest son's cell phone bills—if he uses it to call her once a day.

Robyn Lewis, 56, who raised her two sons after divorcing their father 19 years ago, takes full advantage of the ability to cyber-attach. The Fort Lauderdale, Florida, college recruiter often starts her mornings by turning on her computer and logging on to the linking bank accounts she shares with each of her sons, Ethan, 24, and Brendan, 22.

"My significant other says he can tell when Brendan has spent too much money," Lewis says. "He'll say, 'You go, *Sh-damn,* and switch to e-mail mode, and I hear the keys clicking, *What's this $60 at Café Bola?*'"

After checking what her adult sons have been spending, Lewis e-mails each a to-do list for the day. "I have access to their college e-mail passwords, so I know what grades they're getting and if a teacher has e-mailed them because they missed a class. I can say, 'Hey, what happened? You didn't meet with your adviser yesterday.' Or 'I notice you're missing a quiz in psych.' I know almost every minute detail of their lives." Once a month, Lewis drives two and a half hours each way to clean Ethan's dorm kitchen, buy his groceries—eggs, orange juice, etc.—and take care of his laundry. (Brendan is in school 3,000 miles away, or she'd do the same for him.) Lewis says she does it so Ethan can get extra sleep, but she acknowledges that she helicopters at least in part for herself. "I get a sense of control—of *something.* You can't change politics. You can't change the environment. But you can create something really terrific with your own children."

As terrific as Lewis believes they both are, she's having a hard time accepting that Ethan will not call home as often as she'd like. So she's started checking on him via his new girlfriend. "I e-mailed her yesterday: *Amanda, is Ethan all right? I haven't heard from him in a couple of days. Did he meet with his adviser?*"

The young woman wrote back that Ethan had a headache but was otherwise fine.

Perhaps the most shocking thing about Lewis's story is that her sons do not appear to feel smothered. For the most part, they seem to be as attached to her as she is to them. In April 2008, 24-year-old Ethan sent his mother an e-mail. He typed in the subject line, "Urgent you call... Where are you?" The e-mail continued with a request: *Hey, merm, Here's the stuff.... I didn't have an appointment, but I could register for classes at 3:00 P.M. Sign me up for all the classes except Japanese right now.... Ethan.*

Lewis did register him for his next semester's classes. That same day, 22-year-old Brendan e-mailed her the following note:

Hey...I need some motherly advice.... The girl you met at Goodwill...I took her to the best French pastry joint in town. I was drinking wine on Tommy's tab but I overplayed my hand and bought a bottle of wine for the two of us to share.... I'm sorry, I was a little buzzed when I thought I could play "Big Man" and impress her and now I feel stupid and tremendously guilty....

Anyway, the problem is that she is AMAZING.... She's honors college, Fulbright, wealthy family, polyglot, down-to-earth, outdoorsy, nonreligious, cute, inhibited but sexy. The two prob-lems are that she's nowhere close to on-par aesthetically with other girls I've been used to dating.... The other problem is that I'm leaving.... I think she was made for me.... Can you reflect on all this and get back to me? Love, Bren.

The e-mails suggest a closeness that most people over 30 never had with their mothers and raise questions about 21st-century parenting: How much should you do for your grown children? How do you know if you're doing it to help them—or to make yourself feel better? Just how close should you be?

Helicopter parents tend to have a particularly hard time when their children go away to college. To help alleviate parental separation anxiety (and, one assumes, to cut down on calls to administration), colleges from New York to Minnesota have recently installed what are best described as grown-up mommy-cams on their campuses. Students can stand or sit in front of "Hi, Mom!" Webcams located in common areas while calling home on a cell phone—a makeshift videophone. The University of Rochester actually has three sites, the "Hi, Mom! Balcony," the "Hi, Mom! Bridge," and the "Hi, Mom! Close-up." Cornell University's "Hi, Mom!" Webcam page gets as many as 60,000 visits a month, making it one of the most popular pages on the school's Web site.

After being flooded with phone calls from concerned parents, the Universities of California at Davis and Santa Barbara created special handbooks available on their Web sites to help with issues about campus living—for mothers and fathers. "We had a family who rented a house here for two weeks," says Emily Galindo, interim director of student housing at UC Davis. "Their daughter was coming and they wanted to help her settle in."

Parents like these want to make sure their children get the most out of college from day one, but few parents understand what "the most" means. George Kuh, PhD, however, has been thinking about that topic nonstop for almost a decade. Since 2000 he has conducted the annual National Survey of Student Engagement (NSSE), which measures what conditions make for the most beneficial college experience.

In 2007, for the first time, Kuh, an Indiana University professor of higher education, had his team ask undergraduate students (about 9,000 on 24 campuses) how often they were in touch with their parents, as well as the effect of that contact. The findings surprised members of the team: "The bottom line," Kuh says, "was that, contrary to popular opinion, students with involved parents tend to study more, have more frequent contacts with faculty, report greater gains in critical thinking during college, write more clearly, and talk to their peers more often about substantive issues than students with less involved parents."

Kuh finds it extremely interesting that the students benefited from contact with parents whether their parents were college educated or not. "That's counterintuitive," he says, "because kids of highly educated people usually have advantages. Not just money but social capital."

Although his findings indicate that parental involvement offers across-the-board advantages, Kuh believes there has to be "a tipping point between beneficial contact and the kind that stunts personal growth." Where exactly that point is, his survey can't measure. In their 1990 book, *Parenting with Love and Logic,* Fay and Cline argued that helicopter parenting actually failed to prepare children for the pitfalls of adult life, but it will take years to determine if their suspicions were correct.

In the meantime, university-parent relationship consultant Helen Johnson says you can recognize a child whose parents have been too enmeshed in his or her life. "Some become 'hothouse' children," she says. "They feel they can't do anything on their own, because they simply never have." Others can't take criticism because they think everyone should love them unconditionally, as their parents always have. By far the most commonly reported problem facing helicoptered children is an inability to cope with the normal, inevitable frustrations of early adulthood.

"[This generation is] incredibly capable," says the Fortune 500 recruiter. "They're very technologically savvy, very aspirational, and they are very efficient because they've grown up with three things attached to them at all times—a BlackBerry, a cell phone, and a computer. But they want to be on a fast track very quickly. They want to know: What are the five things I need to do to get from point A to point B? And, if I do those five things, will point B come a little bit sooner for me?" These young adults expect an express lane to the top.

Last summer a young intern, four weeks into his job at a multinational bank, e-mailed the CEO to say he was disappointed because he had been in on very few client meetings. He asked the CEO to contact him directly to resolve the issue, says the still shocked recruiter.

This sense of entitlement poses huge problems for both young workers and American business, says Dan Nagy, an associate dean of the Fuqua School of Business at Duke University. "A generation ago college graduates stayed in their first job an average of four years. Today they stay an average of two years. And that two years becomes one year if the environment isn't rewarding enough." As Nagy explains, that high rate of turnover isn't good for the company or an individual's career.

Given that the NSSE survey found that about 75 per-

cent of college students frequently follow their parents' advice, the newest catchphrase in corporate HR departments and at universities is "parents as partners." The accounting firm Ernst & Young—which hires about 5,500 college graduates a year—now offers students a flash drive with information about the company, its employee policies, benefits, and possible bonuses to give to their parents. The company hopes that being parent-friendly will make it more appealing to top candidates.

Betty Smith, university recruiting manager for Hewlett-Packard, has even found herself negotiating a benefits package in a conference call with a new employee and her mother. Some Enterprise Rent-A-Car locations reportedly send letters to parents of prospective employees, explaining positions and offers.

At least one college administrator thinks corporations are going to have to do a lot more than send letters and make phone calls to help today's twenty-somethings transition to adulthood. As assistant dean of students at Florida State University, Patrick Heaton hires college students to give campus tours. He had to ask several guides to stop chatting with one another and focus on the task of helping new students during orientation. They didn't like the way he corrected them. Heaton was baffled. He had not yelled or been harshly critical. Heaton asked the students how they thought he should have done it. They said they liked the "sandwich" method. "You have to say something nice, then give the criticism, then say something nice again," he explains.

Heaton doesn't think corporate America currently has time for the sandwich method. So he feels that part of his job is to encourage parents to prepare their children for a world that might feel a little tougher than home. Recently he received a call from a mother inquiring how laundry is done at the school. She thought she'd missed that part of the campus tour.

There are washers and dryers in the dorms, Heaton told her.

"But how is it done?" the mother persisted. "Who picks it up and delivers it? Or do students have to drop it off somewhere? What is the service?"

"There is no service," Heaton explained. "The students do their own laundry."

The mother was horrified. She said that her son didn't know how to wash clothes.

Heaton told the woman it was a good thing she called when she did—six weeks before school started. She had time to teach her son something really important: how to do laundry. ◍

The Children of Donor X

When her son—conceived with an anonymous sperm donor—turned out to have a mild form of autism, Gwenyth Jackaway went on the Internet and befriended other mothers whose children shared the same biological father and, in a few cases, eerily similar diagnoses. **Emily Bazelon** reports on the reliability (or not) of sperm banks, the vital importance of the Donor Sibling Registry, and—this is the good part—a whole new kind of extended family.

When Gwenyth Jackaway and Theresa Pergola met for the first time three years ago, they quickly spotted the resemblances among their children.

Gwenyth's son, Dylan, was 3, and Theresa's triplets, Anna, Anthony, and Joseph, 2. The mothers saw right off that Anthony and Dylan have the same full lips; Dylan and Joseph, broad foreheads and wide-set eyes. As the kids played in her living room, Theresa noticed the three boys bent over their toys in the same posture, backs curved at a similar angle.

Then Gwenyth pointed out more unsettling resemblances between Joseph and Dylan. Neither made much eye contact. And both were absorbed by letters and numbers, unlike Anna and Anthony. Gwenyth also noticed that when all four kids took off their shoes to run around the dining room table, Joseph was walking on his toes, a telltale marker of autism in young children.

Dylan, Anthony, Joseph, and Anna share the same father—Donor X from the California Cryobank, which is among the largest sperm repositories in the world. (The donor's number is being masked at the request of one of the mothers in this story.) At 2, Dylan tested on the autistic spectrum. Two years later, doctors refined the diagnosis to a form of autism called Asperger's syndrome, which means that while he is highly intelligent, unlike many autistic children who suffer from some degree of mental retardation, he shares some of the classic traits of the disorder—social and communication impairments and narrow interests. When Dylan was a baby, he didn't look at Gwenyth. When he learned to talk, he used words only to identify objects rather than communicating wants or feelings, or calling "Mama." As a toddler he could spend hours watching spinning toys, and at around age 3 he became obsessive about subway maps and lists of words and numbers, which still decorate every wall of his room.

Gwenyth, who grew up in a small family, first contacted Theresa out of a longing for Dylan to be part of a larger community. Once the women connected through a Web site called the Donor Sibling Registry, Gwenyth quickly opened up about her son's autism. Theresa had just begun to notice troubling signs in Joseph. He was 22 months old, and his speech seemed to be shrinking rather than growing. Unlike his brother and sister, he didn't respond when his name was called. And he regularly lined up blocks, videotapes—anything he could. Still, Theresa

wasn't sure. "I was a little bit in denial," she said recently. "I kept going back and forth in my head on whether it was really true."

A week after the two mothers hung up the phone, Gwenyth and Dylan were on a train from New York City out to Long Island to visit Theresa and crew in the suburbs. The living room of their three-bedroom Nassau County home, which Theresa shares with her mother and sister, is covered with portraits of the triplets at 9 months. When Theresa broached her fears about Joseph's development, Gwenyth responded by talking about the traits Joseph and Dylan seemed to have in common—and stressed the benefits that early diagnosis and specialized therapy were having for her son. Theresa couldn't help feeling defensive. "She was being gentle, but it was definitely scary," she remembers.

About a month later, prompted by her own questions and Gwenyth's observations, Theresa had Joseph tested. He, like Dylan, received a diagnosis on the autistic spectrum. Theresa didn't wait to call Gwenyth. She cried, and Gwenyth comforted her, and then they got down to business and talked about how to navigate the special education system to get Joseph the help he needed.

A couple of years later, they are still strategizing. "In some ways, I look at her as an older sister, someone who listens and guides me," Theresa tells me when the families meet up again for another weekend playdate. "I'd have gone crazy if it weren't for Gwenyth."

This time, Theresa and the triplets—who were 4 and more portable—made the trip to Gwenyth's Manhattan apartment, which is chic and artfully spare, the living room painted a cool blue, with a huge Monet print on one wall. Theresa stands in the door to Dylan's room, where he and Anthony send cars down a track; Joseph is hunched over another toy in the corner, and Anna tries to open a tube of paint. Gwenyth walks over to help her. A 47-year-old associate professor of communication and media studies at Fordham University, she has reddish ringlets piled on top of her head and wears a silver choker and toe ring. Theresa, who is 39 and works in human resources, is dressed for schlepping—jeans, a flower-and-glitter-covered T-shirt, her dark hair falling loose at her shoulders.

With a laugh that is infectious, her speech filled with the sound of Long Island, Theresa says she decided to have a baby when she was in a serious relationship with another woman. They've since split up, but the triplets see their "other mommy" regularly. Theresa also has a new girlfriend, whom she's planning to move in with.

Gwenyth had a string of relationships in her 30s with both women and men, and as each fizzled she toyed with the idea of having a baby on her own. Two months before her 40th birthday, 9/11 hit the city, and she called the Cryobank. When she gave birth to Dylan, a good friend who'd become her labor coach was there to cheer her through an emergency C-section. He is one of Dylan's two godfathers, but Gwenyth has raised her son on her own, dating only occasionally in the past five years.

When Dylan was first diagnosed, Gwenyth went through a mourning process. As she puts it, "You have to grieve a child you thought you were going to have. And then this whole new life gets handed to you." In hindsight, though, she thinks the panic she felt could have been at least partly eased. Autism is not a monolithic diagnosis. Some of the children struggle mightily and find their lives constricted as they become adults. Others without impaired intelligence, however, can learn to get along, often with the help

> Gwenyth and Theresa have a word for their relationship: *sister-moms.* When Elizabeth heard it, she began to cry. "They feel like family to me."

of specialized therapy, and even to pass for "normal." Dylan has shown steady improvement, moving from a specialized preschool to a mainstream one. And in many ways he's exceptional. Before the age of 5, he was reading at a fourth-grade level, playing two-handed compositions on the keyboard, and adding three-digit numbers.

Joseph's status is even more fluid. His diagnosis, pervasive developmental disorder-not otherwise specified (PDD-NOS), is a catchall term for children who exhibit some, but not all, of autism's attributes. In his case, the symptoms seem relatively mild. When he was 2, Joseph received one-on-one therapy five days a week; as he progressed, he only went twice a week. He attends a mainstream preschool with Anna and Anthony; by that summer, teachers expected he would no longer need special help.

And then there's David. About a year after Gwenyth helped Theresa get through the shock of Joseph's diagnosis, she found herself in an eerily similar phone conversation about another child with developmental problems. Elizabeth (who asked to use only her middle name) is a

Gwenyth

Theresa

Anna, 4

TALL, DARK, AND ABSENT: Although the man whose sperm created this family is not here, everyone else was excited to show up for their first group gathering in New York City.

Joseph, 4

Anthony, 4

Dylan, 5

Victoria and Victor, 4

Elizabeth and David, 4

Dixie

One couple with 4-year-old twins

Sydney, 4

David's brother, 2

speech pathologist who lives in western Massachusetts and also conceived with Donor X, twice. Her son David (a pseudonym) was born three months premature with bleeding in his brain, and for a long time doctors thought his behavioral quirks were a result of his birth. But Elizabeth stopped thinking that David would "grow out of it," as one of his teachers said, after she learned from Gwenyth and Theresa about Dylan and Joseph.

When Elizabeth and her son came for a visit one day, Gwenyth watched David open and close a CD player over and over again. Then Elizabeth walked into Dylan's room. "I saw that he had lists of numbers and Spanish words on the wall," she tells me later when I reach her on the phone. "As soon as David learns something, he wants to know all about it. He learned quickly how to count to 100, and then to 40 in Spanish."

June of 2007, soon after his fourth birthday, David got the same diagnosis as Joseph: PDD-NOS. Like Theresa, Elizabeth called Gwenyth before she told her family—it didn't matter that the women had met only once. They stayed on the phone for more than an hour.

Gwenyth tried to say what she wished someone had said to her—that an autism diagnosis isn't a terrible lifetime sentence, that a range of outcomes is possible, particularly for bright kids who get help at a young age. "It was easier to talk to Gwenyth than anyone else because she understands what this diagnosis means," Elizabeth says. Gwenyth and Theresa have a word for their relationship: *sister-moms*. When Elizabeth heard it, she started to cry. "They feel like family to me," she said, her voice breaking.

In the 1970s and '80s, their early days, sperm banks primarily catered to couples who could not have their own biological children because of male infertility. Many of these families kept their children's parentage a secret. With a mother and a father accounted for, there was no particular call for honesty. As late as 1995, one study found that none of the parents in 45 sperm donor families planned to tell their children the truth about their genetic origins. Today, however, at least 60 percent of sperm bank users are single mothers or lesbian couples, according to Liza Mundy, author of *Everything Conceivable: How Assisted Reproduction Is Changing Men, Women, and the World*. These women can't fudge the father question so easily, and they've fueled an increasing push for connection and information—especially medical information.

For the Donor X mothers, the drive to find out about

California Cryobank allows up to 25 families to purchase the sperm of one donor.

the paternal side of their kids' family tree eventually led them to the Donor Sibling Registry (DSR). Started in 2000 by Wendy and Ryan Kramer—an enterprising mother and her sperm donor son—the DSR has gone from a small Yahoo discussion group to a sprawling Web site that has matched more than 4,000 children with their half-siblings or biological parents. The site is a nest of personals ads—it's just that the sought-after partner isn't a lover, but a parent, child, brother, or sister. Or perhaps, a "sister-mom," since many of the ads are placed by mothers on behalf of their children. "Some women use the Internet to build this new kind of kinship network," Mundy says. "They're raising their children on their own, but they feel like they have an extended family. The families are often far-flung, and yet the women have these intimate relationships."

Through the DSR, Gwenyth, Theresa, and Elizabeth found each other as well as two other single mothers, a lesbian couple, and a husband and wife who all chose Donor X. For some of them, the decision to join the site was made with a great deal of angst. One mother, who lives in Florida with her 5-year-old son, says that when friends told her she could look for his half-siblings, she wanted nothing to do with it. But later she started reading blogs written by mothers who had connected with the families of their kids' half-siblings, and she found herself craving the kind of knowledge that they had. "We get to know the donor by getting to know the other children," she says.

The married couple, who have twin 5-year-old boys, went through a similar change of heart. At first, registering on the DSR felt "like jumping off a bridge," the mother says. Her kids would never wonder on their own where their father is. What would they make of all these half-siblings, when they were old enough to understand? And yet, once she knew the DSR was out there, the pull was irresistible. Last spring, after initial contact over e-mail, she and her husband conquered their fears and met up with Theresa and her kids when they came to Florida to go to Disney World. The families got together in a park, and as Gwenyth and Theresa had, the three adults marveled at the kids' similarities. Anna and one of the twin boys mirrored each other's facial expressions. They broke the crust off their sandwiches with the same precise gesture. And when they squinted in the sun they looked as if *they* could be twins.

So far, the DSR has connected seven families who used Donor X. They live in five states and have 11 children, two of them girls, nine of them boys (with one more on the way). The odds that three of these kids would fall on the autistic spectrum is about 45 times higher than the chances for the general population.

Gaps in medical knowledge because of unknown genetic history are always a concern, but when a child has health or developmental problems, the issue feels especially pressing. Among the Donor X families, the reports of autism have drawn some of the parents closer—affecting even those not directly touched by it. For the married couple, seeing how much the others were getting from these relationships has strengthened their intention to tell their own sons when they are older that they were conceived with donor sperm—and also, as it happens, donor eggs. "I don't want to mislead them or have them make medical decisions based on faulty information," the father says.

For other parents, the sharing of medical data has already had real meaning. Victoria Boyd conceived a son named Victor with Donor X. When he was about 2, he had a speech delay and significant trouble chewing and swallowing food. Now at 4, the problems have mostly resolved, thanks to early intervention. But Victoria has been grateful to know about Dylan and Joseph, because the information has given her more to go on. "These are his blood siblings, so that was important," she says.

This is familiar terrain for the DSR's Wendy Kramer. "I wanted to respond to our members' stories about struggling to get medical history that the banks won't give them," Kramer says. And so she recently added a new option to the registry. It's a page designed to collect all relevant genetic and medical information that families who used the same donor wish to share among themselves. The donor can also post, anonymously if he chooses. "I wanted to create a safe place where the donor can let the families know if his father dies of a heart attack, or other medically important facts," Kramer says.

Is the bank that sold Donor X's sperm at fault for failing to catch the genetic defect he appears to carry? (None of the mothers of affected children has family members with autism.) No history of the disorder showed up on the three-generation medical profile that Donor X filled out for the California Cryobank. The bank conducts DNA testing for conditions like Tay-Sachs, cystic fibrosis, and sickle-cell anemia, which are primarily caused by a single mutant gene. Autism is a different story. The disorder clearly has a hereditary component (if one identical twin has it, the odds the other will, too, are between 60 and 90 percent), "but there is not a genetic test for autism because we have not yet identified enough genes that might cause it," says Peter Szatmari, MD, a veteran autism researcher and psychiatry professor at McMaster University in Hamilton, Ontario.

There is at least one other case, reported in 2006, of a high rate of autism and related disorders among children with a common sperm donor—four of the seven known children of California Cryobank donor 3066. Other accounts of shared medical problems among donor children have cropped up. Mundy writes of a group of mothers on the DSR who used Donor 1476 of the Fairfax Cryobank in Virginia, and discovered that while he had claimed to be allergy-free, several of the more than 35 children he produced have problems with asthma. And in Michigan, pediatric hematologist and oncologist Laurence Boxer, MD, diagnosed five children born into four different families with the same genetic disease, severe congenital neutropenia, a blood abnormality that highly increases vulnerability to bacterial infections and raises the risk for leukemia. In treating the children, Boxer discovered that all of their parents had used the same sperm donor, from a Michigan sperm bank. The rate of severe congenital neutropenia is one in five million children in the general population, but a genetic carrier has a 50 percent chance of passing it on. Boxer, writing in the *Journal of Pediatrics,* surmises that the donor's malfunctioning gene only showed up in his sperm—a condition known as a gonadal mosaicism—and without genetic testing, he would have seemed perfectly healthy.

The sperm banks have taken hits as a result of these cases. Some parents say they have phoned in their concerns, describing their children's problems and asking if any similar accounts had been filed, only to learn later that the banks kept no record of their calls and continued to sell the donor's sperm. That has not been the experience of the Donor X group. When Dylan got his diagnosis, Gwenyth called California Cryobank and had a long talk with a genetic counselor, Mindy Bukrinsky, who worked there at the time. "She asked a lot of questions. I felt they took it seriously," Gwenyth says. Theresa, Elizabeth, and Victoria followed up with calls of their own. Persuaded that this donor posed a higher-than-average genetic risk, the bank pulled his sperm from general circulation. Cryobank also notified families that had vials in storage about the autism—and contacted the donor himself. "We wanted him to know for his own future reproduction," says

Bukrinsky.

The bank's handling of this particular case seems fairly unassailable. But that doesn't mean the same is true across the industry. In the United States, sperm banks are virtually unregulated. As a result, they function much as adoption agencies did a half-century ago: Secrecy is the norm—the concern more about protecting the donors' anonymity than helping families solve health problems that develop as their children grow. California Cryobank facilitates the updating of a donor's medical history over the years for the benefit of its clients. But as the DSR's Wendy Kramer points out, this is rare. In most cases, the purchase of sperm is a one-time transaction.

Sometimes the banks go to seemingly unreasonable lengths for the sake of a donor's privacy. In 1991 Diane and Ron Johnson wanted to have a second child. So they went back to the California Cryobank for more vials of sperm from Donor 276, with which they'd already conceived a daughter, Brittany, in 1989. The second time around, the bank told the Johnsons that Donor 276 had a family history replete with kidney disease—his mother and aunt both suffered from it. The bank had evidence of this ever since the donor filled out a profile chart in 1986. Brittany became sick with the illness (autosomal dominant polycystic kidney disease) four years later, at the age of 6. The Johnsons sued the bank for initially failing to disclose the information, and to compel Donor 276 to testify about it. They argued that he had information that was crucial to future decisions about their daughter's treatment.

When the donor refused to come forward, the sperm bank joined him in fighting the subpoena. In 2000 the California Court of Appeal rejected the bank's argument and forced the donor to testify, ruling that he could do so anonymously. "There may be instances under which a child conceived by artificial insemination may need his or her family's genetic and medical history for important medical decisions," the court wrote.

By protecting the donor's privacy while demanding that he testify, the California court sought to help Brittany without shredding the guarantee of anonymity. That's what donors are promised in the contracts they sign. Identity protection also appears to be key to a thriving donor market. Despite the financial incentive—at California Cryobank, donors can make almost $8,000 for a year of twice weekly visits—sperm is now in short supply in Australia, the

Netherlands, and the United Kingdom, where laws have been changed to give donor offspring the right to know who their fathers are. Faced with long waiting lists, some foreign banks have even resorted to importing sperm from abroad.

The fear of scaring away future donors complicates the question of sharing medical histories with donor children. Still, advocates argue that there is plenty of room for reform. Wendy Kramer wants the banks to take a first step by tracking live births. As it stands, California Cryobank admits that it doesn't hear back from many of its clients. Meanwhile the bank allows as many as 25 families, each of which may have multiple children, to purchase the sperm of any one donor; after that, he is retired. Without a complete record of births, it's nearly impossible for the banks to notify all the potentially affected families when evidence arises of a genetic risk like Brittany's kidney disease, or Dylan's, Joseph's, and David's autistic spectrum disorders. This is where Kramer hopes the DSR's new medical page will come in. The details of a family's history can prompt a mother to get a child tested, as Theresa and Elizabeth did—no small thing, because with autism, early intervention can matter. And then there are the decisions that parents make about their family's future. The Florida mother whose 5-year-old son has developed normally recently elected to use Donor X's sperm again. Pregnant with a second son and in a long-term lesbian relationship, she says, "I wanted my two boys to be related in every way possible. Since my partner and I can't reproduce without the assistance of a donor, we felt that choosing the same donor was the only logical way to go." But a second Donor X mother, Dixie (she did not want her last name printed), says that she will use the sperm of a different man if she has more children. Her daughter, Sydney, 4, looks like Theresa's daughter, Anna, and has the donor's professed aptitude for music. Still, Dixie doesn't want to take her chances with autism, now that she knows about the risk. "Not that you wouldn't love the child, but why would you want to stack the odds against yourself like that?" she asks.

Natural as that question is, too much focus on a donor's medical history can make a sick or disabled child seem like faulty merchandise. "There is no certainty in a baby. It does not come with a ten-year warranty," warns David Plotz, author of *The Genius Factor*, the

> In the U.S., sperm banks are virtually unregulated: Secrecy is the norm.

history of a sperm bank established to propagate the genes of Nobel laureates and other prodigies. When parents have only their own genes to hold accountable, are they less likely to feel burdened or cheated by a child with health problems?

Gwenyth, Theresa, Elizabeth, and Victoria voice no such regrets. Donor X appealed to all the mothers (and the one father) who chose him for a variety of reasons. Theresa and Elizabeth were attracted to his part–Puerto Rican heritage, which he had in common with the women who were their partners at the time they became pregnant. Victoria is African-American, and the bank offered her few donors of color; Donor X was the one with a strong academic record who presumably looked the most like the men in her family. For other parents, the donor's IQ was his primary selling point: They mention his degree in economics and that he'd also studied astrophysics—although the form he filled out doesn't name the schools and the bank doesn't verify such information as courses taken.

A common perception about autism—especially Asperger's—is that it runs in the families of scientists. Astrophysics, then, could seem like a telling clue in retrospect. But the parents who chose Donor X don't think they missed any obvious warning signs. On paper and in the audiotaped interview he did with the sperm bank, they all say, he came across as socially adept and quintessentially well rounded. He made jokes, said he loved to travel, play basketball, listen to music, and was curious about moviemaking.

For Gwenyth, the deciding factor was the evidence of his imagination. "They asked him, 'Where do you like to travel?' and he wrote, 'To the farthest reaches of the universe.' Some people might think that's weird. But I'm also philosophical and I like to think big picture. For me, that was it." Rejecting the idea that she would have screened him out as a father if she'd actually met and dated him, she told me the first time we spoke, "I feel nothing but a huge, huge debt of gratitude to the donor who helped me create Dylan. This is the luck of the draw, and there are all kinds of happily married adults with autistic children. I hope someday I get to kneel at our donor's feet and thank him. He brought me the best gift of my life."

Still, even if Donor X were the type to have children on

> "I hope someday to kneel at our donor's feet and thank him. He brought me the best gift of my life."

his own, he almost certainly would not have had a dozen of them. "It's true that if you marry someone and have a child, you never know the whole picture about genetic risk," says *Everything Conceivable*'s Mundy. "But because sperm donation has become an industry, a greater number of people will be at risk from a single person's genetic makeup. It's like E. coli at a big hot dog plant as opposed to a small farm: The danger is dispersed over larger numbers of people."

And yet the extended web has its benefits: "I find it comforting to know that Dylan's siblings have similar challenges," Gwenyth says. "It tells me that there's nothing I did that made this happen to him. This is just the luck of the gene pool." She and Theresa see themselves as the driving engine of the Donor X families. Or is it one big family? In January of 2008 many of the parents met for the first time—a great thrill. The kids are still young, and it remains to be seen whether or not they will decide to forge ties with one another as they grow older.

In the meantime, it's the mothers for whom these relationships are paramount. "Are you excited to see your brothers and sister?" Gwenyth asked Dylan three times when Theresa and her kids were on their way over the afternoon that I spent with them. Dylan didn't answer, and it was hard to imagine what he thought about the idea of siblings. But Gwenyth's feelings were clear. She and Theresa hugged and kissed and traded new observations. "See how much better his eye contact is?" Theresa asked Gwenyth, motioning to Joseph. Gwenyth nodded, and then they stood back while the children sang a naming song with Terri Trent, a special education teacher whom Gwenyth had asked to help with the visit. When it was Joseph's turn, he looked directly at Terri and said, "My name is Joseph." Theresa beamed.

Dylan played his part in the song, too. Last year, when Terri started working with him in preschool, he was isolated and couldn't find the words to talk to other children, despite his advanced reading and cognition. At almost 5, Dylan made his first friend in preschool. Socializing still isn't easy for him. He got upset when the triplets wouldn't sit still and listen to him play an eight-song concert on his keyboard. But before that frustration came a peaceful interlude. All four kids played on the keyboard together. Anna and Anthony and Joseph tapped away. Dylan held down a bass note. Gwenyth and Theresa drank in the music. The notes weren't in harmony, exactly, but then families rarely are. ⬤

Dr. Phil: "You love your son, but you hate his decision"

• A parent struggles with a son's divorce • A woman is torn between motherhood and marriage • A husband is jealous of his mother-in-law.

Q | Earlier this year, our son announced that he was leaving his marriage of 21 years; we soon discovered he has a girlfriend. His wife and sons were devastated, as were we. My husband and I are trying to figure out how to stay connected to him without condoning his behavior. His family is struggling to cope, and all our son says is, "They'll be fine." Do we have to cut off relations with our daughter-in-law? Should we keep telling our son that he's wrong? We don't want to meet this other woman—it would feel like a betrayal to our grandchildren—but we're afraid of losing our son if we don't. How do we move forward?

Dr. Phil: Let's deal with the basic facts—you love your son, but you hate his decision. This is difficult because he's behaving in a way that you believe is self-destructive and contrary to your own values, and he's making your grandchildren and daughter-in-law pay the price. As you weigh your choices, you need to think about what's best for your own peace of mind rather than what you can do to control your son, because you can't do that. And by the way, don't waste time feeling guilty that you must have raised him badly. As an adult, he makes his own decisions.

I commend your efforts to stay connected with your son; cutting him off because you don't endorse his actions would be an attempt to manipulate him. Ask yourself this: If he were suddenly afflicted with a life-threatening disease, would you rush to his side and nurse him back to health if you could? Of course you would, so there's no reason to go through the charade of disowning him. You don't have to love everything he does in order to love him.

To be true to yourselves, though, you need to make it clear to your son that you disagree with him. Then you're going to have to compartmentalize your feelings and establish boundaries. He should respect you enough to avoid forcing you to bond with his girlfriend. He also needs to recognize that you love your grandkids and their mother, so you have no intention of severing ties. She may no longer be his wife, but she's still the mother of your grandchildren.

Meanwhile, allow for the fact that you don't know what's been going on in their marriage for the past 21 years. Sure, you know what you've seen and been told, but you haven't a clue what the real dynamics have been. I'm not saying there's anything that would justify your son having an extramarital affair, just that there could be more to the story. Regardless, continue to nurture your connection with your grandchildren and their mother, and know that this unhappiness, too, shall pass.

Q I'm 30 and have been married for almost seven years. My husband is a good person who has always given me what I wanted—except for children. Despite my request for him to wait until we talked things through, he had a vasectomy two years ago. I explained to him that I feel incomplete and lonely, and he replied that if I want children, I need to find another man. I take our marriage seriously, but I'm not sure if I can accept things as they are. Should I forget about having a family and stay with my husband or find someone else?

Dr. Phil: When you're getting ultimatums such as "If you want children, you need to find another man," clearly your relationship has deteriorated severely. The fact that your husband got a vasectomy two years ago despite your objections tells me you've got much bigger problems than where the two of you stand on the issue of having children; his attitude suggests that you're not a partner in this marriage. In fact, he has said as much by telling you to either get on board with his decision or leave.

Face up to the fact that this union isn't working. You're seven years into a relationship that has denied your thoughts, feelings, and needs. I can understand that you take your vows seriously, and if you want to put in the effort to go to therapy and try to heal this situation, then by all means do—I'm a big fan of marital counseling.

But I have to tell you that I think it's too late. The vasectomy means he's made your choice for you. Even if your husband decided he was willing to reconsider, the chances of successfully reversing that procedure still aren't as high as you might like. In any case, I think this guy has behaved like a self-centered jerk who's too thoughtless to even discuss a life-defining issue with you. The clock is ticking; time to move on.

Q My husband feels that we see too much of my mother. Though I disagree, I have already explained to my mom that we need to pare down the time she spends with us and our children. We even came up with a schedule that worked for everyone—or so I thought. My husband still gets very angry when something comes up that requires spending extra time with her. For example, we all celebrated her birthday last Saturday, then she and I had lunch on Sunday.

Now my husband is so furious, he won't speak to me. I think he's being incredibly unreasonable. I can't just forget about it, and the problem keeps resurfacing.

Dr. Phil: You have to approach this scenario by understanding that relationships are negotiations, and the negotiating is never over. As you continue to find a compromise, I believe the best tactic is to try seeing things through your husband's eyes. Why does he object to your relationship with your mother? Have you ever gotten an answer to that question? It's possible he dislikes her on a personal level, or maybe he feels that the time you spend with her is at his expense—which in one way can be seen as flattering in that he values your camaraderie.

This problem keeps resurfacing as a fight most likely because you've never dealt with the underlying issues that are involved, such as feelings of rejection, and have instead simply addressed the safer topic, which is your mother. If your husband feels he's playing second fiddle to her, you will never get past this until you deal with that issue. Once you get real about what's going on, you will be able to come up with a plan that you and he can live with and then have the emotional integrity to stick to it.

You seem to agree with your husband that you haven't set up ideal boundaries with your mother. Either way, it sounds like you both could use a dose of emotional maturity. You've got to stick to the deals you make, and he's got to quit behaving like a child when he doesn't get his way. I suggest that you have a conversation with him along these lines.

Script of the Month:
Acceptable family boundaries
I want to talk to you about my relationship with my mother because it seems to be a source of friction in our marriage. I'd like to find out what your real objection is, and I'm committed to trying to see things from your point of view. If what you want, for example, is for our family to bond more, I can get behind that. But I also need you to see things from my perspective, which is that I love my mother and want her in my life. I would hate to feel as if I had to sneak around or be unkind to anyone, so let's work this out together. I'm sure we can find a way for me to get what I need that isn't inappropriate, intrusive, or at your expense. If we come up with an agreement, I pledge to you that I will stick to it. I hope you'll pledge to me that you're not going to shut down if my mother still comes around every so often, because we won't be perfect at this in the beginning. We owe it to each other and to our kids to figure this out so that her presence isn't a divisive issue that leads to pouting on your part or resentment on mine. Let's talk this through calmly and find a way for us both to be happy. ◐

No Mean Feast

Even in an age of plenty, there are things we hunger for. Celia Barbour takes a lesson from the ghost of glorious Christmas dinners past.

Unlike Thanksgiving, which I approach with the kind of resignation a Sherpa must feel setting out on his umpteenth ascent of Everest, Christmas gives me culinary wanderlust, a desire to go places I've never been, try recipes and piece together menus no sane woman should dare. I suppose I have my mother to thank for this restlessness. From her I acquired an insatiable longing to serve a jaw-dropping, heart-stopping feast on December 25. My childhood

Christmases were overlaid with stories and traditions from my mother's Finnish girlhood, like a double-exposed photograph. Most vivid was the description of her mother's, my *mummo*'s, Christmas Eve ham, a dish apparently so glorious that anyone who tasted it devoted the rest of their life to chasing that high. According to my mother, Mummo spent two months brining it, first in lye—"Lye, mom? Isn't that, um, toxic?" "Yes; shhh"—then several changes of water, then salt and sugar and allspice and, in all likelihood, some primitive Scandinavian form of heroin. "It was out of this world," she says.

But I am suspicious. I wonder if her memories of this annual ham are so vivid not just because it tasted great but because ham was not around for the other 364 days of the year. Growing up, my mother's family ate red meat once a week, generally in the form of meatloaf: ground animal's-something-or-other mixed with liberal proportions of bread crumbs or oatmeal, spices, and onion. She was far from malnourished as a girl. She had plenty of milk and herring, plus lingonberries, mushrooms, and whole grains galore. There was always enough food for her family's needs, but no more—no excess, no snacks, no waste, and very little red meat. So perhaps the secret ingredient in Mummo's ham was deprivation, the exaggerated appeal of something keenly anticipated for months on end. Indeed, the only thing my mother and her siblings looked forward to as much as the taste of that ham was the sheer galumphing size of it. "On Christmas Eve, we could have seconds," says my mom, "and even thirds."

All of which is of no help to me whatsoever as the holidays roll around again, because even if I could force my husband and children to renounce snacks and second helpings from October through December, I could never demand such devotion from the rest of my relatives. Besides, the problem isn't just that we aren't hungry enough. It's also that cravings, like all forms of discomfort in 21st-century America, barely have a chance to materialize before they are knocked flat. Whatever it is you want—pork rind, tzatziki, smoked reindeer—you can get it, if not immediately, then by mail order in a matter of days. Longing never has a chance to build.

I suspect that's why my Christmas dinners have grown increasingly outrageous over the years, in an effort to cut through this unremitting satiety. Yet hard as I work, deep down I know it's futile. My mind may be filled with quixotic gourmet dreams, but my gut knows that even the most extraordinary ingredients, high-tech appliances, and sophisticated techniques in the world can't replicate an experience that has simply vanished from our lives.

Last year, sensing the onset of my annual bout of existential distress, I approached my husband in tears. "This is crazy," I said, shaking at him the sheaf of papers—menu, recipes, preparation schedule—I'd been working on for weeks. "The appetizer alone requires three recipes. It's hopeless...right?"

He regarded me calmly. "Are you excited about making all those things?" he said.

"Yes," I whispered.

"Then make them."

"Oh," I said, sniffling once more, just for effect. "Okay."

And so, with a dozen words, my husband halted a plunging elevator, pried open the door, and helped me off to safety. Oblivious to his heroism, he turned back to his laptop. I sat on the couch and felt the specter of the Unattainable Ham drift away from me. It dawned on me for the first time in my life that I could prepare the Christmas feast just for the crazy, chaotic joy of it; the six-day process of it; the slowly building, flavor-by-flavor anticipation of it. I decided I was going to have fun.

And so I did. I scrubbed and peeled, cut and scalded, caramelized, pulverized, and generally forced my ingredients into states of self-transcendence. On December 25, I served deep-fried, cheese-filled savory donuts over a bed of roasted beets as an appetizer, followed by beef tenderloin wrapped in herbs and pastry, potatoes fried in goose fat, green beans with lemon zest and parsley. For dessert, there was armagnac-prune cake and caramel pots de crème.

The best present I got that year was rediscovering why I'd fallen in love with cooking in the first place. See, every creative act demands that you work hard, push yourself beyond your limits, and risk at least a little bit of your heart. But most such endeavors result in something that sits on a shelf, or hangs on a wall, or is otherwise meant to be displayed, preserved, admired. Not food! Food disappears. For years I'd been trying to make something as eternal as Mummo's ham, something that would be preserved forever in the glass case of memory. But in the end a dinner, no matter how dazzling, marks a moment, nothing more. Which fills my heart with a kind of bright, singing joy, because it means that, with cooking, the act of creation is the whole gift, and a Christmas feast is the finest thing I can give the people I love: a way to celebrate the rare and wonderful act of sitting down together, right here, right now. ◘

"Your Mother Knows a Few Things"

Her mother was cynical, sophisticated—and full of really bad 1950s-style advice. But when the chips were down, she came through with pizzazz. A generation later, Jeanne McCulloch wonders what kind of wisdom she'll pass on to her own baby girl.

My mother and I did not always get along. But there was a time, when I was about 16 and my father was still alive, when we did. Late at night, we'd sit up in the living room, drinking diet soda and smoking cigarettes. I had just learned to smoke then, and I was working for a certain look, a special controlled nonchalance that I saw my mother as having perfected. So I puffed as she puffed, watching her every move. The way she'd inhale deeply, then let the smoke out in a long dramatic waft. The way she cocked the cigarette just so between two fingers, her head leaning on a hand, the elbow casually grazing the arm of the couch. She looked both poised and wise, I thought, even in her pink nightgown and fuzzy slippers, feet up on the coffee table. The topic was inevitably men.

"He left her flat," she'd say about one of her friends, or "With that weight gain, c'mon, she had it coming." Above her head, the cigarette smoke curled languorously, but her free hand cut the air as she spoke, her dark eyes snapped.

High above the honks and shrieks of the New York City streets, my father and sister far away in sleep, this is what I learned those late nights in the living room: that to my mother, after the ballet lessons, the braces, the first pair of high heels, the next essential item was a man. "The army of women" is how she referred to her friends who were divorced, or widowed, who were suddenly alone. "Don't be one of the army of women," she'd warn, and though I didn't know what she meant, I pictured them all: gray, elegant, with shiny black pocketbooks and Chanel suits, shuffling together down Madison Avenue. I believed that was something bad, something to avoid.

But this was long ago, long before my father died, and she followed some years after. Now I have a daughter of my own, Charlotte, a 7-year-old in high-tops and cargo pants, who cruises our neighborhood on a Razor scooter with her baseball cap on backward, her penny-colored hair flying up behind. I can't imagine I will ever be offering her the things my mother offered me those late nights. Certainly not the cigarettes, or the diet soda, or god forbid the particular brand of parental wisdom that made young girls believe they would be nothing in this world

without a man. Yet as I watch Charlotte skirt the bumps and divots in the sidewalk, hop her scooter in the air, I wonder, what can I arm her with that will make her safe from hurt in this world? Once she's done with Razor scooters and cargo pants and other things that make 7-year-old girls happy, no helmet rules or parental controls on the computer are going to protect Charlotte from mistakes of the heart.

As for me, I took my mother's advice. Not long after college, I married the boy next door—if one counts the boy in the next dorm room as the boy next door—and let the wild tide of romance funnel into one settled stream. Dean was a tall, decent boy from Maine. We had never really spoken until a week before college ended, when he stayed up one night until dawn explaining Einstein's theory of relativity to me. By the time the birds were announcing the coming day and we had moved the discussion to my bed, I decided this boy, this New England boy destined for a lab coat, was a better choice than anyone I would muster out of the gang of guys in Shakespeare 101, with whom I spent most of my time. Besides, I liked his cleft chin and his whisper in the dark. Even if what he was whispering that first night was $E = mc^2$. And I liked that he wore a silver earring in his left earlobe. Beyond the earring, the cleft, and the theory of relativity, we could not have been more different. Dean wanted the simple life, and I wanted the most beautiful KitchenAid mixer we could buy. This seems a minor thing, but once we had moved together to Manhattan, we spent entire dazed sunlit Saturday afternoons walking into every hardware store on Broadway and leaving empty-handed because we couldn't agree on a blender or a toaster, let alone a lifestyle. As the appliances broke down, one by one, so did the marriage. At the end, all we had accumulated between us was the desire to spare each other's feelings. Finally, one day Dean said, "I don't know, it's like a house of cards and the cards are just, well, tumbling down." As he said it, his hands fluttered in the air and fell to his sides. I thought of dance class as a child, when the teacher would say, "Think of your hands as the leaves, girls, leaves in the autumn, tumbling to the ground." And I thought, that's it. Dead leaves.

After the dead leaf gesture, Dean took off his wedding ring and it lay in the palm of his hand, a little lost craft. We both looked at it, for a moment, then he shoved it deep in the pocket of his jeans. He left a few days later, a duffel bag slung over his arm, like a kid catching the next bus back to college. I called my mother, who was living in Paris, to break the news. "I am completely undone by this," she said over the phone, the long-distance wires crackling. "I am the only woman I *know* who isn't a grandmother." To my unmarried sister she confided, "Now I'm back to square one with you girls. Jesus Christ." But things change. I like to think that. The next day she called back and invited me to visit her at her house on the beach at the tip of Long Island. "I think I better come on," she said. "Coming on" is what people did in my family in the case of emergencies. They hopped planes, dropped plans, they banded together. "You know I like to give you your 'space,' as you kids call it these days, but I've been brooding."

I could hear the exhale of her cigarette, as if the smoke were drifting lazily through the phone wires, obscuring all my determined boundaries. "Ma, I'm fine here," I said. "I'm doing just fine." But the voice didn't sound like mine. It was a thin egg-shell of a voice saying no, I mean yes, I mean....

"I don't want my baby girl alone," she continued. "My tiny baby girl."

Who's my baby?" I ask Charlotte when I pick her up from her first-grade classroom. "Who is my tiny baby girl?" "Me," she says, and jumps into my arms. I wonder how long it will be before she says, "Mother, please do not address me in that fashion in front of my classmates, or, for that matter, ever." But the truth is, when my mother addressed me in that fashion after Dean and I parted ways, it was quite all right with me that my mother decided it was time to do some mothering. Since my father had died a few years earlier, she had become something of a traveling road show. She liked to tell me about it over the phone: the parties, the plays, the exotic road trips. She was alone suddenly in the world, after my father's death, and she liked to keep herself surrounded. And now the road show was returning to the homeland for a few lessons in showmanship.

In March in New York, you can sometimes smell the dirt thaw. If it is an early spring, the streets give off an odor at once filthy and fresh, as if the promise of budding trees and new life will soon triumph over the long, dark days of winter. The year Dean left, spring came early. My mother came soon after that.

"You know, I can't really help you with this," she warned me as we drove down the Long Island Expressway to her house. "If you had asked me a few years ago the wisdom in marrying a young man who favors his mother's meatloaf over a nice restaurant, well, I might have said some things then." She raised her eyes. "But did anyone ask me?" She seemed to be addressing the car's sun visor above her. "No." She shook her head. "Yet," she told the visor, "it's a mother's role, in a time like this, coming on. I can't help you with that mess. But," her face brightened, "I can help you with this." She pulled out a pile of glossy magazines she had been reading on the plane from France. "Here, look at this." She flicked a long red nail at a page of young women in poufy skirts. "Bubble skirts. Everyone in Paris is wearing them. I got one for you, to cheer you up. Anyway, at a time like this, it's important to be chic. Baby girl," she patted my hand, "we're going to get through this

McCulloch (*right*) with her mother and daughter, Charlotte, New York, 2000.

thing with grace and style if it kills us."

Recently, Charlotte came home from school and told me she was going to die. "Zeke told me I didn't have a heart," she said. Her almond eyes were wide with terror.

"Were you mean to him?"

She flicked her wrist in a way that dismisses a detailed confession and murmured, "Well, maybe a little. He gets on my nerves." The vicissitudes of childhood friendship—in the schoolyard more fleeting, but often seemingly as passionate as adult love.

"So maybe, Charlotte, he didn't mean you were going to die. Maybe he meant you didn't return his affection."

"But if I don't have a heart, I *am* going to *die*," she said, launching into what her older brother, Sam, refers to as one of her "chick fits." "Jeeesh-a," she announced, "like I need this. He's telling me I'm dying, Mom, because I don't like him following me around." In a chick fit, words take on extra syllables. *Situation* becomes "sit-chew-ayy-shun." "I am die-ing-uhn!"

Oh, the maternal heart. Can I save Charlotte from being cool to a towheaded boy with bright blue eyes who loves to trail her at school? Can I save her when some boy in ten years doesn't return her love?

Okay, let's get this done and get this done fast," my mother said. We were in the attic of her house, a late Saturday morning. It was pouring outside. In a house by the sea, the reverberations of a rainstorm are boisterous and spooky, and as a child I loved being spooked, loved it the way you loved something loud, something forceful, something you could never control. The very drama of it put me in a world that was my own: the rain falling in mad sparks of sound against the roof, the echo of the surf, thunder like a rip through the sky. The attic was a ghostly theater when it rained.

Soon after Dean and I were married, we stored all our wedding presents up in the attic. The blue Tiffany boxes, the festive silver bags, various bowed and bubble-wrapped items. We had never gone through them; they had stayed up there, a huddled reminder for five years that we were too young for things like china and crystal. They would wait until we'd grown up. Suddenly, unused and unopened, they were the only things between us to separate, and without my having to say it, my mother realized I couldn't do it alone. She seated herself in the old beanbag chair we

After Dean and I parted ways, it was quite all right with me that my mother decided it was time to do some mothering.

had in the living room in the late '60s. It was orange and hollowed out, the Styrofoam beans flattened with age. She peered into the dim light at all the boxes, the trunks. At one point she had moved all our baby items up here in anticipation of gaining grandmother status. In one corner was our old highchair, white wood, with a pink elephant on the seat. I reached out to touch it and my finger made a long white line in the dust.

"Let's get it done before the weather clears," my mother said. She wriggled herself further into the beanbag. "Then we can take a nice walk on the beach."

The wind was howling. "Ma, it's dreadful out there."

"Oh," she said, "trust your mother." When she had something absolute to say, my mother always referred to herself in the third person. "Your mother knows a few things. It will clear."

The boxes were carefully marked. TWO SALT AND PEPPER SHAKERS, BRASS CANDLESTICKS, SOUP TUREEN, CERAMIC COOKIE JAR (REALLY UGLY), one box was labeled. BRANDY SNIFTERS ($$$) another said. I brought over a box marked SILVER CHAFING DISH. My mother eyed the boxes.

"I hope to god you wrote thank-you notes for all of this."

"It was five years ago."

"Your mother just wants to make sure. There's some pretty good loot here."

I held up the silver chafing dish. "What the hell is a chafing dish anyway," I asked.

"*That* one happens to be very expensive. Who gave you that?"

"I don't remember."

"It's very good sterling silver." She took off the ornate top and held it up. I could see her red lips reflected in the shine. "Take it home. I'm sure it came from our side of the family."

"How are you so sure?"

"C'mon. It shows real taste. Let's give him something he can really use. That life preserver, for example. Who gave you a life preserver?"

"It goes with the canoe." A canoe had been tied to the top of Dean's family's car when they arrived at our wedding. It was their present to us—a beautiful pea green boat. It had spent the last five years accumulating cobwebs in my mother's garage.

"Who gives such presents?" my mother asked. "A canoe

in New York City. What were you planning to do with it?"

"I don't know. Circumnavigate the island?"

"Please," my mother said, shaking her head. She added the life preserver and the canoe to Dean's side of the list. "Bring on the next box."

The next was china dinner plates. A dozen of them, pearly gray. I remember picking them out. Actually, I remember standing in the store, afraid to touch one, as if it would slip through my fingers, shatter right there on the floor and everyone would know the marriage was a joke. A facade. That we were not ready for adult things in life like fine china.

"You never used these?"

"Well, we never had cause to."

"You eat. God knows *he* ate."

"I don't know. It was safer to use the old stuff."

She waved her pen in the air. "Look. China breaks. You have to be careful, but it doesn't mean you don't use it."

Look, a heart breaks. You have to be careful, but that doesn't mean you don't use it.

"I don't know. I guess I was just scared," I admitted.

But if I don't have a heart, I'm going to die!

"Let him have the goddamn china then." She wrote it down: TIFFANY DINNER PLATES. ONE DOZEN. "Fine. Life goes on."

I closed the box. Goodbye, I was thinking. They looked so serene, lying there. I'd lost them and they didn't even break. The cause some ineptitude more abstract than slipping through fingers. Or just that exact. Just that dumb and tragic.

"You don't want these things sitting around haunting you forever," she said, "trust me."

Loss. Sometimes I pictured a box of the stuff, the consistency of powdered sugar, or ashes, stored away like all the items in the attic. If someone came along and offered me more, I'd say, "Loss? Thanks, but I'll pass. Got all I can use right here."

The morning tapered into early afternoon as we finished up. "Help your old ma," my mother said, erecting an arm from the depths of the beanbag. Though her face, at this point, was lined with age, like a sheet washed and dried too many times in the wind, she still held herself strong against the world. To her death, my mother was a woman used to having her way. As we reached the bottom of the attic stairs,

a blast of light shone down the hallway from the window. "Look," she said. She tapped a ruby nail against the pane. "See? I wasn't crazy." We watched the waves break in long blades of foam. The sun made crazy diamonds across the water. "This is all I can give you now," she told me then. "Baby girl, it's going to be a perfectly glorious day."

So how could you be married and then unmarried, Mom?" Charlotte asked me one recent Saturday. We were heading toward Hudson River Park, Charlotte beside me on her scooter. She dragged the toe of her navy blue high-top sneaker against the cobblestones, which is what she does when she asks a question she feels tentative about.

"Sometimes grown-ups make mistakes," I said.

"Like in math or something." Her voice dropped to a whisper. "That's a mistake."

Charlotte had only recently learned that before I married her father I had had a first husband. She had run across a photograph of a tall stranger in a gray morning suit embracing me in a wedding dress. It would have been a hard thing to try to obfuscate, so I had told her the truth.

"So then grown-ups can make bigger mistakes than in math homework. But it wasn't a mistake, after all. If I had stayed with Dean, I wouldn't have you."

"So he's not my father, then? Phew. 'Cause I was worried he must be, and I don't even know him."

"He's not your father. If he were your father you would have to be 20, and you're not even 10."

"I am 7," she declared, as if to end this discussion by making her own point.

"And who is my baby girl?"

"I am."

Once we were safely to the other side of the treacherous West Side Highway crossing, Charlotte tore down the promenade south along the Hudson River, off to meet her friend Zeke on Charles Street; Zeke, who last week she had disdained and this week was her main man. She darted confidently through the oncoming traffic of baby strollers, couples hand in hand, dogs without their leashes, her penny-colored hair flying up behind. "Careful," I wanted to yell, but Charlotte was already well beyond earshot, riding high and free in the early spring light, the morning a seasonal whisper of what was to come. The sun made crazy diamonds across the water. It was going to be a perfectly glorious day. ◑

> She waved her pen in the air. "Look. China breaks. You have to be careful, but it doesn't mean you don't use it."

Shelter from the Storm

Buffeted by change and unexpected sorrow, Catherine Newman finds comfort in a $3.99 crèche.

It's naptime in the manger. The rosy porcelain baby is sleeping quietly beside his mother, who dozes on her back on the barn floor, despite her permanent bent-kneed posture and a broken-off right hand. There's not a soul awake in the stable: An ox snores softly between two kings; the shepherd lies down with the lamb; a camel slumbers beneath his ceramic saddle. It's like the aftermath of a weird frat party. Opium Day at the circus. "It's pretty crowded in there!" I say, and Birdy, my 4-year-old daughter, puts her finger to her lips and

gently shushes me. "I love this crush," she whispers for the zillionth time, and for the zillionth time I whisper back, "I know."

A day earlier, the cashier at the Salvation Army had wrapped each piece carefully in newspaper and said, with understated Slavic enthusiasm, "Good deal, crèche." Indeed. Ten barely chipped figures, shedding thatched stable included, for $3.99: In the thick of the holiday season, I was treating myself to a little bargain therapy. Or maybe I just wanted to watch Birdy play. We were accomplishing all our usual festive tasks—packaging homemade marshmallows for our new neighbors, frying latkes, cracking walnuts by the woodstove while Frank Sinatra crooned "Silent Night" scratchily from the record player. But the holiday warmth was like a thin sweater, and beneath it I felt cold.

We had just moved—moved in the middle of an ice storm, with frozen branches clattering to the ground around us like bones—and our new house was old and drafty. I lay on the couch under a blanket and pined a bit for our old, cozy, too-small house that was always warm. Moving is hard, and the exhaustion was normal. But what about the sadness? We'd strung up the twinkling lights straightaway, lit the candle chimes and the menorah in the echoing emptiness of new rooms. We were just across town from where we'd been a week earlier, and nothing was wrong, not really. Everything was great, in fact. Except that Birdy had one of her endless winter bouts of bronchitis, and we sat up with her in the night, pulled her into the dark of the strange bathroom to steam her in the strange shower, while she coughed and coughed. We were tired. Come morning, we pawed through boxes to look for the teaspoons, to look for the peanut butter. Come afternoon, we forgot to pick up our son from school, and when I finally rushed from the bitter cold to find him in the office, he said, near tears, "Where were you?" I don't know. Probably in the mouse-smell basement studying the baffling new fuse box.

At night I lay in my husband's arms and cried. It was the anniversary of a miscarriage we'd had the year before, and I cried for the baby we hadn't planned and had barely known about. I cried for that microscopic loss and the bigger one: Here in this new house, we would not likely become new parents again. "Birdy was born in the old house," I said, picturing our daughter with her red newborn scalp, her fig-sized fists. "Well, not actually *in* the house," I admitted. "But, you know, it's the house she came home to." Moving felt less like moving on up and more like moving away—away from the wooden win-

Birdy hums a little lullaby, kisses the tops of porcelain heads, and peace washes over all of us.

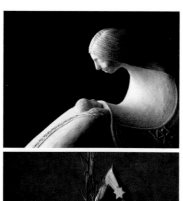

dowsills pitted with evidence of teething, from the measuring wall with the comically low pencil marks, from babies in the house, babies on the way, babies in our future. Now I was weepy and flat-bellied in my lovely new house with my beautiful growing children. I am so glad and grateful, I am; but sometimes the orchestra plays something in swelling chords of luck and joy, and all I can hear is that one violin sawing out a thin melody of grief.

But then there was Birdy, kneeling to unwrap each piece of the crèche like the treasure that it was, lining everyone up on the coffee table with a million questions. As may be typical of agnostic half-Jews, I don't really know the whole story. "Those are the Magi," I say confidently. "The three wise men who brought gifts for the baby." "Then why are there five of them?" Birdy wants to know, and I shake my head, squint at the figures. "This one might be Joseph," I say. "The baby's stepfather. And maybe that's the shepherd whose stable they're sharing? I'm not actually sure." "What presents did they bring?" Birdy asks now, and, when I answer with the mysterious "Frankincense and myrrh," she says, like the Nativity accountant she has become, "Mama, that's only two presents." Before I can respond, Birdy has already moved on. "Why are there farm animals and zoo animals?" she wants to know. "And who's the baby's real dad?"

Jesus wakes briefly, and the ox, remarkably maternal in his bovine way, gets up to cuddle him while snow drifts past our new windows, blankets our new garden beds where, surely, beneath the ice, spring bulbs are dreaming of green. But now it's back to bed for everyone: wall-to-wall kings and shepherds, cows and camels, and an exhausted mother whose happy-sad eyes never close. Birdy hums a little lullaby, kisses the tops of porcelain heads, man and beast each in turn, and peace washes over all of us. However much you might envy Mary her newborn, and whatever you believe or don't believe about Jesus Christ, there is just no getting around the beauty of this little girl tucking everyone in safely over and over again. It's all a kind of Christmas dollhouse to her, sure—but to me it's the timeless and universal idea of *shelter*. And so, finally, I am home. ⊙

Endless Love

By Elizabeth Strout

Love? It can make your mouth dry out so fast your lips stick together. It can make you dizzy in just seconds. It can make you nauseated. It can make you nuts. That's how I felt when I looked out a bus window and saw my baby in a stroller being pushed by her babysitter. I wanted to yell, Stop! Stop the bus, stop the babysitter, stop the traffic—let me grab that child and keep her safe!

She was three weeks old. I was sleep deprived, weepy, and doing a poor job with breastfeeding. ("You're too nervous," the La Leche woman told me.) My mother-in-law had said it was time for me to leave the apartment. "Go do something for yourself," she'd directed. She arranged for a college student to babysit. Dutifully, I had taken the bus to a museum, and sat with a cup of coffee in their café. It puzzled me to think of myself, just a few months before, as a young woman wandering happily through this museum alone. Now the place seemed eerie as a tomb. Did I want to go home? I didn't know what I wanted.

Back on the bus, I looked out the window and thought how everyone on the sidewalk seemed free. Then I thought, *Hey, wait a minute, isn't that the babysitter? Isn't that a baby carriage she's pushing?* I thought, *Wait, do babysitters just take babies out for a walk like they would a dog?* As the bus groaned past, I had a fleeting glimpse of my daughter's tiny face, out in the world of traffic, commotion everywhere.

I had always wanted children. Partly, I wanted someone else to be more important than me; my Self was a burdensome thing to keep carrying around. But I'd been missing that Self since my daughter's birth. I hadn't known it would be so eclipsed by the constant worry—had she burped, slept, peed? ("Sleep when she sleeps," the doctor said. I couldn't. I was too stunned. There were moments in those early days that when she cried, I cried, too.) But that day I saw her from the window of the bus, I almost yelped aloud—not just with worry, with love. Minutes later I sat on the front stoop, and when the babysitter pushed the carriage around the corner, I felt a huge billowing of love that sat like a gigantic, soft helium balloon on my shoulders. I didn't know a person could feel that love, it was so large. But then—a few weeks later, I watched my little daughter wake from her nap, kick her little feet. And—whoosh!—that feeling of love grew exponentially. This kept happening as the weeks went by, and each time I was amazed. How could love be this big? That enormous, soft helium balloon got bigger and higher, until my love filled the skies. *Boundless,* as they say.

Where has that left the Self? Oh, hit by some comets over the years. Obliterated, practically. Maybe I should say transcended. ◐

DO SOMETHING!

making friends with your money

What's Standing Between You and— Ka-ching!—Financial Security?

No matter the roadblock—big worries, small assets—**Jack Otter** has an expert to help you find a way through.

"I have no idea what I'm doing!"

The next time you look at your company's 401(k) options and feel overwhelmed, think about Chris Gardner. As a novice stockbroker at Dean Witter, the *Pursuit of Happyness* author never knew where he and his son would be sleeping at night, but he managed to create asset-allocation plans for hundreds of clients and performed so well that after just a year on the job, he was lured away by Bear Stearns. If a homeless single father with no financial experience can do a credible Warren Buffett imitation, surely you can separate the winners from the losers in your retirement plan.

"It's no less a responsibility than your health," says Gardner, who now runs his own investment company in Chicago. "When something is your responsibility, you've got to get good at it." He tells people to stop saying "I can't" and start thinking *I must*. The first step is to educate yourself. You can click on the investor education section of sifma.org, the Web site of the Securities Industry and Financial Markets Association. Then attend brokerage firm seminars to learn how these companies can help you achieve your goals—but don't commit right away. "Invest your time before you invest your money," says Gardner. "It's your life. Get good at it."

"I can't ever seem to save anything!"

"Prove it to me." That's what Michelle Singletary, *Washington Post* financial columnist and author of *Your Money and Your Man*, tells people when she hears the "I have no money" excuse. "The first thing I do is have them look at their bills." Everyone knows how much they spend on big-ticket items such as rent and car payments, but Singletary says her readers are stunned by their ATM receipts—and all the money they can't account for.

Their problem, she thinks, is that they are unable to distinguish between what they need and what they want. Singletary admits that she tells people this all the time. "When I said it two years ago, people weren't listening," she says, but since the real estate bubble burst, they're suddenly more interested in freeing up some money in their budgets. The key, she says, is to prioritize ruthlessly. "I've talked to people who have no job, and yet they pay for Internet access and ring tones on their cell phone," she says. "They say, 'Don't *you* have a cell phone?' And I say 'Yes, but I have no debt, and the last car we bought we paid for in cash. If you can't say the same, then you should have a basic cell phone with a bill close to $20 a month.'"

Singletary often sees another, linked problem in people who don't have extra cash: an overdeveloped sense of entitlement. "People say, 'I deserve a vacation because I work hard,'" she explains. "And you do work hard, but you don't deserve a vacation if you don't have money to pay for it." Nor does she buy the excuse "My child deserves better than I had." "Any parent whose kid has a cell phone and no college fund should be ashamed of themselves," she says. "Is it a need or is it a want? Keep that phrase in your head and play it like it's on a broken tape recorder, and you'll find that you don't spend as much."

Singletary is proud to be a varsity cheapskate. She laughs when reminded that she dressed her infant son in his older sister's clothes. "What did he know; he was a baby," she says. "He's not going to be scarred." His family has an emergency fund that will cover a year's worth of living expenses, takes two weeks' vacation each year, and tries to avoid any debt beyond a mortgage. His reward will be growing up in a secure financial environment.

"I'm up to my ears in debt!"

The next time you hear the mellifluous voice in the MasterCard ad declare, "There are some things money can't buy…," stop and imagine what that man's life might look like. For the sake of this exercise, let's say he's the owner of MasterCard Worldwide and he's got an adorable baby daughter. Now imagine that he's not worried about a college fund for his child, because you'll be paying a chunk of his child's tuition bills. Because in a sense, you are: The average American credit card holder carries a $6,664 balance; at 14 percent over the next 18 years, that's nearly $12,000 in interest to Mr. MasterCard.

"You've made everybody else rich with your debt," says Farrah Gray, author of *Get Real, Get Rich*. And Gray isn't referring to just credit cards. Interest payments of all kinds are lowering your standard of living while lining the pockets of strangers. "The people who financed your car, those interest payments you make send their children to college," says Gray. By asking his clients to visualize the luxury car they're buying for a credit card executive or the gorgeous tropical beach reserved for guys who finance automobiles, Gray has been able to jolt even die-hard debtors out of their comfort zone. Debt is like any other habit, he says: "We get comfortable in our day-to-day lives and ignore what is truly best for us. Instead, we work, work, work—and pay interest."

Breaking out of the cycle, Gray acknowledges, is not easy. His advice is to find another stream of income to pay off your debt. Whether it's selling stuff on the Internet, baking muffins for a local café, or doing calligraphy for wedding invitations, the sources of income are endless. But what will work for you is intensely personal. "To figure out what you can do, just ask yourself, *What comes easily to me and is hard for other people?*" Gray says.

He knows what the response to his advice will be: Readers tell him they don't have time to do anything else. "There are weekends, there are days off; we all have lunch breaks," he tells them. "People find the time for things that they really want to do."

"I wish I knew—if only I had a clue what I wanted to do for my retirement!"

To plan for life after work, you need two things—a spreadsheet and a dream. Because you can't estimate the cost of retirement until you know what you will be doing, financial planner Paula Boyer Kennedy tells her clients to design their ideal week in retirement. She doesn't let them off the hook with the usual "play some golf, visit the grandchildren" generalities. She wants a detailed plan, with every morning, afternoon, and night filled in for seven days straight.

> "Is it a need or want? Keep that phrase in your head and play it like it's on a broken tape recorder."

"Most people can't get past lunch on Wednesday," says Kennedy, who is coauthor, with Stacey Tisdale, of *The True Cost of Happiness: The Real Story Behind Managing Your Money*. To help people develop a road map for their retirement, Tisdale and Kennedy lead them through questions developed by George Kinder, a financial planner who is credited with starting the "life planning" movement:

■ If you had all the money you'd ever need, how would you spend your time?

■ If you had only five years to live, how would you live your life?

■ If you found out your life would be over tomorrow, what would your regrets be?

As simple as the questions sound, Kennedy and Tisdale say, people are shocked by their own answers. They are so caught up in their daily lives that they've never focused on long-term priorities. The exercise helps them discover what's important to them and what they really want from later life, paving the way to the next step. "Once they have a clear idea of where they want to go," says Kennedy, then the spreadsheets come into play. By tallying the actual cost of their plans, they not only know how much to save but can ask themselves, as Kennedy says, "Is the dream worth the price?" She recalls one client, a New York City woman in her early 60s, who said she wanted to continue to live in Manhattan when she was done with her career. "Looking at her finances, she realized that she could retire tomorrow if she moved back to her native Mexico and live very nicely there," Kennedy says. "But if she stayed in Manhattan, she could probably never retire." The choice then became easy, and she headed south.

For clients who are determined to make their dream happen, Kennedy suggests they give themselves frequent reminders; in her experience, that's what makes people more likely to meet their goals. "You want to go to Australia? I want pictures of Australia in your house," Kennedy says. "I want a picture of that beach in your wallet where your credit card is."

> "We get comfortable in our day-to-day lives and ignore what is truly best for us. Instead, we work, work, work—and pay interest."

"Terror! I'm afraid I'm going to make a tragic mistake!"

You are not alone. Scientists using brain scans have found that financial decisions spark activity in the limbic system, a part of our brains that deals with risk and reward. Researchers have discovered that people feel the sting of a loss twice as acutely as they feel the pleasure of a gain. So even though all available evidence suggests that the stock market will be much higher 20 years from now than it is today, your fear that it will go down tomor-row—which it very well might—prevents you from investing for retirement.

The fear factor is only exacerbated by CNBC. "Many people in the media and the financial services industry present these decisions as winner take all," says Ric Edelman, a financial planner and author of *The Lies About Money*. "The message is that if you don't make the right decision, you'll lose everything." That paralyzes people.

"Investing is not a horse race," says Edelman. "It's a game of horseshoes, where being close can be good enough to win." For instance, by owning a plain vanilla, low-cost index fund such as the Vanguard 500, which basically tracks the return of the U.S. stock market, an investor will get merely average returns. Since 1926, that average annual return is 10.4 percent. If a 30-year-old were to invest $5,000 in her 401(k) every year, get a $2,500 match from her company, and earn 8 percent a year, she would have about a $1.4 million nest egg at age 65. While that's a simplistic example, it's still instructive: Invest diligently in a low-cost index fund, ignoring market downturns and the latest hot funds, and you'll go a long way toward securing a comfortable retirement.

Once clients have a plan in place, Edelman says, you can see their terror melt away. "They feel not merely more confident about their investments," he says. "They feel more confident about their entire lives. Their marriages get stronger; they are able to make better career decisions because they know that the future is secure." **O**

Suze Orman: "Hope is not a sound housing strategy"

● Climbing out from under a too-steep mortgage ● Rebounding from medical costs ● Making barely enough to get by.

Q During the market boom, I locked into two adjustable-rate home loans that I can hardly handle now. I'm a single 34-year-old woman with a job that pays well, but I can't count on a raise, and I'm bringing in just enough to cover the mortgages and my living expenses. I'm looking for someone to rent a room for the extra income. In the meantime, do I ride this out and hope that the housing market makes an upturn, try to sell the place now, or what?

Suze: Hope is not a sound housing strategy. I still think real estate is a solid long-term investment—but only if you can afford what you bought. Let's be realistic about your situation. It's better to get out on your own terms than to be pushed into foreclosure because you were waiting for your luck to turn.

It seems you were seduced, like so many buyers during the boom, into financing your home with two loans: a primary mortgage and a second mortgage that covered some or all of your down payment. The fact that both loans are adjustable is a huge concern. It sounds as though you've already been hit with one rate adjustment that boosted your costs, and another reset could happen relatively soon. You already feel pinched, but realize that things can still get worse.

Selling could make sense if you can't find a roommate soon. If you can get rid of the property at a price that covers your mortgage cost and the 5 or 6 percent commission you will owe your real estate agent, consider yourself lucky. You would be getting out relatively unscathed. Then you can move into a rental and start saving for a down payment so that, next time, you can buy with one standard loan.

But if the price you can get today is *less* than what you owe on the mortgage, talk to your lender as soon as possible. The worst time to ask for leniency is after you're already behind on payments. You may be able to negotiate a deal where you lock into two fixed-rate loans at a better rate than your adjustables.

If that doesn't pan out, ask about a short sale: You unload the house for the best price you can get, and the lender forgives the difference between what you owe and the sale price of the home in today's market. But lenders aren't exactly excited to take a loss. Learn more at housingeducation.org, a terrific resource with plenty of useful information about home ownership.

Q | It's been nearly four years since my husband and I were in a motorcycle wreck. We recovered physically but not financially. We had no insurance, so I charged our medical bills; now the credit card companies are coming after us. Because of the months we spent out of work, we used up our savings. In short, we have about $23,000 in debt, in addition to our monthly mortgage and car payments. Should we go through credit counseling to reduce the amount we owe?

Suze: Your situation is what 47 million Americans without health insurance have to fear every day: How will they cover their medical costs if they become ill or injured? It's my fervent hope that our government leaders will finally make it a priority to address the affordability and availability of healthcare for all. No one should have to go into this kind of debt in order to stay alive.

Now regarding your debt, the credit card companies aren't looking for the $23,000 back all at once. If you could manage to pay just the minimum amounts due on your monthly bills, that would satisfy them. Of course, that could be tough; your minimums probably total more than $700 per month. But you need to be very careful about seeking third-party assistance. A credit counseling service (use only someone recommended by the National Foundation for Credit Counseling; consult nfcc.org) can help you out through various means, but not by reducing how much you owe. *That* strategy is pushed by debt settlement companies, and I don't want you taking that route. They charge a ton in fees, and your credit report will be wrecked for years; after all, the creditors are going to report that you repaid only a portion of what you originally owed. But by striving to meet the credit card minimums, your credit scores will improve, which could help you qualify for a lower interest rate (or possibly a balance transfer to a card with a lower rate).

Next, pull out your tax return from the year of your accident. If your total medical costs for that year—not just from your injuries—were more than 7.5 percent of your adjusted gross income, you were eligible to claim all your medical costs as a deduction. If you didn't take advantage of this tax break, look into filing an amended tax return; any rebate can be used to pay down your debt. (But you need to hustle:

The deadline to file an amended return is three years from the date you filed the original. I'm assuming you still have a little time because you probably didn't file a return until the following year.)

Finally, look at your monthly expenditures for places to cut costs. You mention having multiple car payments; perhaps you can get by with one vehicle for a while.

Q | I'm a 30-year-old stay-at-home mother who is married to a third-year medical resident. My husband earns $52,000 a year—the top of the scale for residency programs—yet we're struggling each month to stay afloat. We aren't frivolous consumers; we use credit cards for necessities and always pay them off in full (but recently had to borrow from our parents to do so). My husband's school loans are more than $100,000, and we have less than $100 in savings on any given day. I know that, because of his career path, we're about a decade behind others our age. Is it possible to make up for years of lost earning potential?

Suze: You're actually in better shape than a lot of people. While it's true that your husband's years of schooling have delayed your savings, his future earnings should help you build up a nest egg fairly quickly once he goes into practice—even with the large student loans to pay off.

You might consider repaying those debts over a long time span (20 years or more); most lenders will offer an extended repayment period. That will keep the installments low enough that you should have some money left over to build an emergency cash fund and start bulking up your retirement savings. Just realize that the longer the repayment period, the more you end up paying in interest. So while this approach can make sense for the first few years, you should make it a priority to polish off the educational debt once your husband is established.

As for your current cash crunch, let's first recognize how great it is that you both have such supportive parents. But if it bothers you to have to borrow from them occasionally, would it be possible for you to go to work? It doesn't sound as though you have a major cash shortfall each month, so maybe a part-time job could keep your bank account in the plus column.

I get that you feel you're lagging behind others your age, but the best thing you can do is forget about where you think you should be compared with everyone else. Focus on what you can do, not what you haven't done. The past is past, but the future is yours to create. **O**

Forget about where you think you should be compared with everyone else.

Money in the Bank: How Does It Get There?

From canceling credit cards s-l-o-w-l-y to how much insurance you really need, **Amanda Robb** has a wealth of unexpected financial advice.

Financial fitness is a lot like physical fitness: We all know what we *should* be doing—eliminating credit card debt, saving for emergencies, socking away dizzying amounts in a retirement fund—but finding a plan that works for the average person isn't easy. Even if we track every dollar spent and saved, swear off lattes and the stupendous but $28 tights, there's *still* that small, tinny voice asking, "Are we covered for flooding?"…"Did I pick the right mutual funds for my 401(k)?"…"Will I ever be able to pay for my kids' college education?"

We realized we needed nothing less than a dream team of experts to go beyond the financial basics, so we enlisted the aid of Eric Tyson (author of *Let's Get Real About Money!*), Susan Burke (founder of the investment management firm Beechtree Capital), and John Claghorn (senior vice president and wealth management adviser at RBC Dain Rauscher). To answer thorny questions about insurance and home buying, we turned to J. Robert Hunter, director of insurance, and Allen Fishbein, director of housing and credit policy, both at the Consumer Federation of America. And, of course, we grilled *O*'s own Suze Orman for black-belt debt-paying tactics and investment advice. On the pages that follow, they tackle the bewildering questions and intimidating calculations that stand in the way of real financial serenity.

"Tell me something I don't know about paying off credit card debt."

 You know that the first thing you have to do is get rid of any debt—and you probably also know to start by tackling the highest-interest credit cards first. But Suze Orman, *O* columnist and author of *Suze Orman's 2009 Action Plan,* recommends that you don't close the newly paid-off accounts: Keep them open but inactive. "About 30 percent of your credit rating (FICO score) is based on your debt-to-credit ratio," she explains. Closing the accounts will reduce your amount of available credit and hurt your FICO score. When you've cleared all the debts, cancel one card each year, starting with those that have annual fees, then those with the lowest credit limit to highest. (She recommends you keep only two cards.) As you're paying off credit card debt, you might be tempted to transfer balances to a card with an introductory 0 percent interest rate. That's a good idea *only* when the cost of transferring is less than the interest you would've paid on the old card. Some cards cap the transfer fee at $75; some charge 3 percent of the entire transfer amount. (bankrate.com has a "real cost of debt" calculator to help you figure this out.)

"Do I *really* have to stash away six months' living expenses?"

 It depends, says syndicated financial columnist Eric Tyson, who suggests you have enough put away to cover…

■ Three months' expenses, if you have family who will loan you money, your employment situation is stable, and you have accounts such as a 401(k) that you can withdraw from—though you might have to pay a 10 percent penalty.

■ Six months, if you can't turn to family or friends and your employment situation is wobbly.

■ Twelve months, if your income fluctuates wildly or if you are at high risk for job loss.

Our experts recommend putting the cash into a high-yield savings account, money market deposit account

239

(MMDA), or a money market mutual fund (MMMF). An MMDA is insured by the government; an MMMF is not, but it is low risk, and generally pays better interest than a typical savings account.

Retirement: Is it ever too early to start worrying about later? What to do in your...

20s You've heard it before: The most important thing is to invest in a 401(k) or other retirement account, and if you can't afford to contribute $16,500 to your 401(k) (the 2009 limit), at least set aside enough to maximize the amount your company will match. The challenge is to pick the right funds. "Choose your employer's most aggressive 401(k) fund," says John Claghorn, at RBC Dain Rauscher (Suze Orman's financial adviser). "The biggest mistake people make is being too cautious, especially when they're young." Susan Burke recommends: "Make sure your 401(k) fund has both U.S. and international stocks. The U.S. economy is growing more slowly than others, so you need to be globally diversified."

30s Now's the time to max out your contributions to your retirement accounts (if you haven't already). The easiest way to choose an appropriately aggressive retirement plan is to invest in a "life cycle" or "lifestyle" fund—one that automatically adjusts your holdings to less risky investments based on the number of years until you retire, says Suze Orman. For a rough idea of how much you'll need for retirement, Eric Tyson offers three scenarios: **1.** You'll need 65 percent of your projected preretirement income if you save 15 percent of your annual income, are a high-income earner (generally more than $100,000), will own your home debt-free when you retire, and plan to live modestly in retirement. **2.** You'll need 75 percent if you save 5 to 14 percent of your annual income and want to maintain your preretirement lifestyle. **3.** You'll need 85 percent if you save less than 5 percent of your annual income, have to pay a mortgage or rent in retirement, and want to maintain your current lifestyle.

40s If at age 26 you invest $20,000 and it earns 4 percent a year, it will grow to $95,000 by the time you reach age 65. If you wait until you're 46 to invest the same amount, it will grow to $43,000. The obvious advice from our panel to anyone who is behind in her savings is to spend less and save more, but John Claghorn has a further suggestion: "If you are going to be working for another two decades, and you are not going to be withdrawing money from your 401(k) or IRAs to buy a home or pay college tuition, invest as aggressively as you can tolerate."

50s "A good investment rule of thumb is: 110 – your age = percentage of plan you should have in stocks," says Eric Tyson. "The rest should be in a bond index fund." After age 50, you can take advantage of the 401(k) catch-up provision and add an additional $5,500 to the $16,500 limit. Another way to beef up retirement savings at this point is to consider downsizing your home. "The IRS lets you profit $250,000 ($500,000 if you're married) tax-free from the sale of your house," says Tyson, who suggests putting much of what's left after the purchase of your new home into retirement accounts.

60s Now is when your attention should begin to include the smartest way to access your savings. At age 59½, you may begin to withdraw money from your retirement accounts penalty-free. (The IRS requires you to take a minimum annual amount out of your tax-deferred accounts once you reach age 70½; this requirement has been waived for 2009.) Our panel says that one of the big mistakes they see clients make is taking out more money than they'll use in a given year (which means they end up paying income tax on an amount they could have left in a tax-sheltered investment).

You can begin receiving your Social Security as early as age 62; the longer you wait (up to age 70), the larger your payment—but there may be advantages to receiving income earlier. Use one of the benefit calculators at ssa.gov to help determine which option is best for you. And as Eric Tyson pointed out, you can always continue to work. "Especially if you enjoy your job, consider retiring at a later age," he says. "You'll get a double benefit: earning and saving more money for more years."

"When should a person like me use a financial adviser?"

■ **SUZE ORMAN**: "You have $250,000 or more to invest."

■ **JOHN CLAGHORN**: "You start investing beyond the basics— beyond a money market, a 401(k), an IRA, a mutual fund."

■ **ERIC TYSON**: "You feel over your head."

 The best way to find a good adviser is to ask friends whose financial acumen you respect—or contact the National Association of Personal Financial Advisors (napfa.org) or the American Institute of Certified Public Accountants (aicpa.org) to find a list of fee-based advisers in your area. "Commission-based advisers are not evil, but they tend to be salespeople," explains Susan Burke. Eric Tyson recommends you ask the following questions (and look for the following answers) when you meet an adviser for the first time: *What is your educational experience?* (Business or finance.) *Do you sell life insurance, options, futures, or commodities?* (No, no, no, and no.)

Will you provide me with personal references from clients? (Yes.) *Do you have liability insurance?* (Of course.) *Will you provide specific strategies I can implement on my own?* (Absolutely.)

"How will I ever be able to buy a house?"

Home ownership: the impossible dream, especially for people contributing to a 401(k) or living in seemingly recession-proof housing markets—or both. But as long as you have not maxed out your 401(k) or IRA, "don't put money in a special savings account for a house," says John Claghorn. "Contribute as much as you can to your 401(k) and retirement accounts at work, which have tax and employer-matching benefits. You can withdraw $10,000 penalty-free from a traditional or Roth IRA for a first-time home purchase, and many employers allow you to borrow against retirement account balances." (Keep in mind that retirement account loans usually have to be paid back within a certain number of years.) Once you have made all your retirement contributions, Claghorn suggests opening a money market mutual fund (which invests low-risk, short- or medium-term investments such as treasury bills, bonds, and commercial paper) to start saving for a down payment. Eric Tyson suggests putting the cash into index funds that are managed by a computer; over ten years, they outperform about 75 percent of the funds chosen by humans. Also, the best-performing index funds are the ones with the lowest expense ratios. Find out which those are by visiting morningstar.com.

Before you even take the step of going to open houses, though, take a look at a buying-versus-renting calculator, suggests Allen Fishbein, director of housing and credit policy for the Consumer Federation of America. The average annual cost of maintaining a house runs about one-tenth the purchase price, but home ownership comes with considerable tax advantages. To determine whether you should rent or buy, check out calculators at hud.gov and bankrate.com, or contact one of the certified housing counseling agencies listed on the HUD Web site. "They can give really good 'Can I? Should I? How do I?' free or low-cost home-buying advice," says Fishbein.

"My pal says his idea will be bigger than Google—should I invest?"

Your great-grandfather made a loan to his neighbor. When the young man offered to repay the loan in cash or stock in his new firm, your grandfather took the money. The company turned out to be IBM. If you don't want to make the same mistake, Eric Tyson says you can certainly consider funding someone else's business if you're investing in a small, privately held company and the amount you're putting in is less than 20 percent of your total financial assets; if you read and understand and totally believe in the company's business plan (it should explain the concept, the business objective, exactly how it will be implemented and at what cost, the background of principals, and how this product or service will better meet customer needs); and if you review a study of model companies in the same field. Finally, if you can afford to lose *everything* you invest, then, sure, go ahead.

"What kind of insurance do I actually need?"

One in four Americans is underinsured for health crises, and about 60 percent of American homes are underinsured. "Most people need to consider five kinds of insurance: health, homeowner's, car, life, and disability," says J. Robert Hunter, director of insurance for the Consumer Federation of America. "Other kinds—from cancer policies to buyer-protection plans—are only worth it if you can't sleep at night without them." First on our list of questions: Who needs disability insurance? "It's only important to have if you are single or if your family is dependent on your income," says Hunter. Most people are best served by a policy that pays out 60 percent of their annual salary, because disability payments are not taxed.

Next up is auto insurance—just how much coverage is enough? In most cases, you don't need collision if your car is worth less than ten times the annual premium. As for life insurance: "Get it if you have dependents," says Hunter. "Term is the best kind for everyone except the superrich. Most people need a policy that pays out five to ten times their annual income. There are loads of policy comparison sites on the Internet. But two of the lowest-cost insurers, Ameritas and USAA (for active and retired military personnel and their families), don't show up on many of them. To see if these companies offer better rates, contact them at ameritas.com or usaa.com."

"How can I afford to pay for my child's college tuition?"

Don't save for your children's college fund, says Suze Orman, until you've met every one of your own financial goals—you're free of credit card debt, own a home, and are on track for retirement—because (1) you don't want to be a burden to your kids when you're old, and (2) you can withdraw money from an IRA without penalty to pay for tuition. Under the current financial aid system, investing in a 529 plan or education savings account can reduce your eligibility. These accounts may, however, have certain tax advantages. Find out more at savingforcollege.com. **O**

Suze Orman:
"Many of us fear that one day we'll end up as bag ladies out on the street"

• Am I too old to buy a house?
• What's so terrible about being in debt?
• Do I need my husband's blessing to start a business?

Q | I'm 50 years old with no children and am interested in buying my first house. I've been looking for a couple of years, and housing prices are just now falling close to my range. I'm self-employed, earning roughly $70,000 a year, with about $33,000 saved for a down payment. Of course, I realize I'd be paying for this home well into my 70s. Am I crazy for wanting to make such a major purchase at this stage of my life? If not, are there steps I can take to do this more intelligently?

Suze: You're not crazy at all. The desire to own a home is all about security. It's about knowing you're in control of where you live rather than being at the mercy of a landlord. This is an especially profound issue for women; many of us fear that one day we'll end up as bag ladies out on the street. Long-term financial gain typically comes from home ownership. Yes, right now there's a lot of turmoil in real estate, but that doesn't change my view of housing—when purchased within your means—as a solid investment.

The challenge is to get yourself into a house you can fully own as fast as possible. When you have a mortgage, you don't own the house; the bank does. That's a harsh reality many people facing foreclosure know all too well. If they can't keep up with the payments, the lender can force them to give up the property.

To own the home outright by age 65 or so, your goal is to buy a place using a 15-year loan rather than the traditional 30-year. With a $33,000 down payment, you can afford a $165,000 house, which would leave you with a $132,000 mortgage. In this market, if you have a high FICO score (above 760), you've got a good chance of qualifying for a 30-year mortgage with a 5% interest rate. That would make your monthly payment $710. If you opt instead for a 15-year mortgage, you'll reap the benefit of a lower interest rate—say, 4.5%—because you agree to pay off the loan in half the time. Of course, your monthly cost is going to be higher ($1,010 in this example), but the point is to own the house free and clear while you are still in your 60s. Another advantage of the shorter term is that your total interest payments would be $50,000, compared with $123,000. At bankrate.com, you can compute your actual costs based on mortgage amount and the length of the loan.

Don't be discouraged if the higher

> **Right now there's a lot of turmoil in real estate, but that doesn't change my view of housing—when purchased within your means—as a solid investment.**

monthly payments seem out of your range; that's just an invitation to get creative. Consider more affordable neighborhoods or less expensive options like condos and townhouses. And be aggressive in your bidding—buyers have the upper hand in today's softening housing market.

Q | I simply don't care that I have debt. I owe $20,000 on credit cards, I have a $165,000 mortgage, a home equity loan, and car payments—but I wouldn't be able to own a house or car without debt. My husband and I have two children, and we enjoy life to the fullest. We spend money on memberships at Disneyland, a local water park, nearby museums, and the YMCA. I don't mind that we're overextending ourselves because I feel these things are important. We may live paycheck to paycheck, but we're happy. What's so wrong with being in the red?

Suze: You aren't living life to the fullest. You're running near empty. First of all, you don't own a thing; your lenders do. All three loans—your mortgage, your home equity loan, and your car note—are known as secured debt. If you fall behind on payments, the lender has the right to repossess the asset. (Read more about good versus bad debt in "IOU 101," *page 244*.)

I wonder how happy you'd be if one of the paychecks you live off of disappeared because of a layoff or illness. Since it sounds like you have no savings, where would you come up with the money to keep the house and the car? Not from your credit cards; they're probably close to tapped out already. And good luck renting if you lose your house—I'm sure your carefree attitude is manifested in an abysmal credit rating, which is a big warning flag for landlords.

Debt itself isn't bad. It's the way you're choosing to handle it that's mind-boggling. If you care one iota for your kids, you need to start caring about money. I wouldn't be surprised if they end up financial disasters because of the example you're setting. There will also be direct costs they'll have to bear as a result of your follies: We both know you're going to be unable to help them handle any college costs. Even worse, you're probably going to wind up at their doorsteps when they're grown because you've failed to save for retirement. They deserve better. That means making sure you have a rainy day fund that can cover your debt payments and living expenses for at least eight months. Can't imagine where you're going to get that money? Start by canceling those memberships. How much you spend doesn't create fullness in life. Real happiness comes from the quality of your relationships and the security of knowing that the ones you love are taken care of.

Debt itself isn't bad. It's the way you're choosing to handle it that's mind boggling.

Though you talk about your zeal for your business, you seem to have no such enthusiasm for your husband's feelings. I would scrap the venture for now as a good-faith gesture that shows you understand the problem you've created. That also gives you a chance to rebuild your relationship. There will be time to try the business again, but if you don't tend to your marriage, it will be gone forever.

Q | Approximately six months ago, I gave up my job to start a business. The one mistake I made was not discussing my plans with my husband first. When he found out, he was livid. The reason I didn't talk about my idea with him is that I'm a risktaker and he's the opposite. I didn't feel that he would've supported my plan, and I was confident I could make it work somehow. Despite all my zeal and faith, the money I started with is gone. We can get by on his salary, but things are tight. Mainly we avoid discussing the situation. I still feel my concept is worthy, but I don't think I can succeed alone. Should I give up and go back to my 9-to-5?

Suze: You're focused on saving your business when what you really should be worried about is saving your marriage. Your complete disrespect for your husband isn't a mistake that can be glossed over. Dishonesty is the most damaging wound one partner can ever inflict on another.

You may be able to smooth things over by telling your husband you'll be filing a Schedule C on your federal 1040 tax return. On that form, you can claim all sorts of deductions for various expenses you incurred from your start-up operation. Each deduction reduces your taxable income—a thin silver lining in your gray situation. If you already filed your taxes, you can fill out an amended return by completing form 1040X. Learn more at irs.gov.

In the future, both of you need to learn how to accommodate, rather than avoid, your differences. Instead of quitting and starting something new on the sly, you could have suggested to your husband that you work together to save up as much as possible before launching. That cushion might have allayed his fears because you would have had the funds to cover some expenses once you got going. It would have also given you a united goal. Without that, no partnership is viable. **O**

IOU 101

Debt is like cholesterol: There's a good kind and a bad kind. Knowing the difference—and managing both wisely—is the key to financial well-being.

■ **Good debt** is money you borrow to purchase an asset, such as a home you can afford. History shows that home values generally rise in step with the inflation rate, so a mortgage is good debt. Student loans are, too, because they're an investment in the future. Census data pegs the average lifetime earnings of a high school graduate at a million dollars below that of someone with a bachelor's degree.

When it comes to good debt, borrow only what you can afford to repay now and in the future. A high FICO score is great for debt management; it will help you get the best deals.

■ **Bad debt** is money you borrow to buy a depreciating asset or to finance a "want" rather than a "need." A car is a depreciating asset; from the day you drive it off the lot, it starts losing value. Credit card balances or a home equity line of credit that's used to pay for indulgences such as vacations, shopping, spa days is bad debt.

■ **Aim for zero bad debt.** If you need a car, buy the least expensive one that meets your needs. You want a vehicle you can finance with a three-year loan; stretching it to four or five years is a sign you should be looking for something less expensive. The objective is to get the loan paid off and enjoy years of debt-free driving. Leasing rarely makes sense. It's just an excuse to get a new car every few years, and it keeps you perpetually in debt. Finally, if you have credit cards that charge a high interest rate on outstanding balances, look into transferring to a card that gives you a 12-month grace period of zero interest (search for one at cardtrak. com). —S.O.

31 Solid-Gold Ways to Save— Without Giving Up Your Latte

Nearly three dozen *geez-I-wish-I'd-thought-of-that-earlier* tactics to help you squirrel away a small fortune by this time next year. By Anne Kadet

Buy the smaller package.

1 Yep, you read that right. Some supermarkets and drugstores charge more per unit for the supersize product. At my grocery store, the price for a 200-ounce bottle of Tide worked out to $3.71 a quart; the 100-ounce bottle, $3.52. Ocean Spray cranberry juice cocktail cost $2.66 a quart in the larger size, $2.29 in the smaller size.

Get a refill.

2 If you're lingering at Starbucks, get refills on your brewed or iced coffee or tea for 55 to 65 cents, depending on the location.

Slash your prescription budget.

3 Have your doctor write you a prescription for pills containing double your usual dose and cut the pills in half. Savings can be considerable: A prescription for 30 pills of a 50 milligram dose of Zoloft at cvs.com costs $96; 30 of the 100 milligram pills cost just $9 more. Some medications work only when swallowed whole, so ask the doc before you start slicing.

Ask for a better rate.

4 You can often get a better deal on Internet service by calling your Internet service provider and requesting a

discount. I called Time Warner Cable and mentioned that their competitor offered better rates. They dropped my monthly bill from $45 to $30.

Check the total.

5 Many online stores make up for their free-shipping policy with higher prices. Zappos.com charged $163 for a pair of Aerosoles boots, for example, that aerosoles.com had on sale for $135 plus $9 shipping.

Purchase glasses online.

6 Using the prescription from your last eye exam, you can order a pair for as little as $40—the better Web sites walk you through the process of taking measurements and selecting the right-size frames. You may not find designer frames, but these cheapies are fine for shuffling around the house before you put your contacts in.

Swap books and CDs.

7 Web sites make it easy to trade used books and records for titles you want. Lala.com charges a dollar per swap for CDs; bookmooch.com arranges book swaps for free.

Join a ticket club.

8 In big cities like Los Angeles, Chicago, Boston, and New York, online ticket distributor Goldstar helps theaters and clubs get rid of unsold seats by offering last-minute discounts to members; tickets are sometimes offered free when a theater needs to generate word-of-mouth for a little-known show. You can also find good deals through stubhub.com, where people resell tickets they can't use.

Choose refurbished.

9 When consumers return products after opening the box, computer, electronics, and appliance manufacturers make any necessary repairs and resell returned goods as "factory refurbished." If you buy direct from the manufacturer's Web site, this lightly used gear often comes with a warranty. I recently found a refurbished $149 iPod nano selling on apple.com for $79. At dell.com, a refurbished 19-inch flat panel monitor was $189, a $60 discount.

Change your calling plan because you can.

10 Until recently, cell phone companies wouldn't let customers convert to a cheaper plan unless they extended their contract another year or two. Sprint, Verizon Wireless, and AT&T have announced that customers can now switch their minute allowance, text, or data options without repercussion.

Scrutinize your bills.

11 You might find anything from unrequested subscription renewals on your credit card bill to accidental double charges from retailers. Looking at my bank statement, I noticed I was being debited $15 every three months for an insurance

policy I canceled years ago. Check the phone and cable bills, too: There's a common practice called cramming in which your own company or another service provider adds charges to your bill that are vague, misleading, or unauthorized, or you're billed for services you didn't receive.

Get free (and souped up) 411.

12 Dial 800-GOOG-411, tell the nice computer what you're looking for, and Google does the rest. When I asked for a French restaurant in Brooklyn, it named ten popular spots, sent a text message containing the address and phone number of my selection, and connected me to the restaurant so I could make a reservation.

Ask for a break.

13 I'm good about paying bills on time, but this year I got slapped with a late fee for missing a credit card payment. When I called to explain the circumstances (a snafu with my online checking account), the customer service rep immediately dropped the late fee—and asked if there was anything else she could help me with.

Outsmart the airlines.

14 The best time to find a low fare is in the morning, says travel site kayak.com VP Keith Melnick. Airfares are sometimes reset overnight, and the best pickings are available before East Coast workers get to the office. Look for flights departing Saturday, when fares are often cheapest; avoid Monday mornings and Thursday evenings, when flights are crowded with business travelers. Book as far in advance as possible—the chance of a price drop is slim, and should one occur, many airlines will credit you the difference upon request.

Rent local.

15 I rent cars from an independent shop that usually charges half what the big chains do—so what if that Ford Focus is a little scratched up? There's a cheap option in nearly every city, like City Rent-a-Car in San Francisco, which offers cars for as little as $25 a day.

Buy a wallet-friendly car.

16 Car costs don't stop with the monthly auto-loan payment: According to AAA, an SUV costs 67 cents a mile to drive compared with 41 cents for a typical small sedan when you factor in such costs as insurance, repairs, and depreciation. Before you head to the dealership, compare the five-year "true cost to own" of any vehicle model at consumer car guide edmunds.com.

E-mail your text messages.

17 It's free to send text messages to a cell phone from your computer— just type your friend's cell phone address into the "to" box in the e-mail header. For Verizon Wireless customers, the address is the number@vtext.com; for AT&T, number@txt.att.net; for T-Mobile, number@tmomail.net; for Sprint, number@ messaging.sprintpcs.com.

Craigslist your overseas stay.

18 Following the advice of friends, my sister and I went to Craigslist Paris to find a place to stay the week. We found a beautiful two-bedroom apartment with wrap-around balconies in the trendy Canal St-Martin neighborhood for $1,100—a fraction of what we'd have paid for a decent hotel—and cooking in saved money on meals. (We checked references from previous renters before sending a security deposit.)

Call Hong Kong for free.

19 Talkster.com lets you chat for free with people around the world for as long as you please. Enter your home or cell number and a friend's number at the Web site. Talkster issues a set of local numbers you can call to connect. The only catch is that you have to listen to a ten-second ad.

Seek out appliance discounts.

20 A number of state and local programs will rebate part of the purchase price of an energy-efficient appliance. The city of Gainesville, Florida, offers a $75 rebate on a clothes dryer or kitchen range; New Jersey provides up to $400 on central air. A list of incentives organized by state can be found at dsireusa.org.

Give a dog a bone.

21 Big rawhide chews cost $9.99 at petco.com. Instead, you can ask the butcher for a beef shinbone—you might pay a dollar or even get it for free. My dog, Louis, loves them.

Discover the coupon.

22 Just about every online store offers discounts through "secret" coupon codes. Find them at coupon sites such as retailmenot.com. While every coupon site offers a searchable database of codes, RetailMeNot uses shopper input to track which codes actually work and under what conditions.

Abandon your cart.

23 Leave that dress in your online shopping cart. Your seemingly feckless ways may trigger the retailer's system to e-mail you a discount coupon—10 percent off is typical. It's hard to predict when this will work, so don't try unless you're willing to miss out on a purchase.

Begin a biweekly payment plan.

24 By sending in half your monthly mortgage payment every two weeks, you make the equivalent of one extra payment a year. Following this schedule on a $300,000, 30-year mortgage would save you $77,000 in interest over the life of the loan.

Arbitrage your gift cards.

25 There are millions of dollars' worth of unused store gift cards lying around. If you have one, you can sell or swap it at plasticjungle.com. You can also buy gift cards at a discount averaging 15 percent off the card's face value. Sample deals: a $1,000 Tiffany gift card selling for $875; a $336 Lucky Brand Jeans card for $245. There's no risk—Plastic Jungle verifies the balance on each card.

Maintain certain debts.

26 In the past 50 years, an investment in the nation's 500 largest companies grew at an average rate of 7.8 percent. Of course, there is no guarantee what future market returns will be, but the long-term historical trend is considered a solid guide. If the interest rate on your student loan or mortgage loan is significantly lower than that, you'll likely have more cash in the long run by investing in the stock market rather than paying your loan off early.

Read the classics online.

27 Project Gutenberg (gutenberg.org) offers more than 20,000 books, like Jane Austen's *Pride and Prejudice,* as a free download.

Ditch the paper products.

28 Cloth napkins over paper is a no-brainer (cloth instead of paper for a family of four = $12 savings per year), but you can also swap your paper coffee filters for a metal mesh filter (saving $8 this year after paying for the new filter, and about $18 annually thereafter), paper towels for dish rags (annual savings: $40), and memo pads for a mini chalkboard ($15 this year). Total savings: $75 (plus a lot of trees).

Get first dibs on sales.

29 Clothing stores typically mark down their inventory on a certain night after they close the store—say, every Tuesday evening. For the best selection, ask a clerk which day is their regular markdown day and show up first thing the next morning.

Check the price by phone.

30 There's a way to find out—as you're standing in the aisle—if the store sale price is a good deal. Call 1-888-DO-FRUCALL and type in the bar code number of the product in question. Frucall's free service will tell you the range of prices that online retailers, including amazon.com, charge for the same item.

Use your flexible spending account.

31 Only a third of eligible employees take advantage of FSAs, which allow you to take a tax deduction on medical expenses your insurance doesn't cover, including copays and therapy visits. A person making $35,000 could save $200 on taxes. **◼**

Sweet Charity

One of the absolutely best things you can do with your money is give some away. **Charles P. Pierce** on the payoffs of paying it forward.

We have become very strange in this country about giving away our money. We only seem to be able to do it unconsciously. Dropping the loose change into the charity jar at the convenience store. Telling someone to keep the change because the untoward jingling in your pocket may disrupt the afternoon staff meeting. As soon as we start thinking about making a donation, we start thinking of reasons not to do it. Money's too tight at home. The person to whom we'll give it will spend it unwisely. The buck in the envelope is just a drop in the bucket. Oh, Lord, the problem's so big and my wallet is so small. The modern reflex seems to be that the worst thing we can do for a problem is to "throw money at it," even though very few problems ever get solved for free.

In fact, as much as we inveigh against it biblically, or deplore the heedless pursuit of it, money is one of the few things that truly unites us. Our common currency is, well, common currency in almost all our essential interactions, including our most beneficent ones. Warren Buffett, eBay founding president Jeff Skoll, and the Google people seemed to realize this over the past couple of years. By giving away their money, they cement together some vital elements of our commonwealth. Smaller transactions have the same effect. Over this past holiday season, a management group in Rhode Island gave its employees money on the express condition that the employees then give it away to someone else in need. The company then asked their employees to share the stories of their charity at a company meeting. Thus does the act of giving away money form a kind of oral history, from giver to recipient and then to the people to whom the story is told. There is a spark of the collective consciousness in that, which heartens not only those people involved in the transaction but those who hear the story and pass it along. There is something like art there.

When giving away your money, it helps to think of it as more than bits of paper and scraps of metal. That's not a $20 bill you're slipping into the envelope there. It's a bagful of flour. It's soup or a blanket or a bottle of medicine. That handful of quarters is a handful of rice. You can even make this art out of raw self-interest. Giving away money can be the most selfish thing you do. With a father and four of his siblings dead from the same disease, I can look at the check I send to the Alzheimer's Association and see something that is every bit as therapeutic as any new therapy that money may help create. I see new drug trials, and respite care, and a light against enveloping darkness.

There is nothing more visceral than cynicism, nothing more brutish than greed. These are reflexes, common and unremarkable, of the undeveloped spirit. But charity in its finest sense is always an act of the creative imagination. ◖

make a connection

Victoria Marsh and Hiromi Awa with (*from left*) Victoria's children, Delaney and Ian, and Hiromi's son Hiro, in New York's Central Park, July 2007.

Finding a Heart

They were mothers from opposite sides of the world awaiting the near impossible—organ transplants for their two critically ill baby boys. What unfolded was a story of life, death, friendship, and a desperate shortage that has many young lives hanging in the balance. By Lisa Wolfe

Victoria Marsh and Hiromi Awa are sitting at a table, poring over Japanese characters. Hiromi has chosen these characters for their sounds and meanings and Victoria is in the process of selecting a pair of them to tattoo on her body that night. Some make a *sh* sound, others an *awn*, and tattooed together they will read "Sean."

"This *sh* means 'everywhere,'" Hiromi explains through a translator. "This *awn* means 'in the clouds.'"

"I like that," Victoria says.

Hiromi shakes her head, dissatisfied. "I worry they are not the right clouds. I fear they may suggest a cloudy day, not the clouds in heaven, which is what we want."

"Then why don't you tell me what you like," Victoria suggests.

"I like this combination," Hiromi replies, pointing to

another set of brushstrokes. She has spent a great deal of time researching the characters, contemplating how best to memorialize her friend's baby boy, and though her voice is sad, it's also confident. "This *sh* means 'flies in the sky.' This *awn* means 'his voice.' If you put them together your tattoo will mean 'his voice as he flies in the sky.'"

"And if you read it out loud," Victoria confirms, "it will say—"

"Sean."

Victoria looks at Hiromi. Hiromi looks back at her. The translator continues to speak, but the women no longer listen. They shift away from her and lean toward each other. Their shoulders soften. Their eyes move with fast familiarity. They are clearly more comfortable communicating without words. This is what they did for weeks in the hospital, while their sons lay waiting for heart transplants. It's what they're inclined to do again now. But this is the first time they've seen each other in the four months since Sean died, and there are many memorial projects to tend to: an origami table they want to set up at the hospital, a story Hiromi wants to write about Sean, and the design of this tattoo.

"If that's what you like, then it's what I want," Victoria tells her.

Hiromi's 3-year-old son, Hiro, squirms in her lap. He was the lucky one. His transplant succeeded. When Hiromi brought him to New York from Japan for treatment, it was unclear whether he'd survive the long flight. He was born healthy but developed a rare heart muscle problem at the age of 1, the translator explains to Victoria. "Really?" Victoria asks. Sean was born with a congenital condition in which half of his heart failed to grow, the translator explains to Hiromi. "Ah," Hiromi says nodding. It's hard to believe the women spent all that time together in the hospital without knowing what was wrong with the other's child. But you quickly come to realize they didn't *have* to know. There were plenty of doctors around with whom to share facts. Far more important was to have someone with whom to share the feeling: the feeling of waiting with your child as he waited for a heart, not knowing whether he would live or die.

"Hiro, you look fantastic!" Victoria cries, smiling warmly at the boy who now has meat on his bones and pink in his cheeks—a color especially precious to heart patients, who tend toward a pearly purple-white.

Hiromi leans over her son and stares at a photo of Sean, which she has placed in a silver frame on the table. Sean was a classically beautiful boy with blue eyes, blond hair, and a mini version of his father's square jaw.

Hiromi sighs. Victoria nods. It just isn't fair that one of the boys should have lived while the other died. But

Victoria has decided not to let this be a barrier in the friendship, and so it isn't. Hiromi slowly starts asking questions for a children's book she hopes to write about Sean. She politely inquires about his birth, his illness, how long he'd been in the hospital before Hiro arrived. But when she reaches the subject of his last night, her reserve breaks like a dam and a torrent of feeling comes gushing out: "Where were you?" she asks Victoria. "I saw the empty bed! I ran down the hall! I wanted to ask the nurses what happened, but I was afraid to hear what they would say...."

The story began when Victoria, who was pregnant with twins, went for her 20-week checkup. The doctor discovered that the left ventricle of Baby A's heart, the major pumping chamber of blood to the body, had stopped growing. The condition was so severe that no one knew whether the child would make it through the pregnancy. If he died in the womb, his twin was likely to die from the physical shock. Victoria, who lives in Stamford, Connecticut, was referred to New York–Presbyterian Hospital in New York City and put on drugs to help her baby's struggling heart.

On a hot August morning, at 36 weeks, Sean and his sister, Delaney, were born. By that afternoon, Sean was having an emergency cardiac catheterization to relieve the pressure in his heart. Six days later, he had his first major surgery to reroute his blood and turn the right side of his heart into the main pumping chamber.

It was a long and challenging operation, but Sean pulled through, just as he'd pulled through the pregnancy. There were intestinal troubles, feeding difficulties, and he had to spend another seven weeks in the hospital getting strong enough to go home. Victoria and her husband, Patrick, rotated shifts so one or the other could be by Sean's side. Though they lived 40 miles away, had a 3-year-old son, Ian, in addition to Delaney, and Patrick had a stressful job in finance, "we wanted Sean to know we were there for him," Victoria says. "And by the way," she adds, smiling, "he did."

Sean finally went home at the end of September, just shy of 2 months old. He didn't smile. He didn't coo. The skin around his mouth was purplish from inadequate oxygenation, and his eyes had the worried look of an old man. But he was rocked, bathed, serenaded with baby songs, dressed as Mickey Mouse for Halloween. Within a month or two, Victoria says, "you could see him start to think, *Hey, maybe I'm not going to be poked or prodded every two days.*" The smiles started. And then the laughs. Almost all the typical baby behaviors but the whining. "If the twins were hungry and I fed Sean first, Delaney would cry,"

Victoria says. "But if I fed Delaney first, Sean would stay calm and watch. His attitude was, *If this doesn't hurt, then what's the big deal?*" By Thanksgiving he was kicking his legs. By Christmas he had meat on his bones. In January he went back to the hospital for his second surgery.

Babies with Sean's condition—officially known as hypoplastic left heart syndrome—typically require three operations, after which at least 75 percent of them go on to live relatively normal lives. The second surgery went smoothly, and five days later Patrick accompanied Sean through a battery of tests to make sure he was healthy enough to go home. "Hey, Seany boy," he'd whisper, as he carried his son in his arms from hospital room to room. The tests went well, but by the afternoon Patrick noticed that Sean's heart rate was climbing: 140, 150, 160. He told the nurses. They said to keep an eye on it: 180, 190, 200, and suddenly Sean gasped, falling limp in his father's arms. It was a heart attack, as unexpected as it was devastating. What little functioning heart Sean had was damaged. His doctor decided there was no choice but to put him on life support and wait until a heart could be found for transplant.

In the United States, when a patient needs an organ, his name and medical profile are entered into a national computer registry. As organs become available, potential recipients are prioritized by region according to blood type and need, among other factors. Because Sean was so young and sick, he went straight to the top of the list. But there was no heart for him. The wait for organs is often excruciating for adults, but for children—especially babies—it can be more punishing still. The median wait for a young child's heart is two and a half months; for a liver, four months; for a kidney, 12 months. Once a child is of elementary school age, he or she may be big enough to accept adult-size organs. But younger children need smaller organs, which come from other children, and are therefore drawn from a narrower pool. Thanks to mandatory seatbelts and car seats, the pool has narrowed further still, while dramatic improvements in neonatal care mean more babies like Sean are being added to the ballooning wait list.

"The encouraging thing about transplant surgery is that the results have gotten so good," says Sean's surgeon, Jonathan Chen, MD, the director of pediatric cardiac surgery at the Cornell campus of New York–Presbyterian Hospital. "More than 90 percent of our patients will go on to live relatively normal lives. It's amazing. Miraculous, really. But though the success of transplant surgery has skyrocketed, the rate of organ donation has remained flat."

And so the long vigil began: Sean lying with tubes in his nose, his arms, his legs, and directly into his open chest, Victoria and Patrick rotating 24-hour shifts to be by his side. One night Victoria noticed a Japanese family arriving in the ward, carrying suitcases. She had heard that a cultural taboo against transplants in Japan makes it impossible for children there to get them and that a 3-year-old boy who needed a heart would be arriving for treatment. What she couldn't imagine was how sick he would look: ghostly white, stick thin, with a belly as round as a basketball from liver failure. "My heart went out to them," she says. "Can you imagine flying across the world with a child so sick to a place where you don't speak the language?"

Sean Robert Marsh, age 3 months, during his brief time home from the hospital between surgeries.

A few days later, one of Sean's nurses saw in his chart that it was Victoria's birthday. She gave her a cake. The Japanese mother noticed and came over with a birthday gift: a mother, father, and baby crane all made of origami. The nurses got to talking about how other Japanese patients had also seemed partial to origami cranes. Curious, Victoria went online to investigate. She discovered that the crane is a sacred bird in Japan and it is believed that whoever makes a thousand origami cranes will be granted a wish.

She ordered a crane-making kit, which arrived two days later. The Marshes were off on their origami adventure— Victoria thrilled to have something to do while she sat in the hospital, Patrick the self-appointed color czar. "I can't say I really cared what color the cranes were," Victoria says, "but Patrick became obsessed. There was a picture on the box of a set of colored cranes and we had to follow the pattern of the colors exactly. And I mean *exactly*."

And still no heart.

At this point in the process, Sean's doctors say, many parents try to protect themselves by spending less time in the hospital. But not the Marshes. They were there as much as ever. Making cranes. When the first thousand were completed, the next thousand began. Doctors, nurses, orderlies, visitors would poke their heads in Sean's room, ask what was going on—and find themselves folding. Out of sensitivity to Hiromi, who is a deep believer in the power of the cranes, Victoria skirts the question of whether she really thought they'd make her wish come true. But she will say they gave her something to do, something people could pop in the room and join with her in doing, something that helped make the terrible wait a little more bearable and a lot more colorful. "A nurse would come in to change one of Sean's tubes and there'd be a really pretty crane hanging from it," she says with a laugh. "I'd say, 'No, don't touch that! Don't you see how beautiful it is?'"

But still no heart.

Time was becoming an issue. Sean's body was weakening with every day on life-support machines. And in a cruel coincidence, Patrick's father, who had been sick with cancer, suddenly died. The four hours of his funeral were the only time in Sean's entire hospital stay that both Victoria and Patrick were absent from his bedside.

And still no heart.

Not for Sean, and not for Hiro, either. As the weeks dragged on, the mothers' bond intensified. Hiromi would bring Victoria origami flowers on toothpick stems. Victoria would bring Hiromi origami birds with crystal droplets. And these were the least of the gifts. Hiromi, whose husband had returned to Japan to care for their two older sons, says Victoria gave her "the feeling of being sisters," and courage. "Sean's situation was worse than Hiro's," Hiromi says. "But Victoria was so brave. When I saw her being brave, I knew I could be brave, too. Sometimes I would go into the shower and cry—it was important for Hiro not to see me cry. But then I would come out, think of Victoria, and smile at him."

Hiromi gave Victoria the comfort of knowing that someone understood how she felt. "You gave birth to this tiny person who's lying in this big, giant bed. His eyes are closed, he's got tubes stuck in everywhere, and you can't even pick him up and hold him. You wait, and you wait, and you have no idea how long you'll be waiting, or if he's even going to make it in the end. Nobody can know how this feels. But Hiromi did."

In Japan, origami cranes are said to make wishes come true.

In late February, on Sean's 29th day of life support, Victoria arrived at the hospital to see many people gathered in his room. She worried that something was wrong. But in fact the news was excellent: Hearts were on the way for both Hiro and Sean.

Hiro's transplant began first. The Marshes didn't learn the outcome of it until later. At the time they were focused entirely on Sean's surgery, which they felt more excited than worried about. "Maybe this sounds crazy," Victoria says, "but it never crossed our minds he wouldn't make it. He'd already come through hell. This was the moment we'd been waiting for. We were thrilled. All the conversations in the hospital were, 'When he gets his heart, when he gets his heart…'"

The surgery went late into the night. Victoria and Patrick took some nurses and doctors to a tapas bar to celebrate. They ate. They drank. "It was the happiest night of our lives," Victoria says. Nurses would send periodic text messages from the operating room: *The old heart is out! The new heart is in! The new heart is pumping!* Victoria and Patrick returned to the hospital close to 3 A.M., elated. That's when Victoria ran into a night nurse who told her that Sean was bleeding. "What do you mean?" Victoria asked her. "The doctors are working to control it," the nurse replied.

Victoria, who was still nursing, went downstairs to a lactation room to pump some milk. At around 3:30 A.M., she heard a knock on the door. "I knew it was bad," she says. "If everything was okay they would have waited for me to go up to Sean's room. But they came down."

Victoria and Patrick were ushered to their child, who was wheeled toward them in a big bed. "People were saying things like 'There was so much bleeding, we tried all kinds of blood clotters,'" Victoria recalls. "I told everyone to stop talking. I said, 'Are you telling me he died?' My friend Alison, a nurse in the OR, looked at me with tears streaming down her face and said, 'Yes, Victoria, he's gone.' I went over to him. I needed to pick him up. I hadn't been able to pick him up for a month. But when I touched him, he was so cold. It didn't feel like Sean. My baby wasn't in there anymore."

Patrick leaned over his son repeating, "I'm sorry. I'm so sorry. I couldn't protect you. I'm so sorry."

Victoria and Patrick took Sean to his room to spend time alone with him. Victoria held her baby tightly in her arms, desperate to finally feel him against her body. "All I wanted to do was hold him," she says. "I could have held him for hours and hours." A nurse came in and suggested they give him a bath. Victoria loved the idea of tending to her child, cleaning him up, rubbing lotion into his battered skin. But Patrick, overcome by grief and feelings of helplessness, began ripping get-well cards off the walls and pleading with Victoria to leave the hospital. As strongly as Victoria wanted to stay, she felt she had to get her raging husband out of there. She kissed Sean goodbye and left. But she returned first thing the next morning. "I had to see Hiromi," she says. "I knew what it would mean to her to see Sean's empty bed." She walked into Hiro's room, where the Japanese boy was recovering in his own bed, and the mothers hugged each other and cried.

Hiro (*center*) with his brothers, (*from left*) Takanori and Katsunori, in Nagato, Japan, October 2007.

Sean's funeral was a pull-out-all-the-stops affair that Patrick described to friends as the boy's birthday, confirmation, prom, and wedding all rolled into one—every party he would never get to have. When it was over, Patrick tried to find comfort by throwing himself into work. Victoria, meanwhile, stumbled around the house, not knowing what to do with Sean's things, or herself. She plastered the walls with photos, put his unwashed blankets and clothes in ziplock bags to preserve his smell, and tortured herself with the thought that if only he had gotten a heart sooner, he would have lived.

Though there is never any guarantee that a patient will survive heart transplant surgery, Sean's doctors agree that his chances would have been better had he not spent such a long time on life support. But the length of his wait—more than four weeks—was typical. There are simply not enough organs for the patients who need them. Between 15 and 30 percent of the children who need hearts die waiting for them. "It's not a crisis of numbers compared to AIDS or cancer," says Elaine Berg, president and CEO of the New York Organ Donor Network, which procures organs for patients in the New York metropolitan area. "But it's a crisis because it's something we can solve. We don't need research or studies. We just need people to donate organs."

But not many people do. Though a Gallup poll shows that 95 percent of Americans support organ and tissue donation, according to the United Network for Organ Sharing, in 2006 the organs of only 8,024 people were actually transplanted after their deaths. Many intend to sign up as donors but procrastinate. Others insist on being buried intact. And a good number fear that if they get sick, doctors might try less hard to save them knowing that their organs could be put to good use. But the system is designed to safeguard against this possibility. The physicians caring for the patients are purposely not affiliated with the organ recovery teams. When a patient dies, the hospital is required by law to report the death to the local organ procurement organization, which then meets with the family to discuss whether the deceased may be a potential donor. "There's a strict separation of church and state," says Martin Woolf, of the New York Organ Donor Network. "There has to be. If this weren't an absolutely transparent system, then no one would donate at all."

It is especially painful, but especially important, to consider donating the organs of babies and children. "One of the many horrible things about our situation," says Patrick, "was knowing that for something good to happen to us, something tragic had to happen to another family." But the fact is that tragedies happen. When they do, parents may be too grief stricken to think clearly about the best course of action. That's why it is crucial to consider in advance what you would do if your child were to become a potential donor, and to realize that the benefits of donating extend not just to the recipient but to the donor family as well. "Losing a child is one of the most painful experiences in life," says Elaine Berg. "People feel so helpless. It can give them enormous comfort to know that something positive has come from their situation. We see it all the time. We're in the room with families when they're going through the unthinkable. When an older person dies, it is also comforting to donate. But when the person is younger, it can be even more meaningful, knowing your child is really living on."

Then of course there's the enormous gift you are giving—the gift of life—to someone like a little Sean or Hiro. The Japanese boy who arrived at the hospital on the brink of death is now a happy 4-year-old, playing with toy dinosaurs and living in Japan, where he and his family have become locally famous. When Hiro was sick, his parents, both schoolteachers, could not afford to bring him to the States for treatment, and so their friends launched a national television campaign, raising more than $1 million. On her return to Japan, Hiromi felt an obligation to go back on television to show people the wonders that can occur when a country supports transplants and its citizens are generous enough to donate their organs.

Hiromi and Victoria have stayed in touch through translators and e-mail, continuing to support each other as much as they can. Victoria is also trying to help Hiromi publish her children's book about Sean, *The Miracle of the Thousand Cranes.* In it, Hiromi writes that even though some people may think the miracle of the cranes didn't work for Sean, it did. His body survived many difficult weeks on life support, and he got a heart. Though he died in the operating room, the thousand cranes led his way up to heaven. Following their flight, Sean was not scared. Now he is an angel, looking down on other children in the hospital.

It is now later in the day on which Victoria and Hiromi have chosen the tattoo. Hiromi has left to put Hiro to bed, and Victoria is walking into the tattoo parlor with Patrick, who is also getting tattooed. Over his heart. They are greeted by an artist who specializes in Asian lettering. Victoria decides to insert a crane between her two characters; Patrick, a cross. As the artist starts copying the characters, Patrick searches the design book for the right cross. But he can't find one. This one is too thick, this one too thin, this one too fancy. Patrick is a man who's used to getting things right. He excelled at school, in sports, and at work, but he couldn't do the one thing that mattered most: save his son.

"I'm okay talking about the facts," he says. "It's much harder to talk about the feelings. You want to protect your child. That's what every father wants. When you can't, you feel like a total failure, whether it was in your control or not. Every time I think of Sean, I feel like I failed him."

If it's been agonizing for Patrick and Victoria as individuals, it's been hard for them as a couple, too. Ever since that night in the hospital when she yearned to stay and he begged to leave, they have responded to the tragedy in different ways. "You assume you had this child together, so who'd be a greater comfort to you than your partner?" Victoria asks. "But we grieve in opposite ways." She looks incessantly at photos of Sean; it pains him just to see one. She needs to immerse herself in her baby's memory; he needs to clear a path in order to move forward.

This is why the tattooing feels promising—something quirky they are doing together to honor their son. Even more meaningful is the foundation they have set up in his name to raise awareness of organ donation and to support families whose children need transplants (see "If You Want to Help," *below*). "I need to make sense of what happened," says Victoria. "Sean was so strong. So brave. He was such a determined little fighter. Why did he die? I need to find meaning. I tell myself he made it through the pregnancy so Delaney could be born. And maybe he made it to the transplant so we could spread the word, tell parents to please, *please* think about donating their children's organs. Who thinks about this stuff? No one ever wants to think about this stuff. But life can be so unpredictable, you just have to." ◘

If You Want to Help

One person can save or improve the lives of as many as 50 people through organ and tissue donation. To become a donor, log on to the Web site of Donate Life America (donatelife.net), choose your state, and follow the simple instructions. It's important to inform your family of your choice. In many states, next of kin are asked to give authorization before donation takes place. When family members are clear about your desires, it can give them great comfort to know they are fulfilling your last wish.

Children can be registered as donors in many states, but the final decision to donate rests with the parents if the donor is under 18. So parents should carefully consider (and make sure they agree on) how they would like to respond in the event of a tragedy. "I have grandchildren," says Elaine Berg, of the New York Organ Donor Network. "I hate to imagine them being in the position to donate their organs. But what if they needed one? That's how you have to think about it."

To support nationwide organ and tissue education programs, visit donatelife.net and click on How You Can Help. Contributions can also be made to the Children's Organ Transplant Association (cota.org), which provides fund-raising assistance for children who need transplants; Little Hearts (littlehearts.org), which helps families affected by congenital heart defects; and the Sean Robert Marsh Pediatric Heart Foundation (P.O. Box 4820, Stamford, CT 06907), which supports research and helps families finance transplant operations.

Chokora Love

By Uwem Akpan

That hot Kenyan Saturday afternoon, I was thirsty and exhausted as I returned from my routine walk into the endless Kibera slums. Into the valleys and over the hills covered by shanties, I plodded through the maze of busy dirt roads. I was angry with myself for venturing too far and was running late for lunch at Hekima College, the Jesuit seminary where I was studying for the priesthood. My T-shirt was drenched in sweat, and my flip-flops were covered by brown dust. I usually dressed down to fit into the slum crowd. Also I seldom spoke to anybody, so my Nigerian accent wouldn't betray me. There were lots of artisans hammering away on scrap metals, and the roads were hemmed in by petty traders' mats selling tomatoes and used clothes and *sukuma-wiki*. But my mind was on the lunch of Nile perch, rice, and *ugali*.

Suddenly someone was running behind me. I braced myself, instinctively sticking my hands into my pockets to guard my wallet. A boy ran past, stopped and turned to face me. He was a street kid, a *chokora*, about 7 years old and hungry-looking. He wore brown shorts and an oversize yellow shirt that had lost its buttons; when he ran the shirt spread out behind him like malformed wings. He had big eyes and his face was dusty as if he had been sand-bathing all day. He was holding something in a white dirty soggy paper cup. He held the cup high. Occasionally, he took a sip or pretended to take a sip, then wiped his mouth with a long tongue, which created a clean circle in his dusty face, a moustache of sorts.

"*Sasa!*" he greeted me, standing in my way.

"Yeah, *sasa!*" I responded with the little bit of Kiswahili I knew and walked past him.

He caught up with me, and felt my soaked shirt, sympathizing with my fatigue.

"Yogurt...yogurt!" he said, trying to offer me the paper cup.

"No...*asante,*" I thanked him.

"Drink...yogurt."

"No, I'm not thirsty," I lied and shrugged.

Looking intently at me, he said, "Me...me...*broder,* cheers!"

I remembered him and stopped. He was one of the two *chokoras* whom I had mistakenly invited into Our Lady of Guadalupe Church one rainy evening a few months back. I remembered how they, seeing the faithful receiving the Eucharist, had slipped into the Communion line to take advantage of free wafers. I remembered the warm feeling I left Mass with because of the risk they'd taken to march in that line of "saints."

Now I reached forward for a handshake. He moved the cup gently to the left hand, offering his right. I grabbed it feebly because his fingers were wet from whatever was in the cup. He smiled, pleased that I'd recognized him, revealing dirty teeth. We chatted a bit, and I gave him 40 shillings.

"*Asante sana...asante,*" he thanked me profusely.

"You're welcome. Well, see you around Adams Arcade. I need to hurry back to Hekima."

"Wait...yogurt, yogurt!" He pushed the cup against my fingers, his eyes begging.

"No," I said.

"No?"

"Yes, no."

"No, *bwaanaaaaaa*...take! Smile, cheers, *sasa,* huh?"

> He was a street kid, about 7 years old and hungry-looking. He wore brown shorts and an oversize yellow shirt that had lost its buttons; when he ran the shirt spread out behind him like malformed wings.

"Not yogurt!" someone called, laughing a mischievous laugh. "Leave *broder* alone! He don't like *chokora.*" When I looked up, it was a band of *chokoras* waiting anxiously under a guava tree. Also a few people on the road were watching us now; I felt my cover had been blown. He ignored his friends. They laughed at him. *Why didn't they mob me asking for a hundred things as usual?* I thought. *Why was he so insistent on giving, when* chokoras *were always interested in receiving? Was I about to be a victim of a prank? How many germs were in this cup?*

I gave him 20 more shillings and reminded him his friends were waiting for him. He thanked me but wouldn't go away. He was no longer sipping the yogurt. The *chokoras* followed us from a distance, roughhousing and loud like street dogs. Little gusts of wind swept the roads, bound into tiny whirlwinds of dust and trash and dead leaves, and blurred Kibera. I could hear buses groaning along the windy Kibera Drive. I tried to convince him that I wasn't thirsty or tired. I summoned all my strength to show this in my walk. I told him not to feel bad, that I would drink his yogurt another day. I laughed out loud to prove to him and the crowded road that I wasn't afraid of *chokoras* or of all the crazy things that could happen in Kibera. He hung his head and said nothing. Did he understand me? Didn't he understand me?

Finally, nearing home and not knowing how else to dismiss him, I stopped and took the cup from him. He gazed at me, his big eyes seeming to double in size, his mouth ajar, his hands at a ready as if I might change my mind and drop the cup. He glanced at his friends, who had stood frozen with surprise once I accepted the cup. I sipped his melted yogurt, returned the cup and thanked him. He received it back, his eyes teary and calm. He drank up the yogurt, tilting the cup till the last drops landed on his tongue. He turned away slowly from me and lifted the cup high like an Olympic torch, jumping and dancing and yodeling. Then he bolted toward his friends, bolted past them, his yellow wings spread in the joy of acceptance. His friends erupted after him in excitement. ◖

Roll Up the Light of Love

By Lorene Cary

We drove from Philadelphia to the New Jersey shore in a rented 15-passenger van. It had a big chassis and a lurching, truck-y feel. I preferred to drive my own Dodge minivan. I knew it; I knew exactly where its front, back, and sides were when I parked; I knew how long it took to stop in the rain. But although we had no more than half a dozen regulars in the Church of the Advocate youth group, I had

to plan on more: Inevitably they brought their siblings and friends. Lionel, a short boy with a slight build, always brought one, sometimes two, of the string of big girls he fell in love with. "Ms. Lorene, this is my friend. She said she never been to the seashore."

"Hello, darling. And who's this?"

"This my other friend."

While we loaded the big white van, they vied for the "shotgun" seat and radio control. I shouted for seat belts: one body, one belt; put it on and keep it on, period! They made their standard jokes about my adhering to a fictional "Sunday School handbook" and argued over radio stations. I had to turn down the volume in my head. The music was loud, and their voices slammed against it and bounced off the hard, metal interior. Someone at church had suggested that I use permission slips, like for school trips, but then I couldn't have accommodated the last-minute add-ons. Each time the ungainly van ollied over a pothole and the kids sang, "Oooooh!" in amusement park chorus, I was sorry I hadn't.

Each of us has needs, and they had many. A brother and sister had lost their mother in a fire. Years later the girl called to tell me that she was prosecuting her father for repeated, forced sexual abuse. Another boy won a bicycle when our group competed in a bike race. Within a year his mother sold the bike for drug money. Some of the kids had great parents who were absent because they worked two and three pieces of jobs. Without medical insurance, these kids received spotty health and dental care. Family therapy for the oceans of grief through which they waded only entered their lives in crises.

People in church smiled to see the youth group growing, but I suspected that churches only tolerate teens until their sexuality revs up, until they question the whack way grown-ups run things, or until they ask us to do more for them.

'Look up, sugar pie,' I'd say after a boy had mouthed the words to a bible verse. Then I'd read back to him, with emphasis, the words that he'd said.

They asked, reasonably, for Saturday trips. Having taught at my old New England boarding school, I knew in my heart of hearts that Sundays-only work with teens was insufficient to their needs. But as the Buddha and my mother had told me, people are lazy.

"Saturdays?" Like I didn't understand.

Angel was the most articulate: "Sundays are fine for church, but really, Ms. Lorene, we need more than that."

Of course they did. We were huddled in a circle of battered folding chairs in a soup kitchen parish hall that smelled of bad digestion, swabbed over with ammonia. It was where we had coffee hour, as if in solidarity with those for whom the church universal prayed each week: "For the sick, the friendless, and the needy...for our family, friends, and neighbors, and for those who are alone...." Shame on me for making a 14-year-old spell it out.

When I entered kindergarten, my public school had just begun "turning," as we called it. White residents moved to near suburbs ahead of the expanding black tide—us. Stranded in blackening schools, white teachers seemed to

be asking outright and sideways: "*What is wrong with you children?*" We understood that we were not smart or talented enough, neither sufficiently self-disciplined nor as delightful as their old students were. That's why dear Marlon, one of the sweetest boys in school, had to stand in the back of the room holding his arms straight out until they sagged with fatigue. "Get 'em up. Get 'em up! And maybe next time you'll think twice" before doing something—I cannot remember what—that any other 7-year-old would do in a heartbeat.

We'd be okay if we were prodded and pushed and molded. We needed to have things instilled in us, which was sometimes misspoken as "installed." They had to instill/install things in us, as one installed a carburetor into a defective engine.

But in 11th grade, I attended St. Paul's School, where the cost to educate and board each child runs to seven or eight times the public school per-child allotment. There, on scholarship, I learned what it felt like to be among children of bankers, lawyers, and businesspeople. We were cherished; we were "great kids." Teachers, administrators, and alumni said it with assurance: just a *great* bunch of young people. Within each of us lay something *won*-derful that teachers were determined to find and help us develop. We were *mar*-velous. That's why they worked us so hard, and ran us into the ground at sports, and made us rewrite and practice and calculate and experiment. One day we'd be leaders, and it was their privilege to teach us. Even at our most despicable, when they had to hold up the mirror to reflect back to us the worst of our faults, it was *because* they knew that we could and would do better next time.

I fell into this extreme educational luxury just as the boy in my Chinese fairy-tale book fell underwater into the gorgeous jade palace of the ocean prince. I returned to St. Paul's to teach in my 20s. By the time I got to the Church of the Advocate at 30, I knew that if these North Philly children had been given what I had in Concord, New Hampshire, they, too, could thrive in America. Instead they were granted constant stress and a half-assed education. There was no need for me to make it worse with a half-assed spiritual experience. All they were asking for was Saturday.

But we humans are lazy.

From a selfish point of view, I'd already given up Sundays: church proper, that is. I'd given up the slow, regal Anglican ritual studded with African-American spirituals. I'd traded our vaulting French Gothic sanctuary hung with huge black arts–era murals for the low-ceiling mop-water funk of the parish hall. I'd given up the easy company of parishioners I'd come to love, older people who petted and spoiled me, for kids who now wanted and would always want more.

Worship helped me to connect, if even for a moment. "Only connect!" as E.M. Forster wrote in *Howards End*, "...the prose and the passion, and both will be exalted, and human love will be seen at its height. Live in fragments no longer." But body and soul could so easily peel apart. That's why I listened to Thelonious Monk's recording of the song of the same title. He understood. One breathy topaz sound finishes, achingly, before we hear the next, which should have been—and really still was—connected to the first, if we could imagine and let go our impatience: clinging, clinging, clinging, gimme now. Like the spaces in Monk's music, like the communion bell, the Advocate's ritual called me to awareness.

The Advocate lived radical welcome: the artist-designer who wore black-watch trousers hallooed me with irreverent swearing; the painfully shy, heavyset woman with a salt-and-pepper wig who spoke in formal sentences; white suburbanites who loved the liberation ministry; and our rector, Ike Miller, who reminded us weekly that God's power working among us could do more than we could "ask for or imagine."

And when he'd say it, in a rumbling deep voice that rolled along the six-story-high ceiling and dropped into my ear, it was as if I could imagine *any*thing. Writing a book about the Underground Railroad, I saw the characters in that church, I heard them making love; I listened from inside her head as a woman calculated whether to leave her master, knowing that they'd kept her baby in Virginia as surety. I knew the story, but it was in that place that I *felt* it. With my eyes closed and Eleanor Farmer singing, *Blessed is he who comes in the name of the Lord,* I understood that the baby left behind was her easy baby. She'd call him her "best baby," the one who nursed easiest, the one they were most likely to sell.

In the Advocate, among those people, with those gorgeous, buck-wild murals and hand-carved stone faces around me, the top of my head opened up to allow images and words to pour through me like light. Live in fragments no longer. Thy kingdom *come* indeed. Thanks be

to God.

Teaching Sunday School and Youth Group required that I give up that experience and hang out with the kids and their attitudes in the parish hall. We read the lesson of the day to start. Only a few could read on grade level. A few really couldn't read at all. They could sound out words but not put them together.

"Look up, sugar pie," I'd say after a boy had mouthed the words to a Bible verse. Then I'd read back to him, conversationally, with emphasis, the words that he'd said. A wealthy man threw a banquet, but all his friends made excuses why they couldn't come, so he sent his servant to bring in anybody off the street: "What's it talking about?"

"Ms. Lorene, the boy can't read!"

"You can't read, either. You can't do a lot of things."

"Okay, okay, okay. Tell me what this verse is saying to you. Listen to it again, will you?" I kept eye contact. *Stay connected.*

"Did they mean *anybody?*"

"Tol' you he can't read."

"Anybody who'd come," I remember saying. "So, he'd have come here to the soup kitchen and invited everybody who hadn't gotten a ticket yet."

"Oh, snap!"

"That's a shame you don't have no friends to come party with you."

"What's it talking about?" I asked again, two or three times, while they laughed at the idea of the wealthy landowner loading up the regulars.

"Listen, hey! What if he came this morning to get us?"

My mind went through our congregation. Two men from the soup kitchen were likely there that day: one, a tall, aloof man who heard voices and collected girls' barrettes off the street to decorate his lapel; the other, a short, grunting character with a bad eye that swoll up and oozed a creamy yellow discharge. He would try to come to Sunday School and get in on the discussion sometimes, but we didn't let him because he frightened the younger ones.

("I'll just sit by the door. 'S all right if I just sit by the door, isn't it?"

"Sure.")

"It means," Jason said, "that Jesus tried to get all the regular people, but they were too big and impor'ant, so then he came for e'ybody else."

"That's you, boy. He came for you."

Laughter breaks out suddenly like rain. Or tears.

We left the Advocate after 15 years. My husband, profoundly touched by the spirit of the place, went into the seminary. We followed as his career took him to other churches, first as a seminarian, then a curate, and now as rector of his own parish. At first we cried. Now we're clergy family.

Okay, guys, two commandments: Love God, love people. Give it up.

Sometimes I meet the young adults who were once at the Advocate. In the years since our beach trip, the boys are as likely as not to have spent time in jail. The girls have had babies. One is being raised by someone else. They struggle: to help raise younger siblings, to earn a living, to make relationships better than those they inherited. They always recall that trip to the beach—the big, splashy sunshine and the cold salt water.

And when they do, I recall my terror as they rushed into the surf.

"I could swim," Jason assured me, shouting, his voice cracking.

No he couldn't; any fool could see that. I remember feeling big and vulnerable. I was pregnant with our younger daughter. But even without the pregnancy, I could never have swum well enough to save them.

I remember that revelation—Jesus!—that I could only save myself. What kind of adult would go through life with just enough for herself? Just enough swimming skill, or time or love or money? Why pray for abundance and live out of scarcity? What would I do if the undertow sucked one of them down and out? Why had I brought them here in the first place?

My kid could swim, of course. She whispered it to me, as if reading my mind. "I could get him."

She was 8.

"Everybody out! Out! On the beach. Now!"

Uh-oh. Now we're in trouble. Jesus, we just got here.

"I'm going to go into the water," I said. "And I'm going to place myself at the edge of where you can go. No farther. I can't protect you otherwise."

My daughter, the athlete, looked at me as if to ask whether this dictum could possibly refer to her, too. At 3, in this same ocean, she told me, "Don't touch me, Mommy!"—then looked around to make sure that I stayed just behind her, absorbing the shock of

waves. *"But don't let me fall."*

But I wasn't protecting these children. I hadn't taught them to read. I hadn't taught them to swim. All we had done was pray together. We had meditated: *Roll up the light of love in a ball at your feet, pull it over your legs and body and face.* One tiny girl who acted as a parent to her brother asked to be allowed to imagine him inside the light with her. We'd held up a mirror, and they'd said to the dark faces that they only partially approved: *I am made in the image of God.* We sang to carve into the place our covenant: Here, in this space, no adult would harm them: *This little light of mine / I'm gonna let it shine.*

I wished to have given them more. Saturdays were not enough.

No doubt those children had everything to do with my founding, at the Advocate, an organization to infuse our inner city with the healing and educational power of African-American arts and letters. In the past ten years, Art Sanctuary has mushroomed into a full-time not-for-profit with a staff of six and year-round programs that reach up to 10,000 people a year. I hadn't planned on running a business, but that's what was required. The North Stars teen after-school program is only one component, but it's the one that most closely mirrors the aims of that first youth group. Its handpicked team of fabulous faculty teaches love and discipline along with the poetry, dance, and music. North Stars has transformed the lives of hundreds of young people, a *great* bunch of kids. All but one have graduated from high school, and nearly 90 percent have gone on to higher education.

Last year the child with whom I was pregnant on the white-van beach trip joined the program. And my older daughter, now in her 20s, has added to her university research job a weekend gig leading inner-city youths in northern New Jersey on rock-climbing wilderness excursions. The journey to connection is longer than we could have known, stretching unbroken, like the ocean from our little New Jersey beach to Lisbon, Portugal, offering the hope of love but no guarantees. ◑

> In the years since, the boys are likely to have spent time in jail. The girls have had babies. They always recall that trip to the beach—the big, splashy sunshine and cold water.

The Voyage Out

By Sarah Broom

Up until my time in Burundi at Radio Publique Africaine, I was best at setting myself apart, as a monument of sorts, so that no one could enter inside and look around for themselves. I looked best and often for the thing to separate myself from the person I was loving, whether by background, age, race, or availability. And in that solitary space, I felt wide open and most primed for reinvention, a trait I have long prized.

I did this not only with those I loved romantically but, perhaps more important, with childhood friends and family. Friends like Alvin Jarvis, whom I grew up with and who died at 22 in a car accident. The last time I saw Alvin I was home for a summer break from college in Texas.

Alvin broke away from his hard-looking friends and walked over to me and grabbed at me in an embrace, but my grasp remained loose. I did not hold tight onto his back, the way he held mine, but rather beat it a few times as if it were a drum. He asked me how school was. I said, "Fine," looking down at my toes. Alvin was still in New Orleans and I was not, and I let that be the chasm. I understood without *understanding* that by avoiding Alvin, I hid from myself.

But in Burundi, looking down or away never worked. I had arrived in that tiny Central African country unmoored, without a familiar language or geography, and let loose from my personal mythologies. All I had to go on was myself. Even at work at the radio station, I was forced to rely on my Burundian coworkers for more than I had ever needed before. And that forced an internal movement. Whenever I tried to look down or around or away from a person, they became more curious than before.

And a few other things happened: I met a man whom I recognized but didn't yet know, and in time he helped show me to myself without my looking to him to do so, and without my asking for it. Sometimes a person can do that, pull you up from the depths. He loved me, and I felt thoroughly and keenly myself in his presence. But it was not only this person but also the country and its people who showed me a kind of caring that taught me the value of looking straight onto things.

Like the time I was stranded on the side of a mountain road on my way upcountry, waiting alone while my flat tire was being fixed. It was broad daylight, and surrounding me were young boy soldiers wearing fatigues and carrying sawed-off shotguns with the barrels wrapped in tape. At first I was full of fear, and for reason, but then I began to notice the slow way the men began to surround my car as I waited hour upon hour and life passed me by—women carrying babies on their backs and plastic containers of palm oil on their heads. And suddenly someone had sugarcane and was offering me some. No words spoken, but the sucking and spitting out of sugarcane while the radio played a Phil Collins song. And how in that moment I learned something of brotherhood and trust and the human condition. All of us together like that.

And later, a Gloomy Sunday when I was sitting in my African house, the solitude burning, with no place to go and no one to talk to. With the banana trees shimmying outside the window and the sound of rain beating down on the roof drowning my thoughts, I opened up a novel and out of it fell a Polaroid of Alvin, my childhood friend. I was surprised and set off-center by the image falling out like that.

James Baldwin once wrote: "To encounter oneself is to encounter the other: and this is love." It took me a long time to know what he was talking about, but Alvin's picture that day forced me to think about the enormous costs of pushing him away, and that felt like a waste of good love. I took the picture and sat it right where I could see it. It is now, always, right where I can see it.

I know this: It is possible to stumble upon oneself in the process of looking onto and receiving others. I had perhaps come into the world alone, but it was populated with other people when I arrived. People who might love me, see me, teach me things. And so I glimpsed, somehow, in Burundi, the nature of connection, which is to say, the nature of love. And there cannot be, I have come to know, one without the other. Simple sounding, yes, but not actually, and I have traveled quite a long way to understand that. ◖

Not to Look Away

By Marie Howe

Ten minutes into my friend Jason's funeral, the rabbi's cell phone started ringing. Jason would have told that joke a thousand times. But his body lay in the coffin, and now we tell the joke.

Is this what a story can do? Emerge from the most painful event and transform it into something else, too? So sad. So funny. Both. And life is there, for a moment, almost adequately represented.

I'm looking for the gate, Jason used to say when he was in pain. I can't find the gate, but I'm looking. What was this gate my friend Jason was looking for? Maybe he wanted to find the door in the room of suffering, so that he might walk through it into another story. If my being in pain would relieve someone else, Jason said, then I would bear it gladly. I want to be present, he used to say. That's all we can be, he would say, present—and kind.

How difficult it is to be present. A few weeks ago, in one of those drooling late-night states trolling through the e-mails, exhausted, depleted, clicking through the Internet, I clicked on a line on the AOL home page that promised to show me Angelina Jolie's split leather pants. Before the page materialized, I turned the computer off and put my head in my hands. And in the sudden quiet of the dark apartment—the blue screen extinguished, the radiator hissing, my 8-year-old sleeping—I noticed death and life sitting quietly beside me, waiting for my attention. Jason's death and my own.

Oh who wouldn't want to look away? The cell phone rings, another American Idol is belting it out, the war is on, and the glittering Web sparkles like the Milky Way in a box—promising that if I keep clicking and clicking, I might finally get to what I long for, to the message, the rug, the T-shirt. I will move beyond suffering and beyond time, beyond the limits of my money and my story and life.

But that place? It's not there—it's virtual—it's nowhere. The days and nights of my life walk by, arm in arm with time, and the gate to the new story stands just outside the circle of my attention. Sometimes I lie here, Jason said, and walk through the old house of my childhood, through all the rooms, and look out all the windows.

This might be the most difficult task for us in postmodern life: not to look away from what is actually happening. To put down the iPod and the e-mail and the phone. To look long enough so that we can look through it—like a window. Jason looked up one day last week and said, This is unendurable. Then he said, I like that black sweater.

How do we learn this kind of attention? A lot of his friends were with Jason during his life and the last three years of his illness. Everyone has stories. Lucie told us this one. She picked up Jason from the hospital and drove all night to get to Provincetown; he wanted to go there for maybe the last time. Walking slowly through the fog on the beach in the very early morning she said, We will always remember this day. And Jason, who was pretty well practiced by then, said, I am remembering it now. ◖▮

I Believe in You

By Hill Harper

I come from a legacy of service. My grandfather on my mother's side was a pharmacist who served the African-American community in a small town in South Carolina. My father's side, the same thing: My grandfather had a farm and was also a doctor who built the first hospital in a four-state radius, specifically to serve African-American families. About 12 years ago, I started getting asked to give talks to young people. I was invited because of my background—public schools in Iowa and California, then to Brown and two graduate degrees from Harvard, and now an acting career. Young guys and women would ask, "Hey. You're talking about goals and dreams, and I'm the first person in my family who has a chance to go to college, but I don't have any money. You said I could do anything—so what can I do?" And I'd say, "You know, I can't answer that question in a sound bite. Go stand over here." By the time I'd finish with these talks, I'd have 40, 50 kids waiting over there. I would try to exchange e-mail addresses with them, and I would try to do some type of e-mail mentoring.

I can't tell you how many young people I meet who, when I ask how they're doing, mumble something. They can't even look an adult in the eye. They don't feel that they're worthy of the connection. So I say, "You're magnificent. You're brilliant. There's nothing you can't do." I ask them, How many times has an adult male ever said, "I love you," and expected nothing in return? A good six to eight times out of ten, the answer is never. In their whole

life. You have to remember most of the kids I talk to are being raised by single moms, so Nana's around, Auntie, Mom—and they say "Baby, I love you"—but oftentimes the men aren't there. That's what all my work is, the talks, the mentoring, the two books I wrote of the best advice I'd been given and had to give: It's love and hugs on paper—that's all the books are.

I was fortunate that I had people in my life who de-

Hill Harper, after a writing workshop he held for teens in Atlanta, Georgia, July 2008.

manded that I live up to my potential, and that's what I try to do with the young people I'm fortunate enough to meet. I tell them they're excellent, so they have to excel. I always ask them what my Uncle Russell used to ask me: "What are your grades?" When they tell me, I say, "How are we going to turn those into straight A's? I can see that you're a straight A student." And they've never heard anyone say that to them before.

Young people are extremely savvy and they can see through b.s. in a second, so they know if you have it in your heart or not. People ask if this is exhausting, but I believe that love expands. As you give love out, it's received and reciprocated—and it grows. That's the beauty of it. Love is an energy. You can feed it to people, and they in turn feed it to others, and eventually it comes back. **O**

—As told to Mamie Healey

WHAT I KNOW FOR SURE: OPRAH

"To know that people care about how you're doing when the doings aren't so good—that's what love is."

BeBe Winans sings for Oprah's audience, November 13, 2007.

I've gotten a new taste of what love is while trying to right the wrongs at my school in South Africa. A dormitory matron was accused of sexual and physical abuse at the Oprah Winfrey Leadership Academy for Girls. Seeing how emotionally draining this time has been for me, people reached out with their encouragement. People I knew well and many I had never met built a bridge of support allowing me to laser-focus on doing what was necessary, moment by moment, to help each girl.

Yes, I was devastated—devastated times 150 trusting hearts. I couldn't stop thinking about the girls, every single one of them...remembering when I first interviewed them to come to the school, and their high hopes and happy smiles the day they were accepted. So many of them had already had such difficult lives: poverty, death, violence, grief. I wanted their lives at the school to be not just better, but easier and free from all harm.

So that dream was temporarily thwarted.

But I can say today (as I write this, I'm on a plane to Africa once again) that the sweeping changes instituted since the report of abuse have put us on the path to a more stable and secure future than we had before. The crisis has forced the school's staff, administrators, teachers, students—and everyone associated with their well-being—to create a more open and collaborative environment.

Throughout this process, I've been sustained by my abiding faith in a power greater than my own. I've recognized in every dark moment that *this too shall pass.* That's the mantra that's kept me going from the moment I received the first phone call of suspected abuse.

After many days of constant conversations and working through a multitude of concerns, I was worn out, but my spirit has never faltered. I've remained encouraged by the grace and love of friends who've e-mailed, written, or called. So many people asked, "Is there anything I can do to help?"—not knowing that they already had, just by

asking. Gayle was as exhausted as I but still attended every meeting with police, and parents. Maria Shriver left daily messages reminding me to hold firm to my intentions in building the school.

Every note or message felt like an embrace, like the greatest valentine anyone could receive. None came with frills or fancy bows—just its own heart-spoken truth. This last line in a handwritten letter from Sidney Poitier spoke volumes: "The universe and all your friends have your back."

To know that people care about how you're doing when the doings aren't so good—that's what love is. I feel blessed to know this for sure.

One day while I was doing the show, my friend BeBe Winans appeared in the audience. "BeBe, why are you here?" I asked during a commercial break. "No one told me you were coming!"

"I just came to see you, see how you were doing," he said. *That's strange,* I thought, but continued with the show. Afterward he followed me to my office and said, "There's something I came to tell you." And as I sat behind my desk, he started singing what he knows is my favorite spiritual: "I surrender all. I surrender all. All to thee, my blessed Savior, I surrender all."

I sat silently, closed my eyes, and opened myself to accepting his magnificent and humble offering, this gift of love and song. When he finished, I felt a release of all pressure to *do* anything. I was content to just be. And for the first time in weeks, I experienced pure peace.

When I opened my eyes and wiped away the tears, BeBe was beaming. He started laughing his *huh, huh, huuuagh* laugh, and gave me a big hug. "Girl," he said, "I just came to remind you, you don't have to carry this load all by yourself. You can surrender all."

And in that moment I did.

Oprah

giving back

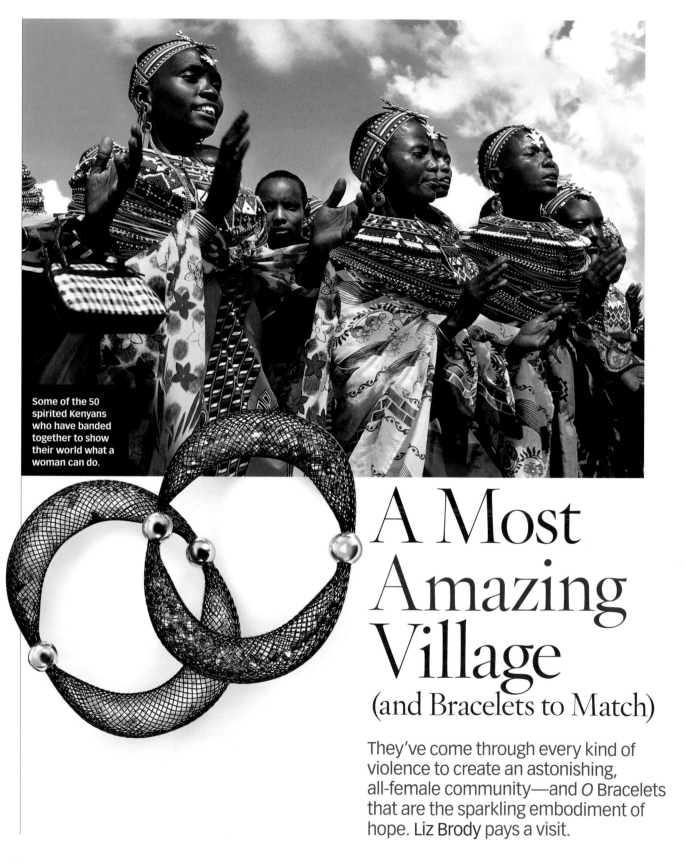

Some of the 50 spirited Kenyans who have banded together to show their world what a woman can do.

A Most Amazing Village
(and Bracelets to Match)

They've come through every kind of violence to create an astonishing, all-female community—and *O* Bracelets that are the sparkling embodiment of hope. **Liz Brody** pays a visit.

I spot her down by the river filling a jerry jug, the sass in her eyes catching my attention, which admittedly has wandered. (*Where's that crocodile from yesterday? How can you see one coming? The water is so muddy—god, they* drink *this stuff?*) Hoisting the yellow plastic container on her head and walking—no hands—with a "watch this" flare of adolescence, she lets me follow her home.

At 14, maybe 15 (it's hard to know with a birthday like "born during the bad rains"), Senteyo Lenaiyasa may be the youngest member of Umoja, an all-women's village in a remote pocket of Kenya. From what I'd heard, this community is making history—a gutsy anomaly of female bonding in a world where women are still treated as livestock.

Stooping to enter her dung-roof hut made of sticks and mud, I take the seat she offers—a can of vegetable oil sent by a U.S. relief agency—the only furniture in this cozy dark surround, smoky from maize porridge cooking over an open fire. Through Jen, a teacher from a nearby village who joins us to translate (the area is so isolated, few speak Swahili, the national language, relying instead on their tribal tongue, Maa), Senteyo describes a grinding childhood spent herding cattle and lugging firewood with her six siblings, all brought up by a widowed mother. Nobody went to school. When Senteyo was 12, maybe 13, her uncles married her off for a few cows. "Empe," she says emphatically when asked about the customary circumcision. "Razor," echoes Jen knowingly, married herself at 9. The blades, I will come to learn, are often rusty. Because of infections, some girls die.

In animated bursts, Senteyo tells me how she bled down her legs for a while, but that was nothing compared to seeing her husband for the first time. She freaked. He already had four other wives, and—she takes the smooth skin of her forearm and, with her other hand, scrunches it, not waiting for Jen to translate—wrinkled! We all burst out laughing.

"And then what?" I ask.

"I ran," Senteyo says, her smile flashing, eyes saucy with indignation.

"What was going through your mind? How did you think you could do better?"

She shakes her head. All she knew was: *He's so old. How can I stay with him? How can I talk to him when I'm younger than his children?* With only a piece of goatskin wrapped around her waist, without an idea of what to do, she bolted, slipping away from the one village she'd ever known, asking anyone and everyone if they could tell her where she might sleep, until somebody finally pointed her toward Umoja.

Started 18 years ago by a handful of wives and mothers bucking their abusive Samburu culture, Umoja—"unity" in Swahili—is a haven for about 50 women who have built their own houses, set up a preschool, and are supporting themselves by making beaded jewelry for occasional tourists. When Senteyo arrived bare breasted and hungry—pregnant, too, at this point—she told her story to one of the head women, who called the others around and said, "Here is a child. She is running away with nowhere to go." After consulting among themselves, the villagers invited the girl to stay until her family came. But nobody did, so they taught her how to bead and helped her build her hut. Now, three years later, she's earned enough to own three goats and several colorful skirts and shirts. And she's raising a daughter who, like all the girls here, will not get circumcised or sold into marriage, but rather go to school and dream of doing everything a man can do.

When I first heard about Umoja I thought, *What a great place to create the next O Bracelet* (see page 273). If it takes a village to change a culture, these intrepid women out there in the middle of Africa seemed to be doing it. But I was a little hesitant to actually go, knowing how stories like this often fall short when you get up close, the inspiration turning out to be a mirage. It didn't help that people kept describing the villagers as "fierce." Rebecca Lolosoli, the leader, had—I believe the word was—"punched" a female journalist. (Something about the interviewer being too exploitative.) Nevertheless, I headed to Kenya with two members of Madre, a nonprofit organization that teaches women their human rights and has been helping Umoja since 2001, and with three colleagues from Fair Winds Trading, our partner for the 2 years in the *O Bracelet* series.

After driving five hours north from Nairobi, across the equator, we pulled into what looked like a random spot on a relentlessly dusty, parched plain, coughed out from the lush highlands. A stingy landscape, for sure, but then the women emerged from a circle of about 20 huts, drenching us with color—blood reds and clanging oranges, flecks of devious indigo and green. They were dancing, laughing at us and with us, tossing manes of beads around their necks. *Fierce, yeah, in the cool way,* I thought, drawn, as everyone is, to those beads. I would find out later what they symbolize. A traditional Samburu wife wears only the necklaces her husband gives her; they're a sign of her worth to him. These women adorn themselves with as many as they want. "We all have beads in Umoja," Rebecca says, "because we are taking care of ourselves."

The village came to life "slowly by slowly," says Rebecca, 44, or thereabouts. Her stance has the settle of an oak—"You'll have to go around"—leaving no question who runs the show here. Pointing to the cock-eyed sticks of a hut going up, she explains that the women in Umoja, which has no running water or electricity, prefer their traditional homes to the sturdier cabanas they've just built for tourists—never mind that the dung leaks in the rain, and there aren't enough cows to repatch. She tells me this with a warm laugh, as her cell phone goes off—an erratic connection to the outside world, dependent on when she can find a recharge. Days go by when she's out of touch.

The Samburu are seminomadic pastoralists and one of Kenya's many marginalized tribes that came under the international news spotlight early in 2008 as flawed presidential elections convulsed the country in ethnic fighting. The violence Samburu women know all too well, however, comes not from other groups but from their own men. In Rebecca's case, after a relatively happy childhood during which she was lucky enough to attend primary school, it started at 17 when she was circumcised.

"I almost died," she says. "In Samburu, they cut everything, the clitoris, both sides, labia minora, all. And then they put their finger inside to see if there's anything left and, even after several hours, they will take you and cut again." She spent three weeks in the hospital, then married the man she'd been cut for, a stranger who'd given her family 18 cows, a few goats, blankets, and other commodities. The new couple moved into his family's home.

Her husband, Fabian, it turned out, was a good man who would later get a job at Barclay's Bank. He didn't beat her. But his family did, regularly and viciously. "I am just like a hyena there, like an animal," she says, her voice softening. "Nobody cared about me. My husband should have been asking why are they beating me? But he wasn't."

If there was any moment that cocked her daring to take such a heretical step as starting a village without men, it was when she asked her father-in-law why he'd sold one of her cows without consulting her and kept all the profit. His answer: "You are a woman and cannot say anything in my home."

Then why am I here? she thought.

In 1990, when Rebecca gathered 15 women on what is now Umoja, the land was vacant. "We didn't have food," Rebecca says. "We just worked and lay down, often faint, very weak." Every little success proved a battle. After they began selling their jewelry, the other villages tried all kinds of tactics, some violent, to divert business from Umoja. When Rebecca attempted to buy the 13.6-acre plot, she says the local government told her, "How can women own land? We have never heard of this here." But with a smile

"We were very thin; we looked old. Now we look our age."

that could net a school of sharks, she has a way of working things: 200,000 shillings later (about $3,000 paid over time), the place was theirs.

What about all these babies, I ask her, looking around the place. How does that work with the women-only concept? "We don't care if somebody goes outside and visits a man, or has her boyfriend come," she explains. "We just don't want the man to come here and talk badly to her or start beating her." In fact, men from other villages do sneak in at night to assault Umoja's women and steal their livestock, although in the past year or two, the attacks have somewhat diminished. Building a fence is high on the to-do list. Each house has a new padlock, but if you pull hard enough it will come off in your hand, probably right along with the rickety door.

What the women have—and no one can rob them of now—are their rights. And that's thanks to Madre's Vivian Stromberg, who has traveled with us, despite a bad heart, diabetes, and a bum hip requiring a cane. When Vivian and Rebecca met seven years ago at a conference, they could barely speak (Rebecca later learned English from tourists), but from one tough, funny woman to another, they made a connection. Since then Madre has held several trainings at Umoja; before their session on AIDS, most of the women, including Rebecca, didn't have a clue they could get it.

"When you know your rights," says Vivian, "instead of begging for something, you start asking that it not be taken away. Your whole body language changes; you stop crying." In Umoja, they actually make a point of laughing—in tough times, sitting down and asking each other what will make them happy. "We have been so sad for so long," Rebecca explains. "Men become annoyed because when we work, we talk, we have

The river they drink from is infested with crocodiles and disease. Ten percent of the money from the *O Bracelets* goes toward a water system.

Above left: What really thrills the mothers of Umoja are the possibilities they're creating for their daughters. **Right:** Rebecca Lolosoli has faced death threats for starting Umoja. "Okay, just kill us then," she's told the men who have tried to chase them off the land. "We're not moving."

fun. But they know that before, their wives were very thin; they looked old. And when we came here and got food, and we started our life, we began to look our age again. So now the husbands are admiring us. That's why they come and beat us and try to take us back.

"Well," she takes in a gleeful moment, "they can't! It's too late."

To spread Umoja's newfound strength, Rebecca is networking with 60 other women's groups in the area. "We are proud, us womens," she says—always adding the *s* as if she can't bear to miss the chance to express the power of the plural. "And it's not just the girls: We don't want our boys to be like their fathers, because they are the husbands of tomorrow." For her part, Rebecca has stayed married, but in name only. "Fab," as her husband is known, lives about 25 miles away and is quick to say that he supports Umoja 100 percent. You can see he's in a tough spot, though. "Yeeaaah," he says with a strained smile, "I've gotten a lot of talk about, 'Oh, this man is making the woman grow horns,' what have you. 'The woman is controlling the husband.'" Even their 13-year-old daughter, Sylvia, has stood up to him. When his parents instructed her that it was time to get circumcised, she refused. "I told them, 'If you touch me, I will call the police and you will eat bad food,'" she relays in perfect English—a story the women in the village can't get enough of.

Umoja still has a way to go. There's a two-room nursery school in the village, but at age 6, the children have to start walking quite a distance to class. "And the men get them in the bush and rape them," says Margaret Ejejo, 28 years old by her estimate, the village's sharp-witted Number Two. "Some of the girls are getting pregnant. It's a big problem. And one little boy was going to school when a herd of elephants came and crushed and killed him. Lions, too. Things are happening all the time." The nearest doctor is about 124 miles away. A van, clearly, would help all around.

No one is offering up a vehicle, but Margaret is ready if they should. She just got her driver's license, the first Samburu woman ever to do so. The next breakthrough she and Rebecca are plotting is running for local office.

Meanwhile, all the women in Umoja are triumphant to be running their own lives. "Before, I didn't have anything that was mine," says a girl named Servicio, who like Senteyo, showed up a couple of years ago in only a goatskin. "But now I am eating well, my child is getting an education, and whether I have money or not I will go to the hospital, because the other women will stand for me.

"And also now," she says, "I have a voice." **O**

Project *O* Bracelet

To those of you who have already bought *O* Bracelets, thank you for helping transform the lives of the African women who made them. On top of paying the women for their work, sales of the jewelry have raised almost $50,000 to help build a water system in Umoja, Kenya.

For this collection, the artists of Fair Winds Trading (FWT), which develops markets for artisans all over the world, used the inspiration of Umoja to come up with a completely novel design: The bracelets are made with an exclusive woven mesh that represents the amazing web of women coming together in strength and unity to make change.

Inside, different colors of Swarovski crystals tumble around, expressing the brightness of spirit that refuses to be dimmed.

Next, FWT arranged to get all the materials to Umoja, along with someone to teach the women how to make this design. FWT also secured a generous grant from the Kind World Foundation to supply the village with tools and training (before, all they had was a single pair of plastic scissors). Then the women went to work. Because of the instability in Kenya, we also employed our previous bracelet team in Rwanda, who were happy to support their Kenyan sisters now facing ethnic violence. The money raised by the bracelets breaks down as follows: Fifteen percent goes directly to the women involved in the production in Umoja (or Rwanda); 10 percent is donated to Umoja to help them set up the water system; 5 percent goes to Rwandan staff and trainers for the extra production there; 10 percent for FWT administration costs of running the project in three countries; 15 percent covers materials; 10 percent for packaging (boxes, tags); 15 percent for shipping between Africa and the U.S.; 5 percent for ground transport within Africa; 15 percent for Macy's to set up their Web site and handle orders. No one is making a profit except the women. To link arms with them by wearing an *O* Bracelet, go to macys.com/obracelet to order.

You can also donate directly to Umoja via madre.org.

The Eco-Makeover

Saving the Planet One Bag, and Ice Cream

Ice caps are melting, coral reefs are shrinking, islands are sinking.... What to do? We can go directly to despair—or we can learn how to be a part of the solution. Eco-activists Laurie David and Matthew Modine drop in on two families to give them easy, effective, and inexpensive ideas that—really!—can make a world of difference. **By Aimee Lee Ball**

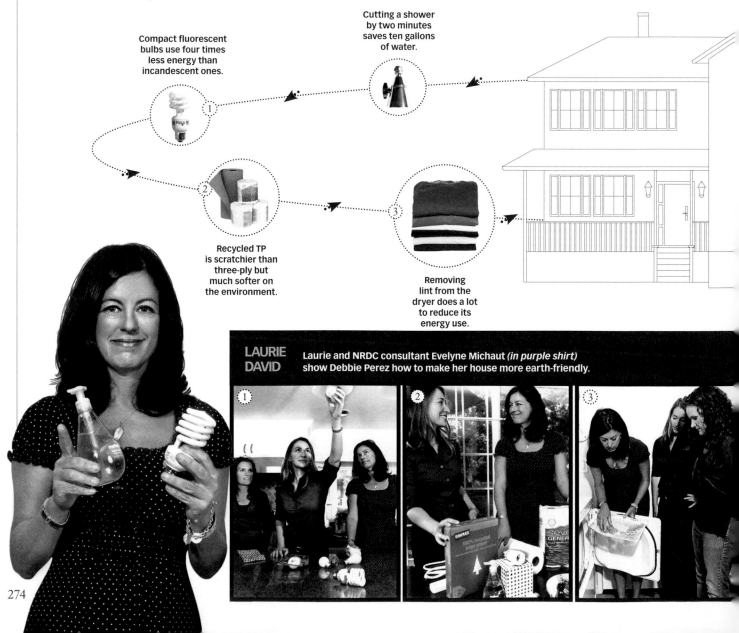

Cutting a shower by two minutes saves ten gallons of water.

Compact fluorescent bulbs use four times less energy than incandescent ones.

Recycled TP is scratchier than three-ply but much softer on the environment.

Removing lint from the dryer does a lot to reduce its energy use.

LAURIE DAVID Laurie and NRDC consultant Evelyne Michaut (*in purple shirt*) show Debbie Perez how to make her house more earth-friendly.

Lightbulb, Grocery Cone at a Time

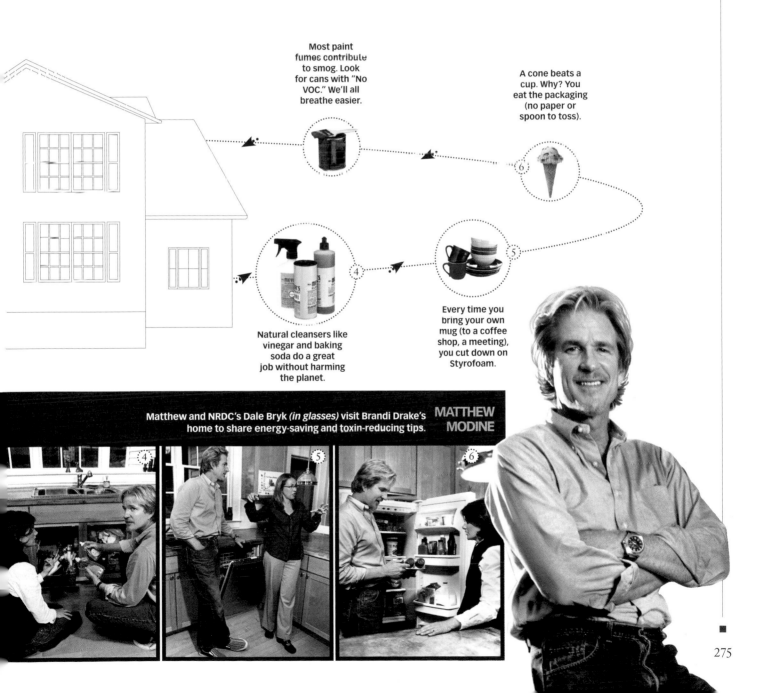

Most paint fumes contribute to smog. Look for cans with "No VOC." We'll all breathe easier.

A cone beats a cup. Why? You eat the packaging (no paper or spoon to toss).

Natural cleansers like vinegar and baking soda do a great job without harming the planet.

Every time you bring your own mug (to a coffee shop, a meeting), you cut down on Styrofoam.

Matthew and NRDC's Dale Bryk *(in glasses)* visit Brandi Drake's home to share energy-saving and toxin-reducing tips.

MATTHEW MODINE

HOME, SWEET
GREEN HOME:
Laurie David in San
Clemente, California,
with the Perezes
(*clockwise from far
left*): Billy, Debbie,
Mark, Mary, Delaney,
and Teddy.

There's nothing like a visit from a movie star for inspiration to spruce up the house, which is why the smell of fresh paint is apparent as Matthew Modine arrives to meet the Drake family of Montclair, New Jersey. And this visit has special significance: Today Matthew is wearing his well-earned hat as an environmentalist, dropping in on the Drakes to offer simple, gratifying, inexpensive ideas for living greener.

It's easy to feel overwhelmed by the prospect of environmental disaster. As Nobel Peace Prize laureate Al Gore said in his Oscar-winning documentary, *An Inconvenient Truth,* "People go from denial to despair without pausing at the intermediate step of actually doing something." Cars, factories, and power plants trying to handle the modern demand for energy have created potentially catastrophic global warming, with the release of carbon dioxide literally heating and thickening the atmosphere of the planet it was meant to protect. So what can one per-

son, or one family, do about the melting polar ice caps, anyway? The answer is a resounding "plenty." Operating on the premise that lots of people would embrace some important changes if armed with the know-how, *O* magazine found two families who agreed to open their doors and their drawers for an eco-makeover.

Our guides for this odyssey are both Hollywood activists and passionate promoters of earth-friendly policies. The genesis of Matthew's green interest was a summer job in the early 1970s, when the drive-in theater his father managed shut down and he earned a little money by collecting copper wire from the speakers for salvage, which got him thinking about what gets thrown away. He is a veteran of more than 40 films including *Birdy, Full Metal Jacket,* and *Married to the Mob,* as well as Showtime's hit series *Weeds,* and his short film about reducing carbon fuel emissions was shown at the World Economic Forum. Recently he created Bicycle for a Day (bicycleforaday.org), a worldwide campaign to promote transportation alternatives.

Laurie David's eco-consciousness was raised as a new mother in the 1990s. Her husband at the time, Larry David, was on a soundstage seven days a week helping create *Seinfeld* (and later *Curb Your Enthusiasm*), and as she pushed a stroller around her neighborhood with a colicky baby, she became aware of how many SUVs were on the road. A little research revealed a loophole in the law that classified SUVs as trucks, allowing them about half the gas mileage and double the pollution of regular cars. Since then, she has written books about the climate crisis including *The Down to Earth Guide to Global Warming*, created the Stop Global Warming Virtual March (stopglobalwarming.org), and was a producer of *An Inconvenient Truth*.

For our home visits, Laurie and Matthew were joined by experts from the National Resources Defense Council (NRDC), a group of lawyers and citizens devoted to safeguarding the planet. Environmental issues are complex, and sometimes the most well-informed people debate the best course of action, but our makeover teams can start all of us thinking about what we might do to make a difference.

4 Things You Can Do Right Now to Help Your Planet

1. **Bag it** Get reusable cloth bags for the grocery store and the dry cleaner. More than 100 billion plastic bags are thrown away every year.

2. **Stop junk mail** Every year 100 million trees are chopped down for junk mail sent to American homes. Contact the Direct Marketing Association at **dmachoice.org** to remove your name from mailing lists of their members.

3. **Shut down** The average computer left on all day uses nearly 1,000 kilowatt hours of electricity a year, producing more than a ton of carbon emissions. So turn off your computer anytime you're not on it, and eliminate the screen saver function, which uses more energy than the sleep mode.

4. **A mug of your own** Every year Americans throw away 25 billion polystyrene cups and 25 billion individual water bottles, most of which end up in landfills. Instead buy a reusable to-go mug and a bottle that you can refill with filtered tap water.

The Perezes

On the day that Laurie David meets the Perez family of San Clemente, California, she is distressed by two news items: The Chicago marathon was halted after just a few hours due to abnormal heat that precipitated one death and several hundred injuries. And the opening of the skating rink at Rockefeller Center in New York City was marred by record-high temperatures, with pooling water instead of a frozen surface.

In the past, such alarm bells would have gone unnoticed by the Perezes: Debbie and Mark, both 37 and former teachers (Mark now works for a nonprofit organization called the Grove Center that supports church-based art), and their children, Billy, 11; Mary, 10; Delaney, 8; and Teddy, 6. But Laurie is helping them see how they are connected to that overheated marathon and melting ice rink. "We're all contributing to this problem," she says, "every day when you turn on a light or drink from a plastic water bottle. There are things the government has to do, but individual citizens also need to be part of the solution."

Sitting at the kitchen table of the family's split-level house, Laurie looks up at the recessed fixtures in the ceiling with more than a dozen lightbulbs. "To me, they're really heat bulbs," she says. Compact fluorescent lightbulbs (CFLs) use only a quarter of the energy that incandescent ones do. Australia and Canada have already voted to ban the use of incandescent bulbs by 2009 and 2012, respectively. If every American family substituted five CFLs for incandescent, it would be equivalent to taking eight million cars off the road for a year. They cost a little more up front, but they last up to ten times longer.

Debbie has prepared a typical school lunch, packed in a paper sack. "This will be used for one day, and then it's going in the garbage," says Laurie, "but this"—pointing out her own daughter's metal lunch box—"will be used for five years. When you see paper, think of a tree." According to the NRDC, Americans throw away enough paper every year to build a 12-foot-high wall stretching from New York to California. Every two seconds, somewhere in the world, a forest area the size of a football field is destroyed—all for things like paper towels, napkins, printer paper—and the loss of those trees is disastrous for the environment. Trees absorb carbon dioxide and convert it into oxygen. During its lifetime, a single tree can absorb the amount of CO_2 released by the average car that's been driven 4,000 miles. "This is a petroleum product," says Laurie with obvious distaste, pointing to a one-shot water bottle. "It's made from oil. It's shipped on a truck spewing fumes. And two and a half million plastic bottles are thrown away every hour." Inside the "greener" lunch box are re-usable containers for sandwiches, snacks, and drinks, made of metal or plastic. The family agrees to start questioning the products they buy: How far has this traveled to get here, and how many resources does it re-quire? The oldest child, Billy, is the most aware and concerned about envi-ronmental issues. He shows Laurie a bag inside his closet where he keeps bottles for recycling, but she encour-ages him to expand his horizons. By the next day, he has already spoken to his principal about setting up collection bins at school.

At Laurie's suggestion, Debbie has timed her family's showers. Mark is the worst culprit—11 minutes—"and he doesn't even have to use conditioner," Mary protests. Low-flow showerheads would be a big improvement. "If

> "Being green is not about being perfect; it's about being conscious and trying to do something."

they're well designed, the pressure should still feel good," says Laurie, "and for every two minutes you shave off your shower, you save ten gallons of water." Delaney agrees that she can turn off the faucet while brushing her teeth. But the whole family winces at the prospect of giving up their three-ply toilet tissue for the scratchier stuff made from postcon-sumer wastepaper (printed material that's been recycled). This is okay with Laurie. "Being green is not about being miserable; it's about being conscious," she says. "It's not about perfection; it's about everyone trying to do something." Still, despite the initial hesi-tance, Debbie reports a week later that everyone has ac-tually adjusted to the new TP. It's like switching from whole milk to skim: After a while, the beloved original seems over-the-top.

With six people living in almost 3,000 square feet, there are dozens of appliances in the house—TVs, computers, hair dryers, toasters, coffeemakers, lamps, cell phones with chargers—and each is drawing electricity when plugged into a wall socket, even when it's not in use. This is called phantom power—a little like a vampire sucking out energy. It's estimated that the amount of electricity used nation-ally each year by idle equipment roughly equals the output of at least 12 power plants. "The idea is to connect the dots," says Evelyne Michaut, the NRDC green building consultant who has accompanied us. "Think of each device as plugged into a coal mine." A power strip makes it easy to turn off up to half a dozen appliances at once.

WHERE TO RECYCLE

APPLIANCES	recycle-steel.org
BUSINESS CLOTHING	dressforsuccess.org
CARPETS	carpetrecovery.org
CELL PHONES AND RECHARGEABLE BATTERIES	rbrc.org
COMPUTERS	sharetechnology.org
ELECTRONICS	mygreenelectronics.org
EYEGLASSES	neweyesfortheneedy.org
FLOPPY DISKS AND VIDEOTAPES	greendisk.com
FORMAL DRESSES	www.operationfairydust.org
PACKING PEANUTS	loosefillpackaging.com
PAINT	earth911.org
TIRES	epa.gov/garbage/tires/live.htm

An old refrigerator can cost up to 50 percent of your monthly bill, according to power company Con Edison. The Perezes have two fridges, the second one in the garage, considered indispensable because the fam-ily stores food for an orphanage in Mexico. When they're ready to replace this ten-year-old model or any other big-ticket appliance, Evelyne and Laurie direct them to look for the Energy Star label, which indicates that the prod-uct meets government energy-efficiency standards. Meanwhile, nobody should be standing in front of any open fridge trying to decide what to eat. The Perezes' washing machine is relatively new, but choosing cold water and doing only full loads will definitely benefit both the environment and their budget: More than three-quarters of the energy used to launder clothes comes from heating the water, and the hot water cycle generates five times more greenhouse gases than cold. Laurie scrapes a big handful of lint from the dryer's filter—it builds up after every cycle, reducing the machine's efficiency. And living in Southern California, with a backyard, the Perezes have the perfect opportunity to hang a clothesline. "Air-dried towels are fantastic," Laurie raves. "Everyone in the family will be fighting for them."

Two of the family's biggest energy drains stand in the driveway: a 1998 truck that gets 13 to 15 miles per gallon and a 2002 van that gets just ten to 12 miles per gallon. Together the two gas guzzlers were driven almost 20,000 miles in the past year, generating more than 30,000 pounds of greenhouse gases. Evelyne approves the Perez plan to "run them into the ground" before replacing, "and by then there will be even more electric and hybrid options," she says, with federal tax credits available for some models. But she also points out that maintaining a vehicle properly makes it more fuel-efficient. The manufacturer's recommendation for tire inflation (in a unit of measure called PSI, or pounds per square inch) is often written inside the door frame or in the owner's manual. Tires can lose about a pound of pressure in a month, and for every three pounds below the recommended pressure, fuel economy goes down by about 1 percent. The NRDC estimates that if all Americans kept their tires properly inflated and bought replacements of the same quality as the originals, we would save more oil than is available in the Arctic National Wildlife Refuge. How you drive is important, too: Flooring the gas pedal and braking hard dramatically decrease gas mileage and lead to more pollution. According to the American Council for an Energy-Efficient Economy, one second of high-powered driving can produce nearly the same volume of carbon monoxide emissions as a half hour of normal driving. Speeding along at 75 miles per hour instead of 65 lowers your fuel economy by about 10 percent. And carrying around an extra 100 pounds of cargo reduces fuel economy by about 1 percent.

Perhaps the most important message for the Perez family—and possibly yours—is about looking beyond one's own backyard. The leaders of more than 600 American cities have signed the U.S. Mayors Climate Protection Agreement, launched in 2005 with a goal to cut greenhouse gas emissions. Portland, Oregon, has built hundreds of miles of bike paths. Austin gave tax breaks for green homes and businesses. Salt Lake City converted more than 200 traffic signals to energy-efficient bulbs. If your hometown isn't on the list at coolcities.us, Laurie suggests writing to your mayor. San Clemente is not part of this admirable action plan—in fact, the Perezes must go to another town just to recycle—so a letter is in the mail.

Great Green Sites

Greenercars.org
Gives a green score for every car, minivan, pickup, and SUV on the market, based on official emissions and fuel-economy tests, plus good driving and maintenance tips.

40mpg.org
Calculates how much money you'd save and how much less pollution you'd generate if your vehicle got at least 40 miles per gallon, like the Toyota Prius and Honda Civic Hybrid.

Greenhotels.com
Directs travelers to B&Bs, inns, motels, hotels, and resorts with earth-friendly policies.

Greenearthcleaning.com
A nationwide source for finding the nearest environmentally sound dry cleaners.

Greenfeet.com
Lists sources for green products ranging from hemp coffee filters to nail polish remover made from vodka.

Greenhomeguide.com
For home buyers or refinishers, with products such as reclaimed hardwood flooring and paint without volatile organic compounds.

Saveourenvironment.org
A collaborative effort to raise awareness of environmental issues; includes a gardener's guide to global warming, with action plans (reducing water consumption, use of gas-powered tools) for your backyard and your community.

Green-e.org
Find suppliers of renewable energy for home or business across the country.

Dsireusa.org
State-by-state guide to tax credits available for using renewable energy.

Preventcigarettelitter.org
Keep America Beautiful sponsors cigarette litter prevention through public education and details how communities can take action. If you needed another reason not to smoke, the fibers in cigarettes look like cotton, but they're cellulose acetate, which is man-made and doesn't biodegrade.

Carsharing.net
For people who live in cities and don't need a car 24/7.

Csacenter.org
A database of community-supported agriculture, listing local farms that emphasize soil conservation.

THE DRAKES

When Matthew Modine shows up at the charming 19th-century, New Jersey home the Drakes have been renovating, the fresh paint is their first eco-lesson. "There are so many chemicals flying out of that paint," the actor says. According to the Environmental Protection Agency, architectural coatings such as paints and varnishes are one of the largest sources of fumes from volatile organic compounds, substances that evaporate at room temperature and react in sunlight to form photochemical smog. (Automobiles are the biggest culprits.) "No VOC" paint is better for the environment and humans.

All sorts of greener options are available to renovators, home builders, and do-it-yourselfers like Brandi Drake, 39, the associate pastor of Grace Presbyterian Church, and her husband, Evan, 41, a neuropsychologist at Columbia University, the parents of two young boys. Matthew is partial to an insulation material called Bonded Logic that's made from recycled denim scraps. It contains no formaldehyde, as most fiberglass does, and requires very little energy to manufacture. Landscaping can help temperature control as well: If the Drakes planted trees strategically on their property, they could have summer foliage to block the infrared radiation that otherwise makes the house hotter, while bare branches in winter would let this heat source through. Looking around inside, the NRDC's Dale Bryk, who works on energy policy issues, suggests a programmable thermostat, set for one or two degrees higher than what the family is used to in warm weather, and one or two degrees lower in the cold. "Check the seals on your doors and windows," she says, "so whatever temperature you're trying to create is not flying out."

In 1994 Matthew basically halved the paper use in Hollywood by getting the William Morris Agency to print movie scripts on both sides of each sheet (double-sided scripts are now an industry standard), and he talks to Evan about fostering a similar policy at the university. Even switching to recycled paper (rather than the kind made from virgin lumber) uses up to 90 percent less water and half the energy, producing about one-third fewer greenhouse gases. Dale recommends that the family pay bills electronically. And the Drakes can visit the Direct Marketing Association's Web site to "opt out" of most junk mail.

Three other backyards abut the Drake's property, and Matthew is enthusiastic about the possibility of cooperative composting. When organic matter ends up in landfills and decomposes without air, it produces methane, a greenhouse gas 20 times more potent than carbon dioxide. Every ton of organic matter that's diverted from the garbage prevents the creation of more than 1,000 pounds of greenhouse gases. "Let's work this piece of land," says Matthew, who encourages composting even for black thumbs, and a kitchen compost for urban dwellers. "You don't have to be a brilliant gardener. The healthiest thing you can do is put your hands in the soil," he says. "And it's great for kids."

ECO-ACTOR: Matthew Modine with the Drake family in Montclair, New Jersey. Brandi Drake holds son Miles. Their other boy, Ethan, leans on his dad, Evan.

Even children as young as the Drakes' sons, Ethan, 5, and Miles, 3, can start practicing some environmental awareness. "If you get an ice cream cone instead of a cup, then you're eating your dishware instead of using plastic," says Matthew. "It's all about consuming less, using fewer of the resources needed to make products and packaging. A smaller ribbon of toothpaste will do. You can dilute shampoo and dish detergent by half. A short wash usually takes care of dirty clothes." As Matthew scans the laundry room supplies, he suggests avoiding chlorine bleach, an environmental toxin, and brings up the idea of using natural, homemade cleaning solutions. "There are so many things you can clean with vinegar and baking soda," he adds. "And a little vegetable oil and lemon juice makes a great wood polish."

When Brandi hears about Nike's Reuse-a-Shoe program, which grinds the rubber, foam, and fabric from old athletic shoes into materials for playground surfaces, she can't wait to tell the boys' preschool about it. As Matthew and Dale check out the boys' closets, the conversation turns to greener choices in clothing. Growing cotton requires tremendous amounts of water plus chemical insecticides and fungicides. Matthew favors industrial hemp, one of the oldest and most efficient sources of textile fiber, no longer grown commercially in this country because of its erroneous asso-

> Every two seconds, a forest the size of a football field is destroyed—all for things like paper towels.

ciation with marijuana (although the two are from the same plant, they are cultivated differently). Industrial hemp has no illicit uses. "I'd like to change the face of hemp in the world," says Matthew. "Almost every canvas in the Louvre is made from hemp. It was an important crop in the United States until after World War II, made into ropes and cloth. But then it got this connotation of 'reefer madness.'"

By the time Mexican takeout arrives for lunch, every-one's "wasteful" radar has been turned up. "It's ironic to get so many paper napkins and plastic utensils," Brandi comments, realizing that it's easy to tell any restaurant delivering food not to send them. She also likes the idea of a "bring your own mug" policy for coffee hour at the church, saving endless numbers of Styrofoam cups. "Our town won't re-cycle cardboard that has touched food," says Evan. That means pizza boxes get thrown away and end up in a landfill. "Some political person is making the decision that recy-cling costs more than landfill replacement," says Matthew, urging the Drakes to speak with municipal authorities about changing the rules. And he asks the family to con-sider a meatless meal every week, limiting the amount of feed and water necessary for the animals as well as reducing the manure polluting rivers and streams. (Here's a statistic any adolescent boy would love: The Worldwatch Institute estimates that flatulent livestock emit 16 percent of the world's annual production of methane.)

Clean water is an increasingly endangered commodity in our world. And toilets are water hogs: About 40 per-cent of the water used in the average home gets flushed away. That amounts to more than four billion gallons of water in the United States each day. Federal law now man-dates that all new residential toilets be low-flush models, which consume 1.6 gallons of water or less per use, com-pared with as much as five gallons for the conventional kind. In one of the Drakes' bathrooms, Matthew and Evan peer into the tank to see if there's room for a brick—an old-fashioned but still viable idea for reducing the amount of water used. There's not, but a plastic jug filled with water or pebbles will serve the same function.

Matthew's enthusiasm for transportation alternatives is infectious, and the American way of getting around is in creasingly hard to defend. If people who live less than five miles from work or school rode their bikes instead of driving, they would cut their CO2 emissions by a ton each year. If just one mem-ber of each U.S. household did this, they would eliminate more than 115 million tons of global warming pollution annually. Brandi's church and the boys' school are both within a mile of the Drake home, so Matthew plants the biking idea for spring weather. Evan's commute is 25 miles, but he could consider carpooling with neighbors. If each commuter car carried one more passenger once a week, gas consumption would go down by almost eight million gallons.

The point made in so many ways is that everyone can do something—at home, at school, at work. What's im-portant is creating a new paradigm and a new conscious-ness. If you often take home a doggie bag from a restaurant, could you bring a container so you avoid using Styrofoam? Can you think twice about disposable anything, from ra-zors to cameras? (Or at least buy rolls of film with 36 shots rather than 12 to reduce packaging?) Might you consider a return to handkerchiefs rather than tissues? Or wrapping gifts with pages from magazines? And Matthew gives an eco seal of approval to a much-maligned practice: "I have absolutely no problem with regifting," he says with a grin. If ever there was a global issue that requires all of our brains and hearts, it is this one. We are in it together, for better or for worse, for the future. ◑

How Long Does it Take to Biodegrade?

BROWN PAPER BAG
1 to 5 months

CIGARETTE BUTTS AND FILTERS
12 years

PLASTIC BAGS, CAPS, AND LIDS
decades

ALUMINUM CANS
2 to 5 centuries

STYROFOAM CLAMSHELLS
virtually forever

Willa Shalit meeting this year with weavers at the Gahaya Links training center she helped build in Rwanda.

The Good-Buy Girl

Who says you can't buy hope? Willa Shalit is proving that shopping can transform other people's lives. Gretchen Reynolds reports.

Willa Shalit has been put on this earth, I think, to allow the rest of us to pretend that our most grasping, selfish impulses are actually noble. Through her company, Fair Winds Trading, she has managed to make shopping meaningful—a way to load up on gorgeous, exotic objects de lust while furthering peace and justice, not to mention improving lives around the world. Bless the woman.

A pioneer in a growing social-entrepreneurial move-

ment, whose mission in part is to provide unique products to U.S. consumers—and, at the same time, sustainable wages to the Third World artisans who make them—Shalit has been collaborating for a number of years with the women of Rwanda. As a result, Fair Winds Trading now imports their handwoven baskets, African-gemstone jewelry, textile bags, and table linens, and has recently branched out with products from Tanzania, Cambodia, and Indonesia.

All of which makes Shalit a stylish godsend for those of us with inchoate longings to be better people, to do more, to change the planet—without having to join the Peace Corps and relinquish decent plumbing.

If the name Willa Shalit sounds vaguely familiar, that's because her given name pays homage to the novelist Willa

Cather, while her family name comes from her father, Gene Shalit, NBC's longtime and luxuriantly mustachioed film and theater critic. With a Cleopatran face and scads of thick, rumpled, curly brown hair, Willa, at 52, looks 30, although I'd bet that at 30, people thought she was older. There's a gravitas to her that would be intimidating if she didn't smile so often.

Shalit's childhood in prosperous, suburban New Jersey was awash with literary, cinematic, and art world celebrities. One of her uncles, Anthony Lewis, was a prominent op-ed columnist for *The New York Times*; a cousin, Robert Krulwich, is a correspondent for PBS and NPR. "Sophia Loren," she says, "made an occasional appearance."

But the bohemian idyll wasn't perfect. When she was barely into her teens, her mother was institutionalized for the first of what would become a lifelong series of visits to mental hospitals, leaving Shalit and her older brother to help raise their four younger siblings. "Having a family member become ill was an early lesson in empathy," she tells me.

A harsher one, unfortunately, followed. When Shalit was 15, she was raped at knifepoint. "I learned that life can change in the blink of an eye and that security is very illusory," she says with steely calm today. "I also realized there are some experiences that require a lifetime to recover from." It was an understanding that would prove to be deeply constructive, if cruel, training for finding common ground with the women of Rwanda.

"I remember my first meeting with Willa very well," says Terry Lundgren, the CEO, chairman, and president of Macy's, Inc. "It wasn't a meeting I'd be likely to forget." Their conversation would soon change the way he, and others within his enormous corporation (more than $26 billion in sales in 2007), viewed what shopping can accomplish. It also swept Lundgren himself into action. "I had no idea how involved I, personally, would become," he says. "But Willa is hard to resist."

That was in 2005. By then Shalit had cycled through several different lives. For a while and quite successfully, she'd been a sculptor, her subject the human body. In the '80s, Shalit had practiced "life casting"—creating plaster impressions of living people. Many of her subjects were famous, including Sophia Loren, the Dalai Lama, Paul Newman, Sting, and five U.S. presidents (Richard Nixon, whose facial mask is poignant, lonely, and sad, being a noteworthy

achievement from a lifelong liberal like Shalit). The finished pieces, among them full-body casts of the lithe, muscled, and quite naked dancers of the Alvin Ailey American Dance Theater, appeared in multiple museum shows and toured the country in an exhibition called *Please Touch!* targeted to blind art lovers as well as the sighted.

It was thrilling work, Shalit remembers, allowing her to showcase raw, unvarnished human beauty (you can't wear makeup under a facial cast) and to get her hands gratifyingly dirty. But the project ran its course, and Shalit, wanting to do something different yet still artistic and meaningful, moved into theater. In the late '90s, fiercely concerned with women's issues, she was drawn to Eve Ensler's play *The Vagina Monologues* and, as its coproducer, mounted the work off-Broadway. In 1998, with Ensler, she also began a series of V-Day events to raise awareness of violence against women. The events garnered not only global attention for the cause but, to date, more than $50 million to fund women's programs around the world. "Willa is a wildly creative and passionate woman," Ensler says. "Her faith, vision, and commitment were hugely important to the birth of V-Day."

Increasingly, though, Shalit became convinced that achieving real change hinged on income generation—antiviolence programs offered feeble protection if the women couldn't make money. Which is how, in 2003, she found herself saying goodbye to her husband, Michael Schneider, and their 14-year-old daughter, Natasha, in Santa Fe, and arriving in genocide-ravaged Rwanda alongside members of the UN's Development Fund for Women. They were there to explore how the country's surviving female weavers might start businesses. And it was on that trip that Shalit's life was completely recast.

In Rwanda, Shalit, who had at times felt disconnected from mainstream American culture—"as a Jew, as a woman, as someone who obviously wasn't blonde"—discovered a strong cross-cultural kinship. "I'd spent my childhood hearing about the Holocaust," she says, "so I knew something of genocide. Many of these women had been raped. I'd experienced how powerless that can make you feel. I don't want to sound sanctimonious, but we understood one another."

As she met with a group of weavers who were genocide widows, she realized what a treasure their handmade

"I thought, If I can sell people on vaginas, I can definitely sell them on these baskets."

baskets were—a tradition that had been passed from mother to daughter (and occasionally son) for generations. These baskets were striking, with natural dyes and quietly intricate patterns. Most important, they were a symbol—and a progenitor—of peace, woven by women from the two once-warring Rwandan tribes, the Tutsi and the Hutu, now working side by side. The single most common pattern, Shalit noticed, was a zigzag of parallel lines, moving across the background like friends companionably walking together. It was called the Peace Basket.

WEAVING PEACE: The baskets are helping Rwandan women recover from the genocide.

Shalit immediately envisioned a huge market for such baskets in the West, and knew that she could shepherd the sales. "I thought, *If I can sell people on vaginas, I can sell them on these baskets,*" she says. Sitting down with the women, she started drawing up a rudimentary business plan. She'd go back to America and talk to sales outlets. The Rwandan women would work on the baskets. From the first, they discussed such new ideas as livable wages and profits, a concept known as "trade, not aid."

"I did not want to make this enterprise a charity" or a not-for-profit, Shalit says. "All of us, myself and the Rwandan women, wanted it to be a business, with sales goals, quality control, training, all of that. The basket weavers would receive money for their efforts." And the money, with luck, wouldn't evaporate, as purely charitable donations so often do. "We'd be creating something that would sustain itself," Shalit says. "And if it failed, I'd suffer, too. We were all stakeholders."

After working with a small importer for a couple of years, Shalit decided to pay a visit to Macy's. Lundgren, who'd known Shalit's father for years, listened politely. "Willa talked about these women and about Rwanda," he says. "It was incredibly moving. When she stopped, I asked, 'What can I do to help?'—thinking she'd ask me for money, which I was more than ready to give." Instead, she said she'd like Macy's to start selling the women's baskets, dramatically pulling one out of her bag as she spoke.

"I said, 'Wow, we can sell these,'" Lundgren remembers. And a for-profit partnership was born.

Since then, sales of the baskets through macys.com/rwanda have steadily increased—from $50,000 in 2004

to $1.5 million in 2007. The number of Rwandan women employed has passed 3,000, most of the full-timers earning close to double the average national income. Fair Winds Trading, too, has grown to a hard-driven team of five and works intensively to help design new patterns, shapes, and colors twice a year that will appeal to Western customers. To further creativity, they have helped their Rwandan partners, Janet Nkubana and Joy Ndungutse, build a training center. And most recently, after collaborating with local textile manufacturers, they're exporting a new collection of vividly patterned bags.

There have been growing pains, of course. But Shalit doesn't have time to pay much notice. Traveling back and forth between the company's offices—in Manhattan, Santa Fe, and Kigali, Rwanda's capital—she was taking her vision further. In the fall of 2008, Fair Winds Trading began importing silk accessories (purses, clutches, jewelry cases) from Cambodia, handcrafted (using ancient techniques) by artisans, some of whom are battered women and land mine victims. Indonesian bowls and picture frames made with seashells, bamboo, driftwood, and coconuts have also been added. "I like to find objects that suggest something about the country from which they come," Shalit says. "The women of Rwanda created their baskets as a way to weave a kind of peace. The people of Indonesia, who have faced so many natural disasters, use pieces of their environment to see meaning in what's happened to their nation. I find that very powerful. Stories—that's what sells these items."

That, and—not to be shallow—good looks. "It would be a different business if the things Willa finds weren't of the highest quality and extremely attractive," Lundgren says. Because they are, Macy's is putting a major push into a new online boutique called Shop for a Better World, in partnership with Fair Winds Trading. "If you shop wisely," Shalit says, "you get to own this really wonderful object and also transfer money to those who need it—in a straight line. It goes right from you to people who may have lived only by barter and never held cash in their hands before. That's a very direct way to effect reform. It's not abstract; it's not a fantasy. It's real. Let's hear it for consumers! You have the power to change the world." ◖

The Congo committee (*from left*): Elissa Hecker, Katie Carron, Sarah LeBuhn, Keira Smith, Stefy Hilmer (*partially visible*), Kelli O'Donnell, Young-Yi Clinton (*partially visible*), Jennifer Williams, Tara Taylor, Stacey Breckling, Jane Nadasi, Catherine Kelley, Heather Bancroft.

Band of Sisters

You can read about something unimaginably vicious—say, the rape epidemic in the Congo. You can feel horrified, helpless. Or, like Jennifer Williams, you can leverage your emotions, time, and talent, gather your friends…and surprise even yourself with how much good a determined group of women can do. **Lisa Wolfe** reports.

Jennifer Williams was thrilled the Sunday morning her husband said he would take care of their 3-year-old and 4-month-old sons so she could have some quiet time to herself. She sat down on the sofa with a mug of coffee and *The New York Times.* But her giddiness quickly disappeared when she read a front-page story about the Democratic Republic of the Congo, where, as a result of a civil war that has ravaged the country since 1998, soldiers from foreign militias and the Congolese army have been raping, torturing, and mutilating tens of thousands of women and girls every year. Many of the victims are so brutally attacked that their digestive and reproductive systems are left beyond repair. "It got me," she says. "I couldn't move on. I think having just had a baby made me feel this was intolerable—and people needed to say so."

She e-mailed the reporter, Jeffrey Gettleman, asking what she could do to help. Then she e-mailed old friends from college, new friends from the neighborhood, and former colleagues from work to draw their attention to the story. Within a few days, Gettleman wrote back with the name of Panzi, a local hospital that Jen could send money to, and the contact information for two aid workers familiar with its needs. Jen e-mailed the aid workers and forwarded Gettleman's e-mail to her friends. Wasn't it awesome to have heard back from him, she asked, and what were their thoughts on trying to help?

A conversation was started. It continued by e-mail, telephone, at stolen moments during school drop-off, pick-up, and playdates: Let's send money to the hospital. Let's throw a party to raise money for the hospital. But wait, we can't ask people to wire money to an African bank account. Better to help the hospital through an established charity.

One of the aid workers wrote back suggesting Jen contact Avocats Sans Frontières, a group of lawyers and legal professionals working to end impunity for rapists in the Congo, as well as V-Day, the global movement started by playwright Eve Ensler to stop violence against women and girls. Jeffrey Gettleman added the name of a United Nations officer in Africa who was closely following the issue. Jen contacted everyone, and was slightly stunned when they all replied. She had worked on Wall Street for 13 years before quitting her job to take care of her son. "When I used to make calls from work, I would say, 'Hi, this is Jen from Morgan Stanley' or 'Hi, this is Jen from Barclays.' Now I was just Jen," she says.

But she was passionate, and impressed people with her eagerness to learn. "She did not pretend to be an expert on the Congo," says Kate Burns, senior policy officer for gender equality at the United Nations. "She asked a lot of questions. Getting the UN to open its doors is not easy, but Jen was very enthusiastic, and I think people like her—regular citizens, not involved in political organizations—have a special role to play in getting others to open their hearts and pockets." The UN agreed to cohost a fund-raising event. So did V-Day. Eve Ensler agreed to speak. The filmmaker Lisa F. Jackson volunteered to show a clip from her Sundance-award-winning film, *The Greatest Silence: Rape in the Congo.*

With support growing, it was time for a meeting. Husbands babysat while their wives gathered in Jen's living room for wine, cheese, and brainstorming. After more phone calls, e-mails, and meetings, a plan was finalized: They would hold a fund-raiser at Cipriani in New York City for 300 to 500 people. The evening would include a silent auction, an art show, and a performance by an African jazz vocalist. The goal was to raise $100,000 for Avocats Sans Frontières and the City of Joy, a center for recovering rape victims being built by V-Day and UNICEF in partnership with Panzi, the hospital Jeffrey Gettleman had mentioned.

Though no one can recall Jen exuding anything but confidence at every step of the planning process, the troops admit they began to feel nervous. They had never done anything like this before. They were afraid of looking like amateurs. "I was worried we'd have a great space, great speakers, but we wouldn't be able to put bodies in the room," says Sarah LeBuhn, a mother of two who knew Jen

from preschool. But Jen refused to entertain negative thoughts, and with her encouragement each woman eventually gravitated to a job she felt comfortable with. Sarah, an actress, felt she'd be terrible at asking people for money but took on the role of producing the event. Kelli O'Donnell, a mother of three who also felt she needed a behind-the-scenes job, became known as the "database queen." Stacey Breckling, a college friend of Jen's, took charge of the finances because this was a job she could do at night when her children were asleep. Catherine Kelley, executive editor of *O,* wrote press releases and Web site pages. Tanya Scholl, Jen's sister who works on Wall Street and couldn't make it to meetings, solicited donations from her friends in finance. Everyone made calls to almost everywhere she had ever shopped, eaten, vacationed, or gotten a facial to ask for silent auction donations. Some, like Jennifer Crossland, a psychologist and mother of two, found this difficult. "I am not a natural salesperson, so I had to focus my calls on a few places that I knew well," she says. Others, like Tara Taylor, who came up with the idea of asking art students to create work to sell, discovered a talent for fund-raising they never knew they had. "The key is to feel great about the reason you're calling," she says. "You have to believe in your heart that if this was your money, you'd give it, too. People pick that up from you."

As the party got closer ("Five weeks!!" "Four weeks!!" read the subject lines of Jen's e-mails in a running countdown), the jobs intensified. Husbands came home early from work so wives could attend last-minute meetings. Meals got simpler—"definitely lots of chicken nuggets," says Stacey Breckling—and laundry baskets overflowed. But if the women found it hard to juggle fund-raising with the demands of toddlers, babies, and full- and part-time jobs, no one complained. Steeped in stories of girls attacked until they became incontinent, women gang-raped as their children were forced to watch, and 70-year-old women abused by groups of boys young enough to be their grandchildren, who could complain? "You read so many horrible stories in the newspaper it can feel overwhelming, like there's nothing you can do," says Jane Nadasi, who worked on communications

Jennifer Williams and *New York Times* reporter Jeffrey Gettleman at the Women of the Congo gala, June 12, 2008.

for the event. "This experience taught me you just have to put that feeling aside. You *can* do something, everyone can do something—it's just a matter of being brave, of not being afraid to make those calls."

It also felt good to know that they were teaching their children an important lesson. "All of us have to be the people we want our kids to be," says Jen. "When my husband came home from work, my 4-year-old said, 'Mommy worked on her Congo party today.' My husband asked, 'Do you know why Mommy is making a Congo party?' And my son said, 'Because the people there are crying.'"

As it turned out, Mommy's Congo party was a greater success than even Mommy, with her boundless optimism, could have predicted. The elegant Manhattan ballroom was pulsing with African music, waiters serving drinks on silver trays, guests bidding on silent auction items, art students proudly explaining the meaning of the works they had created in honor of the event. More than $150,000 was raised and at least 400 people attended, including Jeffrey Gettleman and representatives from the United Nations, the U.S. State Department, and the New York mayor's office.

Looking gorgeous in a navy blue dress, Jen worked the room with a masterful mix of focus and charm, paying particularly close attention to her notable guests. It clearly meant a lot to her to have "VIPs" in the room, as if their presence confirmed the importance of the event and also, perhaps, the seriousness of the stay-at-home mom who, in her words, "spent the last year and a half building Legos." What she didn't seem to realize as she fussed over her important people was that they were making an even greater fuss over *her.* "I got 150 e-mails about my story," says Jeffrey Gettleman. "But nobody picked up the ball and ran with it like Jen. There are lots of starters in the world, people who start things but then lose steam. Jen followed through."

"She followed her gut," says Eve Ensler. "All these women did. They heard the call. They responded. That's what we all need to do. Follow your instincts. Rise to what is inside you. That's how to change the world." ◼

Join a Giving Circle

The "Band of Sisters" are just one example of a giving circle, a trend that combines the social and intellectual exchange of book clubs with old-time traditions like barn raisings and African-American and Asian mutual aid societies. These circles take many forms. The basic premise is that individuals (who tend to be women) come together to pool their money and skills to make more of a difference than they could just writing a check. "For people who want to give, circles are a great way to meet with friends and share ideas on issues you care passionately about," says Caren Yanis, executive director of Oprah's Angel Network.

According to a recent survey by the Forum of Regional Associations of Grantmakers, the U.S. has 400-odd giving circles in some 40 states—up from 200 in 2004—that have raised more than $90 million. Some consist of a few friends who casually get together for potluck dinners; others have grown into 400-member organizations with tax-exempt nonprofit status. Donations vary widely, from less than $100 to more than $100,000 a year—minimum contributions may be required or left to the donor's choice, or tiered to what each member can afford. A circle may devote itself to a single cause or pick a new one each year, with many circles inviting experts or foundation directors to speak so they can make their philanthropy more strategic. Typically members work together reviewing proposals from nonprofit organizations, sometimes arranging fund-raising events and action campaigns. If you're interested in starting your own circle, these five steps will help (also check out oprahsangelnetwork.org):

1. Define your mission. Do you want to set up the group first and then recruit members? Or would you rather gather members before deciding on a goal? How will you develop consensus? Who's an appropriate member?

2. Decide your scope. You can choose a single issue or vary your choices. Also discuss whether you will focus on community or national or international issues.

3. Choose a size and structure. Do you want four members or 400? Set a schedule for meetings, and decide whether members must attend to earn a vote.

4. Remember the extras. How will you cover additional costs, including meeting expenses, paperwork, perhaps legal or bank fees? Who will be in charge of which responsibilities?

5. Figure out resources. What are the expectations of the group in terms of donating time, expertise, and money? Will you create one bank account or write checks individually for grants? If the latter, make sure members make each check payable to a nonprofit grantee rather than another member so that everyone gets a charitable tax deduction. Should you want to formalize the circle as a nonprofit corporation, get advice from a local community foundation or an accountant. Such tax-exempt status has advantages but requires annual filings and other legal procedures.

—Joanna L. Krotz

RAOLAT ABDULAI · NADINE BEAN · DÉBORAH BEREBICHEZ · DAWN BILLINGS · ROSLIND BLASINGAME-BUFORD · CHRISTINE BRECK · AMY CALLIS

REBECCA DALLET · JEANNE DASARO · CERELYN DAVIS · ANDREA DEAN · TAMMY DOBREZ · ANNE DODGE · SARAH DOUGHER

EVELYN FERNANDEZ-KETCHAM · STEPHANIE FIALLO · CATHERINE HEDGEMAN · SONYA HENDERSON · SUE HILDICK · SHEILA HODGKIN · TORI HOGAN

NANCY ROLDÁN JOHNSON · JULIA KEFFER · MICKI KRIMMEL · ELIZABETH LINDSEY · YARA LORENZO · SHANNON LYNBERG · NANCY MANSFIELD

JAMEELAH MEDINA · TANYA MOORE · ANNETTE MORALES · IRMA R. MUÑOZ · NNEKA NORVILLE · EBELE OKOBI-HARRIS · MORGAN OWEN-CRUISE

BOBBI PIASECKI · MICHAELLE POPE · RHONDA PRIEST · LORI-ANNE RAMSAY · BETHANY ROBERTSON · THENA ROBINSON · LINDSAY ROSS

JENNIFER STIMPSON · JOANNE TAWFILIS · JUDI TOWNSEND · YESICA TRUJILLO · CAROL WAGNER · CAROL WATSON · CARY WEATHERBY

AUTUMN DAVINESS

JANEEN COMENOTE

MICHELLE COTE

ERICA COURTNEY

CHRISTINA MELTON CRAIN

MILDRED C. CRUMP

CAMILLE CYPRIAN

LISA DUNSTER

JENNIE DURANT

PENNY BROWN HUBER

JENNY HWA

CHERYL MATHIEU

BINDU MAYI

TAMARA OYOLA-SANTIAGO

RESHMA PATTNI

Women Rule!

A CRASH COURSE IN CHANGING THE WORLD

More than 3,000 women with great ideas applied for the first-ever *O*–White House Leadership Project contest. The 80 winners got to attend an inspiration-packed three-day program, with coaching by some of the top women trailblazers in the country. **Aimee Lee Ball** watched as our winners learned to "make it happen."

EVAN RYAN

CHRISTINA SAINT LAURENT

ELIZABETH ASAHI SATO

ANJULI SHERIN

JORDAN SILVER

FREYA SPIELBERG

ARCHANA SRIDHAR

LEA WEBB

MOLLY WICKWIRE-SANTE

DIANE WILLIAMS

ERICA WILLIAMS

RAHAMA WRIGHT

CHUE YANG

ELIZABETH ZAPIEN-PLATA

n a warm June evening, Cerelyn Davis is scanning a hotel ballroom in New York City, acclimating herself to the surroundings like Dorothy just landing in Oz. A major in the Atlanta police department, she's seen plenty during her career of more than two decades—but nothing like this astonishing scene. Across the room, there's a similar gaze of anticipation on the face of Janeen Comenote, who works for a Native American foundation in Seattle. And in another corner, a self-described "ordinary mom" from suburban Minnesota, Cary Weatherby, is wondering how she got here. Dinner has been served with a rousing welcome by O's Gayle King and a stirring performance by Grammy-winning singer Angelique Kidjo. But the palpable exhilaration isn't coming from the stage; it's pulsing among the crowd: Davis, Comenote, Weatherby, and the other remarkable guests, all winners of an unprecedented leadership training contest called Women Rule!

It's no secret that now is a time when women's strengths are urgently needed in their communities, in business, and in the world. It was with this in mind that O magazine partnered with the White House Project—a nonprofit organization committed to advancing women from all backgrounds into positions of power—to create Women Rule! Over the past decade, the White House Project has perfected the art of teaching leadership skills. And with a sponsorship by American Express, its staff customized a star-studded training program specifically for O's winners.

The contest got off to a start in our April 2008 issue with a call to women who had already initiated a project—a nonprofit, business, public policy initiative, or run for political office—and wanted to take it to the next level. More than 3,000 entered, despite the extensive application, and it took weeks to select the 80 standouts, who were then invited to New York City for three days of leadership training.

Now the lobby of the Affinia Manhattan hotel is buzzing with women from all over the country, ranging in age from 18 to 69, burning with ideas and wild dreams. Déborah Berebichez wants to launch a TV science series for girls, encouraging interest in "the physics of high heels" and "chemistry in the kitchen." Nadine Bean has a plan for social work students to help rebuild the spirit of New Orleans's beleaguered Lower Ninth Ward. Rahama Wright hopes to expand the fair-trade shea butter cooperative she's started in Mali. Lea Webb intends to get her underserved upstate New York neighborhood a grocery store. And Joanne Tawfilis is creating a pyramid in Egypt from 12 miles of murals by worldwide artists to celebrate International Day of Peace 2010. "I need a business plan because I'd like to turn Art Miles into an income-generating, self-sustaining project," says Tawfilis, a mother of nine children, seven of whom are adopted from other countries. "My family is tired of seeing me with paint on my clothes."

The staff of the White House Project have forsaken business attire for Women Rule! T-shirts—"and anyone wearing a T-shirt, consider her your new best friend," says national program director Erin Vilardi at the orientation. The women are in for an intensive weekend of lectures, workshops, and individual coaching by top leaders in business, philanthropy, and politics. But the truth is, they will probably glean as much from one another as they will from the experts, according to Marie C. Wilson, founder and president of the White House Project. "If the energy and vision in this room were applied to world problems," she says at the opening dinner, "the morning paper would look completely different."

That energy and vision were clearly evident in the three women we chose to follow through the weekend:

CERELYN DAVIS

s a girl, Cerelyn Davis watched *Police Woman* so often that her whole family knew she would become an officer herself. But while she has succeeded in earning the rank of major in the Atlanta Police Department, the climb has been a struggle in a male-dominated world (according to the National Center for Women & Policing, women today constitute only 13 percent of the country's officers). "I've had to work above and beyond," says the 48-year-old Davis, "to deal with men not accepting me as a credible leader. A policewoman doesn't get respect until she runs a robber down. But women in these roles contribute so much. I've had experiences where my presence prevented the situation from turning into a shoot-out. And there are some things I can tell a battered woman, things that aren't so protocol." Davis's conviction that women's peacekeeping is essential to police work lies at the heart of her initiative, Sisters-in-Law—a support network for women in law enforcement that also encourages girls to consider the profession by offering real-life role models.

On Saturday morning, Davis and the other Women Rule! winners are divided into breakout groups of five. Led by experts the White House Project has selected, the groups will meet several times during the weekend to focus individually on each woman's project and determine the next steps to move it forward. Davis's facilitator is Aliza Mazor, a consultant for nonprofit start-ups, who begins by going around the table asking, "What is your biggest obstacle right now?" Davis explains she's put out feelers to a few police departments about adopting Sisters-in-Law as an in-house program. "But the men think that I'll bring in an army of women screaming about equality," she says. The group suggests that she change her presentation: Rather than emphasizing the need to serve and uplift women, she should highlight Sisters-in-Law's value to the force, articulating how it will make a department better. Davis pauses to take in the idea. "You're absolutely right," she says. "Just sitting here, I'm already tweaking what I'm going to say."

At dinner that night, Davis listens raptly to a presentation by Julie Gilbert, a senior vice president at Best Buy. "It was a boy's toy store, designed by boys for boys," she says. Gilbert decided that if she wanted to make the store a good place for women to shop, it had to be a good place for women to work. So she started the Women's Leadership Forum—WOLF—to develop a female contingent of innovators within the company. At one point she consulted a male friend in management. "Do you need money?" he asked, trying to be helpful. Realizing that she was about to encounter resistance from on high, she answered, "No, I need a heat shield." Later Davis says she almost wept

> "If the energy and vision in this room were applied to world problems, the morning paper would look completely different."

hearing this story—a heat shield is exactly what she could use in the police department. She also heeds Gilbert's counsel: "Think about all the possible reasons for hearing no, and write them down. It helps you get clear in your own mind."

After the breakout groups reconvene for their next session on Sunday, Mazor asks, "When you push for what you want, what do you feel others are thinking?" There's a simpatico laugh at the response of Evelyn Fernandez-Ketcham, who started a neighborhood center for disconnected young adults in Manhattan's mostly Hispanic Washington Heights (see "Leading Ladies," page 292, for more about her project). "I probably make people angry," she says, "but I need to let them react and not worry that they're thinking, *Oh, she's PMS-ing.*"

Davis tells the others that her female colleagues are hesitant to "make waves;" Mazor counters by suggesting she look at the younger women—this new generation assumes job satisfaction as a birthright, and they are probably ready to join her. "Form a group and brainstorm around the idea, What is women's policing?" says Mazor. This way Davis can start speaking publicly about the program as a new concept. They discuss how Sisters-in-Law could be organized along the lines of the Police Athletic League, with officers going out in the community to work with girls. Do some research, Mazor suggests: Measure the program's potential impact and demonstrate that it will not distract officers from their other work. As the session wraps up and each woman states her intentions for next steps, Davis says her six-month goals are to establish a stakeholder group (including, everyone jokes, one token "alpha male" to keep things lively) and develop a mission statement that she can hand to the chief.

CERFLYN DAVIS

Hometown:
Douglasville, Georgia
Project: Sisters-in-Law
Challenge: Getting buy-in from her male colleagues on the police force
➤ **Breakthrough:**
Changing the way she presents her idea is key
Takeaway:
A six-month plan

➤ LEADING LADIES

To meet all 80 winners, go to oprah.com/omagextras. For a sneak preview, take a look at these seven....

EVAN RYAN Last year, The Associated Press reported the results of a study showing that unemployment among recently discharged military veterans is 18 percent, three times the current national average. The news shocked Ryan, a 37-year-old consultant to Education Partnership for Children of Conflict, an NGO cofounded by Angelina Jolie. "There seems to be little gratitude on their return," says Ryan, who lives in Washington, D.C. "The war in Iraq may be controversial, but our veterans shouldn't be." She has begun the groundwork for a conference called Home of the Brave that will bring together veteran groups with government officials and the Veterans Administration to troubleshoot why so many men and women are still falling through the cracks. "I want to play a part in welcoming vets home," she says, "but I want to do it in a way that gives them a hand up, not a handout."

ROSLIND BLASINGAME-BUFORD Raised by a single mother, Blasingame-Buford started drinking, smoking dope, and hanging out with gangs as a young teenager in Minneapolis. "I should be a statistic," she says. Her saving grace was a YMCA Black Achievers Program that helped her imagine other possibilities. Today the 32-year-old is paying it forward with Building Futures, a Chicago-based college prep and career readiness program for high-risk inner-city youth that is now six years old. In 2007 an astonishing 97 percent of her 1,000 protégés graduated from high school or were promoted to the next grade, and 86 percent went on to college. "In the Chicago public schools we target, the counselor-student ratio is about 1 to 400," she says. "But I believe that given the proper tools and support, at-risk youth can succeed."

AMY CALLIS A vacation in India turned into a destiny for 41-year-old Callis, of Atlanta, who ended up volunteering for two years at a Calcutta hospital where Mother Teresa cared for tuberculosis patients. "Even in her frail state," Callis says, "when she came into the room, the energy changed." Determined to continue meaningful work, in 2007 Callis cocreated the Darfur Stoves Project, which produces efficient portable cookers for refugee women of this war-torn region so they don't have to leave their camps in search of wood, risking rape. Ultimately Callis, a freelance communications consultant, would like to find other simple technological solutions to problems in the developing world. "I've never been an out-front leader," she says. "But the stove is a good intervention right now, until the best one: peace in Darfur."

EVELYN FERNANDEZ-KETCHAM Growing up in New York City's heavily Hispanic Washington Heights, Fernandez-Ketcham, now 41, was struck by the ironic proximity of a world-class educational institution, Columbia University, and the area's many illiterate and unemployed residents. She started the New Heights Neighborhood Center to help young adults in the community develop their skills and get meaningful jobs at the university and other local facilities (all while earning a master's degree, putting her husband through law school, and raising four children). After hearing Minnesota state senator Mee Moua speak at Women Rule! she is considering a run for political office in New York. "It's the policies that effect long-term change," she says. "After the senator spoke, I thought, *Wow, this is really possible.*"

TORI HOGAN As a premed student in 2002, Hogan went on a class trip to Lebanon. While working in a refugee camp there, she called home to say, "Mom, guess what; I'm not going to be a doctor." She realized that aid money was often being wasted and people's lives were not improving. With her project, Beyond Good Intentions, 26-year-old Hogan, now a graduate student at Harvard, is determined to mobilize the next generation of aid workers in a debate about what really works, by creating educational programs and a documentary of successful organizations around the world. "Coming from the West, we don't always know what's best for people in other cultures," she says. "We have this idea that if it worked in Cambodia, it must work in Uganda."

CHERYL MATHIEU Although she hadn't been particularly close to her grandparents, Mathieu, 44, became the point person in her family, responsible for their care as they aged. "The gift they gave me at the end of their lives was the realization that I relate really well to older people," she says. And from that gift came her vision for AgingPro, a one-stop online resource for elder care, including everything from support groups for caregivers to directories of medical specialists and assisted-living facilities. "There's a maze of senior services that's so difficult to navigate," says Mathieu, who lives in Long Beach, California, and went back to school in her 30s to earn a PhD in social work. "I want to be the Google of elder care."

JENNY HWA As a dancer with the San Francisco Ballet at age 16, Hwa realized her career wouldn't last forever. With a love of fashion and a concern for the environment, she studied design, working with Catherine Malandrino and Armani Exchange, and parlayed her experience into her own organic clothing company: Loyale, a line of sustainable, eco-chic apparel. Even the hang tags are made from recycled paper. Now 30 and living in New York City, Hwa plans to expand the line. "I want to amend the philosophy that says the environment must be compromised in order to make a profit," she says.

JANEEN COMENOTE

A member of the Quinault and three other Indian nations, Janeen Comenote was born in Seattle and spent her first few years in and out of foster care. At age 5, she was taken in by her grandmother, who as a young girl had been forcibly removed from her own family and placed in boarding school, where any child caught speaking a Native language had her mouth washed out with soap. "My grandmother hated the American government—she'd send me out to the mailbox for our welfare checks saying, 'Go get the Eagle s---,'" recalls Comenote, 39, a development officer for the United Indians of All Tribes Foundation in Seattle. "So much of our culture has been co-opted. Probably no one who drives a Jeep Cherokee could tell you where the Cherokee tribe is from."

And many Americans may not know that about 65 percent of our country's Native people actually live off reservations, often facing the same, if not worse, socioeconomic hardship as those who live on them. To give what she calls "the silent population" of Native Americans who reside in cities a voice, Comenote created the National Urban Indian Family Coalition, which represents 24 organizations in 19 cities and has already hosted national summits. Her dream is to raise awareness among policymakers and convince Congress to dedicate funding for much-needed services. "Part of my motivation is wanting to help my own family," she says. "My sisters ran away when they were 11 and 12 and started having kids soon after. My sisters are in prison, so I have all these nieces and nephews in foster care that I've never met."

At Women Rule! Comenote can't believe it when she learns that the facilitator of her breakout group, Elisabeth Garrett, is also Native American. Another high point of the session for Comenote is sharing what she's learned about designing her Web site (using an experienced tech consul-

tant) with fellow winner Roslind Blasingame-Buford, who has started a college prep program for at-risk inner-city kids (see "Leading Ladies").

In a workshop about public speaking with Ora Shtull, president of MAXIMA Coaching, Comenote learns that body language, delivery, and wardrobe choices have more impact than the actual words. "In fact, when you communicate, you transmit as much as 93 percent of your information nonverbally—gestures, tone of voice, volume—and as little as 7 percent verbally," Shtull says, "and you have seconds to establish credibility." When addressing a group, she coaches: Keep your feet in line with your shoulders and hands above your waist, make eye contact with multiple members of the audience, and occasionally connect to the back of the room. Shtull strongly advises every woman to have an "elevator pitch" handy for meeting a potential donor or anyone who might support her cause. "Summarize your venture, mention one or two accomplishments, and tell me why I should care," Shtull says. "Too often people stop at features and don't move on to benefits."

In a lecture about time management, Comenote has a moment of clarity about her compulsive e-mail checking. "It puts you in a reactive mode rather than addressing your own agenda," says presenter Julie Morgenstern, author of *When Organizing Isn't Enough: SHED Your Stuff, Change Your Life*. "Wait an hour in the morning before opening your in-box." But

> "Think about all the possible reasons for hearing no, and write them down. It helps you get clear in your own mind."

Comenote realizes her problem is larger than e-mail: With a full-time job, hectic travel schedule, and an inability to say no when others ask for her time, she's allowing an overstuffed life to keep her from focusing on her project.

Morgenstern offers a number of concrete strategies: "Every time you feel out of control, fill in the blanks: I spend way too much time on _____. I procrastinate whenever I have to _____. If there were a 25th hour in the day, I'd use it for _____." Energized, Comenote starts practicing: *No. I'd love to do it, but I'm simply too busy at this time*—words that are "a huge evolution" for her. "And I know I've got to learn the fine art of delegation—the idea that yes, someone else really might be able to do this as well, if not better," she says. Vowing never to get a BlackBerry—"it would be fatal"—she declares herself ready to "do nothing less than change the face of Indian country."

CARY WEATHERBY

Several years ago, Cary Weatherby, of Bloomington, Minnesota, salvaged a huge box of alphabet stickers that were headed for the dumpster, castoffs from a local business that had changed filing systems. She delivered them to a grateful kindergarten teacher at her children's school who had exhausted her minuscule budget for supplies. Then

CARY WEATHERBY

Hometown:
Bloomington, Minnesota
Project: Companies
to Classrooms
Challenge: Fear of
fund-raising
➤ **Breakthrough:**
  She can't take
  rejection personally
Takeaway: Skills
for making the "ask"

Weatherby thought, *There's probably more of this stuff out there,* and Companies to Classrooms was born. Now the 52-year-old "stay-at-home" mother, who spends most of her time running the nonprofit, wants to create "free stores" stocked with surplus business products to help teachers across her state.

At the conference on Saturday morning, she finds signs posted around the ballroom describing different emotional reactions to negotiating: "It's a piece of cake." "It makes me feel powerful." "I try to avoid it." "I worry about how others are going to react." Linda C. Babcock, PhD, a professor of economics at Carnegie Mellon University and coauthor of *Ask for It,* has instructed the women to stand near the sign that best expresses the way they feel. Weatherby plants herself next to: NEGOTIATING IS LIKE GOING TO THE DENTIST. But listening to Babcock, she realizes that she should ignore the voice in her head saying, *Watch out; don't be pushy* or *Are you sure you're good enough?* "It's not the voice of experience or common sense," says Babcock. "It's not even your own voice. It's the voice of society. It's holding you back, it's cutting you off from the opportunity to broaden your life, and it's costing you money."

The part of negotiating that's most like a root canal for Weatherby is "the ask": actually requesting money from individuals or institutions. She hates getting turned down, takes it personally, feels debilitated. But in a Sunday seminar, Julia Pimsleur, a veteran fund-raiser who has worked for more than ten years in nonprofits, suggests a different mind-set. "You're offering something that stirs your passion, and anyone would be lucky to be involved," Pimsleur says. "When you get a no, it could mean, 'We don't know you well enough' or 'It's not a priority right now.'"

➤ AND THE INSPIRATION FLOWED

The women who mentored and advised our 80 winners know what it's like to wrestle a dream into reality. Meet a few key players who shared their knowledge.

1 The idea for **Women Rule!** started with **MEREDITH BLAKE:** Straight out of UCLA School of Law, Blake founded Break the Cycle, a nonprofit agency that helps teens prevent and end dating abuse and domestic violence. Ten years later, in 2005, she joined Participant Productions (now called Participant Media), which makes films such as Al Gore's Oscar-winning documentary, *An Inconvenient Truth.* Inspired by the power of the media to spread important messages, Blake founded Cause & Affect, a company that designs high-impact social action campaigns around issues ranging from the environment to human rights to women's leadership. When she took on the White House Project, she contacted *O*'s health and news director, Liz Brody. "Making your dream a reality almost requires an obsession," Blake says, "a feeling that your idea really, really matters and that you are the one to make it happen come hell or high water." To that, she adds: "You also need a ton of chutzpah and a Teflon skin. You must have, or quickly develop, the ability to forge ahead in spite of naysayers and, ideally, leave them in the dust."

2 **MARIE C. WILSON** took Blake and Brody's enthusiasm and ran with it—agreeing to expand the White House Project's political training to a leadership program in various fields. Wilson had launched the White House Project ten years earlier, when she was president of the Ms. Foundation for Women. "I have never known anything about any field I entered," she says with amusement. A mother of five children, she says there's still a deep ambivalence in the world—and inside women—about ambition. "It's not that women can't dance; it's that women are waiting to be asked," she says. Wilson insists that we must encourage one another to take the lead. "Within the next 24 hours," she says, "you should call up a friend and say, 'Have you thought about becoming a leader in your community or running for…?'"

3 **CHERYL DORSEY, MD,** immediately agreed to take part in Women Rule! when she was contacted by the White House Project. In the early 1990s, while studying to be a pediatrician at Harvard Medical School, Dorsey saw a photo in a local paper of a poverty-stricken mother leaning over the grave of a child. It was her "moment of obligation"—the realization that a particular issue is so important you have to do something about it, "that you are *accountable* for it, that you *own* it." Dorsey launched Family Van, a mobile health unit for Boston's inner-city residents. That endeavor was financed by Echoing Green, a global nonprofit that provides seed money to social entrepreneurs with bold ideas. Today Dorsey is its president. "Ideas without execution are simply daydreams," she says.

4 Minnesota state senator **MEE MOUA** joined the Women Rule! lineup as inspiration for anyone considering political office. She was born at the height of the Vietnam War in a bamboo hut with no electricity in a jungle village of northern Laos. Her family immigrated to the United States in 1978, where they faced the common postwar hostility toward Asians. "I've always been guided by my mother's words: 'No matter how American you become, some people will never like you because of the way you look. That is why you must study hard, go to college, come back, and be their boss.'" Moua did just that, becoming a lawyer and then winning a seat in the Minnesota senate by contacting every single household in her district, reaching out to the most disadvantaged and disenfranchised. "We should infuse our hearts and our souls into this political world that we live in," she says. "Just look around and see what the world has come to without our presence at the decision-making table. We must be audacious, we must be strategic, and we must be ambitious about taking up the mantle of affirmative leadership because we know we can do better."

5 Philanthropist **LIBBY COOK** agreed to help support Women Rule! financially, then came to check out the participants, counseling a number of them during and after the conference. Cook, with her husband, turned a local health food store called Wild Oats into a billion-dollar company before selling it to Whole Foods in 2007. "I had no business experience and made every mistake in the book—at least twice," she says. "At one point we were trying to be everything to everybody—we were trying to be a crossover store, introducing customers to natural foods without scaring them. But people were wondering: *What's your real message?* Sometimes it's important to start small and be really focused." Wild Oats provided the means for Cook to create Philanthropiece, a foundation that supports international programs focusing on education, health, and the environment, with an emphasis on local communities (Cook took a particular interest in several participants, including Lea Webb, Micki Krimmel, and Rahama Wright and has been working with them to develop their projects). "You have to surround yourself with the right people," she says. "I didn't care about having marquee names on my board. I knew not to ask, say, the dean of a business school because he's too darn busy. I looked for people with the same passion I had."

1. MEREDITH BLAKE

2. MARIE C. WILSON

3. CHERYL DORSEY

4. MEE MOUA

5. LIBBY COOK

➤ THE SCIENCE ROCK STARS Three winners are putting a new face on math, physics, and chemistry—and they want girls to notice.

When **DÉBORAH BEREBICHEZ** told her family she wanted to study mathematics, they said, "But you'll never get married. No man wants a wife who's smarter than he is." Their reaction was typical in the Mexico City community where Berebichez grew up, but she paid no heed, earning a PhD in physics at Stanford in 2004. Now 34 and living in New York City, where she's a consultant for MSCI Barra, a financial risk analysis firm, she is determined to make science more appealing to the next generation of girls. Her videos, with titles like *The Physics of High Heels,* demonstrate ways in which science applies to daily life and how fun it can be to learn. If her dream comes true, the series will become a TV show.

TANYA MOORE remembers being told by a high school teacher that she didn't belong in the advanced math class. Moore, 35, now has a PhD in biostatistics from UC Berkeley and wants to challenge the idea

Chemistry is hot! Jennifer Stimpson *(second from left),* back home in Dallas, gets her students fired up about science. Here she shows *(from left)* Phantasia Preston, Richia Campbell, and Chelsea Grant how to determine the number of calories in a peanut.

that "only some people can do math—usually white males." Her project, an Infinite Possibilities Conference, will support and encourage minority women and girls in mathematics by offering role models and mentors. "Math provides a framework to organize information and interpret data," says Moore, who is program manager for

the City of Berkeley's Division of Public Health. "Even if you're not going to use geometry in your life's work, it gives you tools for decision making and critical thinking."

JENNIFER STIMPSON, a 36-year-old chemistry teacher from Dallas, calls herself a "new-millennium science nerd." Stimpson is developing a K–12 program called Get a KIC Out of Science (KIC stands for Knowledge in Chemistry). "It shows that everyday people use chemistry," she says. "Your pharmacist is a chemist, your neighborhood baker is a chemist, and your air conditioner guy has to have some knowledge of chemistry. KIC makes science relatable and tangible."

The trio bonded during the conference. "We're women, we're minorities, we're scientists, and we don't have that geeky look," says Stimpson, "so here's our message: You can be black, Hispanic, or Asian, you can wear Manolos, you can be fly, hip, and dynamic and be a scientist. When a 12-year-old thinks you're cool, that's like getting a million-dollar check."

D uring Pimsleur's session, Tori Hogan asks what standards donations should meet—she's raising money for a project that will assess international aid programs to determine which ones really work. "Choose two or three issues you won't compromise on," says Pimsleur. "Personally, I don't feel comfortable taking money from pharmaceuticals, tobacco, or alcohol. But too broad a list is unnecessarily limiting." Weatherby has faced the same funding dilemma—to seek investors and go into debt or to work with a limited budget—that is raised by another winner, Cheryl Mathieu, who has created an online resource for caretakers of the elderly (see "Leading Ladies" for more on Hogan and Mathieu). Pimsleur throws a question back at them: "Do you want to own a big piece of something small or a small piece of something big? It's hard to take your company far and fast on your own, but with help you can become the biggest player." Ignoring the negative voice in her head, Weatherby realizes that player could be her.

Perhaps the most striking aspect of the conference, true to Marie Wilson's prediction, is the cross-pollination of ideas. Evan Ryan, who works for an organization that

helps provide books, supplies, and teachers to children in areas of conflict around the world, is thrilled to meet Cary Weatherby. And because Ryan's project is a plan to help returning Iraq vets, she's also excited to meet Amy Callis, who has turned her attention to another war zone, providing stoves to Darfuri refugees. And when Jenny Hwa meets Callis, she has a brainstorm: Hwa's line of eco-clothing could incorporate a Darfuri flower print, with a portion of the proceeds going to the refugees (for more on all these women, see "Leading Ladies").

On Sunday evening, the participants return to the hotel ballroom. Responding to a random name call, each woman stands and delivers a one-sentence mission statement—a "lite" version of the elevator pitch. ("Through Sisters-in-Law, policewomen will gain invaluable training and professional support in achieving leading roles in their agencies," says Davis. "Companies to Classrooms gets surplus office supplies and equipment into the hands of teachers," Weatherby follows. "The National Urban Indian Family Coalition will improve the lives of Native people in our cities," asserts Comenote.) As they speak, they fulfill the Hopi proverb that says: The one who tells the stories rules the world. Many of them had mothers who directed the show from the backseat, raised to believe that leading would take them away from their duty. Now these daughters can comfortably take charge, front and center.

For a closing ceremony, the women form a circle and, one by one, offer a word to sum up the conference: "Strength." "Strategy." "Invincible." "Network." "Possibility." Hugs are exchanged along with business cards, as they rush off for trains and planes. "I loved the theme of getting knocked down but finding a way to pick yourself up and navigate your way through obstacles in a positive fashion," says Evan Ryan, heading for the Metroliner to Washington, D.C. "Focus, focus, focus—it's the results that matter," says Cheryl Mathieu on her way back to California. "It's okay to be of service to people and make money. The world needs me and my story—yes, me!"

The application for Women Rule! asked: What would you do if you knew you could not fail? As these new leaders head out to change the world, they now have some answers to guide them. We'll be following their progress. ▣

Thanks to everyone from the White House Project who worked tirelessly on Women Rule!, including Marie C. Wilson, Joan Hochman, Jaime Peters, Elizabeth Hines, and Tiffany Dufu; also to Shifra Bronznick, a leadership consultant for the White House Project who collaborated on the training agenda.

Additional reporting by Polly Brewster, Kristy Davis, Lauren Dzubow, Brooke Kosofsky Glassberg, Dorothea Hunter, Kate Sandoval, Blythe Simmons, Sara Sugarman, and Carolyn Wilsey.

Support for rooms and meals was provided by Affinia Manhattan Hotels, Philanthropiece, and the Sunshine Fund.

➤ SKILLS TO GO The Women Rule! experts have some wisdom about making your own dreams happen.

5 Tips on Fund-Raising

It can be intimidating. But if you can talk, you can fund-raise.

1. Ask frequently, ask big (more than you think you can get), and ask specifically (focus on individuals and organizations that are more likely to care about your project because they have similar priorities).

2. Avoid cold-pitching whenever possible. You can be more brilliant with your preparation and documentation when a potential donor is expecting you.

3. Protect donor privacy by asking their permission before sharing their information with anyone.

4. Spend 90 percent of your time on the 10 percent of your donors who have the potential to give 90 percent of the money.

5. Keep in mind that, although there's a lot of competition, around $300 billion of money is given away every year.

Secrets of Public Speaking

If you love to talk in front of an audience, you fall into a minuscule percentage of the population—people like Lisa Witter, who turned her extrovert disposition into a career as chief operating officer of Fenton Communications, which provides communication strategies for clients such as MoveOn.org and Women for Women International. Here's her advice on how to make an impact:

1. What people want most from a speech is authenticity; you can't project that if you're reading from notes or a teleprompter. Have a stump speech perfected, memorized, and ready.

2. Practice out loud and get feedback from family or friends.

3. Don't thank people at the beginning of a speech. It's boring.

Create A Million-Dollar Business

Women own 10 million businesses and employ more than 13 million people in this country, says Susan Sobbott, president of OPEN from American Express. OPEN helps women entrepreneurs through a program called Make Mine a Million $ Business. (It provides money via loans and lines of credit, as well as mentoring, marketing, and technology tools.) "Having a million-dollar mind-set includes setting a goal and being serious about it," says Sobbott. "A woman who has it can describe what she's doing succinctly and compellingly, having honed her focus so she can sell it to anyone, whether customer, creditor, or investor. Clarity of thinking is what allows you to cultivate believers who buy into your success." Sobbott's best advice:

1. Figure out what only you can do, then get other people to do the rest. "Women tend to be good at multitasking but have trouble delegating, probably because of their sense of accountability."

2. Balance passion and profit. "You must advance your cause but have an appreciation for the bottom line."

3. Success is driven in part by the ability to manage stress. "Perspective and detachment are critical, which means stepping back from a challenge, looking at it objectively, and figuring out how to make it work for you. If you're stressed, you won't be at the top of your game. Instead of being mired in the problem, your energy needs to go to solving it."

Oprah Talks to Denzel Washington

The two-time Academy Award winner, one-time Sexiest Man Alive, and second-time director opens up about his close-call adolescence, his close-knit family, falling into acting, falling in love with directing, and (after his mother finally stepped in to negotiate the deal) making a movie—*The Great Debaters*—so powerful it cost Oprah three tissues and totally wrecked her eye makeup.

T he first time I read the screenplay for *The Great Debaters,* I was riveted. But I wasn't prepared to be so deeply moved by it a second time, when I watched the film (which is co-produced by my company, Harpo Films) with its director and star, Denzel Washington. He showed me a rough cut; three tissues and one makeup-smeared face later, I had what I call an emotional headache (and I mean that in a good way).

The story is inspired by the life of Melvin B. Tolson, a professor at Wiley College in Marshall, Texas, one of the first black Southern colleges. Tolson formed a champion debate team that dared to challenge segregation by debating white college teams in the 1930s, a time when lynch mobs were still commonplace. Along with Denzel as Tolson, the film stars Forest Whitaker and Kimberly Elise, as well as three incredible newcomers who play the members of the debate team.

After more than 30 years of acting and two Oscars—Best Supporting Actor for *Glory* in 1989 and Best Actor for *Training Day* in 2001—Denzel has discovered a new passion: directing. *The Great Debaters,* which opened in

At the Sony Studios in Los Angeles, where Denzel showed Oprah a rough cut of *The Great Debaters*.

December 2007, is the second film he's both directed and starred in (the first was *Antwone Fisher* in 2002). Yet he says his most significant role is played away from the film set: He's the father of four—John David, 23; Katia, 20; and twins Olivia and Malcolm, 16—and he has been married to actress-singer Pauletta Washington for 24 years.

His own parents, Denzel Sr., a Pentecostal minister, and Lennis, a hairdresser, divorced when he was 14. When Denzel began to get into trouble on the streets of Mount Vernon, New York, Lennis, though barely able to get by on her wages, scraped together the money to send him, his older sister, Lorice, and his younger brother, David, to boarding school in upstate New York. After graduating, he attended Manhattan's Fordham University, where he made a decision to try acting in the school's production of *Othello*. His successes have been building ever since.

When he was a young man, Denzel was told by an influential visitor to the Boys & Girls Club that he could be anything he wanted to be. That sentiment and Denzel's deep spiritual beliefs, as well as his belief in the importance of education, are pivotal elements in his life, and he has instilled them in *The Great Debaters*.

OPRAH: How did you feel the first time you read the script for *The Great Debaters*?

DENZEL: The reaction you had in the screening room is the one I had. Man, it just moved me. I felt an emotional connection. What I learned while doing research for the film is that many black colleges, like Wiley and Morehouse, opened during the decade following the 1863 Emancipation Proclamation. That's because education was believed to be the way out, so when millions of black people were finally let go after almost 250 years, boom, we opened schools. And that's partly why Melvin Tolson's debate team was able to beat these other national teams in the '30s: Great thinkers such as W.E.B. Du Bois and Melvin B. Tolson couldn't teach at schools like Harvard or Columbia. But *The Great Debaters* is really about the kids and the journey of one boy in particular.

OPRAH: I'm in awe of how you made the words from the script come alive on the screen. Do you think directing is your gift?

DENZEL: It's my passion. More than anything, I enjoy seeing talented people do what they do well. When you're an actor, you come out of your trailer, do your thing, and then go back in. Directing is about collaboration—the production, the costuming, the script, the actors. I love it. It brings me joy. At 53 years old, I'm blessed to be able to segue into directing. I want to be Clint Eastwood when I grow up!

OPRAH: When you're directing, does it seem like you've

WITH HONORS *Above:* Denzel and his wife, Pauletta Washington, after his Oscar win for Best Actor in *Training Day*, 2002. *Right:* On the set of *Antwone Fisher*, 2002.

accessed a higher part of yourself?

DENZEL: Even a 20-hour day went by like that [*snaps his fingers*]. For a 7 A.M. call time, I was up at 3 and on the set at 4; no one could get there earlier than me. I worked around the clock, even on the weekends. Leadership is quiet, but strong and consistent. As our friend Nelson Mandela has said, a leader is like a shepherd—he sends the fast, nimble sheep out front so that the rest will follow, not realizing they're all being led from behind. On this film, I know there were some of the group who probably thought, *Yeah, right: He's an actor, and now he wants to direct.* But by the time all of the team had arrived, I'd been preparing for hours. I was like, "Where have you all been? I've already made breakfast!"

OPRAH: Great directing is in the preparation and details.

DENZEL: Exactly. I hope I never get to the place where it gets stale. The other day, I was doing the math: I'm 53, and if I direct a picture every five years or so, I could work on six more, if I'm lucky.

OPRAH: How difficult was it to both direct this film and act in it?

DENZEL: Sending your child to Baghdad is difficult; what I do is not hard. But to answer your question: When I'm directing, I can't focus the way I'm used to focusing as an actor, because I don't have the quiet time. I've always taken 40 deep breaths for relaxation before I do a scene. During this movie, 40 breaths was all the time I had to myself! I'm not that great at spinning ten plates at a time. I know that about myself.

OPRAH: When did you know you wanted to act?

DENZEL: When I was doing *Othello* in college. Everyone was coming out of the woodwork to see the show. I was so green, I would look right out at the audience just to see who was there! But I was like, *Wow—all these people showed up. Maybe I'm good at this.* So I already had a drive to perfect the craft.

OPRAH: I can only imagine how many parts must come your way now.

DENZEL: I'm one of the few—whatever you call it, A-listers—who's still available for parts right now because I've been busy directing this film all year rather than reading scripts and signing contracts.

OPRAH: You said "A-listers" under your breath.

DENZEL: Titles have nothing to do with me. That's not who I am. It's like the term *movie star:* What does that mean? It's just a label they give you until they replace it with another one: *has-been.* I don't claim either.

> "I ask, What am I going to do with what I have? I can't take anything with me. You never see a U-Haul behind a hearse."

OPRAH: If you're not a movie star, then who is?

DENZEL: First, I'm a human being. I love my work, but acting is what I do; it's not my identity. I love the way Julia Roberts put it: "I'm just an ordinary person who has an extraordinary job."

OPRAH: Didn't you ever fantasize about being a movie star?

DENZEL: Not so much, because my background is in theater, and in the 1970s, I didn't see anyone I wanted to be like; other than Sidney Poitier, there weren't many African-American film stars. As a kid, I'd wanted to be a football player. Then, after I got into theater at age 20, I saw James Earl Jones do *Oedipus the King* at St. John the Divine on 112th Street in Manhattan, and I was like, Wow. I sneaked into his dressing room and looked at his props and his rings while he was meeting people. I thought, *One day I'll make $650 a week and work on Broadway.* It was never my master plan to go to Hollywood.

OPRAH: Now that you've had all this success, how do you feel about it?

DENZEL: I ask, What am I going to do with what I have? I can't take anything with me. You know the saying: You never see a U-Haul behind a hearse.

OPRAH: There's a line I love in *The Great Debaters*, when Forest Whitaker's character, James Farmer Sr., a charismatic minister, asks his son, "And what do we do?" and James Jr. answers, "We do what we have to do so that we can do what we want to do." Where did that come from?

DENZEL: It came from my house—it's what I tell my kids. If one of them walked in right now, I'd ask, "What do we do?" and they'd answer with that line.

OPRAH: The last time you were on the show, we surprised you with a video clip of your son John David, who said, "Because of my dad, I want to be the best in what I do."

DENZEL: You have no idea what his words meant to me that day. Awards and accolades are great, but I'd easily trade them all for a moment like that. My son is fulfilling my dream, playing football like I'd always wanted to [John David plays for the St. Louis Rams]. My daughter Katia is at Yale—a place where I didn't dare apply. I dig seeing them do their thing. I went to watch my daughter sing with her school's a cappella group. She was so happy.

OPRAH: Raising children who are smart, kind, and generous and who know themselves has become more difficult than ever in our consumer culture. Were you ever worried about spoiling your children?

DENZEL: They live well, but we don't just give them anything they want. When our twins turned 16, I bought them used cars. Okay, they're BMWs, but I wanted them in something safe! [*Laughs*] I got them into athletics, which has also been important. They've learned about hard work and fair play. But when it comes to the kids, I give complete credit to my wife, Pauletta. Early on, we decided that we wouldn't drag them around to all the places I go. Pauletta was the consistent one who made breakfast every day and took them to school. She taught them their prayers.

OPRAH: **You've been working very steadily for most of their lives. Were you ever able to be one of those families that sat down and had dinner together?**

DENZEL: I joined in as often as I could. When my parents were together, my father worked a lot, too. He always had two or three jobs, so he was never home either. Children adjust. My kids knew that I was always trying to get home to be with them. I'd tell them, "You have school Monday to Friday, and I have work. We both have our jobs to do."

OPRAH: **You do what you have to do…**

DENZEL: …so you can do what you want to do. Doesn't that line cover a lot of territory? Once your homework's done, even Dad can't say anything about you going to the movies.

OPRAH: **How did you meet Pauletta?**

DENZEL: We met at a hotel restaurant. I was just arriving to start work on the film *Wilma* [the 1977 television film biography of track legend Wilma Rudolph], and it was her last day of shooting.

OPRAH: **Did you immediately know she was The One?**

DENZEL: No—that happened over time. We met, but then we saw each other again at a party a year later. People who say they knew right away are lying! [*Laughs*] It's a marathon, not a sprint.

OPRAH: **Is Hollywood hard on a marriage?**

DENZEL: Hollywood gets a bad rap; it's just a place with some footprints in cement. I don't live there, I live in Los Angeles. But it's probably helped our marriage that we're apart a lot.

OPRAH: **Really?**

DENZEL: Sure. If I were Pauletta, I'd get sick of me! You know, she gets used to running the house without me, and then here I come, messing things up.

OPRAH: **So there's a period of adjustment when you get back from filming?**

DENZEL: Yes. I have a strong personality. I can be a bully. Pauletta and the kids would get used to doing things a certain way, and then I'd arrive and start telling the kids what to do. It was a long time before I noticed her sighing as I did that. I've had to work on it.

OPRAH: **You know, earlier today, you said something that grabbed my heart. When I asked if you'd been nervous about directing this movie, you said, "Everything was already prayer-filled." How big a role does spirituality play in your life?**

DENZEL: The word *role* suggests a compartment. It doesn't play a role in my life; it *is* my life. Everything else is just making a living. If I get away from that idea, I get lost. This business is not who I am. Anyone with a spiritual base understands humility. When you start using the words *I* and *me* too often, you get in trouble.

OPRAH: **Or worse: When you start referring to yourself in the third person.**

DENZEL: How do people get to that point? "Denzel wouldn't do…"—I can't even finish the sentence! I just wasn't raised like that.

OPRAH: **Is it true that, at one point during the financial negotiations for this movie, your mother stepped in?**

DENZEL: I was out of my mind, going back and forth with Harvey Weinstein [The Weinstein Company coproduced *The Great Debaters* with Harpo Films]. I finally said, "Harvey, what's your mother's phone number? I'm going to ask our mothers to work this out." So they talked, and afterward Harvey said to me, "I don't know what you did, but everything's settled."

OPRAH: **What did your mother say?**

DENZEL: I didn't even ask her.

OPRAH: **Are you proud of what you've done with this movie?**

DENZEL: I don't go there, Oprah. I don't even know what that means.

OPRAH: **Well, I'm so proud of you, Denzel.**

DENZEL: I'm pleased that you're pleased. That's why I asked whether you liked it.

OPRAH: **The fact that I went through three tissues and smeared my makeup didn't give it away?**

DENZEL: I just wanted an answer, and now I can move on. I don't read reviews. It's enough for me that you like it.

OPRAH: **You won't look at the reviews?**

DENZEL: Well…I might sneak a peek.

OPRAH: **What do you most want people to get out of the movie?**

DENZEL: That depends on what they bring to it. As I watched it with you today, I cried—and I haven't cried over this movie in a while. Even the energy of other people in a room can impact the way we see things.

OPRAH: **After winning two Academy Awards, how important is the whole Oscar thing to you?**

DENZEL: I'm about the process.

OPRAH: **You've been nominated many times—**

DENZEL: Five.

OPRAH: **Every time your name is read, even if you don't care about it—**

GLORY DAYS *Left:* Denzel directing a scene from *The Great Debaters* in Louisiana. *Right:* With Ethan Hawke in *Training Day*, 2001. *Below:* In 1998 with (*front row, from left*) twins Olivia and Malcolm, daughter Katia; (*back row*) an unidentified friend, son John David, wife Pauletta, cousin Rita Pearson, and mother Lennis.

DENZEL: I didn't say I didn't care! [*Laughs*] Every young actor wants to win an Oscar. Years ago I was in a parking lot across the street from Spago, and I could see the stars with their Oscars going into the after party. I said to myself, "I want to do that one day." When I was at Fordham, I recall looking at Avery Fisher Hall and the New York State Theater and saying, "I'm going to work in those theaters." I've had those dreams.

OPRAH: What was it like to win the first time?

DENZEL: Kevin Kline was in the wings. He'd won the year before [1988] for *A Fish Called Wanda*. After I got the Oscar and walked offstage, I said to Kevin, "Did that just happen?" It felt like I fell asleep in the mail room and I was going to wake up and find out it was all a dream.

OPRAH: Okay, I have to ask you this: In 1996 you were the first black man to be named *People* magazine's Sexiest Man Alive. At that point, did the sex symbol thing intensify for you?

DENZEL: Nothing changed. It still hasn't. I don't walk around like I'm the sexiest man alive. Then what happens—do you stop being sexy 365 days later? Don't get me wrong: It's nice. But I don't buy into it. It's another label.

OPRAH: Isn't there some part of you that's influenced by the categories you're put in?

DENZEL: Of course. Celebrity itself is an influence. For instance, it can make you more of an introvert—you can't just go places unnoticed. On the other hand, I'm probably more confident, because I don't have to worry about certain things. I try to remember what it felt like to really not know where I was headed or how I was going to eat. At the same time, I've always been a very positive person, and I'd like to think that some of my success came from that. People say you should have something to fall back on, but if I'm falling, I want to fall forward, not prepare to fall back. My religious instruction has taught me that what you believe and speak is what you become. If I constantly say that I'm "struggling to make it through," then that's exactly what I'll do: struggle just to get by.

OPRAH: What role have you been most honored to play?

DENZEL: Oh, I can't pick one. I've played Stephen Biko, Malcolm X, Rubin "Hurricane" Carter, Herman Boone, and now Melvin B. Tolson. I just enjoy the experience. But I do still remember the first time I landed in Zimbabwe to start filming *Cry Freedom* [the movie about the life of South African activist Stephen Biko]. I was alone, I was listening to Janet Jackson on my Walkman, and I was like, *Wow, I'm in Africa. What a life.*

OPRAH: When you first touched ground in Africa, did you feel a connection?

DENZEL: It felt like going home.

OPRAH: At this point in your life, what makes you happiest?

DENZEL: Watching my children grow. Also, my wife recently said, "You love this directing thing; you're happy now." I'm reenergized. As a director, my job is to put great people around me and let them do what they do well.

OPRAH: You sound like a born leader. In all my years of interviewing, I've never met someone who defines himself as a person who likes to see others succeed.

DENZEL: I'm a regular guy. I'm comfortable like this. I may look at my Aston Martin—the one I bought during a midlife crisis—but I drive my truck.

OPRAH: What does a regular guy do to relax?

DENZEL: When I have time, I watch football—but I have to stay busy. I'm not good at doing nothing. I tried it. It's not healthy for me. I need to go somewhere every morning, even if it's just to the gym.

OPRAH: What makes you the most proud?

> "I love my work, but acting is what I do; it's not my identity. I love the way Julia Roberts put it: 'I'm just an ordinary person who has an extraordinary job.'"

DENZEL: I'm careful about the word *proud*; I'm happy to have read the Bible from cover to cover. I'm on my second go-round—I read one chapter a day. Right now I'm digging John. He just had dinner with Mary, and things are about to take a turn for the worse. I tried to instill spirituality into *The Great Debaters*. Remember that old church prayer, God, we come before You, knee bowed and body bent, in the humblest way we know how?

OPRAH: Yes! It reminds me of a poem I performed in high school forensics club. It's called "Listen, Lord: A Prayer," from James Weldon Johnson's *God's Trombones*, and it has that line in it ["...knee bowed and body bent"]. I think it's very important to have this film debut at a time when so many of our children are dropping out of school.

DENZEL: Our children's problems are our fault—we created and allowed this environment for them. But despite all the negative press about our kids, a lot of great work is getting done, and this film is a call to teachers and community leaders to keep fighting. When I was a kid, I was influenced by folks at the Boys & Girls Club, which was a lifeline for me. I was reminded of that while we were filming in the backwoods of Louisiana. I took a drive just to get off the set for a while, and I came across a black family living way out in the woods. I pulled up a chair and chatted with them, and the two girls, each probably around 14, just about passed out! Both were straight-A students; they even showed me their report cards. I said, "Have you thought about Harvard? As smart as you are, you can do anything you want." Those were the very words the mayor once said to me when he came to visit the Boys & Girls Club. I never forgot it.

OPRAH: And those girls will never forget your words. Do you feel positively about the state of the world right now?

DENZEL: Absolutely. I don't mean to be smug, but I'm not surprised by much. It has all been foretold and written. I just stay focused on the question of how I will serve while I'm here. How can I lift people up?

OPRAH: What are you most grateful for?

DENZEL: The opportunity to do that. I hope we can remember that we each have that chance. 〇

Kyra Sedgwick's Aha! Moment

It hit her when she gave birth to her son, Travis: You can guarantee your child a clean, healthy environment for only nine months. After that, what kind of world would he live in? A green one, if she had any say.

I was born and raised in Manhattan. City living never really put me in contact with the earth, and I didn't think I had to count on the land; I *expected* it to provide for me. I assumed that I'd turn on the tap and water that was clean enough to drink would come out, and that I'd always have air that was safe to breathe.

I did take public transportation, but that was for convenience, not because it was good for the environment. My carbon footprint and how I disposed of my garbage weren't issues on my mind.

In 1988, when I was 23, I got pregnant with my son, Travis. It was right at a moment of rising awareness in our culture about global warming and the limit on how long we could exist as a gas-guzzling, throwaway society. It was the cause célèbre of the time.

When you start understanding that garbage doesn't disappear but lies on top of the earth, seeping into the groundwater, you realize that everything you use has an afterlife of hundreds (or even thousands, when it comes to plastic) of years. I became environmentally depressed. As I nested and prepared the house for my son, I had dreams about garbage dumps filling up with disposable diapers and plastic bottles, so I was obsessed with using environmentally sound cleaning products and cloth diapers.

I carried Travis for nine months, providing him with a safe and healthy place to grow inside me, and then I gave birth and fed him my breast milk. Then, when I had to give him over to the world—to food that comes from unknown places and toys that come from irresponsible manufacturers—it really hit me: I felt responsible not only for my child but for the planet.

I became proactive. I got involved in the Environmental Defense Fund and the National Resources Defense Council. I tried to be green and educate others about making environmentally conscious purchases. Unfortunately, the movement petered out in the 1990s, and suddenly I felt like I was the only one shouting, "We have to think about what we use! It's not enough to recycle plastic—you shouldn't be buying it in the first place. What about those nice cardboard takeout containers?" I wasn't alone, of course, which is why the issue has come back to the forefront, but in hindsight, if we had really committed to it back then, our world wouldn't be in the predicament that it's in now.

The Great Law of the Iroquois Confederacy states, "In our every deliberation, we must consider the impact of our decisions on the next seven generations." Thinking that way changes everything: I now have two kids, and they will have kids, and the lineage will go on. I understand that how I walk through my life on this planet will affect the world my children live in. When I go to yoga class with my stainless steel water bottle and see other people bringing plastic ones, I want to scream about it from the mountaintops!

Mothers believe we are responsible for our children from the womb to the grave. We are connected by the longing to protect them after they leave our bodies, so the impetus for making this planet safe for them lies with us. Mark my words: It's the soccer moms who will change the world. ◐

—As told to Rachel Bertsche

An Operation Called Hope

In the desperately poor African country of Zimbabwe, an all-female team of medical miracle workers is changing (and often saving) lives by providing free reconstructive surgery to children with cleft lips and palates. Difficult? Yes. The best thing they've ever done? Without a doubt. Aimee Lee Ball puts on her scrubs.

The people of Zimbabwe sometimes give their babies names that reflect the adversity of their lives in an impoverished and strife-scarred country, where grocery shelves hold little but cornmeal and a policeman earns the equivalent of about $10 a month. So when a group of American doctors and nurses arrive at the pediatric wing of Harare Central Hospital to perform free facial reconstructive surgeries, the children who are brought to be evaluated include those with names meaning Hard Times, No Matter, Wishes, Forget, Otherwise, Again (the ninth

Families wait patiently to see the Operation of Hope surgical team at Harare Central Hospital, Zimbabwe.

child in the family), and Swear to the Sky.

For several months, posters in public spaces have notified people in remote corners of this country about Operation of Hope, the brainchild of Joseph Clawson, MD, a surgeon from Longview, Washington. Dr. Joe, as he's known by patients, retired from private practice when HMOs took over the healthcare system and he realized he wasn't a 15-minute kind of physician. He began traveling to disadvantaged places in the world, starting with Chernobyl after the nuclear power plant disaster, and he kept trying to find the areas of greatest need. Learning that Zimbabwe had a large number of children

with congenital defects—especially cleft lips and palates—he made plans to go in the fall of 2006. The day before his departure, the minister of health called to say, "We don't know if there will be any babies for you," and Dr. Joe said, "If there's one, I'm coming." On that trip, he had to turn away 50 children in one day and made a commitment to return twice a year. Now, for the first time, his medical team—surgeon, resident, anesthesiologist, nurse anesthetist, recovery nurse, floor nurse, and scrub technician—is composed entirely of women.

And that's how I got involved: A year ago, I met Op Hope's executive director, Jennifer Trubenbach, 49, from

Lake Forest, California, when she won the *O* magazine contest to join Oprah Winfrey at Miraval Resort and Spa. Most of the contest winners were deemed deserving of a spa vacation because of serious stress and calamity in their lives—the group included an Iraq-war veteran, an Iraq-war widow, and a woman whose son was killed in a drive-by shooting—but Jennifer won because her life is about helping others. She is Dr. Joe's daughter and gave up a career as a technology consultant for two Fortune 10 companies to run Op Hope. We stayed in touch by e-mail, and when the all-woman team was assembled for Zimbabwe, she called with an irresistible proposal: Come along as a volunteer.

"Mangwanani, chiremba." Everyone on the Op Hope team is wearing a bright blue scrub suit designed by Katherine Heigl of *Grey's Anatomy*. Jennifer persuaded the actress to donate this wardrobe, which seems to merit the native Shona greeting of "Good morning, Doctor" for all of us. The reason for our uniformity is

tional village healer, that children with cleft defects should have been drowned at birth, that such afflictions are payback for some ancestral transgression. They sit on hard benches in an airless room with bars on the windows, the overflow standing in the hall, waiting to be screened by one of the Op Hope surgeons. They sit or stand without complaint or crying, certainly without Nintendos or iPods or other amusement to pass the time. Patience and civility are an ingrained part of their culture; complaining and assertiveness are considered inappropriate. Almost without exception, those who speak English smile broadly and say, "How are you? I am fine if you are fine."

We're fine, except for the palpable tension associated with traveling to a country in chaos. An election was held just a week before we got here, but Robert Mugabe (generally viewed as more despot than president) has refused to cede power, refused even to allow the release of voting results. Zimbabwe's economy is in free fall, with 80 percent unemployment and an official inflation rate of 165,000 percent—yes, all those zeros are correct. One U.S. dollar is worth 50 million Zim dollars the week we

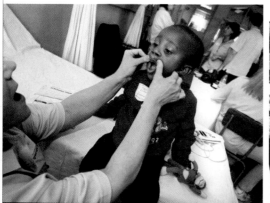

HIGH HOPES *(from left)*: Anesthesiologist Patti Kymer, MD, examining 3-year-old Kelvin Pikayoegore Nyarugwe; Carrie Francis, MD, a medical resident, studying X-rays to decide on possible treatment; Charity Rukasha, holding 2-month-old Shantal, confers with Joseph Clawson, MD, founder of Operation of Hope.

not cosmetic—it's so we can recognize each other down the long, unfamiliar corridors of the hospital. A number of patients and their parents have traveled eight or ten or more hours, by bus or train or the back of a friendly farmer's truck to get here. For some, even the fare of a few dollars is an extravagance made possible only through a collection in their community. Several carry the sort of lined notebook I remember from grade school, containing their medical histories, but many have never seen a real doctor, and they've been told by a *n'anga*, the tradi-

arrive; during our stay, the price of a newspaper goes up from $3 million to $20 million. Life expectancy is less than 44 years. Laws have been passed making it a crime to criticize the president and his policies, and we hear that a 16-year-old girl has been jailed for calling the octogenarian Mugabe an "old man." Most foreign journalists have been banned (I'm here under the radar), and opposition supporters have been killed. A few days before we left home, the front page of *The New York Times* had a photograph of men escaping across the border into South Africa by cutting through a barbed wire fence. We are all a little edgy, and the people here seem a little shocked to see us. But there is work to be done.

There will be two teams, each of which will perform four surgeries a day, Monday to Friday. That's 80 surgeries in two weeks. The surgeons set up a screening clinic in a ward with peeling paint the color of iceberg lettuce: The astonishingly energetic 75-year-old Dr. Joe sets the pace for Lisa Buckmiller, MD, a 41-year-old ear, nose, and throat surgeon from Arkansas Children's Hospital in Little Rock. They wear headlamps that look like miner's lights to assess the children, asking them to repeat words like *cake* and *papa* (because *k*'s and *p*'s test the palate). In the United States, Lisa explains, clefts are often recognized on a prenatal ultrasound and are routinely repaired in infancy. The human face is formed out of three plates that meet in the middle. The ridges above your upper lip are actually the scars left when the tissues join together in the first trimester of pregnancy; a cleft lip results when that fusion doesn't take place. During the same period of gestation, the tongue drops down, and the two segments of the palate "zipper up." A cleft palate is the result of a chink in that zipper. A lot of these children are older than most cleft patients in the United States but look tiny for their age—both poverty and the mechanical difficulty of swallowing has left them malnourished.

cells that carries oxygen from the lungs to the body's tissues) of at least ten. Patti's got a stethoscope and a blood oxygen monitor that fits on the toe, finger, or ear. But with the limitations of language and equipment, she admits, "we're kind of winging it."

Plus she has to rely on a cadre of willing but unskilled volunteers, including two other members of Jennifer Trubenbach's family: 18-year-old daughter Mari, a high school senior, and 48-year-old sister Teryn Bonime, a real estate agent in Portland, Oregon. And then there's me—we're the amateur "info-structure" of this crew, taking histories of the potential patients, often grabbing a passerby who can translate from Shona to English. I'm rather intimidated about getting an accurate body weight since it's an important guideline for administering anesthesia and medicine. But after a while, we're all performing tasks we'd never dreamed of, like mixing powdered amoxicillin

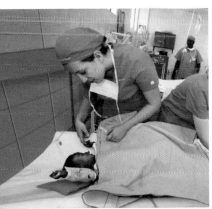   

It's the job of 56-year-old anesthesiologist Patti Kymer, MD, to clear each child for surgery. She was a cocktail waitress in Colorado when she decided to go to medical school ("I thought I might as well do something with my good grades"), but it wasn't until she specialized in treating children that she found her calling. It's easy to see how well suited she is to caring for young patients and their nervous parents. "I'm going to make sure he's asleep and doesn't feel anything," she reassures the mother of one little boy. "We'll take good care of him, but he'll be mad when he wakes up." Sometimes the parents are crushed to learn that their child is too small or too sick for surgery. A common criterion is the "rule of ten": The child should be at least ten weeks old, weigh at least ten pounds, and have a hemoglobin (the protein in red blood

with exactly 74 milliliters of water to make a pediatric dose of antibiotics. The modus operandi is the classic role-up-your-sleeves motto: Do what's needed.

Jennifer has transported 2,000 pounds of medical supplies in military bags (and wrangled for hours with immigration officials at the airport), all of which is stocked on operating room shelves by 50-year-old scrub tech Daisy Dailey. There are syringes and thermometers, bandages and dressings, masks and gloves, acetaminophen and stainless steel surgical blades (numbers 11, 12, and 15), miles of suture (plain gut, chronic gut, and fast-absorbing gut), and "no-no's," which are post-op arm restraints. Jennifer has even brought books about sign language, knowing that several parents will show up with deaf children in the hope that surgery will correct their hearing.

The ORs are dusty, and the gurneys must be tested to make sure they actually have functional wheels. There is no soap at the scrub sinks, just a watery green liquid that smells like industrial-strength floor cleaner. When the autoclave, an apparatus for sterilizing instruments, conks out, Daisy boils water. "Sterility is a relative term here," Jennifer confides. "The water to wash your hands could be worse than what you're washing off."

Nancy Crisler, 50, and Claudia Gibson, 51, are readying their respective domains: the recovery room and the post-op ward. The two women are sisters from Oregon, both of whom came to the nursing profession by circuitous routes. With a degree in community service and public affairs, Claudia went to work for a local health department, "but I had way too much energy to sit at a desk," she admits. Nancy took a summer job with the forest service in a rural community of 1,200 people and stayed to marry a man she met there. "I needed a skill that I could use while living in a small town," she says, "and I figured small towns always have schools and hospitals." The sisters were planning an indulgent trip together to celebrate Nancy's recent half-century birthday but chose to help Operation of Hope instead. "It's such a cool way to travel," says Claudia. "There's no other way you can step into another culture as quickly." The two can communicate with each other in that wordless way that siblings have, and sometimes their communication seems to convey, *What have we gotten into?* But they manage to care for their patients in strange and rudimentary surroundings. When Nancy runs out of plastic bags for her patients' take-home meds, she packs them in the gauzy shoe covers used for the OR.

Like Dr. Joe, 27-year-old medical resident Carrie Francis, MD, originally wanted to be a vet, but a job at an animal clinic in her hometown of St. Louis revealed that she liked only horses and dogs, didn't want to touch anything else. "And I realized I loved talking to people, being a patient advocate, empowering them to take responsibility for their healthcare," she says. "I didn't like dealing with long-term diseases that aren't curable. I wanted to cut out the problem." Surgery seemed the right fit, and a mentor in medical school found her a research project in otolaryngology, the specialty that deals with the ear, nose, and throat. "It's like trying on shoes," she says. "You know once you've slipped into a comfortable pair."

For a young doctor whose training has been 21st-century high-tech, the bare-bones facilities in Zimbabwe are a shock. "In the States, we have machines to do everything for us," says Carrie, "protocols that print out as soon as a patient is brought to the floor, calculators for formulas that people used to do in their heads. It's invigorating to compensate. To actually examine the patients, take a history, and listen to them when you don't have a blood pressure cuff, it's a challenge. But it's fun to become a grassroots physician."

An experienced surgeon, Lisa admits that she has perfected the art of detaching emotionally from the inert patient on the table in front of her. But she has a real and personal connection to the value of humanitarian work: Three years ago, she operated on a little girl brought to Arkansas from an orphanage in central China with a disfiguring birthmark that had hijacked her face; a year later Lisa and her husband went to China to adopt the girl themselves, and Anna is now a thriving kindergartner, described by her mother as Miss Personality. Being in Zimbabwe gives Lisa what she calls reverse culture shock. "I feel absolutely in my element," she says, "but I'm amazed at how people hand their child over to somebody who doesn't even speak the same language. They're entrusting their baby's face to me, and I'm humbled. I have the best job in the world."

No, I have the best job. Everyone on the Op Hope team has brought a suitcase full of toys. I fill one pocket of my scrub suit with boy stuff like model cars and puzzles, another pocket with girl stuff like barrettes and bracelets, then load my arms with stuffed animals and both hands with finger puppets. I go into the ward like Santa Claus, and when the children receive a gift, they clap their hands as a thank-you.

The hardest part of this trip is not the 5 a.m. wake-up calls, the 14-hour days (mostly standing), the strange smells of this bankrupt country where hygiene is a luxury, nor the unnerving rumble of trouble from a government in collapse. (Our hotel is across the park from Parliament, the site of protests from the opposition party, and we discover in concerned e-mails from the States that politically motivated violence is a distinct possibility.) The hardest part is seeing a child frightened beyond my ability to comfort. And I'm not the only wimp: Patti confesses she can't cope when a child cries. So she has a bag of tricks to help. She's brought cherry-flavored anesthesia masks from home, which she puts on the children's faces while making a "yum-yum" sound, and then sings them to sleep—"Blue's Clues" and "Feliz Navidad" and "Twinkle, Twinkle, Little Star."

At 67, nurse anesthetist Bonnie Hilliard is the no-nonsense veteran of the group—this is her 15th humanitarian trip. She lives on 40 acres in rural Oregon with a menagerie of animals and works at a 20-bed hospital, where she never knows what kind of surgery will come up; it takes a lot to ruffle her. She's made considerable effort to anticipate any contingency here, in fact, bringing myriad supplies—from anesthesia drugs to tape for holding down IVs. "I try to keep myself as a unit," she says. "And since we don't have every modern convenience, it's like going back to the old days, when we had to use a more touch-and-feel approach to see how the patient was doing. It's a great chance to use all my skills." But the equipment here is a nightmare—an ancient Japanese anesthesia machine and monitors that may or may not tell her if a patient is in too light or too deep a sleep. At one point, the power goes out in the OR, and an emergency generator comes on. The power is restored in a few minutes, but later a member of the hospital staff says that sometime in the next week or so, the power will go off and it won't come back on. The surgeons will not have oxygen monitors, and they'll have to tell how the patients are doing the old-fashioned way: by looking at their fingernails. "It reminds me of the era when hospitals made you remove your nail polish before surgery," says Bonnie.

After a few days, a natural trust and camaraderie evolves between the American team and the Zimbabwean staff. Their wariness and reluctance to speak about the political situation subsides, and we start hearing what life is really like here. One nurse used to work in a clinic where rebels brought their wounded comrades and demanded treatment on pain of death. A medical student who makes $20 a month has a house payment of $250 a month, so he sold his car, took in relatives, and is now buying and selling sugar on the black market. Daisy, setting up the OR for the next day's procedures, gently teases one of the nurses who's trying to leave early; it turns out that she lives without electricity and is hoping to get home so that she can see her baby in daylight. When Daisy notices another nurse washing her underwear in a bathroom sink at the end of the day, she learns the woman has only one pair, and no running water at home. Before she leaves, Daisy gives the local nurses all the underwear and socks in her suitcase.

Jennifer brings lavender spray to freshen a small, dank space that her sister and daughter have dubbed "the mom room": It's where the parents (mostly mothers) wait for their children in surgery. Every child gets a new going-

We're all performing tasks we'd never dreamed of—the modus operandi is the classic roll-up-your-sleeves motto: Do what's needed.

home outfit, selected from a prodigious collection provided by Jennifer's friends back in California, but they're so small for their age that Teryn has to convert their weight from kilos to pounds to figure out the appropriate size. Mari takes pictures of the moms with the "photo booth" function on her computer and conducts an impromptu art class, with drawings done on hole-punched cards that will be sewn together with yarn as a "quilt." (One card says "Thank you for the job well done in our country." Another has a stick figure and the words "This is a boy"—the girls in this culture tend to have close-cropped hair, and there's been some gender confusion.) Somehow we manage to communicate pretty well despite the language barrier, with a few comical slipups: When Jennifer tells a group of parents, "We'll take you to the floor now," everyone looks down at their feet. When the moms try to comfort their crying babies in the recovery room, they chant a soothing phrase that sounds like "so-ree, so-ree," and Nancy finally asks them to explain the Shona word, only to be told they're saying, "Sorry, sorry."

One of my jobs is helping the parents get into hospital gowns, caps, and booties, so they can walk into the OR with their children. Lisa tells one mom she can kiss her daughter before leaving, but the mom doesn't speak English, so Lisa and her whole team demonstrate with air-kissing. It's crucial that the kids not eat or drink anything within at least a couple of hours before surgery, but for Claudia, just explaining NPO (nothing per oral) orders can be challenging: One little girl has drunk something orange—is it juice? is it soda? is it a problem?—and her surgery must be postponed. The time that I fail miserably to communicate is when a woman arrives at the hospital with her 9-year-old son, too late to be put on the surgery schedule. I give her a "priority card" and, with the help of a Shona-speaking nurse, hope I've conveyed that the boy will be pushed to the front of the line when Operation of Hope returns in six months. Her face is weary and resigned as she accepts the slip of paper and thanks me. A few crazy hours later, I notice the two of them still standing in the hall outside the doors to the operating room. Gingerly, she comes over and says, in halting and heartbreaking English, "Is there hope for him?" I haven't been credible, haven't made her believe that she'll get the help she so desperately wants for her son.

Most problems, large or small, are dumped in Jennifer's lap, and to get through the day she guzzles a vile gel from a tube called Rapid Energy Fuel that provides 50 milligrams of caffeine. Her problem-solving runs the gamut from finding diapers for babies who have only rags wrapped around them to finding an MRI for a patient whose lungs are a concern, but her bailiwick extends to our hotel, where we're being awakened by a ringing phone around midnight every night, only to find nobody on the line. We finally realize that prostitutes in the hotel bar are dialing random room numbers and hanging up if a female voice answers, so Jennifer has a little chat with the management.

There is one problem that can't be solved, not on this trip: Everyone's favorite kid is a 13-year-old named Tinashe, who endears himself with his gentle manner (and his winks when he passes one of the Op Hope women). His soft cleft palate is part of a particular kind of condition called Pierre Robin sequence: His jaw seems to be connected to his neck with almost no chin in between. He's taken into surgery, but when the doctors try to get a tube down his throat, they can't see what they're doing. It's possible that they could operate with a special lighted instrument called a flexible fiber-optic bronchoscope—not exactly standard issue in a place where even Q-tips are hard to come by—but even if such a device were acquired for Op Hope's next trip, it might not be the answer: Tinashe is close to the age when surgery alone would yield little improvement in speech. His brain is hardwired to dealing with his impairment. When he wakes up in recovery, he points to his mouth and is told the surgery didn't happen. The playful boy is gone, silent tears streaming down his cheeks. And as I'm hugging him, in a feeble attempt at comfort, I know this is a moment I'll bring home with me. If Tinashe can't have the surgery, he could still benefit from speech therapy and dental work, both real luxuries in this country. I make a vow to raise funds for him back in the States.

Working under conditions that range from impractical to primitive, Operation of Hope has performed more than 2,000 surgeries but lost only one patient, a baby with a preexisting heart condition. Jennifer still remembers going into the waiting room to tell the mother, who said sim-

"They're entrusting their baby's face to me, and I'm humbled."

ply, "I know." There's a legend in Zimbabwe about a mermaid who appears when a child dies: If the mother cries, the mermaid will take the child to the bottom of the river—not a good resting place. But if the mother doesn't cry, the mermaid will carry the child to the shore and care for it.

Americans who do humanitarian work in places like Africa are sometimes asked why they put their efforts into helping "foreigners" rather than those in their own country. "I get that question a lot, and I understand why people ask," says Jennifer. "But life inside the walls of this hospital is so simple, and the need is so desperate. They don't have surgeons trained to do this work. The face is a piece of art—it's different from a hip replacement—and there is a satisfaction to doing it well that is so pure. A person who's been shunned because of a birth defect will be able to get a job now."

The take-home package for everyone on the team is a profound sense of gratitude and suspension from complaining about the insignificant irritations of a privileged life.

If I ever bitch again about being caught in traffic, or getting the middle seat on a plane, or having "nothing to wear" in my closet, somebody should slap me. When anyone asks in a perfunctory way, "How are you?" I no longer answer with a mechanical "Okay." I say, "Good" or "Fine" or even "I am fine if you are fine." While we were in Zimbabwe, there was a tornado in Little Rock that devastated areas close to where Carrie lives, and a large 100-year-old tree in her yard fell, taking down electric power lines and breaking her fence. "I just took a deep breath and allowed myself to stay peaceful," Carrie reports. "There was no sense of anxiety over things I know I can replace. The line at the bank, the coffee barista taking too long—these things don't seem to be as important. The pace of life we observed, the way people seem to accept what comes, is so different from American culture. We tend to be uptight about things that don't go our way or get in our way. There's definitely been a turnaround in my everyday life." And if you happen to come across Carrie—or any of us from Op Hope—standing in those long lines at the bank or at Starbucks, you might hear us slowly repeating a mantra that sounds something like this: Zimbabwe, Zimbabwe, Zimbabwe.... **◯**

To contribute or volunteer, go to operationofhope.org.

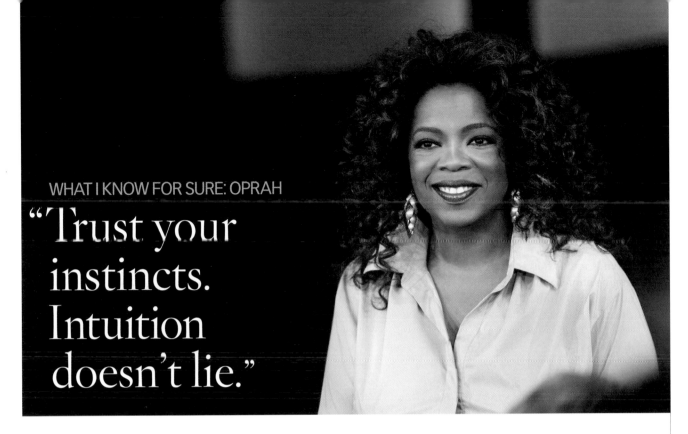

"Trust your instincts. Intuition doesn't lie."

Since the day the late Gene Siskel asked me, "What do you know for sure?" and I got all flustered and started stuttering and couldn't come up with an answer, I've never stopped asking myself that question. And every month I must find yet another answer. Some months I feel I hardly know a thing, and I'm always pressed to make the deadline for this column. This time around, I looked back and came up with my all-time top 20:

1. What you put out comes back all the time, no matter what. (This is my creed.)

2. You define your own life. Don't let other people write your script.

3. Whatever someone did to you in the past has no power over the present. Only you give it power.

4. When people show you who they are, believe them the first time. (A lesson from Maya Angelou.)

5. Worrying is wasted time. Use the same energy for doing something about whatever worries you.

6. What you believe has more power than what you dream or wish or hope for. You become what you believe.

7. If the only prayer you ever say is thank you, that will be enough. (From the German theologian and humanist Meister Eckhart.)

8. The happiness you feel is in direct proportion to the love you give.

9. Failure is a signpost to turn you in another direction.

10. If you make a choice that goes against what everyone else thinks, the world will not fall apart.

11. Trust your instincts. Intuition doesn't lie.

12. Love yourself and then learn to extend that love to others in every encounter.

13. Let passion drive your profession.

14. Find a way to get paid for doing what you love. Then every paycheck will be a bonus.

15. Love doesn't hurt. It feels really good.

16. Every day brings a chance to start over.

17. Being a mother is the hardest job on earth. Women everywhere must declare it so.

18. Doubt means don't. Don't move. Don't answer. Don't rush forward.

19. When you don't know what to do, get still. The answer will come.

20. "Trouble don't last always." (A line from a Negro spiritual, which calls to mind another favorite: This, too, shall pass.)

So thanks, Gene, for asking me the question. The answer continues....

Oprah

ABOUT THE CONTRIBUTORS

CHRIS ABANI is a former political prisoner and winner of the PEN Freedom-to-Write Award. His newest book is *Song for Night.*

UWEM AKPAN is a Jesuit priest living in Zimbabwe. His collection of short stories is *Say You're One of Them.*

CHRISTIE ASCHWANDEN is a contributing writer and editor for *Health, Skiing,* and *Runner's World.*

CELIA BARBOUR is *O*'s contributing food editor.

NAOMI BARR is a research editor at *O.*

EMILY BAZELON is a D.C.-based senior editor at Slate.com, where she writes about law and family.

MARTHA BECK writes a monthly column for *O.* She is a life coach and the author of *The Joy Diet, Steering by Starlight,* and other books.

RACHEL BERTSCHE is an associate producer at harpo.com.

AMY BLOOM is a novelist, short story writer, and psychotherapist. The award-winning author of five books, including her latest, *Away,* Bloom teaches creative writing at Yale University.

JULIAN BOND is the chairman of the NAACP and a leader of the civil rights movement.

KATE BRAESTRUP is the chaplain of the Maine Warden Service and author of the memoir *Here If You Need Me.*

LIZ BRODY is *O*'s health and news director.

GERALDINE BROOKS's third historical novel is *People of the Book.* Her novel *March* won the 2006 Pulitzer Prize.

SARAH BROOM is a writer living in New Orleans.

MICHELLE BURFORD is a contributing writer at *O.*

GEOFFREY CANADA is the president and CEO of Harlem Children's Zone, a non-profit aimed at breaking the cycle of poverty in New York City families.

LORENE CARY is the author of the memoir *Black Ice,* as well as two novels and a short story collection.

FRANCESCO CLEMENTE is an artist whose work has been exhibited at the Solomon R. Guggenheim Museum in New York City.

ARIANNE COHEN is a Manhattan-based writer and author of *The Tall Book,* an exploration of the world of tall people.

SUZAN COLÓN is a freelance writer and a contributing editor at *O.*

KELLY CORRIGAN is the author of *The New York Times* best-selling memoir, *The Middle Place.*

BEVERLY DONOFRIO is the author of the memoir *Riding in Cars with Boys,* which was adapted into the 2001 film starring Drew Barrymore. Her most recent work is the children's book *Thank You, Lucky Stars.*

RODES FISHBURNE is the author of the novel *Going to See the Elephant.*

DAVID FRANCE is the author of *Our Fathers,* about the sexual abuse scandal in the Catholic Church. He lives in New York City.

SUZETTE GLASNER-EDWARDS, PhD, is a clinical psychologist and researcher at UCLA.

JANE GOODALL is the founder of The Jane Goodall Institute, which promotes wildlife conservation and research, and a United Nations Messenger of Peace.

KATIE GOODMAN is the author of *Improvisation for the Spirit: Live a Creative, Spontaneous and Courageous Life Using the Tools of Improv Comedy.*

NANCY GOTTESMAN is a freelance writer based in Los Angeles.

DAVID GRANGER is the editor in chief of *Esquire.*

PENELOPE GREEN is a reporter for the Home section of *The New York Times.*

HILL HARPER is the author of the nonfiction advice books *Letters to a Young Brother* and *Letters to a Young Sister.* He also plays Dr. Sheldon Hawkes on the CBS drama *CSI:NY.*

SARI HARRAR is a writer specializing in health and science.

MARIE HOWE has published three books of poetry, most recently, *The Kingdom of Ordinary Time.*

TIM JARVIS is a freelance writer based in Miami.

ANNE KADET is a senior writer and columnist at *SmartMoney.*

DAVID L. KATZ, MD, is director of the Yale-Griffin Prevention Research Center and a medical consultant for *ABC News.* He writes a monthly section for *O.*

LISA KOGAN is *O*'s writer at large. Her column appears monthly.

JOANNA KROTZ is the founder and editorial director of Muse2Muse Productions, a digital and print communications company.

JANINE LATUS's memoir, *If I Am Missing or Dead,* began as a story in *O* and became a best-seller. She lives in Virginia and speaks on domestic abuse issues.

GABRIELLE LEBLANC is a neuroscientist, biomedical consultant, and writer living in Washington, D.C. Her work has been published in scientific journals, among them, *Nature* and *Stroke.*

AIMEE LEE BALL is the coauthor of four books, including *Changing the Rules* with Muriel Siebert.

JAMES MCBRIDE is the author of the memoir *The Color of Water* and the novel *Song Yet Sung.*

JEANNE MCCULLOCH has been an editor and writer for the literary magazines *The Paris Review* and *Tin House.*

PHILLIP C. MCGRAW, PhD, hosts the daily television show *Dr. Phil* and is the author of six books including *Love Smart: Find the One You Want—Fix the One You Got.* He writes a monthly column for *O.*

CATHLEEN MEDWICK is the author of *Teresa of Avila: The Progress of a Soul* and is a regular contributor to *O.*

ANDREW MELLEN, also known as VirgoMan, is a professional organizer. He travels the country meeting with clients and giving seminars.

CAROL MITHERS is a freelance journalist based in Los Angeles. Her work has appeared in *The New York Times* and *The Los Angeles Times.*

VALERIE MONROE, *O*'s beauty director, is the author of *In the Weather of the Heart,* a memoir.

RICK MOODY's latest book is *Right Livelihoods: Three Novellas.* His 1994 novel *The Ice Storm* was made into a feature film.

CATHERINE NEWMAN, author of the memoir *Waiting for Birdy,* writes a food and parenting column, Dalai Mama Dishes, on family.com.

SUZE ORMAN, host of CNBC's *The Suze Orman Show,* is the author of several books on personal finance, including *2009 Action Plan: Keeping Your Money Safe and Sound.* She writes a monthly column for *O.*

JACK OTTER is a columnist at *Newsday* and the deputy editor and finance expert at *Best Life* magazine. He has written for *The Wall Street Journal* and *The New Yorker.*

CHARLES P. PIERCE is a staff writer at *The Boston Globe Magazine* and a contributing writer for *Esquire.*

SARA REISTAD-LONG contributes frequently to *Esquire, Gourmet,* and *Self.* She lives in New York City.

GRETCHEN REYNOLDS is a writer living in Santa Fe.

AMANDA ROBB is an *O* contributing writer.

GEORGE SAUNDER's most recent work is the essay collection *The Braindead Megaphone.* He teaches creative writing at Syracuse University.

ELAINE SEXTON is the author of *Causeway,* a collection of poetry.

THEA SINGER is the president of Critical Change LLC, a management consulting firm.

PATTI SMITH is a singer and poet. Her latest album is *The Coral Sea.*

JUDITH STONE is a contributing writer to *O.* She is the author of *When She Was White: The True Story of a Family Divided by Race.*

ELIZABETH STROUT's latest novel, *Olive Kitteridge,* won the 2009 Pulitzer Prize for Fiction. She teaches at the MFA program at Queens University in Charlotte, North Carolina.

DANA SULLIVAN is a contributing editor at *Shape's Fit Pregnancy* magazine. She lives in Reno, Nevada.

ELLEN TIEN writes for the Style section of *The New York Times.*

PATRICIA VOLK's books include *To My Dearest Friends* and *Stuffed: Adventures of a Restaurant Family.* She has written for *The New York Times* and *The New York Times Magazine.*

CORNEL WEST, PhD, is the Professor of African-American Studies at Princeton University and author of *Democracy Matters.*

RITA WILSON is an actress and producer who has appeared in numerous films, including *Sleepless in Seattle.*

JESSICA WINTER is a senior editor at *O.*

LISA WOLFE is a writer living in New York City.

TOBIAS WOLFF is the author of *This Boy's Life* and *Our Story Begins.* He is a three-time winner of the O. Henry Award for his stories *In the Garden of North American Martyrs, Next Door,* and *Sister.*

PENNY WRENN, a former editor at *Esquire* and *Redbook*, is a writer in New York City.

EMILY YOFFE is a contributing writer for Slate.com and the author of *What the Dog Did.*

PHOTO CREDITS

INDEX

©2009 by Hearst Communications, Inc
O, The Oprah Magazine is a trademark of Harpo Print, LLC.

Published by Oxmoor House, Inc.
P.O. Box 2262, Birmingham, Alabama 35201-2262

ISBN-13: 978-0-8487-3283-7
ISBN-10: 0-8487-3283-9
Library of Congress Control Number: 2008942160
Printed in the United States of America
First printing 2009

To order more books, call 1-800-765-6400.

O, *The Oprah Magazine*

Founder and Editorial Director: Oprah Winfrey
Editor in Chief: Susan Casey
Editor at Large: Gayle King
Executive Editor: Catherine Kelley
Production Director: Kristen Rayner
Associate Editor: Brooke Kosofsky Glassberg
Assistant Photo Editor: Kathy Nguyen
Art Assistant: Carolyn Wilsey

HEARST BOOKS

VP, Publisher: Jacqueline Deval

OXMOOR HOUSE, INC.

VP, Publisher: Jim Childs
Director, Direct Marketing: Laura Sappington
Managing Editor: L. Amanda Owens
Brand Manager: Terri Laschober Robertson

TIME INC. HOME ENTERTAINMENT

Publisher: Richard Fraiman
General Manager: Steven Sandonato
Executive Director, Marketing Services: Carol Pittard
Executive Director, Retail & Special Sales: Tom Mifsud
Director, New Product Development: Peter Harper
Director, Publicity: Sydney Webber
Associate Counsel: Helen Wan

Dream Big!

Editor: Susan Hernandez Ray
Project Editor: Vanessa Lynn Rusch
Senior Production Manager: Greg A. Amason

CONTRIBUTORS

Designer: Suzanne Noli
Copy Editor: Carmine B. Loper
Indexer: Mary Ann Laurens
Project Editor: Emily Chappell
Interns: Georgia Dodge, Christine Taylor

SPECIAL THANKS TO:

Kristy Harrison, Jennie Whitman